Changing Subjects

Playing the Texts, 7

Series Editor
George Aichele

Changing Subjects

Gender, Nation and Future in Micah

Erin Runions

SHEFFIELD ACADEMIC PRESS
A Continuum imprint
LONDON • NEW YORK

To my parents, Mae and Ernie Runions,
who have never let me stop thinking differently.

Copyright © 2001 Sheffield Academic Press
A Continuum imprint

Published by Sheffield Academic Press Ltd
The Tower Building, 11 York Road, London SE1 7NX
370 Lexington Avenue, New York NY 10017-6550

www.SheffieldAcademicPress.com
www.continuum-books.com

British Library Cataloguing-in-Publication Data

A catalogue record for this book is available from the British Library

Typeset by Sheffield Academic Press
Printed on acid-free paper in Great Britain by Bookcraft Ltd,
Midsomer Norton, Bath

ISBN   1-84127-269-8 (hardback)
          1-84127-270-1 (paperback)

Contents

Abbreviations

AB	Anchor Bible
ASOR	American Schools of Oriental Research
BDB	F. Brown, S.R. Driver and C.A. Briggs, *A Hebrew and English Lexicon of the Old Testament* (Oxford: Clarendon Press, 1907)
BHS	*Biblia hebraica stuttgartensia*
Bib	*Biblica*
BibInt	*Biblical Interpretation*
Bsac	*Bibliotheca Sacra*
BN	*Biblische Notizen*
BTS	*Bible et terre sainte*
BZ	*Biblische Zeitschrift*
BZAW	Beihefte zur *ZAW*
CBQ	*Catholic Biblical Quarterly*
FOTL	The Forms of the Old Testament Literature
HAR	*Hebrew Annual Review*
HSM	Harvard Semitic Monographs
HTR	*Harvard Theological Review*
IEJ	*Israel Exploration Journal*
Int	*Interpretation*
JBL	*Journal of Biblical Literature*
JNSL	*Journal of Northwest Semitic Languages*
JSOT	*Journal for the Study of the Old Testament*
JSOTSup	*Journal for the Study of the Old Testament*, Supplement Series
KB	L. Koehler and W. Baumgartner (eds.), *The Hebrew and Aramaic Lexicon of the Old Testament* (Leiden: E.J. Brill, 2000)
KJV	King James Version
LXX	Septuagint
MT	Masoretic Text
NIV	New International Version
OBT	*Overtures to Biblical Theology*
OTG	Old Testament Guides
PMLA	*Publications of the Modern Language Association of America*
RB	*Revue biblique*
REB	Revised English Bible
RevQ	*Revue de Qumran*

RHPR	*Revue d'histoire et de philosophie religieuses*
SBL	Society of Biblical Literature
SBLDS	SBL Dissertation Series
SBLMS	SBL Monograph Series
SBLSP	*SBL Seminar Papers*
SBLSymS	SBL Symposium Series
SBT	Studies in Biblical Theology
SJT	*Scottish Journal of Theology*
SJOT	*Scandinavian Journal of the Old Testament*
ST	*Studia Theologica*
TOTC	Tyndale Old Testament Commentary
VT	*Vetus Testamentum*
VTSup	*Vetus Testamentum*, Supplements
WBC	Word Biblical Commentary
ZAW	*Zeitschrift für die alttestamentliche Wissenschaft*

Preface

This book has been a long time coming. Though most of the work was done as my PhD dissertation at McGill University, the first seeds of the project grew out of my work with non-profit organizations in Vancouver, especially working for a brief time with marginalized youth, and wondering how they could ever escape the systemic oppression that formed them. In addition, my political and activist work in Montreal proved fertile ground for this project. Working with others to resist unjust policies and neo-liberal agendas being implemented by local and national governments has fed my desire to see how ideology and subject positions might be challenged, particularly through text. At the same time, this project has enabled me to clarify my own political thinking and positioning.

Many people have been instrumental in seeing this come to completion. My first thanks goes to my dissertation supervisor Robert Culley, who not only intervened in my first months as a graduate student at McGill and took me on as a student when I was ready to pack up; but who also gave me my first academic 'permission' (and helpful resources) to go my own way in thinking about text; he then ensured, through careful and challenging commentary on many revisions, that I actually learned to do this. His patience with my impatience was remarkable. I also need to thank several people for their help in reading drafts, whose feedback and encouragement were vital: Maxine Hancock, Roland Boer, Loris Mirella, Elizabeth Castelli, Andréa Schmidt, Fiona Black. I am indebted to Matt Bergbusch for pointing out the undocumented connection between Winnicott and Bhabha, and for taking the time to clarify a number of details about object relations theory. I am also grateful to Ehud Ben Zvi for letting me have early access to his commentary on Micah. Special recognition goes to my editor, colleague and friend George Aichele for his most excellent editorial help and his encouragement from early on; and to Philip Davies, Sarah Norman and the folks at Sheffield Academic Press for their care with the text. Thanks also goes to le Fonds FCAR who provided a grant for one year of the project when it was a dissertation, and another postdoctoral grant for time partially spent revising it into a book; to Elizabeth Castelli and to the Center for Research on Women at Barnard College, Columbia University for institutionally supporting me for the past year; and to the staff, past and present, at the McGill Faculty of Religious Studies who kept the place together (especially Helen Shepherdson, André Lafleur, Sami Khan, Luvana Di Francesco and Marina Costain). And finally this could never have been done without the community I have around me who make this kind of thing possible and have been my support: Mae Runions (with welcome to John Pratt-Johnson), Teresa, Matt, Olivia, Hannah and Jordan Weaver, Paul, Patti and Rebecca Runions, Max and Ruth Runions, Leola Calderwood, Adrienne Gibb, Anna Kruzynski, Rosemary Toye, Scott Kline, Alyda Faber, Andréa Schmidt, Geneviève Leclerc, Erika Jacques-Bedard, Marie-Eve Lamy.

Erin Runions
March 2001

Introduction

Preamble

In this study, I examine gender, nation and future vision in Micah, using the theoretical work of Homi K. Bhabha to explore how these textual configurations might affect readers' positioning in ways that engender resistance to oppression. My purpose is to run the difficulties in reading the text of Micah through a theoretical mill of complex questions on text, reading and ideology; this requires both fairly dense theoretical writing as well as detailed reading of Hebrew text. Thus, this book will provide some theoretical background on Homi Bhabha and also on Louis Althusser, Jacques Lacan and Slavoj Žižek whom I use Bhabha's work to engage. These key figures in cultural studies will be engaged through reading biblical text and scholarship on Micah. I am primarily concerned with the text of Micah as it relates to the sorts of questions about the reading process that arise from literary, ideological critical, and cultural studies approaches to the Bible; but because I am feminist, and because Bhabha is a postcolonial theorist, my project also contains strong gender-critical and postcolonial theoretical elements.

The larger issue at stake here is the question of texts' ability to influence readers for justice. Can texts affect readers' understandings of themselves in the world, and the choices these understandings provoke? Or to put it a little more pointedly, can texts have any real political effect; can they be strategically employed in struggles for justice, and against oppression (such as sexism, racism, colonization and so on)? Can texts successfully position readers to work toward justice? It may seem obvious that they can, yet there are so many ways of understanding texts and readers, as well as the interaction that takes place between the two, that such queries become complicated rather quickly. Are texts 'determinate', with a fixed range of outcomes for readers? Or are they more 'indeterminate', depending on readers' viewpoints? Are readers 'determined', destined always to read according to their own political or religious world-view? What are the processes by which readers' own biases, points of view and opinions come to be fixed? Is change possible, and if so, what would be required to achieve it? Where would text fit into this process?

The text of the minor prophet Micah, celebrated as it is for its call to justice, seems a fitting place to start an exploration of these larger questions of text, reading and justice. These seven chapters of Hebrew verse are evidently meant to be persuasive in some way, as signaled by their imperatives, dictums, threats and promises; but given the aforementioned uncertainties of texts and readers, it is not a foregone conclusion that this text can have any real impact, let alone political impact, on contemporary readers. The problem with Micah is that on the level of text, the Hebrew poetry is complex (see Chapter 4 for details), resulting in what seem to be constantly shifting identities of addressee and addressor, unclear relations between the various participants, blurred lines between gender, and ambiguous prospects for the future (hopeful or bleak). The meaning of the text is often difficult to ascertain. The rather indeterminate, or at least indeterminable, nature of Micah, it would seem, renders the text somewhat infirm as a persuasive force for justice.

On the other hand, the study of Micah opens up the door for pondering the possible political impact of an 'indeterminate text', along with all the issues of interpretation that such an inquiry raises. But this is a line of thought that cannot avoid consideration of the reader. In order to think about influence or change for readers, the way in which readers come to think, speak and act as they do—to be 'subjects'—must first be taken into account. Evidently, to think through this fully would be a rather inordinate task and one that could never be dealt with in a single study; yet if one is to ponder texts' impact on readers, the question of readers' positioning must be considered at some level. One possible, if perhaps provocative, way of looking at the question of the formation of individuals' ability to speak and act has been proposed by Marxist and structuralist theorists. These thinkers see the *subject formed in ideology*. In this view, the individual is positioned to speak and act through a set of *identifications* made with societal discourses and practices functioning to normalize certain roles, norms and behaviours that serve particular—often oppressive—interests. Though this is not the only way to understand the way readers are positioned as they come to a text, because it considers the possibility that particular and perhaps oppressive interests may be at work in forming subjects, it does provide a useful account of an issue that is readily integrated into discussions about justice. I have found it fruitful, therefore, to bring together the notion of the reader formed as subject in ideology with the question of textual indeterminacy, in reading the ambiguous text of Micah.

Statement of Purpose

My specific project, then, is to look carefully at the shifting signs of gender, nation and future vision in the book of Micah in order to suggest that readers' negotiation with the text's ambiguities might be able to

reposition, or reconfigure, their subject positions—that is, their positioning as agents of speech and action formed through identification with
ideological discourses. I will consider the role that readerly identification
plays in interpretation and will suggest that the text's constantly modu-
ating images might provide new points of identification for readers that
are able to interrogate their positioning as subjects. This process, I
submit, has the dual effect of shifting those positions, even slightly—
bringing new awareness of oppression and urging resistance to it—and
of impacting the way in which the text can be understood.

The theoretical framework that enables me to think about the larger
questions of text, readers and justice, while focusing on the smaller
details of the textual configurations in Micah is provided by the work of
postcolonial theorist Homi K. Bhabha. Since Bhabha's writing is primarily concerned with the negotiation of difference between and within
cultures in colonial and postcolonial contexts, he may seem a strange
conversation partner. However, Bhabha explores a number of issues that
might be applied to readers, texts and struggles against oppression:
liberation from (colonial) oppression, cultural difference, agency through
indeterminacy, forms of identification and political subversion. Further,
because Bhabha develops his thinking by engaging contemporary
theoretical debates on subject formation and language, his theory is
productive for considering the effect of *text* on readers' subjectivity.

Since Bhabha's writing is far too dense, and too extended for me to
give a full exposition of it within the confines of this project, I have
chosen to give an exposition of some of the key themes that appear in
his writing, themes that I feel are pertinent to the work I am doing. In
particular, I will be focusing on the contrast he makes between what he
calls 'pedagogical objects and discourses' (cultural icons, national histories and stereotypes) and what he calls 'performative practice' (the
ways in which these stereotypes and icons are repeated in actual cultural
practice). I will look at the distinction between pedagogical objects and
discourses and performative practice as it connects to several other of
Bhabha's concepts related to subjectivity and political agency ('hybridity',
'time-lag', 'third space', 'outside the sentence', 'liminal identification'
and 'agency'). In applying Bhabha's work to Micah, I use it first to
illumine how some scholars have read the text in ways that construct
icons of national identity ('pedagogical objects') which seem to valorize
certain norms of domination and gender; then to think about the way in
which the text disrupts these images and norms through repeating them
differently ('performative practice'); and finally to consider how readers'
identification with these differently repeated signs could possibly affect
their subject positions, as well as their understanding of the text.

Overview

This book is comprised of two parts: 'theory' and 'readings'. Part I situates my theoretical discussion within a number of other discourses both inside and outside of biblical studies. It also outlines my theoretical approach to the text, including an extended discussion of Bhabha and of some of the thinkers whom his work engages. Part II focuses on the details of the difficulties and ambiguities in the text of Micah, the way they have been read by scholars, and my own reading of the text following the approach suggested to me by Bhabha. I begin, therefore, in Chapter 1, with a discussion of the biblical and literary scholarly discourses from which my project arises, moving from discussion on Micah through discussions on textual determinacy, hermeneutics and the reading process. Here I summarize my basic stance concerning the text, maintaining that I am not interested in trying to make it cohere, but rather in seeing how the difficulties and differences in the text affect the reading process. I also summarize my stance concerning readers, indicating that, following materialist analyses of culture, I understand people (and therefore readers) to be formed as subjects in ideology. Through all of this, I try to show how I have arrived at these positions through consideration of questions posed in biblical studies.

In Chapter 2, as a way of setting up my problematic and introducing my use of Bhabha, I give an exposition of the notion of 'the subject', understood within certain (structuralist, Marxist) views of ideology. My discussion here does not pretend to be a thorough discussion of structuralist and Marxist/materialist notions of subjectivity and ideology, but rather, it outlines the starting-point for my use of Bhabha, and it lays out the issues at stake in thinking about the possibilities for readers to be repositioned as subjects. I try to draw out the problem that the notion of the subject fixed in ideology poses for reading and for change, and to indicate how Bhabha's theory might address this problem. Here Slavoj Žižek's re-reading—by way of Jacques Lacan—of Louis Althusser's description of the formation of the subject in ideology is particularly helpful for introducing the theoretical terms and issues that Bhabha's work engages. In Chapter 3, I give an exposition of some of Bhabha's key concepts: 'pedagogical objects and discourses', 'performative practice', 'hybridity', 'time-lag', 'third space', 'outside the sentence', 'liminal identification' and 'agency in indeterminacy'. As I go, I relate Bhabha to my previous discussion of subjectivity and ideology, considering how Bhabha enables thinking about negotiation and identification with difference as a means to shift subjects' positioning in liberating ways. To conclude the chapter, I consider the usefulness of Bhabha's work for thinking about Micah and the possibilities for readers to be repositioned as subjects in the process of reading.

Chapter 4 marks the shift into Part II, which is concerned with readings of Micah. Here I give an exposition of the text of Micah and many of its difficulties, paying particular attention to the shifts in its representations of gender, nation and future. My main concern in this chapter is to show Micah as a site of *difference*, with which the reader is obliged to negotiate in order to interpret the text. I also show the various solutions that have been proposed by scholars in order to smooth over the differences in the text. In Chapter 5, I look more carefully at how three biblical scholars (Lamontte M. Luker, James Luther Mays and Charles S. Shaw) have interpreted the text, reading the nation as a punished, passive and suffering woman waiting for her divine male hero to lead her into a glorious future of dominion over other nations. I give these as examples—though more pronounced—of a fairly common kind of scholarly reading of Micah that seems to rely on dominant gender constructs, and on an understanding of Israel's nationhood as based on covenant and a right to the land. I argue that these readings correspond to Bhabha's notion of 'pedagogical objects and discourses' (cultural icons, stereotypes and historical narratives) operating within the construction of national identities, as well as to Žižek's notion of ideological pinning points with which subjects identify.

In my final chapter, I draw all these issues together to show how readerly identifications with the 'pedagogical object' produced in scholarly interpretation of Micah might be disrupted by the 'performative practice' of the text, in particular by the changes in the repetition of the signs of gender, nation and future in the book. Looking in depth at several examples from the text, I suggest that the differences in the textual reiteration of the commonly understood image of the nation in Micah create a space for the negotiation between text and reader ('time-lag', 'third space', 'outside the sentence') in which 'hybrid' figures emerge. I look at a number of these figures as they appear throughout the book, and then move to look in detail at the hybrid figure of the nation as both colonizer and colonized in Mic. 5–6 and as both male and female, human and divine in Mic. 4.8-14. These hybrid figures, I contend, offer up new points of identification for readers ('liminal identifications') which can bring a reader's own positioning as subject into view, questioning it and possibly shifting it. Further, such identifications open up other possibilities for understanding the meaning of the text, possibilities which I explore with reference to the visions of the future in the book. I conclude by proposing the ways in which this sort of study might open out into larger considerations of ideology, texts, readers and interpretation.

Part I
Theory

1

Reading Micah: Text, Interpretation, Readers

My question is: how can an indeterminate or ambiguous text like Micah affect predetermined readers? In other words, how can an ambiguous text influence readers, when readers' ability to speak and act—that is, their position as 'subject'—is understood to be determined by the way that they identify with various societal practices and discourses that make sense of the world (ideology), which are in turn determined by economic and historical factors? With this line of questioning, I am choosing to engage a particular debate and a particular understanding of how readers develop their initial stance toward the text, by starting with the idea that readers are formed as subjects in ideology. While the details of this particular theoretical framework and the way I use Bhabha's theory to engage it will be dealt with in Chapters 2 and 3, in this chapter I would like to show how my thinking about Micah, Bhabha, subjectivity and ideology is situated with respect to various facets of scholarly discourse, and to show how I have come to situate my question as I do.

More specifically, in this chapter I would like to show why the problems raised in studies of Micah lead to consideration of the problems of text and reading, which in turn lead to questions of textual determinacy, readerly ideology and subjectivity. These latter have been explored tentatively within biblical studies from a Marxist critical perspective taken from critical theory, a theoretical trajectory that also rejoins cultural studies, which is where I begin my thinking with Bhabha. As a way of organizing this overview of the theoretical background, both within biblical studies and without, I will begin with 'text', looking briefly at the text of Micah and its treatment by biblical scholars; I will then move to 'interpretation', looking at how a consideration of ideology fits into discussions of textual determinacy and hermeneutics;[1] finally, I

---

1. I use the term 'hermeneutics' here because in this chapter I take Ricoeur's thinking as a *starting-point* (only), from which I move on. The scope of this project does not permit me to engage all the philosophical debates that 'hermeneutics' implies, nor the relation of these debates to the study of ideology, or to poststructural theory which Bhabha takes up. Following my discussion of Ricoeur, for the rest of the study, I use the terms 'interpretation' or 'reading' somewhat interchangeably. For a more technical discussion of some of the relationships between hermeneutics, psychoanalysis and ideological criticism, see Žižek (1994a).

will turn to 'readers', looking at how questions of individuals' relation to ideology and their 'subjectivity' have been framed within the theoretical discourse of cultural studies, as well as where Bhabha fits into this discussion.

Text

Micah

I initially chose to study Micah because I thought it might be the kind of text that would confront readers and influence them to do justice. Indeed, the text of Micah has often been considered a text that celebrates and advocates justice (Alfaro 1989; Brueggemann 1981; Brueggemann, Parks and Groome 1986; Gutiérrez 1973: 293; Limburg 1988; Mays 1983; Sakenfeld 1985: 101-104, 148-49; R.L. Smith 1984), with its famed call, 'He has shown you, O human, what is good, and what Yahweh seeks from you: to do justice, and to love faithfulness and to walk wisely with your God' (Mic. 6.8); and with its exaltation of peace, 'Their swords will be beaten into plowshares and their spears into pruning knives; nation will not lift sword against nation, and they will no longer learn battle' (Mic. 4.3).[2] Micah would seem the perfect text, then, with which to think through the possibility of positioning readers in a way that orients them toward justice. Thus I began work on Micah rather idealistically, hoping to find the text calling readers to identify with subject positions and identities poised to do justice at every turn.

But having read and reread the text, I have come to realize that the call for justice in Micah, while undeniably present, is not uncomplicated by ambiguities within the text. It is true that the text seems to lament warfare, conquest and conflict (1.8-16; 2.8; 4.3, 10-11; 7.4-6), to condemn deception as well as wrongful extortion of land and resources (2.1-3, 9; 3.1-12; 6.10-13), to exhort justice (6.8), and to envision a glorious, peaceful and egalitarian future (2.12-13; 4.1-8; 5.1-4; 7.7-20). On closer scrutiny though, these images seem to fade in and out of another scene which includes valorization of (male) conquest and rule (1.3-7; 2.12-13; 5.5-8), colonial invasion (6.4-5), totalizing assimilation of other nations to the rule of Yahweh (4.1-4; 5.6-7; 7.12), and violence against Israel in figurations both female and male (against female figures: 1.6-7, 11-16; 3.12; 4.14; against male figures: 2.1-4; 5.9-14; 6.13-16). The ambiguity in the book is further compounded by the difficult Hebrew structures: ambiguous referents, odd and difficult phrases, and frequent switches in gender and person, addressor and addressee (for details see

---

2.   All translations of the text of Micah are my own.

Chapter 4). In addition, the book contains several dramatic shifts in mood, from announcements of doom (1.5-16; 2.3-5, 9-10; 3.6-7, 12; 5.9-14; 6.13-16; 7.1, 13) to comforting images of hope (2.12-13; 4.1-8; 5.1-8; 7.7-20). And almost as if to make the process of reading more laborious, there is no obvious narrative or poetic flow which would help interpret the difficulties.

Reading for Coherence: Micah Studies

It is hard to know how to approach this text. Given the ambiguities, how does one understand what is meant in the text, let alone be influenced by it? Does one emend textual discrepancies to make them more comprehensible, or does one try to find ways to read the text as it stands? Certainly I am not the first to notice the ambiguities in Micah; as I outline below, scholarship on Micah has long been concerned with accounting for the book's textual difficulties. Since the end of the nineteenth century, scholars have been suggesting readings that ease the discomfort of the dramatic reversals in attitude in the book ('hope' versus 'doom'), as well as the discordant Hebrew syntactical structures. Solutions to these 'problems' have included readings that divide the book into original and later materials, hypotheses of unifying themes for the text, and emendations of textual discrepancies.[3]

Those scholars who have resolved the problems by viewing the text as a compilation of original and later prophetic works—often debating how to group chs. 1–3, 4–5, and 6–7 together as discrete linguistic and thematic units, and proposing various relations between these units[4]— have tended to do so in the context of redaction criticism. For very recent examples of this, see Theodor Lescow, who identifies various redactional stages through an analysis of key words (1997: 20-22); and William McKane, who argues that the original text of Micah (chs. 1–3) has been augmented by later prophets as it suits their thinking about Israelite society (1998: 7-19). These scholars pick up on a well-developed tradition of redaction criticism in Micah studies. For instance, Ina Willi-Plein (1971) traces the stages of the book's growth from the time of Micah into the post-exilic era, and the prophetic reinterpretation of certain passages during this textual growth. B. Renaud painstakingly details

3.   For overviews of interpretation from the nineteenth century onwards, see Willis (1966: 1-100); Jeppesen (1978, 1979); Luker (1985: 5-123); Cuffey (1987: 8-87); Mason (1991: 27-42); Shaw (1993: 1-18). Shaw identifies two general tendencies in Micah scholarship, the first to attribute Mic. 4–7 to later dates, the second (within which he situates himself) to try to read the book as in some way coherent.

4.   For a good overview of the various proposals, see Hagstrom (1988: 13-27); Shoemaker (1992: 32-33).

the pre-exilic and exilic redactions, final structuration, and a final rereading containing anti-Samaritan elements (1977: 383-473). James Luther Mays uses form and literary criticism to discern redactional units which correspond to the concerns of historical settings from Sennacherib's invasion, to the Babylonian crisis, to exilic and post-exilic periods (1976: 22-33). Hans Walter Wolff posits a redactional formation of the book, starting with original sayings of Micah, then moving to deuteronomistic commentaries, postexilic collections and redactions, with a final edition preparing Micah for liturgical use (1990: 26-27). Itumeleng Mosala looks at the class biases of the various redactional strata, from ruling class ideology to critiques of that ideology from the point of view of the oppressed (1989: 101-53). And A.S. van der Woude argues that the book is for the most part a coherent debate between true and false prophets (chs. 1–5), with chs. 6–7 being the work of a northern prophet, redacted with deuteronomic intent (1969; 1982: 49-50).

Some scholars also combine redaction criticism with the search for unity in the book. For instance, John T. Willis posits a coherent whole and suggests that the final form is a compilation for liturgical use, reflecting the theological concerns of a sixth-century redactor (1966: 123-24, 194, 312). Likewise, James Limburg suggests the final form was designed for liturgical use (1988: 162). Lamontte Luker has considered how redactional unity is accomplished through a new montage of older Divine Warrior, lament, and woman–city traditions (1985: 224-28; 1987: 285).

Luker's approach, especially, reflects a trend in many of the more recent commentaries and dissertations that look at the book as a coherent whole, whether or not written by one author. Some scholars have sought coherence either by positing historical contexts as frames enabling the diverse parts of the book to hang together in a meaningful way, or by positing literary structures that hold the book together. Delbert Hillers, who posits a 'millennial movement' in eighth-century Judah (1984: 4) as a background to the book, is a good example of those using historical context to give the book coherence. Likewise Bruce Waltke (1988: 149) and Peter Craigie (1985: 2-3) argue that the book dates to the time of the Assyrian invasions, and is mostly, if not entirely, original to the eighth-century prophet. Helmut Utzschneider (1999) finds most of the book (Mic. 1.1–4.7) to be a kind of drama between Micah, his rivals and Yahweh, including addresses (with quoted speeches of others), monologues and responses. David Noel Freedman finds the disjunctions in the book to cohere with the person of a historical prophet who, he proposes, alternates between ecstatic vision and calm poetic reflection (1983: 157). Along more political lines, George Pixley

(1991) uses Norman Gottwald's peasant revolution theory to suggest
that Micah was a revolutionary, and that the text reflects the conflict
between his politics and those of the leaders of Israel.[5] Most recently,
Ehud Ben Zvi has contended that the text was written by and for the
literati (1998: 104) as a coherent text (2000: 58), most likely in the post-
monarchic Persian II period (2000: 10), though set in the monarchic
period. He suggests that the text is designed to explain the past, influence the present and articulate a hope for the future (2000: 5).

The emphasis on unifying themes in the book also appears in the
kinds of literary accounts of coherence in Micah that have become quite
prevalent over the last twenty years.[6] For instance, David Hagstrom
posits that the book is structured by two disputes (chs. 1–5, 6–7) which
are both made up of judgment and salvation (1988: 27). Kenneth Cuffey
argues that that 'the remnant passages are the center of integration for
Micah' (1987: 247), each remnant passage responding to the doom that
goes before it, creating a book which reflects on God's care for his people. Leslie Allen suggests a concentric structure with parallel sections
alternating around hope and doom (1976: 260). Walter Kaiser sees the
book as structured by the 'Hear' imperatives at the beginning of chs. 1, 3
and 6, with 'common themes, recurring motifs, repeated uses of similar
rhetorical devices and linking words from one section to the next' (1992:
25-26).[7] Kenneth Shoemaker outlines the various units and types of
discourse in the book by paying special attention to who is speaking to
whom; his argument is that the text is a highly sophisticated literary
work which uses various types of discourses yet maintains coherence
(1992: 19-24, 424-31), and that if these units of discourse are not

5.   For a range of other scholars who have also suggested the 'Hear' imperatives
as important to the structure of the book see Hagstrom (1988: 27 nn. 34, 36).
Hagstrom also suggests that the 'summons to hear does play a role as a structural
indicator in the book of Micah' (1988: 27), but he argues that it is not able to 'bear the
weight of the structure of the book of Micah when considered alone' (1988: 25-27).

6.   The most recent of these, the new Anchor Bible commentary on Micah by
Francis Andersen and David Noel Freedman (2000), was not yet available until after I
completed my own study, and so is not incorporated throughout. They argue that the
text is a unified composition held together by key words, structural features and
overarching concepts, divided into three parts: The Book of Doom (chs. 1–2); The
Book of Visions (chs. 4–5); and The Book of Contention and Conciliation (chs. 6–7).
They state that their analysis of the composition of the book affects the decisions they
make about text critical and form critical issues, and leads them to '*solutions* different
from those enshrined in the older commentaries and text-critical apparatus' (2000:
29, emphasis mine).

7.   Willis proposes that this is the structure around which redactors arranged the
book (1966: 314).

properly identified, the text appears disjointed (1992: 425, 428). All of these accounts of literary coherence aim at unifying the text in some way.

In all of these ways of accounting for the discrepancies in Micah, it seems that the practice of textual emendment begun in the nineteenth century has not been abandoned as a way of problem solving, but remains a consistent solution to the most difficult textual problems, no matter what the overarching method. A glance through the textual notes in almost any analysis of Micah (see Chapter 4) shows that scholars often tend to maintain or slightly modify suggestions for emendment made by earlier commentators, or, having discussed the options for emendation, make their own. When the Hebrew is very difficult, which it often is in Micah, scholars tend to consider the text damaged in some way and correct it (e.g. Hillers 1984: 34; Mays 1976: 48-49, 68). Even some of those who try to avoid emendation can be found saying, 'emendation is unavoidable' (Shaw 1993: 70 n. 4) or, 'the text appears confused...the emended reading not only makes sense, but also restores parallelism' (Hagstrom 1988: 26 n. 49). Shoemaker is another who argues for caution in emendation and careful text-critical work in doing so (1992: 222, 229), as this would affect participant analysis; yet he seems to adopt emendations quite freely, without necessarily noting text-critical sources (e.g. 1992: 124 n. 82, 129 n. 104, 179 n. 268, 232 n. 41).[8]

Reading Difference in Micah

For my part, rather than approach the text to 'solve its problems', in an effort to produce a unified reading, or to ascertain something of its historical context, its redactional process, or its literary unity, I am choosing to look at the possible impact of this text, as it stands in the Masoretic Text (MT), with all its fascinating nuances and fissures. This is partly because I feel that others have done readings that posit historical and literary contexts and coherences, and done it thoroughly. But it is also partly because it seems to me that the kind of reading that solves problems or enables unity has the effect of homogenizing texts and erasing or disavowing difference within them. I would rather not presume the text to be unitary, knowable and 'fixable' with the 'right interpretive key' (that is, if I can discern the proper context, I can understand or emend the text). This is not to say that I do not acknowledge that the MT is the result of a long process of textual transmission into which scribal errors

---

8.   Shoemaker does however provide a good overview of the text-critical sources and known variants (1992: 222-29); see also Hillers (1984: 9-10); Allegro (1968); Collin (1971); Sinclair (1983).

and opinions may have crept, perhaps accounting for some textual disjunctions and discrepancies.[9] However, I would say that it seems very difficult to sort out what is error and what is 'original' without imposing some external standard for both detecting and solving problems. Thus my concern is not to see how the various parts of the book cohere or can be made to cohere with any pre-fixed notion of the original, correct and unified text.

To my mind, it is more interesting to attend to the many voices and shifts in the text, without trying to subsume them into one 'unifying theme' in order to see what effect the ruptures in the text might have on the reading process. I wish to consider the textual difficulties in terms of the interpretive process and its relation to readers' positioning as subjects. As stated above, I am choosing to look at how the differences, difficulties and reversals in the way participants are addressed in the book—specifically with respect to gender, national identity and vision for the future—might operate to re-situate the reader with regard to her own subjectivity. It might be objected that my focus on these themes is only another way of unifying the text, and this may be so in one sense, since these themes prove interesting focal points around which to think the issues of address in the text. However, I am not trying to fit the text into these categories, but am using them as heuristics for readerly identification and positioning as subject. Further, since gender and nation are both pervasive—and I would argue ideological—constructs within which present-day readers are situated, and since they are often enacted with reference to the future, these categories will provide useful starting-points for the kind of larger inquiry into texts' impact on ideology that I will eventually pursue.

Such an approach to Micah that attends to difference is not without any precedents, four of which I would like to draw attention to below: (1) Ehud Ben Zvi's work on Micah, culminating in his commentary, *Micah* (2000, see also 1998, 1999); (2) Itumeleng Mosala's use of Micah, in his *Biblical Hermeneutics and Black Theology in South Africa* (1989); (3) Anthony Petrotta's *Lexis Ludens: Wordplay and the Book of Micah* (1991); and (4) Timothy Beal's article, 'The System and the Speaking Subject in the Hebrew Bible: Reading for Divine Abjection' (1994, see also 1997a).[10] What is interesting about all of these readings is their

9.   See Culley (2000) for a discussion of prophetic texts as complex composite texts that mark the way major themes have been dealt with differently through various time periods and compositional traditions (oral and scribal).

10.   Beal has developed his original article to serve as an introduction to *Reading Bibles, Writing Bodies* (Beal and Gunn 1997). This reworking asks questions pertinent

attention to the shifts in the text, and in the cases of Mosala and Beal, the use of Micah to challenge totalizing (univocal, bourgeois, patriarchal) understandings of the text in the desire to crack the binding of ideologically coherent readings, through pressure on 'the tiny cracks and fissures' (Beal 1997a: 1-2).

As already noted briefly, Ben Zvi looks at the differences within the text to show that it was composed as a complex literary text, rather than deriving from oral sources. Ben Zvi's overarching concern is historical, which is not my own, but his method of demonstrating his point is unusual in its attention to differences within the text. He considers the text to be purposefully indeterminate, arguing that the shifts in pronouns and address in the book are part of a deliberately ambiguous stylistic technique designed to catch readers' and re-readers' attention and to draw links between ideas. For Ben Zvi, the openness or indeterminacy of the text allows re-readers to relate to the text and to develop new understandings (2000: 37, 54). Further, he suggests that the 'consistent blurring of differences between the speakers, on the one hand, and the addressees on the other, by means of areas of overlap and identity confusion is not only a stylistic device to get the attention of the (re-)readers of the book, but serves the purpose of associating certain "entities" with one another' (1998: 114). Throughout his work he notices how the ambiguities in the text function to associate ideas and personas in the book (e.g. 2000: 31, 126-27, 139, 143). He therefore does not try to correct the text, but rather looks at how the blurred identities might be intended to affect the reader. While my concern is not so much the *intention* behind the style as its possible *effect*, the ideas of overlap and identity confusion are motifs that I will pick up on, in quite different ways, as I think about ideological identification and repositioning of the reader.

Mosala, like Ben Zvi, looks at differences in Micah from a historical point of view, but he does so in order to argue, using Micah as an example, that any attempt to use the biblical text for liberation must take into account the 'oppression and oppressors, exploitation and exploiters' (1989: 33) inherent in the production and presentation of the biblical text. Mosala looks at the shifts in the text to demonstrate the method of exposing 'the underlying material relationships [which] throw light on the problems of which the biblical texts are a solution' (1989: 5). He scrutinizes the text for what it leaves out, for the struggles that have been

to a book on bodies and identity, and takes into account Kristeva's subsequent reading of the Bible in *New Maladies of the Soul* (1995); however, the force of this article for Micah studies remains substantially the same.

silenced, or that appear only faintly, suggesting that careful historical-materialist reconstruction can help in detecting the various forms of oppression latent in biblical texts. He writes:

> As is true of most of the Bible, [Micah] offers no certain starting point for a theology of liberation... However, enough contradictions within Micah enable eyes hermeneutically trained in the struggle for liberation today to observe the kindred struggles of the oppressed and exploited of the biblical communities in the very absence of those struggles in the text (1989: 121).

Thus in his discussion of Micah (1989: 101-53), Mosala separates out the various redactional strata and analyses them for their class and ideological affiliations. From this analysis, he looks at the potential for black working-class people in South Africa to identify with the various strata of the text. He finds texts of the ruling class that uphold the dominant ideology (1989: 127-34); texts that are produced by scribes to critique the ruling class (1989: 134-43); texts directed against the ruling class (1989: 143-49); and finally texts that are a combination of the latter two (1989: 149-52).[11] Mosala's reading is interesting, not only because it puts (parts of) Micah to liberatory purposes, but because it uses a Marxist hermeneutic of suspicion to think about the contradictions and incoherences in the text as indicative of the contradictions present in the social and economic conditions within which the text was produced.

Petrotta, on the other hand, comes at the text from a completely different angle, focusing on the differences within the text as wordplays with rhetorical purpose. Petrotta does not look at the text in its historical context, but purely from a literary point of view. Through careful attention to the sound plays (alliteration, assonance and so on), puns and irony in the text, Petrotta traces the rhetorical and literary force of a number of the passages in the book. One operative element that Petrotta frequently points out in these kinds of rhetorical wordplays is *ambiguity*, whether lexical or syntactical (e.g. 1991: 118-23). He suggests that there is often a kind of deliberate indeterminacy in the text (1991: 123), and he demonstrates how certain meanings are not excluded by the text. He illustrates how the various possibilities that are offered to readers may be used to draw readers in and then change their expectations, surprising them—as is typical of wordplay—with an 'alternative and incongruous reading of an utterance' (1991: 37); he calls these 'reversals'. This, he argues, is part of the affective and cognitive work of wordplay (1991: 5), that is, the emotional and persuasive effect of the

---

11. Mosala is following Robert Coote's analysis, in *Amos Among the Prophets* (1981), of A, B, and C texts in Amos.

text on the reader (see his chs. 7–8). Thus Petrotta adds to an analysis of the text's intent a more particular focus on the effect, and affect, of the text on the reader. While he seems to assume a 'universal' reader, which a discussion of ideology would problematize, what I find interesting in his project, beyond his careful work on wordplay, is his understanding of the way the ambiguities in the text can confront or reposition the reader.

Beal's approach also opens up new ways of thinking about the text, through engagement with contemporary critical theory. Beal uses Mic. 1.8-9 to critique Julia Kristeva's notion of the biblical God as the patriarchal, 'stable guarantor of the entire system' (1994: 176). He makes this argument using Kristeva's own discussions of intertextuality (the understanding of texts as continually interacting with other texts) and the abject (the 'jettisoned', 'radically excluded' object that disturbs, yet is somehow fundamental to, 'identity, system, order') (Kristeva 1982: 2, 4, 13, 15).[12] Beal suggests that Yahweh, as the lamenting, speaking subject in Mic. 1.8-9, internalizes the abjection which is inherent to the symbolic order set up in Israel and in Micah. He goes on to consider how reading Yahweh as abject establishes intertextual links with other passages, such as Isa. 42.14, where Yahweh is depicted as a woman in labour. Thus this image of Yahweh is transposed in a way that challenges the notion of a stable, univocal and patriarchal God in the Hebrew Bible. In the later reworking of the essay, Beal argues that this kind of reading can unsettle readers by first unsettling understandings of 'the social and symbolic order of the Bible...[with] its centerpiece, foundation and guarantor of the One God, whose divine prohibition against the mother...is the basis for the formation of identity' (1997a: 4). By questioning the identity of Yahweh as guarantor of the patriarchal order, he asks a question that resonates with my own line of questioning: 'Is it conceivable that [Scripture] does not simply serve the formation of the subject within a particular system or politics of identity? Might it also articulate a crisis in identity, a crisis that is capable of opening to new possibilities for political transformation?' (1997a: 2).

---

12.   As is well known, Kristeva was one of the first to use the term 'intertexuality' in this way, and she develops an understanding of this term from Bakhtin's dialogism, 'the open-ended, back-and-forth play between the text of the sender (subject), the text of the addressee (object), and the text of culture' (Beal 1992: 29, cf. Kristeva 1980: 65). Intertextuality is, then, the text in dialogue with other texts (Beal 1992: 30), the 'transposition of one (or several) sign system(s) into another' (Kristeva 1984: 59). In this way a text is endlessly augmented by the transposition of other texts into it: 'any text is constructed as a mosaic of quotations; any text is the absorption and transformation of another' (Kristeva 1980: 65).

Thus Beal, Petrotta, Mosala and Ben Zvi all look at the question of differences within the text and consider in some form or another the kinds of identifications readers make with text. In the work of Petrotta and Ben Zvi, the 'discrepancies' in the text are considered deliberately indeterminate; and though in the end this implies that the text is actually determinate for meaning, it is an approach that at least opens up the idea that indeterminate text can have some kind of real impact on the reader. In the work of Beal and Mosala, analysis of differences in the text moves toward thinking about the biblical text's capacity to provoke a questioning of identity in a way that urges political change. It is this latter line of inquiry that motivates my own work on Micah, but I would like to do it with the kind of detailed attention that Petrotta and Ben Zvi pay to the textual ambiguities.

Interpretation

Textual Indeterminacy

The question of the ability of textual ambiguities to affect readers has certain affinities with another line of questioning that has been taken up in literary and biblical criticism for a number of years now, under the auspices of textual determinacy. One of the more important and pro-vocative questions dealt with in these discussions has been: 'Does the text control the reader or does the reader control the text?' (Fowler 1985: 13), or put another way, how does one deal with the 'gaps', the unknowns, in a text? This question has circulated amongst literary critics since the mid 1970s, and was initially raised in biblical studies by reader-response criticism.[13]

The full range of responses has been explored by biblical scholars, from Meir Sternberg's insistence that the gaps in the text are part of the Bible's strategy as a foolproof text, carefully controlling the reading pro-cess and preventing counter readings (1985: 7-59); to Fewell and Gunn's careful work on the way in which the multivalent meanings of texts can be used to read against their own grains (1993); through Edgar

---

13. Biblical scholars began questioning, along with literary critics like Stanley Fish and Wolfgang Iser, how the 'gaps in the text' are interpreted. For Iser, both the processes of finding gaps and filling them are largely determined by the readers' expectations, however the text does present fixed points or schemata (1974: 276, 282). For Fish, the gaps themselves open up differently according to the interpretive context of the reader (1981: 7). For a more thorough introduction to these issues, see the debate between Iser and Fish in *Diacritics* 11 (1981); Fowler (1985, 1992); McKnight (1988); Sherwood (1996: 25-34); and the Bible and Culture Collective (1995: 20-69).

McKnight's position that the gaps created by textual omissions and ambiguities are filled in by the reader who searches for coherence (1988);[14] to Julia O'Brien's fully reader-oriented autobiographical exploration of how her own life situation changed her understanding of Malachi as an abusive text (1995).[15]

In turn, this question of readerly control sparked debates in biblical studies on textual indeterminacy, opening the door for the exploration of poststructural ideas such as intertextuality and deconstruction. In particular, attractive but troubling ideas for biblical scholars have been Roland Barthes's conception of a writerly (plural, open, reversible, indeterminate) text (1974: 4-6, 260; Beal 1992); Kristeva's intertextuality, that 'intersection of textual surfaces' (1980: 65) in which text is endlessly augmented by the transposition of other texts into it (Beal 1992; Fewell 1992; Phillips 1992); and Derrida's understanding of text as a fabric of endlessly deferring traces (1979a: 84) 'constituted on the basis of the trace within it of the other elements of the chain or system' (1981b: 26; Phillips 1995).

In thinking about text as an endlessly referring chain, a number of scholars have turned to Derrida's notion of the undecidable, that is, a point in a text that has 'a double and opposite meaning, which allows (indeed invites) the reader to read the text against the grain of its main argument' (Sherwood 1996: 177). Gary Phillips, in his article ' "You are Either Here, Here, Here or Here": Deconstruction's Troublesome Interplay' (1995), suggests that perhaps attention to Derrida's undecidable is a way to move away from the disturbing either/or logic of textual in/determinacy. An example of this kind of attention to undecidables is Yvonne Sherwood's work in *The Prostitute and the Prophet* (1996), where she shows how the notion of the limitless, constantly referring text is for Derrida part of the undecidability of borders (see her excellent discussion of undecidables, 1996: 176-87). She goes on to show how undecidables, which often appear with the aid of intertext, might be usefully employed to challenge typical patriarchal and oppressive readings of biblical text (in particular, she works on Hos. 1–3).

Although whether and how *meaning* can be located in the continuous chain of signification and multiple codes is a question still open for

14. McKnight's position strongly resembles that of Iser, upon whom he draws heavily; see Iser (1974: 235-39; 258-59).

15. For a different kind of reading of the gaps in a text see Todd Linafelt's 'Margins of Lamentations' (1997), where he reads the absence of God's voice in Lamentations alongside of Jabès's reflections on the absence and white space inherent to texts, in order to reflect upon the constant deferral and supplement that this void provokes.

debate, the attention to undecidables moves away from the text/reader dichotomy (*either* the text *or* the reader controls meaning) and urges an exploration of the negotiation between the two. Indeed it seems that by now many scholars agree that reading is a 'dialogical process', a negotiation between text and reader, where both have a role to play in establishing 'meaning'. However, work within biblical studies on theorizing this dialogical process has most often stayed focused on the questions of *textual* interpretation and the production of meaning and has only begun to touch on how this negotiation might affect *readers*. Some of the recent work on the ethics of reading (see Fewell and Phillips 1997a, in particular the articles by Fewell and Phillips, Heard, Snyman, A. Smith) moves in this direction, discussing the kinds of identifications with the text readers might make, and how this affects their reading.

Text and Reader 'in Front' of the Text: Ricoeur

The idea that texts can affect readers and readers' positioning as subjects, however, is not new to biblical studies. Paul Ricoeur's description of the self's confrontation with the world of the text has been influential for biblical study over the last twenty years (see Ricoeur 1975, 1980; Vanhoozer 1990; Wallace 1990). In his *Hermeneutics and the Human Sciences* (1981), Ricoeur proposes a way of thinking about how the text might challenge the reader's ideology,[16] by making the self more aware of its own positioning. Though I do not build on Ricoeur explicitly in this present study, his ideas bear some attention at this point, as they have played a vital role in opening up the various new avenues along which other biblical scholars and I are able to think about the relationship between text and reader.

As is often pointed out, in *Hermeneutics and the Human Sciences*, Ricoeur argues that meaning is produced neither in the projection of the reader onto the text (1981: 182), nor in the 'hidden intention' of the

---

16. Ricoeur uses the terms 'ideology' and 'subject' in a more humanist or 'anthropological' (1986: 120, 153-57) vein than Althusser. For a thorough discussion of this see Ricoeur's readings of Althusser in his *Lectures on Ideology* (1986), where he argues that the base–superstructure model is not adequate to deal with claims to legitimacy which he sees (after Weber) driving ideology (1986: 89, 95, 107). For Ricoeur, claims to legitimacy involve psychological factors (beliefs, motivations) that cannot be reduced to a causal model (1986: 154); as I understand it, by this Ricoeur wants to affirm individuals' agency (individual motivation). Ricoeur does want to adopt Althusser's notion of overdetermination, especially overdetermination of meaning, but this he feels can only be done adequately within a motivational, rather than causal, framework (1986: 128).

text, but somewhere in between, 'in front of the text'. In the process of interpretation, readers *appropriate*[17] the 'proposed world' of the text (1981: 143). For Ricoeur, fiction and poetry create a 'world' in which other possibilities for 'being' exist, in which 'new possibilities of being-in-the-world are opened up within every day reality' (1981: 142). Because poetry and fiction (especially) refer not to everyday reality but to some other imaginative reality, they abolish the first order of reference (to reality), and provide 'the condition of possibility for the freeing of a second order of reference' (1981: 141), that is, reference to a world unique to a given text.[18] For Ricoeur, the world of the work is that which the work 'unfolds, discovers, reveals' (1981: 142) in 'front of the text' (1981: 143). The world of the work is then 'a *distanciation* of the real from itself' (1981: 143, emphasis mine). 'Appropriation', on the other hand, is the 'dialectical counterpart' of distanciation; it is what enables the reader 'to actualize the meaning of the text' (1981: 185), to enter into relation with it. 'Appropriation' is Ricoeur's translation of the German noun *Aneignung*, from the verb *aneignen,* meaning ' "to make one's own" what was initially "alien" ' (1981: 185).

It is here that Ricoeur's views on subjectivity come into 'play' (to use a Ricoeurian turn of phrase). Appropriation 'gives the subject new capacities for knowing himself' (1981: 192) through entry into the world of the work, as well as new capacities for discovering the possibilities for 'being' opened up within this world. In this way, the world of the work 'opens up its readers and thus creates its own subjective *vis-à-vis*' (1981: 143). Because the world of the work is 'in front of' the work, understanding is a matter of *understanding oneself* in front of the text (1981: 113, 143). 'It is not a question of imposing upon the text our finite capacity of understanding, but of exposing ourselves to the text and

---

17. Ricoeur addresses what he calls the dialectic between distanciation (the distance of the text with respect to discourse) and appropriation (the reader's interaction with the text). In other words, Ricoeur deals specifically with the way readers interact with the discourse encoded in text. Ricoeur points out that when discourse is turned into text, 'there is no longer a speaker, at least in the sense of an immediate and direct self-designation of the one who speaks in the instance of discourse' (1981: 149). Though it is still a form of discourse, writing is detached from specific utterances and references, requiring specific responses. Ricoeur terms this distanciation. In this way, writing is 'freed from the dialogical condition of discourse' (1981: 139).

18. Ricoeur is building from Husserl and Heidegger here. He argues that the second order of reference created by a text 'reaches the world not only at the level of manipulable objects, but at the level that Husserl designated by the expression *Lebenswelt* [life-world] and Heidegger by the expression "being-in-the-world" ' (1981: 141).

receiving from it an enlarged self' (1981: 143). Thus Ricoeur distinguishes the '*self* which emerges for the understanding of the text' from
the '*ego* which claims to precede this understanding. It is the text...which
gives a *self* to the *ego*' (1981: 193).

Not only does appropriation enlarge the subject, enabling greater self-
understanding, but at the same time, appropriation has the effect of
destabilizing the subject. First, the process of appropriation requires that
the self must distance itself from itself (1981: 113), or 'unrealise itself'
(1981: 94) in order to allow for the new subject positions presented by
the text (Ricoeur calls them 'imaginative variations of the *ego*' [1981:
94]). In order to appropriate the matter, or world of the text, the subject
must 'exchange the *me, master* of itself, for the *self, disciple* of the text'
(1981: 113). This enables a partial critique of the subject's ideology, or
as Ricoeur puts it, of 'illusions of the subject' (1981: 94), because in the
process of self-distancing, the subject also distances itself from its
ideological conditioning (1981: 190-91, 243-44; 1978: 58-59).

Second, the subject is destabilized in appropriation through 'play'.
Ricoeur borrows the concept of play from Gadamer in order to signify
'the mode of being of appropriation' (1981: 185). Play is not the activity
of the subject, but rather what takes place when the subject enters the
world of the text (1981: 186). Ricoeur likens reading to entering a game:
the reader plays, but more to the point, the reader is played (1981: 186);
to read is to 'abandon ourselves to the space of meaning which holds
sway over the reader' (1981: 187). Play is what enables the destabilization and metamorphosis of the reader through the work: 'play shatters
the seriousness of a utilitarian preoccupation where the self-presence of
the subject is too secure' (1981: 186).

Ricoeur's world of the work therefore opens up a space for negotiation between text and reader and urges consideration of how that negotiation might shift the reader's subject position. Through the notions of
appropriation and play, he approaches an understanding of the self-
awareness, destabilization and transformation possible in an interaction
between text and reader. But Ricoeur's work seems also to assume that
the world of the text is discernible and readily available to readers,
which has not been my experience with Micah. Because Micah does not
always make its referents and objects of address clear, the world of the
text shimmers and changes at best, and at worst, lies in fragments on the
floor of the reader's imagination. My own work, therefore, moves on
from a Ricoeurian perspective. I am trying to understand what the kind
of understanding of self and text that Ricoeur proposes might look like if
texts are considered indeterminate, and selves (subjects) are understood—in the light of insights brought by structuralism, poststructuralism

and cultural studies—as culturally, structurally and ideologically produced and defined.

Indeterminate Text, Ideology and Determinate Readers: Beal

A slightly different approach to the negotiation that takes place between text and reader has been put forward by Beal. In 'Ideology and Intertextuality: Surplus of Meaning and Controlling the Means of Production' (1992) he suggests that it may be the reader's ideology that controls the play of the text. However, he also questions what effect the biblical text might have on loosening readers' ideologically-bound interpretive strategies.

Beal's article, the questions it raises and the theoretical lead that it offers, has played an important role in leading to a Marxist Althusserian framework as a starting-point for understanding the question of the relation between text and reader. It may be helpful at this point to state briefly that Althusserian position, as a way of orienting the following discussion. Althusser argues that people (and thus for my purposes, readers) are formed as subjects within ideology. By this he means that the position from which an individual speaks and acts is determined by the way she responds to, and identifies with, the practices and discourses offered to her by various societal institutions (churches, schools, families and so on) in order to make sense of her material conditions ('the relations of production'). Ideology is not separate from any of these structures and practices, but is produced in them and by them; it is 'overdetermined', that is, both determined by and determining for them. Beal's article points toward adopting this kind of Althusserian starting-point for taking the exploration of textual (in)determinacy in new directions. For this reason, I take the time here to follow the theoretical trajectory, following from Beal's article, that has led to the framework which I lay out more fully in Chapter 2, with which I work for the duration of the study.

Beal suggests that, given the endlessly productive possibilities for 'intertextual' readings of texts, perhaps it is the reader's ideology which acts as a *strategy of containment* to limit the production of meaning. Working from Derrida's notion of a general text, a 'total and limitless fabric of text which constitutes our linguistic universe' (Beal 1992: 27), and Kristeva's notion of intertextuality in which 'the text is always a playful "intersection of textual surfaces rather than a point (a fixed meaning)" ' (Kristeva 1980: 65), Beal questions how meaning can ever be fixed (1992: 30). But following the definition of ideology as 'a strategy of containment which imposes meaningful structures on the totality' (1992: 31), he is able to say that the reader's ideology limits the possibilities for

intertextual relations in order to produce a coherent interpretation.[19]
According to this view, neither the text nor the reader would control
meaning, but rather the reader's ideology; the reader would only control
textual play to the extent that she would be able to control her own
position within ideology. Given these restrictions on the possibilities for
meaning, Beal asks, 'how can one's recognition of the dialogic, polyvocal
dynamics of biblical writing dynamite [ideological] strategies of containment and loosen their control over the processes of production?' (1992:
36). Or put slightly more pointedly, is it possible that the process of
reading biblical text might free readers from their entrenchment within a
particular ideology, given that they read and interpret according to that
ideology? This is the question that I ultimately try to work out with the
help of Bhabha. However, it is by reading Beal through an intertext that
he offers that I also find the framework in which to use Bhabha.

Beal takes the definition of ideology as a 'strategy of containment'
from a discussion in Fredric Jameson's *The Political Unconscious* (1981)
on the analysis of ideology operating in texts. In this discussion, Jameson
lays out several understandings of ideology; of these, the one to which
Beal refers, is Georg Lukács's description of ideology (1981: 52-53). As
Jameson describes it, Lukács argues that ideology is not just imposed on
the totality of a text, but produces that totality. Jameson writes:

> Lukács' achievement was to have understood that such strategies of con-
> tainment...can be unmasked only by confrontation with the ideal of
> totality which they at once imply and repress... [A] strategy of contain-
> ment...allows what can be thought to seem internally coherent in its own
> terms, while repressing the unthinkable...which lies beyond its boundaries
> (1981: 53).

Jameson later contrasts Lukács's view of ideology as totalizing to
Althusser's understanding that ideology inheres in structures, and can be
discerned through 'structural difference and determinate contradiction'
(1981: 56). Quoting Althusser at length, Jameson shows that Althusser's
view of ideology is related to his understanding of 'structural causality',
in which structure is inseparable from content:

> The structure is not an essence outside the economic phenomena which
> comes and alters their aspect, forms and relations and which is effective on
> them as an absent cause, absent because it is outside them...the effects are
> *not outside* the structure, are not a pre-existing object...*the structure is*

19. David Penchansky offers a similar account of the role of ideology in interpretation (1992: 38-40), though he is not dealing specifically with containing intertextual
relations. Conversely, Michael Fox argues that while ideology may 'bias readings...
most often ideology is not relevant to interpretive choices' (1995: 185).

immanent in its effects (Althusser 1970: 188-89; cited by Jameson 1981: 24; emphasis mine).[20]

Jameson suggests that Lukács's notion of totality is similar to what Althusser rejects as an absent cause. In the end though, Jameson finds both approaches useful for analysing ideology within texts, saying, 'I have found it possible without any great inconsistency to respect both the…concept of totality or totalization [Lukács], and the quite different attention of a "symptomal" analysis to discontinuities, rifts, actions [that show up structural difference] within a merely apparently unified cultural text [Althusser]' (1981: 57).

Beal, in making the move from a consideration of ideology operative in texts (so Jameson) to a consideration of ideology operative in interpretation, suggests that the reader's ideology contains (totalizes) intertextual play, which would, according to Jameson's discussion at least, follow Lukács. Yet to my mind, Beal's argument urges a more Althusserian approach,[21] though this will take some spelling out. To begin, if Beal's appeal to Derrida is taken seriously, then it would also follow that if ideology is part of the 'total and limitless fabric of text', it is not outside of 'text', and therefore *is not outside* of the intertextual relation. In this case, ideology would have to be considered a textual formation just like any other text or set of texts. What Beal calls ideological 'interpretative rules' (1992: 32) would need to be understood as prescribed, inscribed and circulated in textual discourse, as part of the general text. If this logic is followed, the interpreter's ideology cannot be considered a strategy of containment that controls or contains the play of text *from the outside*, but rather would have to be seen as thoroughly integrated into that play.

But if ideology is thus located, I arrive full circle at Beal's original question about intertextuality: what limits the production of intertextual

20. Althusser takes his understanding of structural causality from Marx, whom he argues is the first to think of the whole as structure, and the effect of the whole on its parts as the effect of the structure on its parts. Althusser shows the inconsistencies in Marx in developing this conception, yet argues that it is nevertheless a novel and important conception, over against mechanistic or transitive causality (originating from Descartes) which 'could not be made to think the effectivity of a whole on its elements, except at the cost of extraordinary distortions' (1970: 186); or expressive causality (originating with Hegel and Leibnitz) which thinks of the whole in terms of inner essence and the effect of the whole on its parts in terms of the effect of this essence on its parts.

21. In fact, Beal does follow Althusser's general definition of ideology as 'the imaginary representation of the subject's relationship to his or her real conditions of existence' (Althusser, cited in Beal 1992: 37 n. 4).

relations? If ideology cannot be considered the structure that controls reading from the outside, what is it then that allows one text, or set of texts, to have influence over another? If the controlling structures for interpretation are elsewhere, the question is where? It seems clear to me that Beal is correct in arguing that biblical texts are often interpreted in the light of ideology. My question is: what is this interpretive operation if it is not a case of containment from the outside; further, might this interpretive operation also be able to work in the other direction so that biblical texts can also affect ideological texts in ways that might subvert hegemonic norms?

It seems to me that any theory of reading biblical texts that tries to take into account the three important issues Beal raises—(a) the problem of interpretation given the endless play of signifiers; (b) the impact of ideology on the indeterminacy of texts; and (c) the possibility that texts might challenge readers' ideology—must grapple with the details of the intertextual relation that takes place between the ideological text of the reader and the biblical text (which is of course in itself ideological text). That is, if both 'limitless text' and 'readers' positioning in ideology' are to be taken together seriously, then ideology must be read as part of the general text, and a new intertextual relation must be studied: the relation between ideological text and biblical text.

What Althusser has to offer the discussion is the notion that the structures cannot be separated from their effects. If structures are immanent in their effects, and if both texts (ideological and biblical) and readers' positioning with respect to ideology are effects of structures, as Althusser (and other Marxist critics) might suggest they are, then I might say, tentatively at least, that textual interpretation is a negotiation between various intersecting structures and their effects (texts and readers, who are also structured by language). This will bear a closer look in Chapters 2 and 3. What I will argue there, building from an Althusserian position, but with the help of Bhabha and others, is that interpretation is the negotiation between the structures of language that form texts and readers.

Readers

Readers' Formation as Subjects

Quite evidently, these kinds of discussions about text and reader cannot proceed without some recognition of *what a reader is*. However, if Althusser's view of ideology is taken seriously, one also has to reckon with his notion that individuals are formed as (historically-bound) subjects within ideology. While biblical scholars interested in reader-response theory have discussed the kinds of readers that texts assume and the level of readers' 'competency' (McKnight 1988; Fowler 1985, 1992), little work has been done within the field that takes into account the reader's formation as a self, or an agent, and the impact that this might have on reading. Likewise, discussions of the impact that a 'dialogical reading' might have on the self or subjectivity are rare, though scholars such as Beal (1997a, as discussed above), Jan Tarlin (1997) and Carol Newsom (1989) have moved in this direction.

One important article that should be mentioned here is Carol Newsom's 'Women and the Discourse of Patriarchal Wisdom: A Study of Proverbs 1–9' (1989). Newsom builds on Althusser's notion of ideological interpellation, discussing the process by which Proverbs 1–9 ideologically interpellates, or calls, readers into the position of the 'son'—thus aligning them with patriarchal ideology—through the use of the pronoun 'you'. She notices, however, that the father teaches 'you' the son to resist interpellation into other ideologies, and she suggests that this resistance can be applied to the text itself, so that 'the problematic nature of the discourse itself' (1989: 159) is revealed, with its silent son and its dissident and marginal 'strange woman'. Newsom provides a clear account of the way that texts might interpellate readers, and of the way that through that interpellation the reader might also learn to resist the ideology of the text. Although Newsom does not describe in detail the mechanics of the process by which a reader comes to be in a position to resist textual ideology, her article suggests a sort of negotiation of textual and readerly ideologies. As her article models, there is a kind of identification with the strange woman that might take place, perhaps in defiance, when the resisting reader is subjected to the text's ideological demands for identification as a son with the father; for contemporary readers, perhaps women in particular, it may be a sympathetic identification, with liberatory potential, that would perhaps not occur had the reader never encountered this text.

Cultural Studies

Newsom's article moves in important directions, but as mentioned, not too much has been done in biblical studies to expand on this kind of inquiry. However, as I see it, biblical studies' recent travel along the route of cultural studies (see Exum and Moore 1998; Segovia 1998a) has come to a turn that opens up onto the question of ideology and subjectivity. This theoretical vista is a space in which the role that the reader's ideology plays in reading, and the possibility for the text to affect the reader's subject position can be interrogated. One of the major concerns in cultural studies—especially early on—has been to explore how the self or 'the subject' has been situated and determined by ideology and attendant cultural objects, including various kinds of cultural discourses, as well as what effect this might have on agency. While I cannot hope to outline all of the discussions in cultural studies on this topic here, I will say that many of them have tried in various ways to combine a Marxist structuralist view of ideological analysis (subjectivity and ideology determined by material factors and economic structures, i.e. means and relations of production) with a Lacanian psychoanalytically based analysis of the subject (subjectivity determined by the interaction between 'libidinous' drives and culture/language). Such discussions often take as a starting-point Althusser's combination of Marxist and Lacanian thought, and in particular, his notion that individuals are always-already formed as subjects through their response to ideology. These discussions thereby draw out the Lacanian underpinnings of Althusser's discussion of ideological interpellation. The possibilities for repositioning subjects through subsequent interpellations (for instance, by film, text or political discourse) have been posited (e.g. Hall 1988; Grossberg 1997; Silverman 1983: 194-236), and have tended toward understanding the *desires* evoked by such cultural objects and the identifications made with them.

It is within this realm of cultural studies that I find Bhabha, who, in his discussions of the negotiation of cultural difference in colonial and postcolonial contexts, draws heavily on Lacan and Derrida. Though he makes much use of Lacan's descriptions of identification and subject formation, he also brings a primarily Derridean deconstructionist critique to bear upon it. Bhabha's theory also intersects nicely with another cultural theorist, Slavoj Žižek, who provides an important link to Marxist structuralism here, and therefore to my question of the possibility for shifting the reader's subject position, always-already formed in ideology. Žižek rereads Althusser's theory of ideological interpellation by extending and fully explicating its more muted Lacanian foundations, focusing on the kinds of psychic identifications that take place in intepellation (see Chapter 2). Because Žižek uses Lacan in this way, his work opens up a space for applying Bhabha's Derridean critique of Lacan to a discussion of ideology and interpellation. I will argue that Bhabha's theory has interesting implications for Althusser's (and Žižek's) description of the subject's interpellation into ideology and subsequently for the reading process in general (see Chapter 3).

While this may sound rather large, I am actually only proposing to take one small step toward thinking through these kinds of questions with respect to biblical text. Thus I read the text of Micah, replete with its own shifting metaphoric and syntactic subject positions, to theorize—

building on certain notions taken from Bhabha—how these shifts might interpellate and reinterpellate readers and what affect this might have on readers' 'subjectivity'. Can the shifts in the text—paying special attention to the changing forms of address in the text—also shift readers?, I ask, and suggest that they can, if readers make the kinds of identifications urged by these shifts.

Negotiating Readerly Subjectivity and Textual Indeterminacy: Bhabha
Bhabha's work provides a way of thinking about interpretation and the space 'in front of the text' (what he calls the 'third space'), while at the same time taking into account textual indeterminacy and the infinite play of text (using Derrida), as well as the formation of the subject in language and ideology (using Lacan and Žižek). Bhabha's work is able to handle these questions because it is largely concerned with the problem of agency within indeterminate (postcolonial) contexts, and with the different 'times' and 'spaces' in the negotiation of difference within which this agency can be inaugurated (see Chapter 3 for details). As will be discussed, Bhabha, in speaking of the negotiation of cultural difference, argues for the *inability to define or to determine* 'culture' and 'cultural identity'. For Bhabha, within every 'culture' there is only difference, and difference within difference; it is not possible to pin a culture down with one image or historical narrative, because these images and narratives get lived out very differently, if at all, by people or groups within a culture. But he does not want to submit to the idea that this kind of indeterminacy leaves people out at sea, that agency and solidarity are impossible. So he tries to show that negotiation with the indeterminate can bring about subversive agency, subversion of dominant structures, and revision of oppressive histories; this he calls 'the indeterminacy that makes subversion and revision possible' (1994a: 179). Because he draws on theorists that explore questions of language and subjectivity, Bhabha's discussions of the negotiation of cultural difference are able to furnish something like a model for thinking about how reading indeterminate text might affect readers' subjectivity in a manner that engenders resistance to oppression.

As acknowledged earlier, it may seem strange to use Bhabha, a postcolonial theorist, in a project that does not deal explicitly with modernity and its relation to colonialism. However because Bhabha deals with questions of language and text, and particularly with the way in which structures of language are related to agency, his work is useful for considering what impact texts might or might not have on readers' agency. He reads colonial and postcolonial texts to show how they embody a kind of subversive negotiation of cultural difference; it is his *description* of the process of negotiation, and his use of the language metaphor in this description, that is helpful for thinking about texts and readers.

This is not to say that Bhabha's work is without its own problems. In fact, Bhabha's work has been critiqued for its possible collusion with oppressive hegemonic power structures.[22] One of the main questions that has been raised about his work is his unproblematized use of the western canonic psychoanalytic and theoretical thinkers like Lacan, Žižek, Barthes and Derrida, as well as the effectiveness of using psycho-analytic categories for liberation (Moore-Gilbert 1997; Young 1990; Parry 1987). The relationship, or possible collusion, between postcolonialism and late stage capitalism set out by Dirlik (1994) and Ahmad (1992)—for example, the similar emphasis on translation and transnationalism in big business and in Bhabha (Dirlik 1994: 348-49)—also raises questions about the possibility of using this kind of theory for liberation. Further, a number of critics have raised questions about Bhabha's use of Fanon, and whether or not he leaves behind the historical and revolutionary context of Fanon's work, diminishing Fanon's call to armed resistance, and focusing on the psychoanalytic and discursive sides of Fanon's work (Moore-Gilbert 1997; Parry 1987; Holmlund 1991). Certainly his open-ness to various kinds of resisting agencies does seem to be limited. For instance, in discussing political actions of oppressed groups in an inter-view, he says, 'oppressed people resorting to guerrilla tactics are always archaic, premodern, bestial, or at best impulsive, lacking in ethical sense because they participate in violence'. Though his point is that as such, these 'profoundly regrettable' actions are troubling to notions of pro-gress and modernization (Bhabha 1993b: 6), it does not present militant struggle in a very positive light. Bhabha's article in praise of the way Lady Diana constructed her public image (1997d) also opens the question of his political affiliations.

These are important critiques that could, and indeed should, prob-lematize my use of Bhabha. Most particularly, this study *does* operate within the realm of western canonical texts, which may put into question the possibility of advocating for identification with difference ('liminal identification') in any real sense, given a centrist starting-point. This is a contradiction I am willing to inhabit, if uneasily, because Bhabha's theory brings together a number of issues that appear in recent debates in biblical studies on text and readers in ways that I believe can take these debates in productive directions. I use Bhabha's theory, therefore, not as something that can be straightforwardly read off the page and

22. For a general overview of critiques of Bhabha, see Moore-Gilbert (1997: 130-51).

applied to biblical text, but in the deconstructive spirit of working from within a (western, hegemonic) tradition, using its own problematics to try to push a little beyond its confines. It is my contention that Bhabha's theory provides a way of *critically negotiating* with canonical texts of psychoanalysis, literary theory and philosophy to which, as I have shown above, biblical scholars are increasingly turning.

Bhabha and Biblical Studies

To date, very little work has been done using Bhabha in biblical studies. I am uncertain whether Bhabha would wish to apply his thinking on postcolonialism to the process of reading ancient texts, especially a text like the Bible, which has been a tool of colonization. Yet, for the very reason that the Bible has been central to much of western colonialism, Bhabha's work may be crucial to reading biblical texts. Jim Perkinson's 'A Canaanatic Word in the Logos of Christ; Or the Difference the Syro-Phoenician Woman Makes to Jesus' (1996) is the most extended use of Bhabha in biblical studies that I have found.[23] Perkinson's article is interesting because he takes up Bhabha's work on cultural hybridity and performativity. Perkinson rereads the story of the Canaanite woman's encounter with the Israelite Jesus (Mk 7.24-30; Mt. 15.21-28) in terms of Bhabha's notion of the hybridity which takes place in the cultural contact between colonizer and colonized. The cultural moment in which the colonized speaks the words of the colonizer comes with the woman's repetition of Jesus' proverb. Her performative repetition of his proverb explodes his pedagogy, making his words new, hybrid, and thus undermines their original authority. Thus the woman wins the argument with Jesus. By reading the story in this way, Perkinson introduces biblical scholars to Bhabha's work and provides an exposition of the liberatory force of his argument, demonstrated through biblical narrative. I would like to take this one step further, and because I have more space, provide a longer exposition of Bhabha, as well as apply his theory to the reading process itself.

Reading for Liberation? Complicating the Question

I would be remiss, however, if I did not mention the strong influence of liberation theology in formulating the larger questions motivating my project, as well as the issues raised for it by the work that is being done with respect to ideological, feminist and postcolonial criticism of the Hebrew Bible. On the one hand, I am motivated by liberation theology's

---

23. See also S.D. Moore (2000); Runions (1998, 1999, 2001).

use of the Bible to raise consciousness about oppression, to provide liberating metaphors, to shift attitudes and to build community (e.g. Croatto 1981, 1998; Gutiérrez 1973; Hendricks 1995; Mosala 1989; Richard 1998; West 1991; West and Dube 1996). In addition, liberation theology's demand for readers to come clear about their own ideological commitments has played an influential role in conceiving this project (Oosthuizen 1988). On the other hand, I am influenced by the hermeneutic of suspicion employed in feminist criticism (e.g. Brenner 1993–95; Day 1989; Schüssler Fiorenza 1995), postcolonial criticism (e.g. Segovia 1998b; Segovia and Tolbert 1995a, 1995b; Sugirtharajah 1991, 1998a, 1998b; Warrior 1989), and ideological criticism (e.g. Bible and Culture Collective 1995; Gottwald 1992; Gunn and Fewell 1993; Jobling and Pippin 1992; Jobling 1992). This work has been vital for exposing the oppressive ideologies of class, race and gender which permeate the Hebrew scriptures, and for expounding the political implications of understanding and possibly subverting these ideologies.

Though I am interested in the *interaction* that takes place when the reader's ideology is confronted with the textual ideology, I wonder, given the kinds of ideologies that scholars have uncovered in texts, do I really want the text to have an impact, do I really think it will be liberatory? This returns to the question raised by Mosala and others: can a text built on oppressive ideologies be used for liberatory purposes at all, or should they be discarded? Of particular concern when thinking about liberation is how the Bible, a book (still) used to justify great oppressions, might also be put to use in a way that resists and undoes oppression rather than promotes it. I wonder if it is possible for the biblical text to help subvert the kinds of oppression often 'legitimized' by reference to it. At the same time, I must take seriously the position advocated by David Jobling and others which recognizes that 'any "authority of the Bible" as cultural critique [any liberatory impulse] must be a *production* rather than an *a priori* assumption' (Jobling 1990: 102). This echoes Mosala's point that it is in no way a given that the biblical text, in this case Micah, is *de facto* liberatory. Jobling makes the important observation that 'as being, in an almost unique sense, the book of the West, the Bible will be implicated in whatever structures, and in whatever subversion of structures, the West has generated. There can be no liberation through the Bible which is not at the same time liberation from the Bible—and vice versa.' Thus my work looks at some of what I consider to be the oppressive tendencies within Micah, and tries to see a way beyond these tendencies (though to be frank, this is where many of my doubts about this project lie). I also try, as R.S. Sugirtharajah suggests is necessary, to pay attention to 'marginal elements in the text' that can subvert traditional meanings and bring to the fore forgotten voices (1998a: 294).

In Sum: Negotiation

To my mind Bhabha's work is appropriate because it leads to a model that does not prioritize either the ideology of the text or of the reader, both of which could be considered ambivalent with respect to liberation (as much as readers may wish to work for liberation, they are always already caught in oppressive systems which seep into their readings—in my case, my white, educated, middle-class privilege cannot be dismissed or disavowed). However, in applying ideas taken from Bhabha to the question of reading, I will be arguing that the impact of the text is not the triumph of one ideology over the other, but of the production of hybridity. This process of negotiation between ideologically divergent symbolic orders (that of text and reader) produces a hybrid ('third') space which is neither the one nor the other, but something in between (see Chapter 3), and which can critique both. In other words, readers are not ideologically re-situated according to the ideologies inherent in the text, but are, rather, re-situated in a place 'in front of the text' from where they might better understand their own ideological positioning, and in which they might make new types of ideological identifications. In this process the text can be reread in ways that may be liberatory. It is my hope that this interaction will become clear as I proceed from theory to text in the chapters that follow.

2

Subject Formation: Identifying with Lack

The question at stake in this project, then, is how to think through the possibility of texts affecting readers' positioning in ideology, while affirming both a Derridean view of text as an endless chain of sliding signifiers (indeterminate text), and an Althusserian approach to ideology (which implies ideologically determined readers). Put another way, picking up on issues coming out of recent biblical scholarship, I am interested in whether the text can hail (interpellate) readers so as to disrupt the way they have already responded to ideology. Specifically, can the indeterminate text of Micah trouble readers' previous interpellations into ideology, and the identifications that are made in this process?

At this point, in order to prepare the way for my use of Bhabha in considering the possibility of repositioning the (ideologically determined) reader through text, I need to outline more fully the basic terms of the (Marxist-psychoanalytic) Althusserian framework. I use Althusser as a starting-point for understanding how people come to be positioned to speak and to act (i.e. as subjects) within their particular societal framework (i.e. ideology). The specific trajectory of this theory that I wish to outline here is Slavoj Žižek's rereading—by way of Jacques Lacan—of Althusser's theory of the subject's formation in ideology. Through reference to Althusser, Žižek and Lacan, I set up the theoretical problematic that I use Bhabha's theory to address, that is, the problematic of the fixity of subjects' positioning within language and ideology. I do this to prepare the terrain for Bhabha's critique of understandings of *the fixed colonial subject* and for his argument that indeterminate processes of identification in subject formation can disrupt and undermine oppressive forms of power and knowledge.[1]

I take the time and space to go over theoretical arguments other than those made by Bhabha because in subsequent chapters I will draw on

---

1. Where it is necessary to use a pronoun to refer to 'the subject', I have chosen to use the neuter 'it' for clarity's sake, in order not to get mixed up in problematic, classic psychoanalytical questions of gender and subjectivity. (For a clear exposition of these problems, see Kofman [1985]; Irigaray [1985].) I am aware though, that using the neuter may gloss over the problem of the inherent masculinity of Althusser's and Žižek's interpellated subject (and indeed the western subject in general).

this theory of subject formation to show how Bhabha's work modifies it in ways that are helpful for thinking about texts, readers' subjectivity and ideology. In discussions of cultural difference and national identity, Bhabha thinks about agency and indeterminacy, combining psychoanalytic terms (taken from psychoanalysts Lacan and Winnicott) with post-structural understandings of language (following Derrida). Though I am in no way engaging the theory on a clinical psychoanalytic level (i.e. on the level of detailed individual unconscious psychic processes), Bhabha's use of generalized psychoanalytic images and concepts along with post-structuralist theory will enable my use of his theory in thinking about how a shifting text like Micah might reposition readers' subjectivity.

Briefly to configure my eventual argument here: Bhabha reads Lacan and Derrida together in a way that, when set beside Althusser's and Žižek's reading of ideology, critiques any hint of a notion in these latter that the subject is destined to return interminably to its same always-already positioning in ideology. When this theoretical argument is applied to a discussion of reading texts, it opens up the possibility for thinking about how the indeterminacy of texts allows for, even encourages, different kinds of identifications to be made with the text (instead of the same old habitual identifications dictated by external ideological formations). Such new identifications may actually put into question readers' ideology and their position with respect to it. Bhabha's theory supports the idea that readers (as subjects) are not fully self-determined but operate according to their positioning with larger systems and structures. At the same time, his work takes seriously the notion that these structures are inherently indeterminate. Thus his theory is able to suggest the possibility for *agency formed in negotiation with indeterminacy*. In short, the idea I will work out, with the help of Bhabha's use of Lacan, Žižek and Derrida is that if the reader's identifications with the text are made with *difference* rather than with the famous Lacanian '*lack*' (see below), the reader's always-already positioning within ideology might be affected in some way. To this end, I take the time here to introduce the Althusser–Lacan–Žižek trajectory, which I use Bhabha's theory to engage in Chapter 3.

The problem to which Althusser's, Žižek's and Lacan's descriptions of the formation and positioning of the subject tend, and which Bhabha's thinking on indeterminacy and agency addresses, is the problem that a structuralist understanding of the subject *determined by* ideology poses for conceiving of possibilities for re-forming or repositioning that subject. There are, however, moments which I will note within these thinkers' work that seem open to conceiving of a more fluid, or less predetermined positioning of the subject; these are moments on which Bhabha's

work builds. Because my argument will eventually focus on the identifications that the reader makes with the text, I attend especially to the
processes of identification that are part of the subject's formation as
described by Althusser, Žižek and Lacan.

Two qualifications are in order. First, Althusser, Lacan and Žižek have
each written a great deal, and their entire corpuses can clearly not be
fully explicated here. However, it is useful to have a handle on some
basic terms and ideas from limited parts of their work. My point is not so
much to argue with these thinkers' positions, as it is to set out some
specific processes which relate to each other, and also to indicate the
points in the theory which Bhabha engages. Though in some ways the
terms and ideas that I present here are central to these thinkers, they
must be understood as snapshots. As any prolific writer, each theorist
moves through various positions and formulations within the course of
his writing, and what I present here momentarily freezes this movement
for my own purposes. For Lacan especially, it is very difficult to give an
'accurate' presentation. Further, because he is such a fluid and cryptic
writer, he is often more intelligible through those who take up, explain
and interpret his work in their own, including Žižek, whose work I use
primarily. I do, however, take recourse from time to time to other
expositors of Lacan besides Žižek (most often Kaja Silverman,[2] and sometimes Derrida), for clarity of explanation.

Second, these frameworks are by no means the only possibilities for
coming at the questions of subjectivity or its relation to the reading
process, but they are ones which make sense to me *as starting-points*,
and which Bhabha's work takes in interesting new directions. Although
ultimately I bracket the question of the material nature of ideology in
order to look more closely at the processes of identification that take
place in language and in reading, I begin within the context of materialist
theories of ideology so as to be able eventually to reopen the discussion
of material practices and their relation to the kinds of identifications
which I pursue in this study.

The Subject

The question of what constitutes the 'subject' is huge, and it is almost
impossible to speak of 'subject' or 'subjectivity' apart from the theoretical

---

2.   I have found Kaja Silverman's readings of Lacan, in *The Subject of Semiotics*
(1983), *The Threshold of the Visible World* (1996) and *World Spectators* (2000)
particularly helpful in understanding Lacan, in part because she applies Lacan to
reading (cinematic and philosophical) texts.

frameworks in which these terms are conceived. Though I do not write from the position of one involved in all the intricacies of philosophical debate, it seems clear, when looking at the broad strokes of the philosophical discussion over the last 250 years or more, that epistemic and ontological questions of subjectivity have become central preoccupations of philosophers. Questions about the definition and formation of the subject have been posed one after the other: following the Enlightenment, questions of autonomous and transcendental individuality; after Hegel, the question of the relation of the Self to its Other; after Marx, the question of the relationship between subjectivity, systems, historical processes and relations of production; after Nietzsche, the question of subordination and *ressentiment* in the formation of subjectivity; after existentialism, the questions of freedom, responsibility and the limits of being; after phenomenology, questions of consciousness and perception of self; after psychoanalysis, the question of the relation of agency to the unconscious; after structuralism, the question of the subject's mediation through language and discourse; after feminism, the consideration of what women's experience and exclusion brings to the notion of 'the subject'; after poststructuralism, the question of whether the subject might hold only one, or many subject positions; finally, after deconstruction, the question of the viability of even speaking of 'the subject'.[3]

Within this range of questions, I might say that the point to which Bhabha will lead is located somewhere between structuralist, psychoanalytic and deconstructionist positions. In order to situate and engage Bhabha's work though, I begin with expositions of Althusser, Lacan and Žižek, all of whom might be described as more or less structuralist theorists. (Often Lacan has been labeled poststructuralist because he describes a split or 'decentered' subject; however, he sees language as a determinative structuring force and so, to my mind, remains within the structuralist camp.) In fact, Žižek's rereading of Althusser and Lacan could even pull the project away from a structuralist framework toward one that favours a more traditionally transcendental approach (autonomous unified subject etc.), since Žižek strongly eschews poststructuralism in favour of a return to Kant and Hegel (by way of Lacan). But Bhabha's Derridean critique of Lacan, when applied to Žižek, balances this tendency. By using Derrida, Bhabha invokes the deconstructed,

3. For various discussions of theories of subjectivity see: Belsey (1997); Butler (1995b, 1997c); Cadava, Connor and Nancy (1991); Copjec (1994); Coward and Ellis (1997); Derrida (1995); Hall (1981); Laclau and Mouffe (1985); Levinas (1994); Ricoeur (1992); Silverman (1983); P. Smith (1988).

decentered subject,[4] but does so in the context of questions posed by structuralist discourses: questions of determination, agency and politics.

Ideology, Materiality, Subjectivity: Althusser

I begin my discussion of readers fixed within ideology with Althusser, who brings together psychoanalytic theory and Marxist structural theory to propose *the subject formed in ideology*. It may be best to begin with Althusser's definition of ideology. In his famous essay, 'Ideology and Ideological State Apparatuses' (1984), Althusser defines ideology as 'the imaginary relationship of individuals to their real conditions of existence …to the relations of production and the relations that derive from them… class relations' (1984: 36, 39, 41). This 'imaginary relation' between individuals and their conditions of existence 'is itself endowed with material existence' (1984: 41), meaning that it is lived out in daily rituals and practices. Ideology is not, therefore, just a complex of ideas existing in an ethereal spiritual realm, but rather, it has material existence (1984: 39).[5] The material nature of ideology is one of Althusser's main contributions to a Marxist understanding of ideology, and differs considerably from the early Marx's understanding of ideology as simply false consciousness.

Althusser further argues that ideology is governed, reproduced and enforced by apparatuses that give meaning to or prescribe these practices (1984: 43). Althusser uses the term 'apparatus' in the Marxist sense as the State apparatus, where power, mostly repressive power (courts, prisons, army, government and administration), is understood to be situated (1984: 15). Althusser adds the concept of 'Ideological State Apparatuses' (religious institutions, political parties, families, schools, newspapers, unions and so on) which are not repressive, but which function to ensure the smooth operation of the State by offering discourses and images with which individuals identify and understand their positions within the social order and within the relations of production (1984: 18).

One of the most compelling accounts of the subject's relationship to

4.   For Derrida on the subject, see his ' "Eating Well", Or the Calculation of the Subject' (1995).

5.   It is interesting to note that not only has Althusser been influential with regard to theories of ideology, but also with regard to theories of reading. In his reading of Marx's *Das Capital*, Althusser innovatively suggests that Marx reads other writers 'symptomatically', that is, measuring the lapses, the oversights, the lacunae against what appears in the text (1970: 27-28). This kind of reading is subsequently taken up in the study of cultural phenomena (literature, art, media etc.) by Marxist critics such as Frederic Jameson, Pierre Macherey and others.

ideology is Althusser's well-known conception of the subject's formation through interpellation into ideology (from the French *interpeller*, to question someone, or to demand a response). As Althusser states it, 'Ideology hails or interpellates concrete individuals as concrete subjects' (1984: 47),[6] meaning that individuals respond to the call of the ideological order, and in so doing are transformed into subjects. Althusser likens this ideological interpellation to an everyday hailing, perhaps by the police, 'Hey, you there', to which the hailed individual turns around, and in the act of recognizing the call as addressed to her becomes a subject (1984: 48).[7] Thus a person addressed and interpellated by ideology recognizes, or more properly *misrecognizes*, herself in ideology. In simpler terms, this process of interpellation might be thought of as an individual identifying with an image, or name given to her through cultural discourses, and behaving accordingly.

It has oft been noted that Althusser's notion of (mis)recognition is influenced by Lacan's description of the misrecognition that occurs in imaginary identification.[8] Lacan's well-known 'mirror stage', in which imaginary identification occurs, describes how a child looking in the mirror misrecognizes her fragmented experience as whole. The child's identification with the mirror image is essentially a *misrecognition*, because the image is fictive, more coherent and independent than the toddling, dependent child herself.[9] Likewise, Althusser suggests, in interpellation the ideological image or discourse with which the individual identifies is more coherent than actual reality.

6.   For a discussion of Althusser's distinction between individual and subject, as well as problems in cohering with Lacan's theory of the subject, and a critique of interpellation as constitutive for subjectivity, see Heath (1979).

7.   Althusser's use of the metaphor of the police with its inherent implication of the law is not incidental, but reveals the influence of Lacan and Freud, who call the law by the 'name of the Father' (e.g. Lacan 1977: 310-11, 321-23). Two pages after using the metaphor of the police, Althusser uses Freud's image of a child being given the 'Father's Name' before it is even born to describe the always-alreadyness of ideological interpellation (1984: 50).

8.   As Eagleton points out, ' "Imaginary" here means not "unreal" but "pertaining to an image" ' (1994: 214).

9.   For this reason Lacan says that in the mirror stage the *imaginary ego* identifies with the *imaginary other* (see Appendix, graph II). Thus the mirror stage, while providing a point of identification, is fundamentally alienating because the child realizes her distinction from the imaginary other, and her lack in comparison to it as an coherent object (Silverman 1983: 157-58; Lacan 1977: 2). As Žižek puts it, 'to achieve self-identity, the subject must identify himself with the imaginary other, he must alienate himself—put his identity outside himself, so to speak, into the image of his double' (1989: 104).

For Althusser, there is at once a function of recognition and of mis-recognition operative in ideology. The recognition function is ideology's ability to produce a response to itself as if it is completely natural or obvious; the misrecognition function is the way that ideology effaces its operation—as well as its intimate connection to materiality—so that sub-jects think that their responses are spontaneous and free, not ideologically controlled.[10] Or as Althusser puts it, it is 'a peculiarity of ideology that it imposes (without appearing to do so because these are obviousnesses) obviousnesses as obviousnesses which we cannot fail to recognize' (1984: 46). In all this obviousness, individuals misrecognize ideology's reproduc-tion of the material relations of production (1984: 57).

Althusser further makes it clear that the interpellation of the individual into a subject position is not optional, 'individuals are *always-already* interpellated by ideology as subjects' (1984: 49-50, emphasis mine). The interpellation of the subject is always also *subjection* to the dominant order. 'The individual is interpellated as a (free) subject in order that he shall submit freely to the commandment of the Subject, i.e. in order that he shall freely accept his subjection… There are no subjects except by and for their subjection' (1984: 56).[11] This then poses a number of questions for thinking about change. If subjects are always-already sub-jected by ideology, is the subject's position within language and ideology always firmly fixed? Is the subject forever pinned to the same position? Is there any way out, any possibility for ideological change, for re-position-ing subjects, for changing material practices and ways of thinking about material practices? As I see it, Bhabha's theory is able to engage these kinds of questions about the fixity of the (reader as) subject without relinquishing the notion of materially determined ideology.[12]

10.   Ricoeur points out that Althusser's limitation of ideology to the imaginary does not take into account the important relation of ideology to the symbolic order (1986: 157). Žižek also finds this to be a problem, and it is the question of symbolic order that he addresses in his Lacanian reformulation of Althusser's account of inter-pellation.

11.   For an interesting discussion of the limitations of the interpellating voice as a theological and sovereign power in Althusser's work, see Butler (1997a: 30-33).

12.   Properly speaking, in Althusserian terms, ideology is *overdetermined*: it is not just determined *by* economic structures, it is also determining *for* them. Althusser modifies this Freudian term for the work that occurs in dreams or symptoms to stitch together a number of divergent unconscious elements, by applying it to Lenin's con-ception of the effect of the superstructure on the base. For Althusser, overdetermina-tion is the process by which diverse and possibly contradictory elements already determined once by the structure are also made to cohere in ideology. This in turn results in adjustment and reworking of the structure. In this way, superstructural elements (like ideology) also have an effect on the structure (Althusser and Balibar

Ideological Interpellation, Language, Text

Because Althusser's combination of materialism and psychoanalysis takes up a question of much interest to scholars studying contemporary cultural configurations—that is, the question of how the structures of economy and psyche are related—his formulation has had far-reaching effects in cultural and critical theory. However, in order to be able to keep the discussion focused enough eventually to apply to the biblical text, and in order to avoid becoming lost in the many discussions of ideology and materiality which extend beyond the scope of this project, at this point I must bracket the relation between ideology and materiality (means and relations of production, and so on), in order to take up the notion of ideological interpellation *on the level of language*. From here on in, therefore, I will focus on the positioning (interpellation) of the subject through language. For my purposes, the emphasis on language will enable consideration of how texts might interpellate readers in a way that might confront their always-already interpellation into ideology. As mentioned, I do this within the framework of Althusser's materialist description of ideology, because I hope ultimately to touch on the effects of reading on material practices (doing justice in concrete economic terms) in my conclusions.

Although it is no simple theoretical maneuver to move from speaking of *ideology* to speaking of ideological discourses—to move from material practices to linguistic practices—in doing so here I am following others before me (who have deliberated it at some length, [e.g. Laclau and Mouffe 1985: 105-108]). Although Althusser is quite explicit and innovative in relating ideology and subjectivity to material practices, a number of cultural critics and broadly Marxist thinkers have shifted the discussion of ideology and ideological interpellation onto the level of *language* and *text* by emphasizing ideological *discourses*.[13] This move has been made,

1970: 89-127, 233-34). This means that possibly contradictory or divergent material elements, already determined once by the material economic structure, are made to cohere on what Althusser calls an imaginary level (Althusser and Balibar 1970: 233).

13. There are many who have taken up Althusser in debating the relationship between the subject, ideology and language who should not be ignored, but whose work cannot be taken up within the scope of this study. To name a few: the Centre for Cultural Studies in Birmingham produced a good deal of research on ideology, the subject and language during the period that Stuart Hall was director (1968–79); for a sampling, see articles by Morley (1980); Weedon, Tolson and Mort (1980). Likewise, Ernesto Laclau has developed the idea of interpellation to include the 'different types of interpellations (political, religious, familial, etc.) which coexist whilst being articulated within an ideological discourse in a relative unity' (1977: 102); Laclau also questions possibilities for ideological change, arguing that change occurs through

in part, because Althusser's notion of 'hailing' can clearly be related to language.

As cultural critics have noticed (e.g. Silverman 1983: 43-53), the 'Hey you' of Althusser's police resonates with linguist Emile Benveniste's description of the relation between *I* and *you* in language, as set out in his *Problems in General Linguistics* (1971). For Benveniste, language is deeply marked by the expression of subjectivity (1971: 225), to the extent that 'language is possible only because each speaker sets himself up as a subject by referring to himself as *I* in his discourse'. At the same time, with the emergence of the subject as *I*, an other is invoked, *you*. Since *I* and *you* are reversible in nature, the use of one automatically invokes the other: 'The one whom "I" defines by "you" thinks of himself as "I" and can be inverted into "I"' (1971: 199). Therefore, because language is communicative, because the *I* speaks to a *you*, language is conditioned by intersubjectivity (1971: 230). Within the understanding of the reversibility of *I* and *you*, it is possible to think of second person forms creating a space ('eternally present moment', 1971: 227) for a reader to respond as *I*, the subject who speaks, in discourse. Thus it is possible to think of the text's *you* (Althusser's 'Hey you') interpellating the reader, who responds as *I*.

This kind of formal and linguistic take on interpellation lends itself well as a starting-point in thinking about texts and I will return to it in my own reading of Micah (Chapter 6). Indeed, to speak of texts interpellating readers is nothing new. As mentioned in Chapter 1, this concept has been employed in biblical studies by Carol Newsom (1989) and others. Still prior to this, cultural critics considered the way that texts, both linguistic and cinematic, can interpellate readers, or position them for the texts' purposes. For instance, some film theorists —in particular a number of those writing for the journal *Screen* in the 1970s—drew on Althusser to suggest the interpellation of the viewer into the filmic text. Many explored the identifications made through film between the subject of speech (who or what the discourse is about), the speaking subject (that is, the agency of the discourse), and the spoken subject (the subject constituted through identification with the subject of speech) (Silverman 1983: 43-53, 194-236).[14]

class struggle. Michel Pêcheux is another theorist who has taken up these questions, by developing a complex linguistic theory of discourse analysis which takes into account the ideological interpellation of the subject with relation to the discourse of the subject; see his *Language, Semantics and Ideology* (1982: 110-29); or for a brief introduction to Pêcheux, see Morley (1980: 163-66).

14. For the establishment of subject positions following Benveniste, see MacCabe

Along these lines, the analogy was also made between Benveniste's reversal between *I* and *you* and shot/reverse shot sequences in film. Put simply, in filmic terms, the viewer becomes aware, by means of a camera shot, of what, or whom, is not visible, the 'appearance of a lack perceived as a Some One (the Absent One)'. The viewer is placed in the position of this absent person (identification with lack; see below for more on 'lack'). Then with the reverse shot, this absence is filled in by the image of what is missing; the absence is abolished 'by someone (or something) placed within the same field' (Oudart 1978: 37). An identification is forced between the viewer and the reverse shot; in this way the subject (viewer) fills in the lack.[15]

What concerns me here is whether and how these kinds of textual interpellation of subjects (readers) might dislodge previous always-already interpellations. This would mean that interpretation is not always governed by (ideological) terms outside the text, but that the reading process could actually shift readers with respect to those outside terms as well. As I will show in reading Bhabha with and against Lacan and Žižek, the process of interpellation into ideology—and also into text—is more complex than the response, *I*, to the hailing of the *you*; there is also a very involved process of identification that takes place in interpellation. My central suggestion here, following Bhabha's use of Lacan, Žižek and Derrida, will be that if readers respond to the text's hailing by identifying with the text's difference instead of with images that abnegate that difference, their always-already positioning within ideology might be affected, even shifted.

In order first to fill out the problematic of the determined—fixed— subject, I turn now to the more psychoanalytically oriented (neo-Freudian) theory of language, ideology and subjectivity (Žižek on Lacan). This theory *does not*, at first glance, allow for the possibility of textual influence on readers' ideology, positing instead the notion of seemingly predetermined and fixed subject positions. However, it is within this theoretical context that Bhabha's work is able to suggest the possibility

(1976, 1979); for the subversion of subject positions through film see MacCabe (1974); for the way the subject position is manipulated through shot/reverse-shot formations see *Screen* 18(4) (J.-A. Miller 1978; Heath 1978; Oudart 1978), also see Heath (1976).

15. Film theorists termed this filling-in for lack that occurs in the shot/reverse shot technique 'suture', after Lacan and J.-A. Miller. Suture designates 'the relation of the subject to the chain of its discourse' (J.-A. Miller 1978: 25); that is, the way the subject fills in for what is lacking in the discourse of the Other, or the way the subject identifies with the lack in the Other. For further explanation of suture, see Dayan (1976); for a critique, see Rothman (1976).

of repositioning subjects in ways that resist prior stereotypic determina-
tions. To reiterate, because Bhabha draws rather centrally on Lacan, as
does Žižek, his use of Lacan—and in particular his critique and modification of the Lacanian theory of identification—can also be applied to
Žižek's reading of Althusser. This same critique and modification of
Lacanian theory can be further applied to a consideration of how readers
might respond to textual interpellation. In order to lay out theoretical
material to which to refer when explicating Bhabha—ultimately to show
(in the next chapter) how Bhabha's theory takes it forward in productive
ways—for the remainder of this chapter, I will go through Žižek's description of interpellation and identification and the Lacanian theory on
which he draws in some detail.

Ideology, Language, Subjectivity: Žižek Using Lacan

Once ideology is considered discursive as well as material, Žižek illu-
mines the process of interpellation into ideology through language. He
does so by likening Althusser's theory of interpellation to Lacan's psychoanalytic theory of signification, that is, the process by which meaning
comes to be fixed for a linguistic sign. For Lacan, subject formation is
part and parcel of signification: the process by which the subject is
formed and by which language comes to have meaning is one and the
same. Žižek's combination of Lacan's description of signification with
Althusser's description of the subject formed in ideology does not seem
too surprising, given that both deal with the formation of the subject,
and given that Althusser does draw on Lacan.

For Lacan (simplifying somewhat), the subject is formed in language.
The subject is formed when in the course of its development, a child
enters into language; that is, into the realm of Other, the symbolic order.
'Language', 'the symbolic order', 'the Other' are all coterminous here
(and significantly, gendered as female). For Lacan, all signification (as
well as desire) takes place within the realm of the Other. It is through
entry into this realm of language that the unconscious is formed (1977:
284-85), and the individual is formed as subject. As is oft cited, Lacan
calls the unconscious 'the discourse of the Other' (1977: 172, 312; 1981:
131). Language, therefore, and the signifying chains that make up language, exist outside of the subject (as the realm that the subject encounters); but, as will be discussed shortly, 'meaning' does not.

In *The Sublime Object of Ideology* (1989), Žižek redescribes the Althusserian moment of interpellation, using Lacan's notion of the subject's
formation in language. Here Žižek argues that Althusser does not
adequately account for the process by which the external apparatuses of

ideology (schools, family, religion) become internalized. He suggests that this gap in Althusser's thought is filled by the Lacanian account of the subject's passage through, and identification with, the symbolic order (Lacan's Other) (Žižek 1989: 43-44). For Žižek, ideological interpellation is not just a moment of *imaginary identification* with ideological discourse, but is also *symbolic identification*. Symbolic identification takes place in the moment that Lacan describes as the subject's entry into language, that is, the symbolic order.[16] As symbolic identification takes place, several things occur: the subject is formed, the chain of signifiers stops sliding, and meaning is fixed. It is these processes that Bhabha picks up on, in order to posit a kind of symbolic identification with difference that can shake the fixity of the subject.

For this reason, it may be worthwhile to outline these processes at greater length. Because the theory is somewhat complex, I find it useful to do this somewhat repetitively, moving from less complex descriptions to more detailed explanations, always of the same process. My goal is to spell out the relation in this theory between meaning and subjectivity, in order eventually to think not only about the relationship of readers to ideology, but also about the relationship between reading texts (producing meaning) and (readers') subjectivity. So while at first I will be speaking about the Other—following Žižek—as the symbolic realm of ideology in which readers are formed as subjects, I will eventually want to be speaking about the Other as the symbolic realm of the text which might re-interpellate the reader.

Subjectivity and Signification

For Lacan and for Žižek, subjectivity is intimately connected to *signification*. Indeed, according to this theory, it is impossible to separate the process of subject formation from the processes producing 'meaning'. The subject does not come into existence independently of language or the production of meaning. Lacan theorizes subjectivity in terms of signification, by reformulating Ferdinand de Saussure's description, in his

---

16. In Lacan's theory, the encounter with language occurs sometime after the mirror stage. For a visual representation of the process see the Lacanian graphs in the Appendix. While the result of the imaginary identification is marked in the graphs as the ideal ego, e, the result of the completed symbolic identification is what Lacan calls the ego-ideal I(O) (Lacan's reworking of Freud's super-ego) (see Appendix, graphs II, IV). It is from this point of symbolic identification with the Other that 'we observe and judge ourselves' (Žižek 1989: 108). Žižek notes that the imaginary identification 'is always already subordinate to I(O) [symbolic identification]: it is the symbolic identification...which dominates and determines the image, the imaginary form in which we appear to ourselves likeable' (1989: 108).

Course in General Linguistics (1986), of the distinction between the two parts that make up the linguistic sign: the signifier (the graphic or auditory marker distinguishing it from other signs) and the signified (the concept or meaning).[17] As is well known, Saussure draws the relation between the signifier and the signified as *S/s* (signifier over signified), symbolizing a separation between the two. Lacan, however, redepicts this relation as an *intersection between signifying chain and subject* (Lacan 1977: 148-66). Where Saussure's equation, *S/s*, shows two parallel entities, in which 'the linear progression of the signifier runs parallel to the linear articulation of the signified' (Žižek 1989: 101-102); Lacan, on the other hand, draws out the complexities of the relationship between signifier, signified and subject in a series of four graphs (see Appendix).

In the Lacanian graphs, the image offered is of the signifying chain (a string of signifiers) like a horizontal surface, perhaps a piece of fabric, through which the subject travels like a needle and thread, looping through it, up and back down, like a stitch. Previous to this movement the subject appears as a pre-symbolic 'intention' (see Appendix, graph I). As this pre-symbolic 'intention' passes (up) through the signifying chain into the symbolic order—into language—it *makes identifications as it goes* (to be elaborated on shortly) and returns back (down) through the signifying chain as a 'subject'. Furthermore, to continue the metaphor of the stitch, this process 'fastens down' meaning. In other words, it attaches meaning to the signifier; it produces a signified (Lacan 1977: 303-15; Žižek 1989: 101-24). Thus, according to Lacan, in the process of signification two main things occur: the individual is positioned as a subject, and the signifier is supplied with meaning (attached to a signified).

The Retroactivity of Signification

In this theory, signification occurs *retroactively*: *before* meaning is fixed for the sign, the subject *identifies with the Other*. Signification occurs as a result of this process, at a point which *precedes* the intersection of the subject and the symbolic order. Žižek summarizes: 'subjective intention...steps out of the signifier's chain backward...at a point preceding the point at which it has pierced it...the effect of meaning is always produced backwards, *après coup*' (Lacan 1977: 303; Žižek 1989: 101; see Appendix, graph I). Thus, meaning is produced in the process of the subject's backward journey through the symbolic order.

This understanding of the retroactivity of signification is a development of the Freudian notion of *Nachträglichkeit* (deferred action). In

17. See Saussure (1986: 65-67). For a good overview of Saussure's concepts and their importance, see Eagleton (1983: 96-99).

psychoanalytic terms, *Nachträglichkeit* 'includes the paradoxical claim that the earlier event can be the later event's cause only once the latter has happened' (Forrester 1990: 208). Thus, as a result of a later event an earlier memory can be accordingly restructured. Bhabha likewise understands signification to be retroactive, and this concept enables his liberatory and revisionary impulse. Effectively, the retroactivity of signification means that *the past is influenced—can be changed—by the present*. (Bhabha will also see this as disturbing linear time consciousness.) This reorientation of the past in turn has implications for both the present and the future: 'the past dissolves in the present, so that the future becomes (once again) an *open question,* instead of being specified by the fixity of the past' (Forrester 1990: 206, emphasis original, cited in Bhabha 1994a: 219).

Interpellation and Signification
Using Lacan's description of the formation of the subject and meaning as an analogy to the process of interpellation, Žižek argues that the outcomes of the process (meaning and subjectivity) are thoroughly governed by *ideological master signifiers*. In the graphs, the subject does not pass up to 'stitch' through the symbolic order of its own accord, but is *articulated* (or hailed) *by a master signifier* and so pinned to it; Žižek calls this *interpellation* by the big Other.[18] Interpellation by the master signifier causes the subject retroactively to 'quilt' or 'pin down' the constant sliding of the signifiers' chain in accordance with that master signifier (Žižek 1989: 101). For Žižek, it is this pinning that is the moment of ideological interpellation. The master signifier positions the subject ideologically and encodes the subject's subsequent relations in the symbolic order. As Žižek puts it, the subject is 'fastened, pinned to a signifier which represents him for the Other, and through this pinning he is loaded with a symbolic mandate, he is given a place in the...network of symbolic relations' (Žižek 1989: 113). In other words, in being pinned to the master signifier, the subject is given its symbolic mandate. As will be explained in greater detail further on, this takes place through a process of identification with the symbolic order (the Other).

According to Žižek's Lacanian reading of Althusser then, subjectivity is not only related to ideology but also to the production of meaning. This pinning that gives the subject its mandate is all part of the process of signification. The ideological operation not only mandates the subject,

18. Žižek calls this *the big Other*, because Lacan writes it *Autre* (*A* majuscule), in contrast to *autre* (*a* minuscule, the object of desire, which usually remains untranslated as *objet petit a*) (see Lacan 1977: 139, 303-308).

but also halts the continual sliding of signifiers, and gives them ideologically invested meaning. For example, Žižek gives the example of the
master signifier 'Communism'. He writes,

> In the ideological space float signifiers like 'freedom', 'state', 'justice',
> 'peace'…and then their chain is supplemented with some master-signifier
> ('Communism') which retroactively determines their (Communist) mean-
> ing: [e.g.]…the 'state' is the means by which the ruling class guarantees the
> conditions of its rule;…only socialist revolution can bring about lasting
> 'peace' and so forth. (Liberal-democratic 'quilting' would, of course
> produce a quite different articulation of meaning) (1989: 102).

For Žižek, it is the ideologically invested master signifier that determines
the meaning of other signifiers. In other words, the master signifier gives
diverse terms and ideas meaning; it also delineates various terms' relationships to one another. It has a totalizing and unifying function.

A concrete example of this operation can be seen in the 1998 film
Elizabeth (to use a Žižekian trick of explaining theory through popular
culture). At the end of the film, Queen Elizabeth quite consciously
becomes the *virgin Queen* to replace the popular religious icon, the
Virgin Mary, in order to unify the diverse political and religious hopes of
the people of England. Similarly, in recent readings of Micah, the image
of Israel as a woman—first punished and then rescued by Yahweh—
stands in to unify immense textual difficulties and diverse textual
elements (see Chapter 5).

In sum then, in this account of ideological interpellation, a complex
interaction takes place between the formation of the subject and the production of meaning. The individual, as the subject-in-formation, enters
the realm of language through responding to the hailing of a master
signifier. In responding to the master signifier through a series of identifications (see below), the subject is both given its mandate, and meaning
is 'pinned down'.

Texts and Interpellation
The relation of this theory to a discussion on reading texts begins to
come clear here: *if* texts can be said to present ideological master signifiers, then perhaps it would be possible for readers to be interpellated by
the text, and for their subjectivity to be affected at the same time that
meaning is produced. As texts come to mean something for readers,
perhaps they can also affect readers' subjectivity. Yet the proposition that
texts might be able to affect readers' subjectivity is fraught with questions
that need to be worked through. To begin, what sets signifiers off as
ideological master signifiers in the first place? After this, other questions
follow: *can* texts produce ideological master signifiers, or are they

destined always to be quilted by master signifiers outside the text? How, for instance, would a signifier within a text (say Communism) be able to override a previous interpellation by another master signifier (say Capitalism) and be able to quilt other signifiers like 'justice' or 'State' differently? What of the problem posed by the always-already nature of interpellation: how is ideological change possible, if subjects are always-already interpellated by the master signifiers of dominant ideology?

Since the master signifier seems to have the most power within the ideological operation described by Žižek, in order to explore these questions, it may be useful to take a yet closer look at the mechanics by which the master signifier gains this power. In other words, what are the operations at work in the elevation of a signifier to the level of *master signifier*? According to Žižek's Lacan at least, the master signifier seems to be attributed its power through fantasy, which is in turn given power through the subject's *identification* with the fantasy object.

In order to better understand this process by which the master signifier gains its power, I delve further into Žižek, Lacan, and the relation between subject formation, signification and ideological interpellation (subjectivity, meaning and ideology). But because their theoretical writings are vast, I limit myself to noticing the main aspects of the theory on which Bhabha draws. These fall broadly into two categories: the formation of the lacking subject, and identification with the lack in the Other. These moments can be further delineated as: the split between the subject of speech and the subject of the statement (*énoncé* and *énonciation*); the split, alienated nature of the subject; and the notion of 'lack' in the Other, along with desire for that lack. These are themes that Bhabha employs in questioning the fixity of subject positions, and the determinacy of meaning. (The fine points of Bhabha's use of these moments will be covered in Chapter 3; here I only give the theoretical description of them, and indicate how Bhabha will use them.)

As I go, I also draw out what will be important for my own use of Bhabha, namely, the relation of *identification* to the pinning function of the master signifier, particularly through the formation of the split subject and the desire for lack. Though much of the language in these next two sections is not specifically about ideology, focusing instead on the Lacanian system, I continue in the Žižekian vein of considering the subject's entry into the realm of the Other as a reading of interpellation into ideology. It may also be helpful to bear in mind that when I come to applying all of this to text, I will be thinking of the text as homologous to the Other, but as that which re-interpellates the reader.

The Lacking Subject

Enoncé ou Enonciation

In thinking about 'subject' in terms of signification, an interesting problem arises: is the 'subject' the individual person, or the linguistic topic or function? This has been stated in technical terms, by theorists of language and interpretation, as the difference between the 'subject of speech' (*énonciation*) and the 'subject of the statement' (*énoncé*) which can be both the grammatical position, and the subject matter.[19] These 'subjects', though part of the same signifying process, are never self-identical, and this means that meaning can never be fully fixed, neither can the individual's position in language, since there is always something that escapes the particular designation of 'subject'. No subject fills both positions of *énonciation* and *énoncé* at once. Bhabha picks up this distinction, along with the way that Lacan relates it to the alienating encounter between 'meaning' (at the level of the statement) and 'being' (at the level of the speaker), to be discussed presently.

I will also show this split at work when I come to thinking about readers' (re-)interpellation into the text in Chapter 6. The reader can never actually 'be' the 'you' that the text hails. Even if the reader identifies with the image held out to her by the text (for instance, 'you, my people'), there is always something that escapes that designation. It is this 'something', this remainder from the interpellative signifying process, that will be productive for challenging both the received meaning of the text and the reader's always-already positioning as subject.

Split Subject

Recalling that the articulation of the subject by the symbolic order (interpellation) *produces* the subject, it is important to notice that for Žižek and Lacan, the subject that is produced is a *split and alienated subject*. This is because, according to these thinkers, when the subject enters the world of language, it loses direct access to its sexual ('libidinal') functions and needs. In other words, on entry into the symbolic order, the subject is split off from its 'drives' (the routes that sexual libido

---

19. The difference between the subject of the statement (*énoncé*) and the subject of speech (*énonciation*) is a distinction that has been explored by a number of theorists in various ways. For a range of different views, see Benveniste (1971: 218); Lacan (1977: 298-300; 1981: 138-42); Ricoeur (1981: 133, 149, 159, 198); Žižek (1990: 61 n. 10); Foucault (1972: 192-95). For a helpful overview see Silverman (1983: 45-53).

follows, e.g. oral or anal drives) and from the world of the drives.[20] Language splits the subject off from its drives. Perhaps Silverman explains this most clearly:

> Once the subject has entered the symbolic order its organic needs pass through the 'defiles' or network of signification and are transformed in a way which makes them thereafter impossible to satisfy... Moreover, since language speaks no more to the reality of objects than it does to that of subjects, it effects as complete a rupture with the phenomenal world (1983: 166).

Simplifying a little, because language is an arbitrary system of signs that has no direct connection to the individual's libidinal needs and resources (Silverman 1983: 176), on entry into language the subject is alienated from those phenomena.

Thus, because it no longer has direct access to these bodily functions and needs, the subject experiences itself as lacking. The subject is never completely aware of itself, because the drives have become unconscious. This is the much-worked Lacanian concept of *alienation*. When 'pre-symbolic intention' emerges from its entry into the symbolic order, it is as a split, 'lacking', alienated subject (Appendix, graph I); it is alienated from its drives. For this reason, the subject is written in the graphs as the barred or split subject, $, to indicate its insufficiency to itself (Silverman 1996: 76). Ever after this first encounter with the Other, the process begins with the barred subject, $, since the subject is, as Althusser would say, always-already interpellated (see Appendix, graphs II, III, IV). The libidinal needs to which the subject no longer has access—what Lacan and Žižek call 'the Real', to be distinguished from 'reality' (e.g. Žižek 1989: 169-73; Lacan 1981: 53-55, 205-206)—are described by Lacan as 'lost' to the subject, who spends its time trying to regain them through symbolic substitution. This appears in the graphs as $<>D.

In Freudian terms, this is loss of access to the instincts' organization around the loved opposite-sex parent. This loss first occurs in the traumatic primal scene, which is then repressed. For Lacan, the loss is not of a love object, but of being itself (see below) (Silverman 2000: 40). Ever after the original loss, the subject attempts to regain what has been lost through symbolic substitutions; this is what creates desire. Freud, and Lacan after him, give the famous example of Freud's grandson who

---

20. Lacan describes these routes using Freud: 'Freud says that it is important to distinguish four terms in the drive: *Drang*, thrust; *Quelle*, the source; *Objekt*, the object; *Ziel*, the aim' (1981: 162). For further description of the drives, see Lacan (1981: 162-73, 194-97); Freud (1957b).

played a game in which he threw a reel attached to a string and pulled it back to himself, all the while uttering *fort-da* ('gone-there'), to mark its disappearance and return. Freud interpreted this as the child's way of regaining access to his mother who had left the room. This substitution of the object was the child's symbolic way of dealing with the lost love object (Lacan 1981: 62; Freud 1989: 13-16).

The Split between Meaning and Being

Lacan describes this negotiation between language and the subject in another way that becomes important for Bhabha, and in a way that can also be related to the question of interpretation. Here he draws the alienation of the subject in its encounter with the Other as the relationship between meaning (the symbolic order/the Other) and being (the subject). This is also a way of describing the split between the subject of the statement, *énoncé*, and the subject of speech, *énonciation* (Silverman 1983: 46).

To illustrate this split, Lacan uses the example of two overlapping fields: the field of the subject (which is being), and the field of the Other (which is meaning), drawn in a Venn diagram: two circles, side by side, slightly overlapping in the middle (Lacan 1981: 203-29). As Lacan describes it, the alienation of the subject is similar to what happens when a choice is made between the two overlapping fields. Normally, Lacan argues, in such a choice between fields, one is chosen, the other is discarded. However, in the case of overlapping fields, neither can be chosen uniquely. In the choice between 'meaning' *or* 'the subject', if the subject is chosen, it disappears; this is because—according to Lacan—the subject cannot appear without the production of *meaning*, since subjectivity is a result of the signifying process. Meaning is the only choice that can be made, but neither can the subject (being) be discarded from this field since it is integral to it. So being remains as the unconscious—hidden, alienated, within the field of meaning. Lacan terms this hiddenness *aphanasis* (1981: 216) or 'the fading' of the subject (1981: 218). He calls the overlap between the two fields the alienating *vel* of non-meaning. Non-meaning refers to that which cannot be represented, that is, the unconscious (which only appears with the advent of meaning). *Vel* is a term Lacan borrows from logic for 'or'; it is not the 'or' of 'either or', but rather it is the 'or' of 'neither one nor the other' that necessarily occurs in trying to choose elements shared between two joined sets (1981: 211). For Lacan, this space is that part of the subject (the unconscious) which overlaps with, and is eclipsed by, the Other (the field of meaning), it is *neither one nor the other*. The image of a space shared by two fields which is neither one nor the other becomes a very important image for Bhabha; I will apply his use of this image not only to the space between ideology and subject, but also to the space between text and reader in the text's re-interpellation of the reader.

Moreover, in Bhabha's use of this theory, we will see that the split and alienated nature of the subject is a moment within the theory that might enable thinking about the way in which the subject might be repositioned. Since the subject's experience of itself is never fully identical to itself (i.e. it has no access to the drives), it cannot be considered—or consider itself—complete or autonomous. The subject's understanding of its 'lack' is always contingent on something else—on the symbols offered to it in language. There is, therefore, always a *negotiation* that takes place between language (the Other) and the subject, and the result of this negotiation will affect the behaviour of the subject. Though I will return to the notion of negotiation when I come to Bhabha, and also when I come to the reading of Micah, a closer look at the Lacanian-Žižekian description of the relationship between the subject and the Other is necessary to lay the groundwork for this and also to continue to understand the process by which the ideological master signifier gains its power to position the subject.

Identification with the Lack in the Other

Lack in the Other

According to Žižek and Lacan, it is not just that the subject experiences itself as lacking; it is also that it *identifies* its lack with the 'lack in the Other'. The subject realizes its lack and at the same time, it realizes that the Other is also incomplete, lacking. So the subject identifies its own lack with the lack in the Other. When Lacan uses examples from childhood development to describe identification with the lack in the Other, he speaks of the Other as the Mother, and 'the lack' as the lack of phallus. For Žižek the lack in the Other is more abstract: it is that which is non-symbolizable (1989: 162-63), that 'strange traumatic element which cannot be symbolized, [or] integrated into the symbolic order' (1989: 133). This traumatic element is the Lacanian Real, the structuring of the libidinal drives and needs (being) from which the subject has been split off. It is 'the non-symbolizable traumatic kernel' (1994b: 26) which 'gives rise to ever-new symbolizations [including fantasy] by means of which one endeavours to integrate and domesticate it' (1994b: 22).[21]

---

21. Again, in Freudian terms, this is that initial structuring of the drives around the loved object, which is traumatically lost in sublimation, or maybe some other repressed traumatic event to which one no longer has access (and which can therefore not be symbolized), but which compulsively returns in other ways.

Thus the subject is further alienated by identifying with lack in the Other, or the non-symbolizable. As I will argue a little further on, it is the way that this lack is 'filled in' that ultimately gives the master signifier its power in the Lacanian-Žižekian system.

What is important to notice for thinking about the ideological operation is that this lack in the Other is only made apparent *by way of the master signifier*. Žižek, following Lacan, terms the master signifier the *point de capiton* (in English, the less alluring 'upholstery button', or nodal point).[22] As mentioned above, it is a kind of pinning point for the subject and for meaning, that articulates the subject in the first place and gives meaning, by unifying diverse elements. For Lacan and Žižek, the *point de capiton* is a 'pure signifier', a master signifier with no signified, the signifier of a lack in the Other, the signifier whose signified does not exist because it is a 'symbol only of an absence' (Lacan 1972: 54). In this sense, the *point de capiton* represents the lack, giving meaning and unity to floating signifiers.[23] As Žižek puts it, it is

> a point of extreme saturation of Meaning, as the point which 'gives meaning' to all the others and thus totalizes the field of (ideological) meaning…the element which only holds the place of a certain lack, *which is in its bodily presence nothing but an embodiment of a certain lack*… In short, *pure difference* is perceived as Identity (1989: 99, emphasis mine).

When thought of in the light of generally understood semiotics, the place of lack (that gives rise to new symbolizations) may sound like that which might normally be understood as the signified. But as Žižek puts it, this lack is 'the impossible Real'; though it is comprised of some original trauma (the loss of the loved object, or the loss of being), it can't actually be signified, since the subject does not have access to it. This is why the master signifier which refers to it is a signifier without a signified.

Desire for Lack

How then does a subject come to identify with 'lack' in the Other, if it is absent and non-symbolizable, represented only by some external master signifier? According to Žižek and Lacan (and Bhabha picks up on this),

22. Lacan also calls it the 'unary' signifier (see 1981: 218-19); for a clear explanation of Lacan's thinking on the unary signifier see Silverman (1983: 170-74).

23. See Butler (1993: 208-22) for a critique of Žižek's view of the *point de capiton*. She questions whether his consideration of *points de capiton* as rigid designators allows for 'the kind of variation and rearticulation required for an anti-essentialist radical democratic project' which he seems to espouse (1993: 211).

the answer to this question is: *through desire and fantasy*. In the process of the subject's identification with the lack in the Other, *the subject begins to desire what the Other desires*, through fantasy. As I read it, this is also where the master signifier gains its power.

The Other's desires become the subject's desires in the following manner. As discussed, on interpellation into the symbolic order, the subject is pinned by a master signifier that confers its symbolic mandate upon the subject. But something else occurs as well. In this process, the Other addresses the subject with the question, *'Che vuoi?'* ('What do you want from me?') (Lacan 1977: 312, 316). The question is asked as if the subject knows why it has the symbolic mandate bestowed upon it by the master signifier (Žižek 1989: 113). But because the conferral of language is arbitrary and not related to some internal essence, the subject does not know why it has this symbolic mandate. The subject therefore internalizes and reformulates the question as, 'What does the Other want of me?' (Lacan 1977: 316). In internalizing the demand of the Other, the subject also desires what the Other desires. Thus, the subject does not just recognize its lack in comparison to the Other, it is more than this: when the subject identifies its own lack with the lack in the Other, it also desires what the Other desires: 'it is *qua* Other that he desires' (Lacan 1977: 312; 1981: 115, 214-15).

However—and here things get more complex—when the subject internalizes this question ('What does the Other want of me?'), it does not know what it wants because what has been conferred upon it is pure difference (lack); it must therefore respond through fantasy. In slow motion, the process moves as follows. The Other desires what it itself lacks. (For Lacan, using the image of the M/Other and child, the M/Other's desire is for the phallus.) But, because the Other is lacking, the subject can never really know what the Other desires. Because the subject does not know what the Other wants, the only way it can identify with this unrepresentable, unknowable lack is through fantasy.

So the subject fantasizes an object that *represents its own lack* (the libidinal needs and resources to which it no longer has access). Lacan calls this fantasy object *objet petit a* (Lacan 1981: 62). Taking the form of fantasy, the *objet petit a* comes to *stand in for* both the subject's lack and the Other's lack. Lacan gives several examples of the kinds of objects that might be fantasized, starting with the subject's own death. He writes: 'The first object [the child] proposes for this parental desire whose object is unknown is his own loss... The phantasy of one's death, of one's disappearance, is the first object that the subject...bring[s] into play' (1981: 214). Žižek gives another example, of love, taken from

Lacan.[24] Love is the subject's wish to fill in the lack of the Other with itself as the fantasy object, through devotion and sacrifice. 'The operation of love is therefore double', Žižek writes, 'the subject fills in his own lack by offering himself to the other as the object filling out that lack in the Other' (1989: 116). The important thing to notice here, which I will make much of presently, is that these fantasy objects are self-referential.

It is through the fantasy object (*objet petit a*) and desire then, that the subject identifies with the lack in the Other. Since identification with the Other is part of the subject's formation, and since the fantasy object is essential to this process of identification, the fantasy object is therefore constitutive for the subject. Once again, the subject experiences itself as an alienated and split subject, because it does not know what it (or the Other) wants, yet is always identifying with, and desiring, something to fill that lack. This is figured in the upper level of the Lacanian graphs of desire (detailed in Appendix, graphs III and IV). There the desire of the lacking subject for the fantasy object appears as $\$ < > a$ (see also Silverman 1996: 75).[25] So according to Žižek and Lacan, the identification of the subject with the Other is *motivated by desire* to fill its own lack (or in Freudian terms, to fulfill its libidinal needs) but it *also produces desire*. As Žižek put it, the object of desire becomes, paradoxically, both *the cause of desire* and *the desire itself*, produced as a result of searching for what the Other desires (Žižek 1989: 160). For this reason he calls the *objet a* the *object-cause* of desire.

Another way that Lacan and Žižek describe the *objet petit a* is as a little piece of the unsymbolizable Real (lack, or lost being, which resists symbolization) that acts as a screen onto which fantasies are projected (1989: 50-53).[26] It is a little piece of the Real 'which persists as a surplus' after the subject has entered into the symbolic order. It is the remainder, the left over, from the process interpellation/signification. Imbued by fantasy, this remainder comes to 'stand in' for what the subject desires and lacks and also for what the subject thinks the Other desires and lacks. Put another way, fantasy comes to play through desire for the lost

---

24. Žižek does not give a particular source in Lacan for this example of love.

25. Lacan develops these graphs for the purpose of demonstrating 'where desire, in relation to a subject defined in his articulation by the signifier, is situated' (Lacan 1977: 303).

26. Elsewhere Žižek speaks of the *objet petit a* as 'the Thing' (Lacan's take on Kant's *das Ding*) (see Lacan 1988b; Žižek 1989: 180-81). Žižek describes this as the 'Real in the very heart of the subject which cannot be symbolized, which is produced as a residue, a remnant, a leftover of every signifying operation' (1989: 180). For a reading of King David as 'the Thing' and an exposition of Žižek on 'the Thing', see Boer (1999).

object—whether that be the subject's lost being or the M/Other's lost phallus; the *objet a* therefore stands in for the unknowable, yet interpellating, master signifier which represents that loss. Through fantasy, this little piece of the Real is *elevated to the position of pure signifier or point de capiton*, standing in for the whole lack (1989: 71). This is why Žižek calls the *objet petit a* the 'real-impossible correlative' to the *point de capiton* (1989: 95); it is always both the representative of the absent yet interpellating master signifier (the cause of desire) and the fantasy of what is desired to fill that gap (the object of desire).

In short, the *objet petit a* is the fantasy response to the question of the Other, 'What do you want of me?' (*'Che vuoi?'*) addressed to the subject in interpellation. As Žižek puts it, 'fantasy appears, then, as an answer to *"Che vuoi?"* to the unbearable enigma of the desire of the Other, of the lack in the Other' (Žižek 1989: 118). Not only does the symbolic (or ideological) order hail the subject, 'Hey you!', but it also follows this call with a demand. Significantly though—especially in trying to understand how the subject comes to be fixed—it is only through the subject's own identification through fantasy and desire that these appellations by the symbolic order have any effect.

Desire, Fantasy, Ideology, Interpellation

So, following Žižek, when the subject is interpellated into ideology, it is formed through an identification of its own lack with the lack in the Other, the lack in the social order. In making the analogy from the symbolic order to ideology and the social order, Žižek reads the Real, the non-symbolizable lack in the Other, as a fundamental social antagonism.[27] It is an antagonism which 'is nowhere given as a positive entity' (1994b: 22), yet which nonetheless functions. He gives the example of class struggle as this kind of social antagonism.

However, one identifies with the master signifier that represents this elusive antagonism in the social order, by means of fantasy (social images and discourses). More specifically, it is through the production of fantasy objects that master signifiers are elevated so that they are able to 'pin down' the subject. Thus for Žižek, ideology is the fantasy-construction which masks this troubling 'hard kernel of the Real' and which structures social reality around it. We can only gain access to this traumatic element through ideology—ideology is, in a sense, a support for the Real, but hides its functioning as such (1989: 45-49; 1994b: 19-22). It is the involved process of fantasy and desire in ideological identification that

27. Žižek attributes his thinking on social antagonism to the work of Laclau and Mouffe (1985).

facilitates ideological (mis)recognition. This is the Žižekian re-reading of Althusserian subject, interpellated through identification with social discourses offered by the Ideological State Apparatuses.

Žižek gives a more concrete example of a phantasmic social discourse which structures the social order, and with which subjects identify, when he discusses the nation. He describes 'the nation' as that fantasy object (*objet petit a*) that is elevated to the status of pinning point (*point de capiton*). The non-discursive practices of a nation (the little piece of the Real) are taken together and elevated through fantasy to the ideal status of the *point de capiton* (1993: 202). To take a Canadian example, the non-discursive practices—that is the economic uses—of maple syrup, royal mounted police and hockey are, through fantasy, turned into discursive identification points for 'Canada'. The nation 'Canada' then becomes a *point de capiton*, in turn quilting other floating signifiers to make 'Canada' a friendly, healthy nation. This operation effaces the fact that Canadians are hard-pressed to find anything that binds them together (exhibiting an absence), and more importantly, it also effaces things like the economic exploitation of Québec by English Canada implicit in the production of maple syrup,[28] the brutality of the Royal Canadian Mounted Police in 'maintaining the peace', and child abuse in hockey coaching. We will see a similar (though not strictly analogous) operation occurring in readings of the nation in Micah (Chapter 5).

In sum then, interpellation takes place in the subject's entry into, and journey through, the ideological order; it is hailed and assigned a symbolic mandate through a process of identification with an ideological master signifier. For Žižek, fantasy is what clinches the ideological operation. The ideological operation *par excellence* occurs when through fantasy the fantasy object (*objet petit a*) steps in to fill the lack *as if it were* the ideological master signifier (*point de capiton*). The important thing to realize about the *point de capiton* is that, because it holds the place of lack, it is inaccessible except through the *objet petit a* which stands in for it.[29]

<hr />

28. And even this masks another exploitation, that of aboriginal peoples and their lands in the economic program of the sovereigntist Québecois government (for instance, the flooding of aboriginal lands to fuel hydro-power to be sold to the USA to gain economic independence from the rest of Canada).

29. Again this may be confusing in semiotic terms. Though the *objet petit a* stands in for the *point de capiton* (and would therefore seem to render the *point de capiton* as signified) it is still the *point de capiton*, the signifier of that inaccessible lack, that generates the fantasy in the first place. It is not that the fantasy object signifies or represents the pinning point, but that it substitutes for it.

The Problem of the Fixity of the Subject

With all these details in place, the overall problematic that Bhabha's theory addresses begins to emerge: within this framework, is it possible for subjects—determined as they are by identification and fantasy—to be repositioned at all, let alone by texts? It would seem that since 'pinning' master signifiers are related to lack, they could be, according to this view, interchangeable. For instance, Communism could just as easily be inserted in place of the lack of the Other as Capitalism; but each would have a quite different effect on the signification of the same terms (Žižek 1989: 102). The interchangeability of the master signifier might make more feasible the possibility of repositioning subjects. If the subject could just be pinned by a different *point de capiton* then it would come back down out of the symbolic order in a different place, with different meaning. This would mean that texts could supply new master signifiers and pin readers in new ways.

Unfortunately, within this theoretical framework, the process of repositioning the subject is not as simple as substituting master signifiers for each other. As I have tried to show, according to Althusser, Žižek and Lacan, interpellation into the symbolic order and ideology is a complex process of identification that is cognitively loaded in terms of signification, and psychically loaded in terms of desire and fantasy. More specifically, master signifiers gain their power to govern meaning through a conception, or recognition, of lack and the subject's identification with that lack through fantasy. The problem with this is that meaning, and attendant subject formation, is dependent on the way the lack is figured. Paradoxically, the way the lack is figured is both *caused by* and *produces* fantasy. The problem of self-referentiality begins to emerge here.

Lack of What?

This notion of lack is a moment in Lacan's thought that Bhabha reads critically to propose a less predetermined, pre-fixed subject; he does so using Derrida's critique of the *self-referential nature* of the lack. Since I will look at Derrida's critique of Lacan in Chapter 3, when I discuss Bhabha's use of it, for the moment I will only note the *problem* of the narcissistic self-referentiality of signification that Derrida critiques. To be clear, the critique is that the problem toward which this theory tends (specifically Lacan's) is that subjectivity and the production of meaning are always destined to be fixed in the same place, because they are always invariably governed by the same (self-referentially established) master signifier that holds the place of the lack.

The metaphor of the phallus used by Lacan might best illustrate this problem. As noted, Lacan describes the master signifier with the metaphor of the phallus. For Lacan, the phallus is what ensures that the subject (and signification) always comes to rest in its 'proper place'; that is, it always comes to fill the Other's *lack of* phallus (1977: 280-91). As already mentioned, the Other is, metaphorically speaking, the woman ('M/Other'). The woman marks the absence of the phallus.

Lacan develops this metaphor in his 'Seminar on the "The Purloined Letter"' (1972), a reading of Poe's short story, 'The Purloined Letter'. In Poe's story, a letter is stolen from the Queen, and the police cannot recover it, for all their searching; but the clever detective, Dupin, knows where to find it because he knows where to look. He guesses that it will be disguised as a different letter in the thief's apartment. So when Dupin goes into the thief's apartment, he finds the stolen letter, as he expected. It is disguised as another letter, set casually in a card holder hanging from the mantelpiece. Lacan reads this story to suggest that through the efforts of the psychoanalyst (Dupin), 'the letter' (the signifier), even when diverted, always arrives at its proper destination (finds true interpretation), because it (the letter, or signifier) is always found where it should be, filling in for lack.[30]

The way that Lacan describes the letter filling in for the 'lack in the Other' is symptomatic of the problem with the theory. The letter, or signifier, is a 'symbol only of an absence' (1972: 54) and this absence is typified in the female body. He writes,

> so does the purloined letter, like an immense female body, stretch out across [the thief's] office when Dupin enters. But just so does he already expect to find it, and has only...to undress that huge body. And that is why...he will go straight to the spot in which lies and lives what that body is designed to hide, in a gorgeous center caught in a glimpse... Look! between the cheeks of the fireplace, there's the object already in reach of a hand the *ravisher* has but to extend (Lacan 1972: 66-67, cited in Derrida 1975: 62, emphasis mine).

The lack of the woman's body, *for which the letter stands in* is the lack of a penis (phallus). However, the privileged term, the phallus, is nowhere to be seen, and it must be *assumed* by those fortunate enough to somehow realize that it is important,[31] in order for 'the lack' to be noticed and

---

30. Lacan reads the repetitions of the appearance of the letter in the story as repetition compulsion (1972: 39, 44-45). Thus the signifier *compulsively* returns to its proper place, not a very hopeful image for that which determines the subject.

31. Derrida calls this 'psychoanalytico-transcendental topology' (Derrida 1975: 58). Lacan insists that the phallus is not in fact the penis, and there has been a great

for the letter to be found and returned to its proper place (violently—I might note—by a 'ravisher').[32]

The self-referential nature of this operation becomes more fully apparent here: because the lack can only be known by fantasy; it appears as lack of that very fantasy; the phallus appears as lack of phallus. The sign fills that lack *as the phallus*—the sign which fills 'the hole between the woman's legs' (Lacan cited in Derrida 1975: 61). The *point de capiton*, or master signifier, steps in to 'unify a given field', representing the lack of the Other as *itself* (Žižek 1989: 95). It would seem then that signification, meaning and subjectivity are, according to this view, *self-referentially* governed by the phallus, or the absent master signifier.

Affixed by Fantasy

All of this has rather negative implications for the possibility of ever repositioning the subject, since the point where the subject comes back down out of its journey through the symbolic order is determined by the master signifier to which it is pinned, and through which it identifies with the lack in the Other. How could the subject's identification of its own lack with the lack in the Other ever effect a repositioning of the subject, when it is so self-referential (even narcissistic, because the subject also *desires* the fantasy object filling in for lack, thus both identifying with, and desiring, its own lack)?[33] If the master signifier is determined

deal of debate over this by his critics and interpreters; for a discussion and references to the debate, see Butler (1993: 57-91). The fact of the matter is that the 'lack of phallus' is a metaphor for the absence of the *penis*, and as Jane Gallop points out, for this reason it is impossible to separate the two (1988: 125-31). (And as Derrida points out, the use of the metaphor of the missing maternal penis in the 'Seminar on "The Purloined Letter"' is an unacknowledged debt Lacan owes to the psychoanalyst Marie Bonaparte [Derrida 1975: 66-67].)

32. The word here in the French is *ravisseur* (Lacan 1966: 37), with the meaning of 'one who takes by force'. Yet somewhat disturbingly, in reading this as an analogy to analysis, the editor to the English translation elaborates this ravishing as a kind of rape (which of course violently inserts the penis/phallus): 'analysis, in its violation of the imaginary integrity of the ego, finds its fantasmatic equivalent in rape' (1972: 67 n. 38).

33. Lacan alludes to this in an early version of his seminar text, where he describes the letter in the 'The Purloined Letter' as entering into a narcissistic relation to the subject, like a kind of love-letter the subject has sent himself (1988a: 199). This idea is not found in such straightforward terms in the later 1966 version that opens *Écrits* (Lacan's seminars go through some transformation between the time they were originally given—as gathered and edited by Jacques-Alain Miller in *Le Seminaire de Jacques Lacan*—and the time some of them were officially written and compiled for *Écrits* in 1966).

by, and determines, the subject's *own fantasy*, the system would seem rather closed; the subject would be destined to repeat the same identifications over and over, and to come through the signifying chain in the same place, producing the same meaning again and again. In order to change this, one would have to arrive at a way of changing the subject's fantasy. But if fantasy is also determined by an imposed external master signifier which is given its power by that very fantasy, then how does one find a way out?

If, hypothetically, signification of texts and readers' interpellation into texts were understood according to this view, meaning would come through a master signifier's ability to re-present (stand in for) the lack in the text. *Points de capiton*, or pinning points, found in the text would only gain their power to interpellate readers and govern the meaning of a text through a conception of, or fantasy of, lack in the text. The master signifier's ability to represent that lack would arise from the reader's identification of that lack with her own lack through a fantasy object that stands in for both. The problem with this, though, is that meaning, and any attendant positioning of the subject, would be dependent on the shape of the lack which could only be made known through fantasy raised to the level of something outside the text (i.e. an ideological master signifier by which the reader had already been interpellated). This would mean that texts could not be interpreted on their own terms, but would always be dependent on some absence represented by an external master signifier. Meaning and a reader's positioning by a text would be dependent on this self-referentially established external master signifier. How then could one ever hope that texts might reposition subjects?

Indeed according to this view, it seems that I may have come back, full circle, to a view discussed in Chapter 1: namely, the idea, discussed by Beal, following Lukács (in Jameson), that ideology acts as a strategy of containment for reading. There I suggested that if a study of ideology and reading were to take a more Althusserian approach, it would not be able to understand the reader's ideology as controlling (totalizing) the play of text *from the outside*. Rather it would understand structures to be immanent in their effects, and in doing so it would be more compatible with the notion of endlessly playing and indeterminate text. Now having looked at Žižek's reading of Althusser through Lacan, it seems that control executed by an outside term (the master signifier generated by the reader's own fantasy) is required to stop the sliding of the signs of a text.[34] Yet, as I argued in Chapter 1, if the idea of limitless text on

34. This, of course, indicates a line of questioning to be applied to Žižek's reading

which the notion of indeterminate text rests is to be taken seriously, then ideology cannot be considered outside of that limitless text (i.e. the reader's ideological text and the biblical text need to be considered part of the same fabric). Thus the relation between the structure of ideological texts (according to which readers are formed) and that of written (biblical) texts along with their respective effects (interpellation and meaning) must be studied. A tension stands, therefore, between Althusser's understanding of ideology and Žižek's rereading (using Lacan) of the processes involved in ideological interpellation.

This tension will be resolved for me through Bhabha's use of Lacan and his discussion of new possibilities for the subject's identification with the symbolic order. Bhabha picks up on the Lacanian notion of identification with the Other through interpellation into the symbolic order, but in ways that resist the self-referentiality of signification that Žižek and Lacan imply. Moreover, in describing the processes of cultural identification, Bhabha takes up the Derridean critique of Lacan and by doing so, is able to suggest a process of identification with difference that resists forms of discrimination. I will suggest in the next chapter that what Bhabha contributes to an understanding of subject formation is an understanding of identification with difference, instead of an identification with lack. I will use his theorizing to suggest that identification with the differently iterated signs of the text, rather than with perceived lack in the text, can have the effect of reorienting the reader's subjectivity.

of Althusser, one that I am not able to consider in detail here, though I do come back to it, at points, in Chapter 3.

3

Bhabha and the Subject: Identifying with Difference

Thus far in this study, I have tried to outline the more general issues of text and reader that are at stake in reading Micah (Chapter 1), and building from there, the specific problem that the theory of the subject's formation within ideology poses for reading in ways that are not always predetermined (where ideology is understood more or less as Althusser describes it, as images and discourses with which people identify, and as that which they 'practice' in order to make sense of their material circumstances) (Chapter 2). Putting this in simple terms, if one starts from the position that ideology is instrumental in the formation of readers as speaking, acting selves, how is it possible to think that readers might read otherwise than dictated by that ideology in which they were formed, let alone hope that the text might actually affect their positioning with respect to it. Pinned (through fantasy and identification) as the subject is—following Žižek's Lacanian reformulation of Althusser's notion of interpellation into ideology—to certain (self-referentially established) ideological master signifiers, there seems to be no escaping these master signifiers when trying to interpret a text.

In this chapter, I show how Bhabha's discussions of the *negotiation of cultural difference* can be applied to the question of ideologically determined reading. My overall argument is that Bhabha conceptualizes the possibility for the subject to be repositioned through a process of *identification with difference*, and that this is useful in considering how readers' identification with difference in the text of Micah might be able to disrupt their positioning as subjects always-already positioned within ideology. Alongside a detailed exposition of Bhabha, I pursue this argument in a number of ways: I show how Bhabha brings a primarily Derridean deconstructionist critique to bear on Lacan's description of subject formation; I argue that this has interesting implications for Žižek's Lacanian description of the subject's interpellation into ideology, as well as for the reading process in general; and finally, I suggest how all of this might apply to the way that readers interact with the text of Micah.

A number of preliminaries are in order before I embark on this discussion. First, for the purposes of this study, I concentrate my discussion on Bhabha's collection of essays entitled, *The Location of Culture* (1994a), and refer to other of his articles only at rare points for clarification.[1] In the essays collected in this volume, Bhabha draws from myriad theoretical and literary texts, combining ideas and images in a very fluid, poetic fashion, building with theoretical tools and bits and pieces at hand.[2] By combining various ideas, images and terms from a number of different theories, especially psychoanalytic, deconstructionist and third-world texts, he sketches out a number of what I might term 'conceptual metaphors' or 'metaphorical concepts'. These are terms (for instance, 'the time-lag', 'hybridity', 'outside the sentence'), perhaps borrowed from other theoretical discourses, that are given visual, or at least spatially descriptive, connotations (even 'time-lag' is drawn out in spatial terms); they compress dense and difficult concepts into compact theoretical imagery. In each of his metaphorical concepts, Bhabha weaves together various theories of signification, subjectivity and ideology, returning always to pass through the same theme: the negotiation of cultural difference in a way that is liberating for those caught in oppressive situations.

Giving an exposition of any of Bhabha's conceptual metaphors, however, is difficult because of his poetic, intricate and allusive style. He is a difficult writer to 'exegete' fully, and trying to do so is somewhat akin to interpreting poetry (or biblical text): the danger is in unproblematically filling in the 'gaps' with privileged outside terms or texts. Though Bhabha notes many of his allusions, providing most of the sources from which he borrows in endnotes, oft times he uses phrases or images that he has documented elsewhere and so does not document again. To make matters more complex, many of the writers to whom he refers (e.g. Lacan, Žižek, Derrida) also rarely produce texts that are straightforward. I nonetheless turn to some of these sources to aid in my

---

1.   See Moore-Gilbert for an excellent overview and discussion of all of Bhabha's work (1997: 114-51). He divides Bhabha's work into two phases, 'From around 1980 to 1988, [Bhabha's] principle interest is in colonial discourse... Since then, Bhabha has become more preoccupied with the issues raised by the cultural consequences of neo-colonialism in the contemporary era and the complex and often conflictual relationship of postcolonial discourse to postmodernism' (1997: 114). Both these phases can be found represented in Bhabha's collection of essays, *The Location of Culture* (1994a).

2.   This might be best described by the concept of *bricolage*, borrowed from Lévi-Strauss and popularized in poststructural thought by Derrida (1974: 138-40; 1978: 284-86). Derrida's use of the word seems to imply a kind of tearing down, or at least a critique (see 1974: 139); in this vein, Bhabha's use of various borrowed ideas, juxtaposed with other ideas, often confronts the very context from which they are taken.

explication. I have already outlined in Chapter 2 my understanding of
the basics of the Lacanian theory to which I will refer; here I also outline,
where needed and in a very limited way, my understanding of the
Derridean theory and the psychoanalytic object relations theory on
which Bhabha draws.

What makes Bhabha crucial to my project is that all of these metaphorical concepts turn, in some way, around the *possibility of resituat-
ing the subject through the negotiation of cultural difference* in ways
that disrupt oppressive power regimes. Again, this is important for my
argument, because I am interested in the impact of the text of Micah (as
a site of difference), on readers' positioning as subjects (where subjectivity is understood to be related to ideology). Each of these concepts—
primarily concerned with theorizing cultural difference in a way that
resists (neo)colonialism, racism and discrimination—takes up the theory
of the subject in a way that does not privilege 'transcendental' terms and
hierarchies (e.g. the absent phallus), but rather looks at the formation of
the subject as a negotiation of difference. Bhabha's use and modification
of Lacan's theory of subjectivity enables thinking the possibility of
repositioning the subject through *identification with difference* rather
than with *lack*. Theorizing as he does, Bhabha shows the possibility for
negotiating the processes of subject formation; his work implies—or at
least can be read in a way that suggests—that subject formation is tied
up with, but can also disrupt, ideology. Because Bhabha's concepts are
both spatially, temporally and linguistically oriented, they are readily
analogous to the interaction between text and reader.

I proceed then, first by broadly describing Bhabha's project and giving
an overview of the way he uses the discourse of subjectivity in his work. I
then set out his conception of 'pedagogical objects and discourses' (very
simply, unifying discourses) used both in the processes of colonization
and in understandings of the modern western nation in general. I give
the concept of 'pedagogical discourses' as a point of contrast to other of
his metaphorical concepts: 'performative practice', 'the Third Space',
'hybridity', 'outside the sentence', 'the time-lag', 'liminal identification',
and 'agency in indeterminacy'. These latter are all metaphors which he
uses to demonstrate the inherently ambiguous and undecidable nature
of 'pedagogical discourses'. So while for the purposes of exposition—
and eventually my own analysis of text—I break down the theory into
the simplifying formula of 'performative practices' over and against
'pedagogical objects and discourses', in reality Bhabha's theory holds
these things together; they are not separate processes. Pedagogical
objects and discourses are not actually, for Bhabha, as unitary as they
might seem; careful analysis of them, and in particular of the temporality

in which they are formed, shows up the ambivalence and indecidability of the modern nation.

Within my expositions of these concepts, I draw out the liberatory value of Bhabha's work, looking at how he envisions the indeterminate and ambivalent processes of cultural identification as disruptive and undermining to oppressive dominant orders, and as empowering for colonized peoples. I also show how he uses Derrida to modify the Lacanian discourse on subjectivity in a way that critiques the fixity of the (colonial) subject. Finally, I look at how Bhabha's work might affect Žižek's Lacanian formulation of Althusser's interpellation of the subject, and the usefulness of this theoretical encounter for reading in general, and in particular, for reading Micah. Again, it may be helpful to note that in all my attention here to subject and Other, I am looking ahead to thinking about reader as subject and text as Other (though as Bhabha asserts, these polarities cannot always be maintained).

Bhabha's Project

Bhabha's work as a postcolonial[3] theorist critiques modernity's dominant myth of progress, and makes explicit the relations of modernity to nationalism, colonialism and racism. More specifically, he shows how the process of identifying 'other' nations and races denies, or disavows, differences within them; it also denies the dependence of the colonizer's 'self' on (an unacknowledged) identification with the colonized 'other'. This disavowal enables and produces discrimination and antagonism. Oppression and violence, based on a (mis)recognition of some form of stereotypic difference, he argues, are constitutive for modernity. As he puts it, 'forms of social and psychic alienation and aggression—madness, self-hate, treason, violence—can never be acknowledged as determinate and constitutive conditions of civil authority… They are always explained away as alien presences, occlusions of historical progress, the ultimate misrecognition of Man' (1994a: 43). According to Bhabha, this kind of systemically 'constitutive' violence is typically denied along with the difference that might disturb the homogeneous, stereotypic image of a race. All of this disavowal assures colonizers of the 'progress' being made by their colonizing actions.

---

3. Bhabha frames the term 'postcolonial' as follows: 'Postcoloniality, for its part, is a salutary reminder of the persistent "neo-colonial" relations within the "new" world order and the multinational divisions of labour. Such a perspective enables the authentication of histories of exploitation and the evolution of strategies of resistance' (1994a: 6).

To counteract this disavowal, Bhabha is interested in allowing the relations and antagonisms that are constitutive for modernity to be represented. He critiques modernity's universal ideal of the nation as a homogeneous, sovereign, autonomous political entity (1990b: 293), by looking at the articulations of cultural difference within nations. He suggests that narratives of nationhood are, in actual fact, continually disrupted and destabilized by the different everyday cultural locations from which these narratives are spoken (what Bhabha calls the 'enunciatory present'). One of the main goals of Bhabha's project is to work toward an understanding of what it means to negotiate cultural difference in a way that is empowering for those subordinated, displaced or otherwise marginalized. Thus he imagines, in a number of ways, a kind of space (and time) where difference can be recognized as that which is between and within cultures, a space that both constitutes cultures and also disrupts the boundaries between them. Bhabha describes this as 'the cutting edge of translation and negotiation, the in between space' (1994a: 38), the space where meaning and difference are negotiated.

One of the contemporary stances against which Bhabha develops his notion of cultural difference is the liberal celebration of cultural diversity (1994a: 34, 60). Cultural diversity, he argues, is a concept that proceeds from an understanding of cultures as knowable, that is, as objects that can be studied and known empirically (1994a: 34). Such assumptions about culture keep different cultures separate, sealed off from each other according to their respective 'origins'. In Bhabha's estimation, proponents of cultural diversity think of distinct cultures as able to live side by side but separately, distinguishable by their differences; but it is precisely this kind of thinking about difference that authorizes discrimination and oppression. As Bhabha puts it, the notion of cultural diversity is based on a 'rhetoric of the separation of totalized cultures that live unsullied by the intertextuality of their historical locations, safe in the Utopianism of a mythic memory of a unique collective identity' (1994a: 34). The notion of a utopic 'common past' or 'origin', Bhabha argues, is fiction—that glosses over many historical disjunctures—in the service of authority. Through appeal to 'origin', authority can base itself in 'tradition'. In Bhabha's view, separation of cultures based on 'knowable' traditions does not allow for understanding the 'intertextual' links between cultures in the past, nor for new liberatory ways of thinking about negotiation between cultures in the present (1994a: 35).

In contrast to cultural diversity, which sees cultures as homogeneous and knowable through their cultural icons (1994a: 35), cultural difference 'is the process of the *enunciation* of culture as "knowledgeable", authoritative' (1994a: 34). Since difference resides *within* cultures, as well as between cultures, the enunciation, or articulation, of cultural difference undermines the homogenizing tendencies that accompany the idea of unitary and knowable cultures (a homogenization, I might suggest, illustrated by statements like, '*the* Blacks like…' or '*the* Chinese want…'). When attention is paid to the daily practices that take place within a 'cultural group', Bhabha suggests, it becomes very difficult to define it as a knowable 'Other' (1994a: 147-48). In some ways then, in setting out this notion of difference within cultures, rather than just between cultures, Bhabha critiques the very notion of 'culture' itself (1994a: 131-32).

In order to find examples of 'cultural locations' that disturb monolithic images of a nation, Bhabha looks at the kinds of representations that appear in postcolonial texts and cultures, and the kinds of 'identities', or images with which people identify, established there (see especially his essay, 'Interrogating Identity', 1994a: 40-65). He finds that the representations and images presented for identification in postcolonial texts are both defined by colonial power and disruptive of it, and are therefore ambivalent. However, this very ambivalence is what disturbs unitary and homogenizing stereotypes.

The Discourse of Subjectivity

In describing the kind of postcolonial images held up for identification, Bhabha utilizes a Lacanian psychoanalytic discourse of subjectivity. He does so following the lead of the Algerian revolutionary psychiatrist Franz Fanon, who he says, 'suggested an oppositional, differential reading of Lacan's Other' (1994a: 32). Bhabha therefore develops a way of reading Lacan's description of the subject's entry into the symbolic order ('the Other') that does not fix the subject in one place, but allows for liberatory movement away from disempowered positions. He does so both by exploiting the less deterministic moments (outlined in the previous chapter) within the Lacanian conception of subject, and by engaging a Derridean critique of Lacan. Bhabha uses the Lacanian terminology of subject and Other in a couple of overlapping ways that may at first seem contradictory, but are actually in line with his work of erasing binary oppositions between cultures.

First, he picks up on the common usage of the terms 'self' and 'other' to speak of colonizer and colonized respectively; however, his writing works at erasing the oppositions implicit in the usual self/other, subject/object, us/them polarities which he suggests authorize discrimination (1994a: 179). By reading the self/other dichotomy as Lacan's relation between subject/Other, he argues that the alienation the subject undergoes in interacting with the Other, and the lack that cuts through them both are what can also be invoked to destabilize the self/other (subject/Other) dichotomy.

Thus the Lacanian image of the overlap between subject and Other (i.e. the *vel*, the 'or' of 'meaning *or* being') becomes a central trope for Bhabha; it is a place that is neither the self nor the other, but somewhere in between. This image becomes vital to Bhabha's discussion of cultural difference which he describes as those untranslatable, incommensurable moments that cannot be homogenized by the generalization 'that cul-ture'. He calls for a negotiation of difference, a negotiation that refuses homogenization. He sees this as 'a non-Hegelian dialectic', one which does not 'sublate' or synthesize difference into a higher term, in a way that would not value difference for itself (1994a: 26, 173).[4] He therefore likens these dialectical moments—where differences interact without being sublated—to Lacan's *vel*, the space of non-sense between meaning and being, that alienation which occurs when the subject encounters the Other and which runs through both the subject and the Other (1994a: 56, 124-25).

In this dialectic, the colonized other is also read as the enunciating, colonial subject, and this, as I will show, is the second way in which Bhabha employs the Lacanian language of self and other. Here the colonized subject resists the 'pinning' of the colonial order (the Other). The subject can 'unpick' this pinning and find its own authority and agency through a negotiatory process of identification with the margins of that order. This too destabilizes the distinction between subject and Other.

So Bhabha uses the overarching Lacanian metaphor of subject/Other: the colonizing self is only formed through overlap with its colonized other, and the colonized subject can revision its own identity through an intersubjective negotiation with the colonial symbolic order. I hope to show that these conceptual overlaps are productive for thinking about repositioning the reader as subject, through a negotiation with text. Though the reader may seem at points like a colonizer (self), imposing unifying concepts on the text (other), I suggest that the text can become an enunciating subject, and moreover, that the reader, herself pinned by the ideological order (Other) in which she is formed, can also identify differently in this process. The enunciation of the text, I suggest, can help to 'unpick' the reader's pinning in ideology.

Within this framework, as I will show, Bhabha also draws on related

---

4. Roland Barthes, on whom Bhabha draws at different points in his work, also wishes to find a non-synthesizing third term instead of a simple opposition (1975: 55).

Lacanian concepts: the relationship between signification and subjectivity, the retroactivity of meaning, the split subject, the process of identification with the object of desire, and the like. However, these Lacanian concepts are—in good postmodern style—never 'pure' in Bhabha's work; they are almost always put into play through engagement with other theory, most often through the decontructionist theory of Derrida, and the psychoanalytic writing of Fanon, but also through a wide range of other postcolonial literary texts, or cultural and ideological critical theories.

Before continuing, I turn to a brief example of this kind of theoretical mixture, pertinent to Bhabha's use of Lacanian theory. One of the ways that Bhabha reads the space that destabilizes the binary terms of self and Other is through Derrida's notion of the undecidable. An undecidable is, for Derrida, a term or image that 'escapes from inclusion in the philosophical (binary) opposition and which nonetheless inhabit[s] it, resist[s] it, and disorganise[s] it but without ever constituting a third term, without ever occasioning a solution' (1981a: 43).[5] Bhabha describes the Lacanian image of the overlap between self and Other (e.g. the *vel*) as exactly such a place of undecidability, neither the self nor the other, but somewhere in between (1994a: 54, 127, 133). This undecidable space between self and Other in signification and in representation is what, for Bhabha, allows for liberation: 'the time of liberation is…a time of cultural uncertainty, and, most crucially of significatory or representational undecidability' (1994a: 35). Undecidability—the 'ambivalence that haunts the idea of the nation' (1990a: 1)—is a theme elaborated by Bhabha throughout his work on nations and identities.

Pedagogical Objects and Discourses

What Bhabha finds to be undecidable are 'pedagogical objects and discourses'; that is, images, narratives and stereotypes that are used to homogenize identity in the discourses of nationality. As already noted, Bhabha argues that in colonial and postcolonial contexts, there is often an attempt to 'categorize' the Other, to make 'them' all the same, to pin down 'their' identity. This kind of categorization is often aided by cultural icons, national histories or racial stereotypes—what Bhabha terms 'pedagogical objects and discourses'—which gloss over difference in order to make difficult social interactions more manageable. When I come to look at readings of Micah, I suggest that a similar thing happens there:

5. For an excellent discussion of undecidables, see Sherwood (1996: 176-87).

sometimes the figure of the nation within the text is smoothed over, or
pinned down, in just this way, according to images and understandings of
Israel (and of gender in general) that come from outside the text of
Micah. The pedagogical discourse of the nation is, for Bhabha, a sort of
unitary icon, 'a holistic cultural entity' (1994a: 140) which is often used
to identify peoples in order to justify discrimination or colonial policy.
Bhabha calls pedagogical discourses 'continuist' and 'accumulative'
(1994a: 145), because they seek to situate a culture or nation in its past,
to construct a people as an historical or patriotic object, in order to best
'know' that people. The use of these kinds of discourses as strategies for
identifying, 'understanding' and 'managing' a people turns the nation or
culture in question into a 'pedagogical object' (1994a: 147) instead of a
speaking ('enunciating') subject.

Bhabha's main concern (and therefore, so too the concern of much of
this chapter) is always to show the 'splitting' of these homogenizing
images and discourses (1994a: 145-48). Bhabha works to demonstrate
the splitting, the undecidability and tension in the formation of these
unifying icons, by reading Lacan through Derrida. However, before
looking at how he does this, I turn to a slightly more detailed exposition
of how he understands and explains his idea of pedagogical objects and
discourse. It will be important to my more general discussion of ideology
to notice, as I go, how Bhabha uses Lacanian imagery—in a way that
resonates with Žižek's theory of ideology—to show that cultural and
racial difference within colonial rule—like Lacan's and Žižek's lack—
must be filled in, disavowed, made to conform, if domination is to be
successful. Bhabha's conceptions of 'pedagogical discourse', 'cultural
icon' and 'stereotype' all play a role similar to Lacan's and Žižek's *objet
petit a* (the fantasy object that stands in for 'lack') raised to the status of
point de capiton (ideological pinning point): each masks or fills in for
difference, calling it 'other', by portraying it, imagining it, fantasizing it
as somehow related to the self. With the notion of pedagogical object,
Bhabha effectively illustrates, deliberately or not, Žižek's Marxist–Lacanian
description of the *point de capiton* that ideologically pins or buttons
down diverse phenomena in the social order.

Historical Narrative
Bhabha argues that there is often a focus on 'historical origin or event'
(1994a: 145) in pedagogical discourse. Attention to 'national history', he
argues, does two things. First its sets up a 'fixed' point of origin, a sort of
national myth, by which the culture can be read and understood. Bhabha
argues that even though modern nations are 'irredeemably plural' spaces,
made up of the coming together of people from 'different, even hostile

nations' (1990b: 300),[6] they are often understood as unitary through reference to a common past, or formative historical event. This attention to the past forms what Bhabha calls a 'signifying space that is archaic and mythical…turning Territory into Tradition, turning the People into One' (1994a: 149). He gives the example of Rosa Diamond, an English gentlewoman character in Salman Rushdie's *The Satanic Verses* (1988) as embodying this kind of historical pedagogical discourse:

> The pageant of 900-year-old history passes through her frail translucent body and inscribes itself, in the strange splitting of her language, 'the well-worn phrases, *unfinished business, grandstand view,* made her feel solid unchanging, sempiternal, instead of the creature of cracks and absences she knew herself to be'. [She is] constructed from the well-worn pedagogies and pedigrees of national unity—her vision of the Battle of Hastings is the anchor of her being (Bhabha 1994a: 167, citing Rushdie 1988: 130).

As we will see further on, this kind of grounding in national history — which is an appeal to tradition, a return of the archaic—is ultimately, for Bhabha, undecidable and ambivalent (1994a: 143).

Second, this kind of focus on historical event or origin gives the discourse a certain kind of authority 'that is based on the pre-given or constituted historical origin *in the past*' (1994a: 145). By setting up an '*a priori* historical presence' (1994a: 147), nations are able to justify their political actions upon other nations as grounded and justified in the past. Bhabha calls this authorizing moment of origin 'the Great Event…a historical sign of the "people"…that constitutes the memory and the moral of the event *as a narrative*, a disposition to cultural communality, a form of social and psychic identification' (1994a: 243).[7]

Cultural Icons
Bhabha describes 'cultural icons' as serving a function similar to pedagogical discourse. In speaking about 'culture' there is always a 'demand for a model, a tradition, a community, a stable system of reference' (1994a: 35) with which a culture can either understand itself, or be identified by others. Bhabha argues that the kinds of 'cultural symbols and icons' that are produced for this purpose have 'homogenizing effects' (1994a: 35), synthesizing many differences into one unitary symbol. Bhabha contrasts symbol—'the iconic image of authority'—to sign—'the

6. This phrase only appears in the earlier version of this essay, 'DissemiNation', in *Nation and Narration* (1990b).
7. Such an analysis of historical narrative rings true when one considers the way the exodus story is used pedagogically in the Hebrew Bible to remind the people of the formative event of their rescue from Egypt by Yahweh.

signifier that produces that image' (1994a: 149); the symbol or icon of culture tries to unify, or I might say, pin down what Bhabha calls the sliding signifiers of culture: the multifarious peoples and practices that make up that culture (1994a: 148, 237). While Bhabha does not seem to use the term 'national icon', it seems to me that the kind of emblem or icon used to identify a nation, either from within or from without (for instance, hockey in Canada, or the royal family in Britain), functions in this kind of homogenizing and unifying way. When I come to my discussion of Micah, it will be interesting to notice how Zion and the divine ruler are often read by scholars as kinds of 'icons' for the nation of Israel.

Although Bhabha does not explicitly describe, as Žižek does, the discourse of nation as *objet petit a* (fantasy object), he uses language that suggests that he may see the pedagogical discourse of nation this way. Bhabha's statement that 'the nation *fills the void* left in the uprooting of communities and kin, *and turns that loss into the language of metaphor*' (1994a: 139, emphasis mine) sounds remarkably like Lacan's description of the *objet petit a* filling in for the void which is *the loss* of connection to the drives. Using this psychoanalytic image more obviously, he writes, 'the lost object—the national *Heim*—is repeated in the void [of migrant and minority language]…the object of loss is written across the bodies of the people, as it repeats in the silence that speaks the foreignness of language' (1994a: 165).[8] The 'national icon' or 'myth' is a fantasy object that fills in where there is a lack of cohesion; it gains authority as it is raised to the status of *point de capiton*, as it begins to be used to account for national practices or to identify peoples within a culture.

Stereotype
Bhabha speaks more specifically of the stereotype's relation to the *objet petit a* and the *point de capiton* (master signifier), by using Freudian

---

8.   Here in this section of the essay 'DissemiNation', and elsewhere (1994a: 10, 101, 136-37) Bhabha plays with the words *heimlich* and *unheimlich* that Freud uses to describe the uncanny (*unheimlich*). For Freud *heimlich* means familiar, friendly, homely; but also secret (1953: 224-26). The *unheimlich* is a feeling of dread or terror that one has when something is thought to have hidden aspects; this feeling arises when one sees something familiar that has become alien through repression reappear (1953: 241); or when infantile or 'primitive' complexes make themselves felt, after they are thought to be overcome (1953: 249). The uncanny is a kind of haunting remainder. Bhabha reads the figure of the nation (embodied by icons, historical narratives, stereotypes) in postcolonial contexts as something that stands in for a loss (of homeland, of community, of tradition); it is the haunting, archaic remainder of something that was once familiar. Bhabha also plays with this notion alongside the idea of imperfect repetition of culture (see below for details) that 'haunts and hinders' (1994a: 137).

terminology to describe stereotype as fetish (1994a: 68-69, 73-75, 80, 115, 132), that is, as an object of desire, that comes to stand in for lack. For Bhabha, the racial stereotype, like fetish, is a 'fixated' form that 'facilitates' relations between people or groups. The racial stereotype, like fetish, is 'the prop that makes the whole object desirable and lovable, facilitates sexual [or colonial] relations and can even promote a form of happiness' (1994a: 78-79). At the same time the stereotype or fetish is itself often an object of anxiety or horrific fascination. Bhabha gives the stereotype of black people as an example of this kind of object of desire and horror:[9] 'the black is both savage (cannibal) and yet the most obedient and dignified of servants (the bearer of food); he is the embodiment of rampant sexuality, and yet innocent as a child' (1994a: 82). This kind of image of 'the black' facilitates or enables the discrimination and exploitation that is necessary for the functioning of imperialist regimes.

Stereotype operates, therefore, like Žižek's ideological pinning point (*point de capiton*, or master signifier) to pin down differences within the social order. While Bhabha also shows the ambiguity of stereotype as something that is at the same time a recognition and a disavowal of difference, in its *disavowing function*, the fetish is like the *objet petit a*, the object of desire which comes to stand in for lack. And as Bhabha puts it, stereotyping is 'the process by which the metaphoric "masking" is inscribed on lack...[this] gives the stereotype both its fixity and its phantasmatic quality—the *same old* stories of the Negro's animality, the Coolie's inscrutability or the stupidity of the Irish' (1994a: 77). Because Bhabha understands fetish (in Freudian terms) as the disavowal of sexual difference through 'fixation on an object that masks that difference [of the vagina or so-called castration] and restores an original presence [the penis]' (1994a: 74),[10] his notion of stereotype as fetish is very close to Žižek's *objet petit a* raised to the status of *point de capiton* (see 1994a: 115).

In sum then, Bhabha describes pedagogical objects and discourses as those things which, in postcolonial contexts, stand in for the lack of social cohesion, or common language. The pedagogical object is always constructed in terms of a search for a lost origin (in Lacanian terms a phallic absence), for the unified history of a nation. The kind of cohesion

9.   The *objet petit a* as an object of both horror, fascination and desire might best be seen in Žižek's analogy of the *objet petit a* to the endlessly bleeding vagina as wound (1993: 181-82).

10.   While Bhabha locates racial stereotype within the realm of the Lacanian imaginary (partly because skin colour is visual, and the imaginary is related to the scopic, visual realm [1994a: 77]), he describes fetish as a function of the symbolic realm, as suture (1994a: 74, 81).

that is created with this kind of narrative or icon of a people is what gives it authority; there are no visible cracks to investigate critically, everything fits unquestionably together. This is analogous to the way Žižek describes the operation of ideology. When I come to Chapter 4, I will show how these kinds of 'pedagogical objects and discourses' about Israel as a nation function as ideological pinning points that fill in for, and disavow, the difference in the text.

Performative Practices

Bhabha contrasts these kinds of images and discourses that unify and pin down identity with the repetition and difference on which they are built. For instance, he contrasts pedagogical discourse—'the continuist, accumulative temporality of the pedagogical'—with *performative practice*—'the repetitious, recursive strategy of the performative' (1994a: 145). He is concerned with showing how the performative discourse of a nation, with its varied forms of self-representation, disrupts the image of a unitary cultural icon. Performative practice is that 'repetitious, recursive strategy' in which individual people, not necessarily unified in their beliefs or by their willingness to be represented by the national identity, take part in producing national culture differently, through daily activities and through their interaction with, or enunciation of, the national story or identity.[11] Ambivalence is a result of the movement between the pedagogical and the performative. Tension irrupts when the 'pedagogical object', that is, the self-contained national identity, is intersected by the open-endedness of its being-told, its enunciation, by a community that is far from unified. As Bhabha puts it, in performance 'the…Nation *It/Self*, alienated from its eternal self-generation, becomes a liminal form of social representation, a space that is *internally* marked by cultural difference and the heterogeneous histories of contending peoples' (1994a: 148). Put very simply, the pedagogical object cannot hope to be representative of all people within a culture; so when individuals interact with it, or enunciate it, the static 'national identity' breaks open,[12] and becomes less dominant and less definitive.

11. Others have argued along the same lines: see Gallissot, who speaks of the process of identification as an active process, outlining two kinds of identification, one that is participatory and one that is for naming: 'l'identification d'appartenance, l'identification par référence' (1987: 17).

12. For example, in Québec, the sense of national identity that pushes toward a sovereign Québec is an example of a pedagogical object of discourse, based on the historical event of colonization by the English of French Canada, and on all the events accompanying that colonization. Yet within Québec there is a great deal of ambivalence created by the different parties who interact with the notion of a sovereign

The disruptive force of performative practice is part of what Bhabha calls the enunciation of cultural difference. For Bhabha, the enunciation of cultural difference is vital: the ability for a culture to articulate, to be other than an empirical object, explodes neat boundaries and ensures that those articulating are 'subjects of their history and experience' (1994a: 178). The enunciation of cultural difference is effective as an undermining strategy because no culture is so monolithic or so unitary (*they're all like that*) as attempts 'to dominate in the name of a cultural supremacy' would like to purport. The enunciation of difference blurs the lines that hold discrimination in place and allow those objectified in history and discourse to become subjects. Bhabha calls this attention to enunciation a 'liberatory discursive strategy' (1994a: 178), because it explodes the discourse of hegemonic, dominant culture, by introducing other 'times' and other 'spaces' of culture; times and spaces that are liminal and contestatory, that erase binary oppositions between 'us' and 'them'.

Bhabha uses Derrida's notion of *supplement* to explain this 'recursive strategy', speaking of a supplemental doubling of the pedagogical object through daily repetition. For Derrida, the supplement at the same time *adds to* and *substitutes for* meaning (as Bhabha suggests, like *double entendre*; 1994a: 154). For Bhabha, the performance of the national narrative both adds to the national tradition (accumulating historical expressions of it) and substitutes for it, interrupting the tradition, articulating it differently, and allowing for new kinds of identifications with it. Bhabha is emphatic that this does not imply that the meanings of a cultural icon simply become plural in its performance, but rather that the supplemental repetition of the sign *changes the mode of its articulation* (1994a: 154, 163-64).

Derrida's supplement returns throughout Bhabha's writing as the idea of a disruptive 'uncanny doubling' that occurs within the process of

Québec, whether they be sovereigntist or federalist (that is, anti-separation). There is not consensus even within these groups. Within the sovereigntist camp, positions range from those near fascism, to those who truly believe that the systemic oppression of francophones in Canada would be alleviated, and that a social democracy or better could be accomplished through Québec's secession from Canada. Within the federalist camp, positions range from that of anglophones who feel that they are 'oppressed' by this bid for national identity, to the claim of the aboriginal communities who argue that the Québecois must acknowledge their own status as colonizers. This range of stances toward a sovereign Québec reveals what Bhabha would call ambivalence, or 'the complex rhetorical strategy of social reference where the claim to be representative provokes a crisis within the process of signification and discursive address' (1994a: 145).

cultures' signification (1994a: 49-57, 194-97).[13] He calls the supplement 'a relation that is differential and strategic rather than originary, ambivalent rather than accumulative, doubling rather than dialectical' (1994a: 56). Derrida describes the supplement in terms of overturning hierarchy, where the '*subaltern* instance...takes the place' of the thing (1974: 145, emphasis mine). Bhabha punningly applies this to the 'subaltern' postcolonial subject (taking up a term used in postcolonial theory for the silenced, colonized people, see 1994a: 192-93); he suggests the displacement of the 'pure origin' of the nation by the *subaltern* supplement (1994a: 145). In other of his terms, this might be the cultural icon disrupted by the repetitive performative practice on which the icon depends.

By using supplementarity thus, Bhabha can also put the idea of pure origins into question. Supplementarity implies that there can be no pure beginning, no pure meaning for a sign, that what might be set up as an authentic origin can only be seen as such in relation to what exists around it. As Yvonne Sherwood puts it, 'there can be no single starting point that is not dependent on another term for definition' (1996: 183), or put another way, 'in violent hierarchies the superior term is always already dependent on...its inferior' (1996: 182).[14] For Derrida, the supplement adds to and replaces the 'thing' itself; but since signification operates in this way, and since things can only be apprehended through signification, a supplement which adds and replaces is necessary for the functioning of the thing itself (1974: 145). In the same way, for Bhabha, there can be no national identity or cultural icon without performance of it. There is therefore no 'original' national identity possible;[15] the very performance that makes it possible also puts into question its fixity.

The Third Space
Another related way that Bhabha describes the performative production of national narrative is as the linguistic split and overlap between the subject of the statement and the subject who speaks/reads/identifies with it (the split between *énoncé* and *énonciation*; or the *I* of the statement and the *I* speaking it,[16] see Chapter 2). Like the supplement, the speaking subject—

13. See n. 8 above.
14. For a clear discussion of Derrida's supplement, see Sherwood (1996: 182-85).
15. Hence Bhabha can speak of the void which the figure of the nation fills.
16. Bhabha also plays with the overlap between these two subject positions throughout his essay 'Interrogating Identity' (1994a: 40-65), where he speaks of the invisible colonial *I* (eye) that looks but is not seen. He writes, 'Invisibility erases the self-presence of that "I" in terms of which traditional concepts of political agency and narrative mastery function' (1994a: 55). In other words, invisibility disrupts, and yet is

who is also the colonized subject speaking the language (the iconic statements, stereotypes, and so on) of the colonizer—doubles, adds to, and replaces the subject of the statement—all at once. At the same time, the subject written into a statement and the person speaking, reading or identifying with that subject position (in Bhabha's terms 'enunciating' it) inhabit two very different, perhaps even incommensurable, cultural and discursive environments. There is, therefore, both a join and a divide between these two subjects, a linguistic space that both joins and divides (the Lacanian *vel*; see below). Bhabha calls this in-between space the 'Third Space' (and also the space outside the sentence, and the time-lag, to be discussed presently). Like the supplement, it is a space of doubling where the repetition of the sign disrupts a unitary understanding of it.

As already noted, the *articulation* of cultural difference, unfettered by disavowal, is central to Bhabha's project; it is not surprising then that he names this space of difference and doubling the Third Space *of enunciation*, where writing and discourse intersect. The Third Space is the moment when the word, the statement, the cultural symbol (*énoncé*) is articulated, and so crossed by the difference within a particular dis-course or utterance (*énonciation*): the place where both the general (differing, deferring) conditions and structures of language and the specifics of a particular discourse or utterance meet (1994a: 36). Put simply, the way a 'cultural practice' (*énonciation*) is actually performed may be quite different, even radically different from how it is perceived from the outside as a cultural icon (*énoncé*).

The constant sliding from the subject of the statement to the subject of enunciation prohibits the cultural icon from establishing itself as defini-tive or authoritative. The very split in language between the statement and enunciation of that statement 'deprives it [the cultural icon] of the certainty and stability for centre or closure' (1994a: 147). So while the image of a nation set forth in language or narrative—some kind of cumu-lative pedagogical object—may set out to validate a certain kind of authority, the fact that it is repeated differently every time it is enun-ciated makes it difficult for it to be established as definite and final. Thus Bhabha's assertion that 'cultures are never unitary in themselves'

necessary to, the authoritative functioning of the colonial political subject. (Here Bhabha seems also to be picking up and elaborating on Lacan's use of Merleau-Ponty's *Le Visible et l'invisible* to speak of the gaze as a kind of lack which is prior to the eye—it looks without being seen.) For allusion to the Lacanian *vel* in this essay—as Bhabha puts it, 'the overlapping space between *the fading of identity and its faint inscription*'—see especially Bhabha (1994a: 56, emphasis mine).

(1994a: 35) is based not only on the observation of cultural practice in relation to cultural representation, but also on the understanding of difference within the very structures of signification. Bhabha therefore argues that there can be no 'strict causality' between a sign and what it will signify within discourse. Rather as he puts it, 'the sign finds its closure' only after the initiation of a discourse. He cautions, however, against taking this to mean that the sign can signify *anything* as a free-floating signifier. Meaning, he argues, is *negotiated* between the 'event of the sign' and 'its discursive eventuality' (1994a: 182). In other terms, I might say that meaning is negotiated in the moment between the sign's appearance in discourse or text, and its attachment to a signified; this negotiation is mobilized through the subject's entry into, or interpellation into, the symbolic order (whether that be language, or simply the symbolic order of the text). The Third Space then is a space in which 'unifying' signs of culture are both destabilized and renegotiated.

In order better to understand how Bhabha conceives of the Third Space, and eventually to understand the usefulness of this concept metaphor for thinking about the reading process as a space in which ideological pinning points are destabilized and renegotiated, it may be helpful to look at some of the psychoanalytic theory on which Bhabha draws. To start, the Third Space has remarkable affinities with the notion of *potential space* found in the theory of play, developed by object-relations psychoanalyst D.W. Winnicott. In a chapter entitled 'The Location of Cultural Experience' (remarkably similar to the title of Bhabha's book) in his *Playing and Reality* (1971), Winnicott contends that 'cultural experience begins with creative living first manifested in play' (1971: 100). Play helps to bridge the gap between mother and child, in the transition between the child viewing herself as part of the mother, and realizing herself as distinct from the mother (1971: 100). For Winnicott, play is a 'third area' which is neither 'inner or personal psychic reality' nor the external world, but rather 'the potential space between the individual and the environment' (1971: 102-103).

Winnicott's potential space is useful for Bhabha because it considers the relation of self to other in a way that does not isolate either, but shows how difference, even within the self, is related to the other. Through play the child is both 'joined to and separated from' the world around it (1971: 108). The potential space is that space in which, paradoxically, one both finds and creates the world. The objects with which a child plays are both found and created, 'the baby creates the object, but the object was there waiting to be created and to become a cathected object [psychically invested object]' (Winnicott 1971: 89). This is also how the person becomes, in psychoanalytic terms, 'individuated'; that is, through play, the various internal components (ego, id, and so on) become separated from each other, and begin to interact in the type of patterning that makes the individual unique. 'Potential space is a space in which there is interplay between the me and the not-me, where me and not-me are both merged, and always emergent as distinct' (Berg-busch, personal communication). Thus Winnicott writes that play creates the 'place where it can be said that *continuity* is giving place to *contigu-ity*' (1971: 101)—a phrase on which Bhabha draws when he moves into the language metaphor (1994a: 183-87).

Bhabha brings this kind of negotiation between self and other together with the notion of the instability of the sign, by conjoining Winnicott's potential space to Lacan's *vel* of non-meaning. To recall briefly, the Lacanian *vel* is a description of the alienation of the subject on entry into the symbolic order (the Other). As discussed in Chapter 2, the alienation of the subject is the disappearance of being in the overlap between the two circles, meaning and being (it is also the overlap of *énoncé* and *énonciation*). For Lacan, this space of non-meaning in which the self and the Other overlap both *joins and separates*, and is similar in this way to Winnicott's potential space. Bhabha reads it as the space where the self meets the Other, the space that is *neither one, nor the other* (he takes up this Lacanian phrase often and adds the qualifier 'but somewhere in-between' [Lacan 1981: 211; Bhabha 1994a: 25, 28]). Bhabha returns to the Lacanian image of the *vel* again and again,[17] speaking of the non-sense, the 'threatened "loss" of meaningfulness in cross cultural interpretation' (1994a: 125-26). He also describes it as the repetition of one term 'in or as the other in a structure of "abyssal overlapping" (a Derridean term)' (1994a: 186, see also 131). By applying this Derridean term, Bhabha again relates the Lacanian *vel* to a space of undecidability. All of these psychoanalytic and linguistic metaphors that circle through Bhabha's work point to the idea of an undecidable space that is neither self nor Other, a space which is both found and created, a space which both joins and separates through the play of difference in language (the intersection of *énoncé* and *énonciation*, writing and discourse).

Indeed the distinction between self and Other comes undone in the Third Space. Where the colonial self tries to pin the colonized other (object) down through fantasy, in enunciating the position assigned to it, the colonial other/object becomes the subject resisting the pinning of

---

17. See especially 'Articulating the Archaic: Cultural Difference and Colonial Nonsense' (1994a: 123-38).

the colonial symbolic order (Other). As Bhabha puts it, there is a 'double-inscription [of a people] as pedagogical objects and performative subjects' (1994a: 151). Dominant discourse may seem to gain its power, in part, from a 'self' phantasmically assigning the same old stereotypic meanings to 'other' cultural signs (behaviours, discourses, foods, appearances). But the crossing and overlapping of self and Other in the Third Space troubles the positions within this hierarchy. The undecidability between self and Other in the Third Space is what enables the possibility of hybridity (see below for explanation) and catachresis[18] (the reordering and overturning of dominant discourse), ensuring that 'the meaning and symbols of culture have no primordial unity or fixity; that even the same signs can be appropriated, translated, rehistoricized and read anew' (1994a: 37). Thus it is within the realm of the Third Space that the repetition and doubling of signs can challenge and reorder dominant discourse.

By putting Winnicott's formulation of potential space together with the Derridean notion of undecidability and the Lacanian *vel*, Bhabha is able to think about an indeterminate space that is not only constitutive for the *colonizing subject*, but also allows for some agency on the part of the pre-fixed, subjected, *colonized subject* (who is in some senses like the subject fixed in ideology). For Bhabha this is another way to speak about an indeterminacy which allows for agency in liberatory strategies and the repositioning of the colonial subject in empowering ways. This moves away from the notion of predetermined, impossible-to-surpass oppression (1994a: 187), that is, 'strict causality', toward which certain forms of structuralism tend. (Althusser's view on ideology, for instance, illustrates the difficulty in dealing with structural oppression: as one is always-already interpellated, one can never get outside of the structures.) This Third Space is precisely the kind of model that Bhabha needs to take up the question of structural determinism. By playing on border-lines, as he does throughout his work, he acknowledges that there are indeed structures at work in situating subjects (including language), but he argues that disturbing the borders also disturbs the power differentials set up within these structures (binary oppositions, unitary knowable cultures, and so on), and creates a space for the agency of those 'acted upon' or marginalized by such structures.

18. 'Catachresis' is a term Bhabha takes (1994a: 183) from Gayatri Spivak who describes catachresis as 'reversing, displacing and seizing the apparatus of value-coding' (1990: 228, see also 229). In an endnote she gives the dictionary definition: 'abuse or perversion of a trope or metaphor' (1990: 242 n. 29).

Hybridity

The circulation and repetition of signs produces what Bhabha terms hybridity. Hybridity is the concept that Bhabha uses to describe the liberatory potential of the difference between and within cultures, and the overlap between subject and symbolic order. Hybridity displaces, transforms and subverts hegemonic norms in a way that is liberating for those oppressed. The concept encompasses a number of Bhabha's key ideas: ambivalence within the production of discriminatory discourses, revaluation of colonial identity, reversal of domination, questioning of authority.

For Bhabha, hybridity is a result of the ambivalence of the colonizing and narcissistic demand for mimicry (*they should become like us*). In colonial (and postcolonial) contexts the fear of cultural difference— between colonizer and colonized—is diminished by colonizers' belief that their culture is original and authentic, and that other cultures must only learn to emulate this pure and authentic culture. The threat of the real difference between cultures is therefore contained, *disavowed by* 'the fantasy of origin and identity' (1994a: 67) that demands mimicry. However, Bhabha argues, in a colonial context, the mimicry which colo- nizers demand of colonized peoples is never permitted to be perfect; the colonized is never allowed quite to 'become one of us'. This 'desire for a reformed, recognizable Other, as a subject…that is almost the same, but not quite' (1994a: 86) produces something new, something hybrid. That difference be recognized is crucial for discrimination, but it is always understood in a way that is 'entirely knowable and visible' (1994a: 71). The colonized people must be known and categorized as Other, but not too different; construed as a 'population of degenerate types…in order to justify conquest and to establish systems of administration and instruc- tion' (1994a: 70). The very demand for imitation, which tries to establish one culture as 'superior' and 'original', also requires that difference (hybridity) be produced.

The resulting categorization of difference is what produces and justifies discrimination (*those people, not from our origin, not like us*). Thus, produced by the strategy of disavowal that is the myth of origins, hybridity becomes a 'discrimination between the mother culture and its bastards, the self and its doubles, where the trace of what is disavowed is not repressed but *repeated* as something different—a mutation, a hybrid' (1994a: 111, emphasis mine). In other words, the feared difference of the colonized people does not disappear with disavowal, but is made visible through the colonized people's (enforced) imperfect imitation of the colonizing culture. As Bhabha puts it, 'colonialist authority…requires the production of differentiations, individuations, identity effects through which discriminatory practices can map out subject populations that are tarred with the visible and transparent mark of power' (1994a: 111). In brief, the demand for slightly differently repeated colonial culture enables discrimination.

Hybridity, then, is ambivalent in its construction because the mimicry demanded by the colonizing need to disavow difference must also *produce* difference to be effective within the colonial matrices of power: 'the discourse of mimicry is constructed around an ambivalence; in order to be effective, mimicry must continually produce its slippage, its excess, its difference' (1994a: 86). But hybridity is ambivalent in another sense as well: it puts authority, which depends on the ability to discern difference while disavowing it, into question. The imperfect mimicry of 'original culture' has the subversive effect of unsettling the 'mimetic or narcissistic demands of colonial power', by turning the 'gaze of the discriminated back upon the eye of power' (1994a: 112). In displaying the colonial culture, but differently, hybridity puts the 'myth of origins' into question, and so displaces the dominant culture's own notions of self-identity.

This critique of the 'myth of origins' is central to Bhabha's notion of hybridity—and his work as a whole—and once again takes up Derrida's notion of supplementarity. Like supplementarity, hybridity might be said to be 'an indefinite process [that] has always already infiltrated presence [original culture], always already inscribed there the space of repetition and the splitting of the self' (Derrida 1974: 163). By differently repeating the 'original culture', the 'self' of colonial culture splits, revealing its requirement for difference and otherness in order to be established as superior. Bhabha builds the idea of repetition and the splitting of self (original culture) into his discussion of the production of hybridity: 'the problem of cultural difference…is the problem of the not-one, the minus in the origin and repetition of cultural signs in a doubling that will not be sublated into a similitude' (Bhabha 1994a: 245). In simpler terms, cultural 'difference' doubles or repeats 'original culture' in a way that forces a recognition of the normally disavowed components that make its 'originality' possible.

Bhabha illustrates this process of questioning 'original culture' by citing the first encounter between an evangelical (Indian) missionary and a group of less 'orthodox' Indian converts, recounted in the Church Missionary Society of London's *Missionary Register*. In the reported conversation between the two parties, the Bible as the origin and authorization of British rule and demand is questioned over and over: 'How can the word of God come from the flesh-eating mouths of the English?'; 'How can it be the European Book when we believe that it is God's gift to us? He sent it to us at Hurdwar'; and, 'to all the other customs of Christians we are willing to conform, but not to the Sacrament, because the Europeans eat cow's flesh, and this will never do for us' (1994a: 116; see also 103-104). This account exemplifies the hybrid deformation and displacement of the religious discourse being used to give authority to the discriminating and dominating practices of colonization; it also shows a disturbance of the myth of original culture (shown here in the contestation over who had genuine religion) which was used to differentiate between English and Other.

Thus Bhabha envisions hybridity as a step toward freedom, using the very disavowal that holds discrimination in place and that does not allow for the full play of cultural difference. Hybridity can be used to reread and reorder dominant discourses, allowing for subaltern voices suppressed in the stifling of difference: 'hybridity is the revaluation of the assumption of colonial identity through the repetition of discriminatory identity effects. It displays the necessary deformation and displacement of all sites of discrimination and domination' (1994a: 112). For Bhabha this means resistance and empowerment. He writes: 'mimicry marks those moments of civil disobedience within the discipline of civility: signs of spectacular resistance. Then the words of the master become the site of hybridity—the warlike, subaltern sign of the native—then we may not only read between the lines but even seek to change the often coercive reality that they so lucidly contain' (1994a: 121). In short, hybridity can transform those discourses, norms and practices that hold coercion and oppression in place.

Outside the Sentence

Bhabha further elaborates on the themes set out thus far with his image, 'outside the sentence'. He takes the phrase 'outside the sentence' from Roland Barthes's *The Pleasure of the Text* (1975), where Barthes describes being half asleep in a bar, hearing bits of conversation, music and restaurant noise float through him, as if he were a public square (Bhabha's space of non-sense). Barthes describes this as 'a definitive discontinuity' flowing through him:

> [T]his *non-sentence* was...what is eternally, splendidly, *outside the sentence*. Then potentially, all linguistics fell, linguistics which believes only in the sentence and has always attributed an exorbitant dignity to predicative syntax (as the form of a logic, of a rationality) (Barthes 1975: 49-50).

Barthes goes on to speak of the hierarchical, ideological, finite nature of the sentence, implying that the experience outside the sentence subverts or goes beyond hierarchy, ideology and closure in some way (1975: 50-51).

Bhabha is interested in the way 'the hierarchy and subordinations of the sentence are replaced by the definitive discontinuity of the text' (Bhabha 1994a: 180). He wants to see how the bits and pieces of language that come together—with various intersecting discourses—in the (performative) moment of enunciation can subvert those (pedagogical) structures that purportedly give the sentence meaning. Again, subversive, liberatory themes come through in this discussion. For Bhabha, Barthes's experience of non-sense—outside the sentence—suggests a strategy for the negotiation of cultural difference, whereby 'the emergence and negotiation of those agencies of the marginal, minority, subaltern' (Bhabha 1994a: 181) can disturb dominant culture, along with the fixity of meanings and cultural signs that dominant culture wants to inscribe. The circulation and repetition of signs in Barthes's square, not governed by the hierarchical structures of the sentence, serves as a model for cultural difference disrupting dominant western notions of time and space, subject and object, colonizer and colonized. This is a model for what Bhabha calls an 'iterative temporality that erases the occidental spaces of language—inside/outside, past/present, those foundationalist epistemological positions of Western empiricism and historicism' (Bhabha 1994a: 182).

What Bhabha means by 'foundationalist epistemological positions of Western empiricism and historicism' can be found detailed in his article 'Representation and the Colonial Text' (1984), where he argues that historicism is based on an epistemology of 'linear time consciousness' (1984: 96) and that empiricism is based on an epistemology of 'recognition' of a pre-given reality (1984: 99-100). He suggests that both historicism and empiricism are ideologically constructed notions based on belief in the ability to discern 'reality' and represent it 'coherently'. For Bhabha, the way language circulates and repeats in this space of non-sentence/non-sense disturbs typical western language which fortifies 'linear time consciousness' (1984: 96) and the recognition of certain 'objects' (texts, other races, and so on) as distinct from the subject (1984: 99-100, 113-14). In the space outside the sentence, difference is negotiated in a way that undermines both temporal (linear time) and spatial (subject/object) distinctions on which western empiricism rests.

To explain how the negotiation of difference operates within the space outside the sentence as a liberatory strategy, Bhabha once again brings the Lacanian image of a space of non-meaning that joins and separates together with his thinking about cultural difference, by invoking Derrida. As in his discussion of the Third Space, he refers to Derrida in order to suggest that this kind of in-between space is in fact akin to the structure of language, and to the nature of the sign as that which repeats and displaces. Bhabha cites Derrida on the structure of the sign, when he writes that the non-sentence 'opens up disjunctive, incommensurable relations of spacing and temporality within the sign—an *"internal differ-ence of the so-called ultimate element (stoikheion, trait, letter, seminal mark)"*' (Bhabha 1994a: 182, citing Derrida 1984: 10, my emphasis). This citation is taken from Derrida's 'Mes chances' (1984) in which he summarizes his earlier argument in 'The Purveyor of Truth' (1975) cri-tiquing Lacan's 'Seminar on the "The Purloined Letter"' (1972). Bhabha's use of this citation here brings Derrida's critique of Lacan to play in his argument. For both Lacan and Derrida, the 'mark' or 'trait' is the sign; it is the line that divides signifier from signified; it is the marker of differ-ence, that which differs from other signs; it is a margin or border, that which is not inside or outside.[19] But as Derrida points out, where for Lacan the master signifier is indivisible,[20] a unity governing meaning, for Derrida it is divisible like any other sign, part of the repetitious structure of language.

Because this use of Derrida's critique of Lacan is important to my own argument about the way in which Bhabha envisions the repositioning of the subject, I take the time to fill in the details. To briefly recall what I outlined in Chapter 2, Lacan, in his 'Seminar on "The Purloined Letter"', suggests that the letter (or signifier) 'always reaches its destination' (Lacan 1988a: 205); in other words, it always returns to the same place to fill in the lack in the Other. For Lacan the signifier fills in the lack in the Other as the phallus (the sign which returns to fill the hole between the woman's legs). Lack is recognized as *lack of something* (notably the phallus) and filled in through fantasy (the letter), elevated to the status of that known thing (the phallus). Thus the master signifier is self-referential because it is the subject's fantasy *objet petit a* which has been raised to the status of master signifier, or *point de capiton*.[21] Meaning,

19. For a fascinating exploration of this idea, see Derrida's article 'The Parergon' (1979b) in which he blurs the borders of the frame. Also see 'The Double Session' in *Dissemination* (1981b).

20. For example, Lacan writes: 'cut a letter in small pieces and it remains the letter it is' (1972: 53); or, 'the signifier is a unity' (1972: 54).

21. Elsewhere Lacan writes of the phallus, 'the phallus is the privileged signifier of that mark where the share of logos is wedded to the advent of desire… [T]he phallus [is] itself the sign of the latency with which everything signifiable is struck as soon as its is raised (*aufgehoben*) to the function of signifier. The phallus is the signifier of this *Aufhebung*' (1982: 82). Since *Aufhebung* is also the German word used by Hegel for his idea of synthesis, often translated as 'sublation', it may be that Bhabha has Lacan's

therefore, always returns to the same place, because it is governed by the unifying and self-referential master signifier.

Derrida, however, argues that the sign does not always return to the same place, as Lacan would have it. Derrida critiques Lacan's circular and self-referential trajectory of the signifier, which leads, as Derrida puts it, 'from void to void and from the void to itself' (Derrida 1975: 58). Derrida points out that this self-referential predetermination of the sign for Lacan is due in part to his understanding of the materiality of the signifier as that which does 'not...admit partition' (Lacan cited in Derrida 1975: 44): the signifier is indivisible because it only represents an absence; it is therefore 'transcendental...intangible and indestructible' (Derrida 1975: 45).

Derrida argues instead for the eruption of the reign of the unified signifying phallus—Lacanian phallogocentricism—through the rain of dissemination. He appeals to the divisibility of the sign, as he puts it (and as Bhabha quotes), 'the divisibility or internal difference of the so-called ultimate element (*stoikheion*, trait, letter, seminal mark)' (Derrida 1984: 10). Because a *sign* is repeatable, he argues, it is therefore divisible, 're-markable from one context to another' (1984: 16),[22] and this produces difference. The repeatability of the sign gives rise to the continual prolif-eration of the trace, because 'the identity of a mark is also its difference and its differential relation' (1984: 16). Iterability, as part of the structure of the mark, allows it 'to emigrate in order to play elsewhere' (1984: 16). Thus Derrida can write, 'dissemination mutilates the unity of the signi-fier, that is, of the phallus' (1975: 66); the sign is not destined always to return to fill the same lack, there is a chance that it will 'not always arrive at its destination' (1975: 107). For this reason, the subject who is sub-jected to the signifier is also divisible (1975: 107) and is not destined always to identify in the same way.

Bhabha is interested in Derrida's critique of Lacan (which also figures in his discussion of the time-lag) because it considers the internal difference of that which already marks difference. Internal difference softens borders and disturbs 'what Derrida calls the occidental stereotomy [science of the

use of it in mind when he argues for a dialectic that does not sublate (1994a: 126, 173). Derrida's discussion on undecidables also comes to mind: '[undecidables] mark the spots of what can never be mediated, mastered, sublated, or dialecticized through any *Erinnerung* or *Aufhebung*' (Derrida 1981b: 221). One of my major questions about Bhabha is whether his use of thinkers like Lacan and Žižek, who are avowedly Hegelian, contradicts his explicitly anti-Hegelian bent.

22. For a critique of Derrida's critique of Lacan, see Žižek (1989: 158-60; 1991a: 85-91).

cut or division], the ontological, circumscribing space between subject and object, inside and outside' (Bhabha 1994a: 182). This is appealing to Bhabha, who wants to see the cultural difference which inheres *within* cultures (internal difference within the mark of difference), disturbing the dominant orders which justify discrimination. Thus he likens the space outside the sentence to the space within the sign, it 'opens up disjunctive, incommensurable relations of spacing and temporality within the sign… temporally ex-centric, interruptive, in-between, on the borderlines, turning inside outside' (1994a: 182). This notion draws together what his concepts of Third Space and hybridity express: there is a place where self and Other cross, which is within the very sign of culture itself, and which is made visible by the difference—the non-meaning—in its doubling or repetition.

Time-lag

Bhabha takes this further and explores this interruptive division within the sign, what he calls the 'time-lag' of signification. Time-lag is the inner working of catachresis: the process by which the enunciation and negotiation of cultural difference can reorder symbols. As such, it is one of Bhabha's most complex and compact ideas. Time-lag ties together a number of intersecting processes, and serves a number of purposes within Bhabha's argument: it describes the linguistic possibility of reordering or reinterpreting cultural symbols through the negotiation of difference; it suggests the (psychic) process of identification that must take place to allow for such reinterpretation; and it enables Bhabha to account more fully for *agency* within this process, given the indeterminate structure of signs.

The time-lag is the moment between the sign and its signification, or as Bhabha puts it, the moment between 'the event of the sign' and its 'closure', or meaning, in discourse (1994a: 183, 185). Bhabha makes much of the Lacanian notion of the retroactivity of signification here, speaking of the time-lag as the 'retroactive' closure for the signifier, and using the technical psychoanalytic term, *Nachträglichkeit* (1994a: 184). In Chapter 2, I noted that within Freudian-based psychoanalysis, *Nachträglichkeit* means that an earlier memory can be restructured as a result of a later event such that the past can be influenced by the present. Lacan takes this image up in his graphs of desire (see Appendix), suggesting that the subject comes out of its loop through the symbolic order at a point previous to its entry.

Likewise for Bhabha, the time-lag is the 'retroactive' time of signification: the backward momentum of the time elapsing between the sign and its signification in discourse. Though Bhabha does not say it in so many words, his use of Lacanian (and sometimes Žižekian) terms throughout his discussion of the time-lag suggest the time-lag as the moment between the subject's pinning to the symbolic order in interpellation and the moment when meaning is fixed for the sign: the subject comes back out through the signifying chain prior to its point of entry. This means that symbols and subject positions can be reinterpreted, repositioned, given new life: the 'lagging, *impels* the "past", *projects* it, gives its "dead" symbols the circulatory life... *Time-lag keeps alive the making of the past*' (1994a: 254). Further, Bhabha suggests that this disturbs the linear time consciousness of the West, as well as the understandings of history that see 'progress' as an attainable goal.

Using the language of Lacan, Bhabha describes this temporal gap between sign and signification as the moment between the 'subject's accession to, and erasure in, the signifier as individuated' (1994a: 184). This is the moment in which the subject identifies with the Other and is subsequently interrogated by the Other with the question, 'What do you want of me (*Che vuoi*)?' (1994a: 184). Bhabha, quoting Žižek, calls the time-lag the 'realm of the intersubjective...where we "identify ourselves with the other"' (Bhabha 1994a: 184, citing Žižek 1989: 109). As I read it then, the time-lag is not merely the passage of time between a sign and its signification in discourse, but all that takes place within that moment: the pinning of the subject to the master signifier, the identification of the subject with the lack in the Other, and the fading (*aphanasis*) of the subject with the emergence of meaning.

Thus the time-lag is a detailed way of thinking about the interaction of the subject with language. Again, Lacan's overlapping space between the subject and the Other, the *vel* between meaning and being, might provide one pictorial image of the time-lag. Lacan also describes this interaction in his graphs on desire and the subject's interpellation into and loop through the symbolic order (1977: 299-300). To belabour the point a little, since Bhabha's Third Space is modeled on Lacan's *vel*, and since the *vel* is spelled out in another way in the Lacanian graphs on desire, the time-lag can also be considered a detailed way of thinking about the Third Space. The time-lag is the *time and space* between the subject's interpellation into the symbolic order and signification.

The spatial element of the time-lag is, once again, the 'uncanny doubling' of meaning and being, of subject and language, the space of the supplement which both adds to and replaces. It comes as no surprise then that Bhabha uses Derridean terminology here. In Derrida's essay, 'Freud and the Scene of Writing' in *Writing and Difference* (1978), he notes that one of the meanings of the German adjective *nachträglich*, is 'supplementary', linking the more technical psychoanalytic term

Nachträglichkeit to his notion of supplement (1978: 211). Thus Bhabha also writes of the time-lag as both retroactive and supplemental:

> It is a pulsional incident, the split-second movement when the process of the subject's designation—its fixity—opens up beside it, uncannily *abseits* [beside], a *supplementary space* of contingency. In this 'return' of the subject, thrown back across the distance of the signified, outside the sentence, the agent emerges as a form of retroactivity, *Nachträglichkeit* (1994a: 185, emphasis mine).

For Bhabha, meaning is *negotiated* in this process which is the indeterminate space, the time-lag, between sign and signification. As he says, meaning is *contingent on and contiguous with* the various discourses intersecting in this interaction (1994a: 186-90). This can be seen as related to the Winnicottian notion of finding and creating: the retroactive closure of the sign implies that new significance can be given, or created for, a found sign or event. This is catachrestic, reinscribing the 'authoritative' cultural symbols, disrupting their value as authoritative, and enabling the future to be ordered differently (*Nachträglichkeit*).

In this way, the time-lag figures in Bhabha's work as a way of employing the retroactivity of the sign in order to reclaim histories of oppression so that the future is not dictated by the kinds of myths of origins or collective identities (often generated through historical narrative) which give rise to discrimination in an unsurpassable systemic imbalance of power. Theorizing this way works against the idea that oppression is inevitable, because it is determined by a fixed conception of originary and eternal inferiority of the oppressed. In the time-lag the *difference within difference* (the difference within the letter, mark, trait) can be negotiated and reinscribed in historical accounts; this will have dramatic effect for postcolonial situations in which discrimination based on 'history' or 'origin' is rampant. Accordingly, the time-lag is a 'historically transformative moment' (1994a: 242), because in this moment cultural difference can confront disavowal of that difference. He writes: 'with the *projective past* it [the discourse of modernity] can be inscribed as a historical narrative of alterity that explores forms of social antagonism and contradiction that are not yet properly represented, political identities in the process of being formed, cultural enunciations in the act of hybridity' (1994a: 252). In this way, the discourse of modernity—which has given rise to a notion of human progress, without taking into account the silent and silenced series of oppressions and social antagonisms on which this 'progression' is built (1994a: 43)—can be reclaimed in a way that is liberatory for oppressed peoples.

In sum, the time-lag is the space between the moment of signification and the moment when meaning is fixed, when new times and new spaces are opened up. In these times and spaces (outside the sentence, in the Third Space) the unifying and dangerous myth of origins is split, forming a hybrid space which defies the disavowal of discrimination. The time-lag is then the catachrestic Third Space, the space where dominant discourse is reordered and overturned, where 'the same signs can be appropriated, translated, *rehistoricized* and read anew' (1994a: 37, my emphasis).

Liminal Identification

For Bhabha, liminal identification is the process within the trajectory of the subject—within the time-lag—that can reorient the subject, and signification, with liberatory effect (1994a: 185). Glossing a little, the subject, in the process of this retroactive interaction and identification with the Other, is able to negotiate new juxtapositions of difference and to reinscribe the meaning of the signifier to which it is pinned. This process of negotiatory identification can change the place where the subject comes out of its trip through the symbolic order.

In this process, the subject identifies with the margins. Bhabha calls this 'liminal identification'. In Žižek's description of the subject's journey through the symbolic order—or as Bhabha puts it, on 'the return of the subject as agent' (1994a: 185)—the *subject identifies with the lack of the Other*, at the 'point at which he is inimitable, at the point which eludes resemblance' (Žižek 1989: 109). Where in Lacanian terms the point 'eluding resemblance' is the lack in the Other, for Bhabha it is the place of difference within the sign or culture. Bhabha takes up 'the point that eludes resemblance', citing Žižek (1994a: 184), but gives the idea weight in terms of his notion of mimicry, or differently repeated signs.

The term *liminal identification* also resonates with Bhabha's use of Derrida in the discussion of the divisibility of the sign or mark, bringing to mind Derrida's punning quotation of Hegel's *Phenomenology of Spirit*:

> We have come to a remarkable threshold [*limen*] of the text: what can be read of dissemination. *Limes*: mark, march, margin. Demarcation. Marching order: quotation: '**Now—this question also announced itself, explicitly, as the question of the *liminal*** ' (Derrida 1981b: 16, bold original).

Liminal identification is, then, the identification with the difference produced by the repetition of signs. Because Bhabha figures 'lack' (with which the subject identifies) as that undecidable space of the supplement, he can suggest that the subject's identification with that 'lack' allows it to re-identify with the difference within the sign.

Liminal identification draws the idea of the divisibility, iterability and motility of the mark (liminality) together with its implications for meaning and identity. By speaking of *identification*, the phrase suggests the possibility of re-identification, and consequent reordering or redirection of the meaning (destination) of signs. As Bhabha puts it, 'the repetition of the iterative, the activity of the time-lag, is... interruptive, a closure that is not conclusion but a liminal interrogation' (Bhabha 1994a: 191). For Bhabha, liminal identification can reorient the subject, as well as meaning, with liberatory effect; it 'unpicks' the cultural icon (or I might say, the *point de capiton*) and makes new points of identification with difference: 'this liminal movement of identification—eluding resemblance—produces a subversive strategy of subaltern agency that negotiates its own authority through a process of iterative "unpicking" and incommensurable, insurgent relinking' (1994a: 185). Liminal identification is seen as a kind of negotiation that takes place in the time-lag, between the event of the sign and the moment of signification.

As part of the time-lag, liminal identification also relates to Bhabha's Third Space of negotiation, which might be considered a Winnicottian (non-sublatory) formulation of Lacan's and Žižek's (Hegelian sublatory) formulation of lack, the *vel* of incommensurable non-meaning, that splits both the self and Other, but is necessary for 'self-consciousness' (for Hegelian understandings of lack see Lacan [1981: 212-13, 221]; Žižek [1989: 195-96]). The Žižekian Real/lack, the 'point which eludes resemblance' is for Bhabha a negotiatory potential space which both joins and separates (1994a: 184), in which the subject is both formed and has agency through liminal identification. In this way Bhabha can move toward a dialectic which does not sublate otherness (lack) (1994a: 173).

Agency in Indeterminacy
In this way, Bhabha can think of the subject as both indeterminate and determined at the same time: it is indeterminate because in its trajectory it has this possibility for re-identification, that is, identification with the margins and with difference, which will (retroactively) bring it back from its trip through the symbolic order in another place; it is determined because it is necessarily linked to the chain of signification. This suggests a kind of anchored (as opposed to free-floating) indeterminacy which is important for Bhabha's liberatory impulse, because it opens a certain kind of space for change.

Bhabha wants to use postmodern discussion on indeterminacy to move to a place where theory and practice, language and politics supplement each other (1994a: 19-39); but since *practice* requires some kind of *agency*, he is concerned to find a way that agency can be built into this theoretical discussion. Bhabha wonders, 'can there be a social subject of the "non-sentence"? Is it possible to conceive of historical agency in that disjunctive, indeterminate moment of discourse outside the sentence?' (1994a: 183). At this point, Bhabha raises an issue that a number of theorists have discussed with respect to poststructural theory and its continual emphasis on *différance* and indeterminacy. (For instance, he cites Eagleton who wonders about poststructuralism's possibilities for strategic action [1994a: 183].) The notions of time-lag and liminal identification enable Bhabha to incorporate the idea of political agency into the space outside the sentence, as it is a space 'between the event of the sign…and its discursive eventuality…where *intentionality* [agency] is negotiated retrospectively' (1994a: 183, emphasis mine).

By using the notion of time-lag, Bhabha sets agency within the realm of the Other, allowing him to stay away from the discourse of individualism and at the same time to speak of *the agency of the subject* (1994a: 184). Bhabha describes the inauguration of agency as intimately related to signification: 'in this "return" of the subject, thrown back across the distance of the signified, outside the sentence, the *agent emerges* as a form of retroactivity, *Nachträglichkeit*' (1994a: 185, emphasis mine). Agency is not transcendent or autonomous: the agent is an 'effect of the "intersubjective" ' (1994a: 184).[23] For Bhabha, the demand of the Other, *Che vuoi?*, 'What do you want of me?' is what pushes the subject to agency, *to ask the question itself*, to internalize the Other's demand. Because this question is an interaction between the subject and the Other, Bhabha says that the agent is produced in the 'dialogic position of calculation, negotiation, interrogation' (1994a: 185). So the subject becomes an agent as a result of its loop through the symbolic order. Agency is constituted in the intersubjective space of the time-lag, that moment between the event of the sign and signification, as the subject returns on its trajectory through the symbolic order.

Bhabha develops the idea of the agent formed in indeterminacy by playing with two meanings of the word contingent: that which may or may not occur (indeterminate) and dependent, touching (contiguous).[24]

23. For a discussion of the potential problems in Bhabha's discussion of intersubjectivity, see Salomon's article 'Deconstruction, Postcoloniality and Objective Interests' (1995).

24. Thus the contingent agent is the overlapping of a temporal relation (indeterminacy with respect to identification) with a spatial relation (contiguity with the chain of signification). In this way Bhabha takes up Derrida's understanding of the *différance* as temporal, that which divides the present, and also as '*spacing*, the becoming-space of time [and] the becoming-time of space, *temporization*' (Derrida 1982: 13). Bhabha sounds *remark*ably like Derrida when he says, 'the contingent is

Thus the social agent is continuous (touching, identifying, *solidaire*), yet indeterminate (able to break away from totalizing conceptions). The agent, like the sign to which the subject is pinned in interpellation, is not a pre-fixed entity whose existence is strictly causal for outcome (meaning), nor is it completely determined, but rather it is both. By theorizing the agent in this way, Bhabha is able to bring back the notion of solidarity to his emphasis on cultural *difference*. While he insists that cultural difference disrupts unitary forms of cultural identity, he does not want to do away with the ability of people to link together along different lines of identity in struggle, and at the same time he wants to allow for some kind of political agency.

In giving an exposition of these conceptual metaphors—performativity, the Third Space, hybridity, outside the sentence, the time-lag, liminal identification, agency in indeterminacy—I have tried to show how Bhabha rereads the moments within Lacanian theory that hint at the possibility of a less predetermined outcome for the subject. I would like now to draw together the ways in which I understand Bhabha to develop the possibilities for repositioning the subject. Bhabha's application of Derrida's focus on difference within the structure of repetition in language to a Lacanian framework can also be applied to Žižek's use of Lacan in theorizing subject formation.

Bhabha and the Subject's Identification with Difference

To begin, Bhabha makes much of Lacan's conception of the lacking, not fully self-cognizant subject; the lack which runs through the subject and the Other; the retroactivity of signification; and the split between the subject of the statement and the subject of speech. However, he does more than just manipulate Lacan's theory. By using Derrida's understanding of the iterability and supplementarity of language, he critiques Lacan's phallogocentricity, and takes the theory one step further to show the disruptive and potentially liberating undecidabilities that emerge in the interaction between the subject and the Other.

In other words, Bhabha takes up the Lacanian theory of the subject's formation in language, but takes into consideration the structure of repetition in language, as postulated by Derrida. This structure of repetition enables Bhabha to see the overlap of meaning and being in the subject's entry into the symbolic order as a disruptive doubling, an

contiguity, metonymy, the touching of *spatial* boundaries at a tangent, and, at the same time the contingent is the *temporality* of the indeterminate and the undecidable' (Bhabha 1994a: 186, emphasis mine).

imperfect repetition that displays the very operation that makes language and subjectivity possible. Once in view, this operation, which often authorizes oppression unnoticed, critiques itself, gazing back upon the eye of power. Moreover, Bhabha argues that identification with these differently iterated signs of culture is what gives the subject an empowered agency.

To be more specific, by using Derrida's theory in this way, it seems to me that Bhabha revisions the image of *lack* in the Other as *difference*; with such a re-conceptualization, the possibility opens up for the repositioning of the subject through the subject's liminal identification with this difference. For Bhabha, 'lack' is only determined in relation to some supercessional culture (lack of being the original race); but since for him there is no 'original' culture, there is no original lack. This means that for Bhabha 'lack' can only be understood within the structure of repetition and difference in language. Just as 'origin' or even 'master signifier' cannot be understood without some kind of previous contact with the terms which it is supposed to generate, as well as those from which it differs or which it excludes; neither can 'lack' be understood without some reference to the terms from which it is excluded, in comparison to which it is said to be 'lacking'.[25] Bhabha's approach, therefore, would suggest that 'lack'—the non-symbolizable Lacanian Real—might be considered as a function of difference. Difference cannot be symbolized, precisely because any attempt to do so would be to translate it into known terms, depleting it of its difference. It seems that in Bhabha's work, the Real is not figured as lack (which is always self-referential), but as difference, which cannot be symbolized, even as lack.

Like Lacan, Bhabha's work suggests that there is always an impulse to fill in the non-symbolizable (with, for instance, pedagogical discourses); but his work suggests that in this very process, it is the structure of repetition that can prevent the subject from inevitably returning to the same place. On the one hand, it may not seem so, since difference—like lack—must be covered over in order for the dominant order to function: domination requires that difference be controlled, symbolized and disavowed. Pedagogical objects and discourses of the nation (cultural icons, national narratives, racial stereotypes, and so on) mask or disavow *difference* by portraying it, imagining it, fantasizing it as somehow related to

25. Judith Butler makes a similar observation in a discussion of Žižek's re-reading of Lacan; she writes, 'What counts as the "real", in the sense of the unsymbolizable, is always relative to a linguistic domain that authorizes and produces that foreclosure, and achieves that effect through producing and policing a set of constitutive exclusions' (1993: 207).

the self. On the other hand, the repetition required to reproduce the 'originary culture' can never be perfect, and produces a continual slippage, making available new points of identification, new hybrid fantasy objects, for the subject. If the subject identifies with these hybrid figures, the 'original' unifying image loses its ability to pin the subject.

Identification with difference opens up the circuit of the signifier, so that it does not return to exactly the same place that it started. As I read it, Bhabha's conception of liminal identification suggests that if in interpellation the subject identifies with the Other's difference, rather than with lack, then it will come out in a different place in the signifying chain. Identification with the difference produced by the repetition of signs has the effect of disturbing the narcissistic filling of 'lack' with the same. This means that signification can be different—the sign is not always determined to be ideologically pinned by a self-referential master signifier, its sliding always stopped in the same place. Thus, liminal identification also allows for the positioning of subjects in new and empowering ways. The subject is not always narcissistically interpellated by identification with the same master signifier.

This then is liminal identification: identification with the hybrid figure; it is identification with the margins, and with the difference within the margins. Liminal identification is not identification with lack and its masking function (fantasy about the colonized race) which often results in hatred and oppression; instead liminal identification suggests an identification with difference as a liberatory strategy. In Lacanian terms, this would mean that the signifier of lack (phallus, *point de capiton*, master signifier) is not necessarily strictly determining for the outcome of the signified. In Bhabha's terms, this means that the same stereotypes and pedagogical discourses are not destined forever to pin colonized peoples to the same disempowered place. The idea in Bhabha's theory is that history and signification can be revised and renegotiated in the time-lag that occurs between 'the event of a sign' and its 'enunciation', that is, the space between a sign being read, 'understood' and 'known', within a pedagogical discourse and its repetition in performative practice.

For Bhabha, these points of identification can be *negotiated* in the Third Space. Bhabha's conception of the Third Space—in which he modifies the Lacanian alienation of the subject in the space (*vel*) between meaning and being, by reading the split between *énoncé* and *énonciation* as the Derridean supplement—provides another way of understanding the identification with difference. Difference might be seen as that which separates subject and Other; it is the space of non-meaning between the two. I might suggest that, within a Bhabbian framework, it is *difference*, rather than lack, in the encounter with the

Other that alienates the subject. Thus, according to the way that Bhabha seems to read the Lacanian model, it is *difference* that cuts through both the subject and the Other, the space of non-sense. But this space of non-meaning can also be a space of negotiation, where the subject can both find and create new hybrid points of identification.

Bhabha also describes this negotiation as the intersubjective relation with the Other: in Bhabha's view it is intersubjectivity that pushes the subject to agency (the ability to speak and act) in interpellation into the symbolic order. It seems that for Bhabha, agency is determined in that it is linked to the Other or contiguous with it, but the formation of agency is also, in part, indeterminate, contingent on the question demanded by the Other, *Che vuoi?* ('What do you want of me?'). And in reply to the intersubjective demand, the subject is pushed and can choose to identify with unsymbolizable, or in Bhabha's terms, 'incommensurable' difference, in ways that do not homogenize and silence that difference. Because the structure of repetition always produces difference, the subject can *negotiate* with the utterly different, rather than merely fantasizing it as its own lack, and this can produce a slightly altered kind of agency. When new identifications are made, the outcomes of the process—meaning and the positioning of the subject—change too.

Bhabha and the Subject Formed in Ideology

Understanding the subject's formation thus might have some implications for the notion of the subject always-already formed in ideology. Because Bhabha draws heavily on Lacan, and a little on Žižek, and because his work is so suggestive and fluid, his theory lends itself to transposition, at least provisionally, onto Žižek's Lacanian reformulation of Althusser's theory of ideological interpellation. To my mind, Bhabha's focus on difference and the structure of repetition suggests a model for thinking about the possibility that the subject's always-already interpellation into ideology does not have to be static, that there is room for negotiation with the symbolic order.

Recalling briefly what I outlined in Chapter 2, Žižek suggests that interpellation occurs through the subject's identification with a fantasy object that is raised up to fill in the lack in the symbolic order, or in other words, raised to the status of ideological *point de capiton* (master signifier, or phallus). To reiterate, for Žižek, in interpellation, the subject identifies with the lack in the Other, through the fantasy of the *objet petit a*; that is to say, the subject interacts with the unsymbolizable Real of the social order through fantasy, and this is the masking function of ideology.

Bhabha picks up this concept, but recasts it when he shows how the national icon or pedagogical discourse is used as a way of identifying a culture and justifying discrimination. Indeed, as I have been indicating, Bhabha seems to relate the pedagogical discourse, national icon, or stereotype to Žižek's fantasy *objet petit a*, raised to the status of ideological *point de capiton*. But where Žižek suggests that the ideological operation occurs when *the lack* is filled by the self-referential fantasy of the *objet petit a*, Bhabha's focus on the disavowal of difference would suggest that the ideological operation is the *misrecognition of difference as the same*, as something knowable. Following a Bhabhian model then, the ideological *point de capiton* might be understood as something that fills in for difference, rather than for lack.

Bhabha's theory also suggests a slightly different process by which the *point de capiton*—or in Bhabha's terms the national icon—might gain its status. Bhabha's focus on the structure of repetition suggests that the cultural icon or stereotype, which 'pins' the (colonial) subject through its stereotyping, gains its status through continual repetition. He says this another way when he speaks of the performative practice of a nation, which eventually accumulates into 'national identity'. Through constant repetition, the national identity—like Žižek's *objet petit a*—is both created and raised to the point that it seems originary and able to govern, that is to the position of *point de capiton*.[26] It is the structure of repetition, the iterability of the 'mark', that enables the fantasy object to be recognized as 'national icon', or stereotype, and to gain its power as such. If, as Žižek, Lacan and Bhabha suggest, the *objet petit a* as fantasy object is both the object *and the cause* of desire, then this would mean that *fantasy and desire are also produced by repetition*.[27] But once again, this process of repetition means that the fantasy object is by its very nature unstable, divisible, repeated differently, able to disturb the stereotype (see Bhabha 1994a: 37).

The idea of the *point de capiton* as the attempt to symbolize

26. Butler, who also makes use of Derrida's supplement (e.g. 1993: 38-39), makes a similar point in a discussion of Lacan and identification. She writes, 'The excessive power of the symbolic is itself *produced* by the citational instance by which the law is embodied… The priority and the authority of the symbolic is, however, constituted *through* that recursive turn, such that citation…effectively brings into being the very prior authority to which it then defers' (1993: 108-109).

27. This seems like a obvious observation when looking at the advertising or erotica/porn industry where the sexually desirable body or pose is created through continual repetition and consumption. For a more nuanced example, see Aichele's discussion of canon as ideology and the role of repetition in establishing its power as such (2001: 15-23).

difference, and the notion that it gains its status through repetition, both enable thinking *against* the idea of ideology—and also meaning—as determined and therefore immutable (always arriving at its proper destination, as Lacan would have it). If in ideological interpellation the subject identifies with difference, with the margins of the symbolic and social order, perhaps it is not always-already destined to come out from every interpellation in the same place. Where identification with lack inevitably returns to the same in some way (e.g. the phallus returns to lack of phallus), identification with difference could produce something new. Identification with the kind of difference produced by the 'performance' or 'enunciation' of the national identity, or with the hybrid fantasy object is what may enable the subject's repositioning. It is the identification with difference that may be able to reposition the subject retroactively, consequently affecting meaning.

This kind of identification is a kind of intersubjective negotiation with the Other, or in Žižekian terms, with the ideological order in which the subject is always-already positioned. Bhabha's notion of agency formed through contiguity and contingency troubles the idea of a simple, once-and-for-all pinning of the subject by an external master signifier, generated by the subject's own fantasy. Bhabha's use of Winnicott is particularly helpful here (and in mediating the problem that the external master signifier in Lacan and Žižek raises for the Althusserian view of ideology, which does not separate structure and effect). As object relations theorist, Matthew Bergbusch, put it:

> Whereas for Lacan discourse [the Other] is experienced, insofar as it is in a sense imposed from outside, as necessarily oppressive (i.e. ontologically oppressive), for Winnicott, discourse/culture is experienced as simultaneously made and found by the subject in potential space—i.e. paradoxical, but not ontologically oppressive (although specific moments in discourse/ culture may indeed be experienced as politically oppressive) (personal correspondence, 1998).

Using this to gloss the Lacanian–Žižekian system, I might say that though ideology can situate and even oppress the subject, the process of interpellation is not fully determinate because it is contingent on the subject's response to the perhaps incommensurable and indeterminate discourses that make up the ideological order.

In my view, the value of this kind of rereading of Žižek's Lacanian theory of ideological interpellation—beyond the simple relief of at least trying to move away from purely phallogocentric understandings and theoretical descriptions—is in its ability to posit the subject as both determined by ideological structures, and able to negotiate them. A theory which posits the possibility of the subject's repositioning through a process of liminal identification with hybrid signs and figures is certainly more hopeful and politically productive than the idea that the subject is destined always to be governed by the same ideology in which it was formed.

Bhabha and Reading

And, importantly, this reading of ideological interpellation opens up a space for the role of texts in all of this. Texts, as (ideological) discourses that readers 'find' within the social order can make demands on the reader. If texts can 'interpellate' readers (see Chapter 2), then it may be possible that readers can be repositioned as subjects through identification with the *differently repeated signs* of the text rather than with the *lack* in the text. The reader's identification with the images, entities and fantasy objects offered up in the text, as they are repeated *differently* throughout the text, ought to be able, according to this model, to have some negotiatory impact on their always-already positioning as subjects. This would be a quite different kind of reading than the kind discussed in Chapter 2 where the ideological *points de capiton* that have always-already pinned the reader also pin down their interpretations; instead this would be a kind of negotiation with the difference within the text, and of the difference between text and reader.

Difference, the Third Space and Interpretation

I would like to think of interpretation as a possible space for the negotiation of difference within and between text and reader, where the 'difference' within and between the text and reader might be thought of, following Bhabha's use of Derrida, as a product of the repetitious structure of language. If interpretation can be considered a negotiation of this kind of difference, it might be likened to Bhabha's Third Space. In this case, the moment of interpretation could be considered a space of difference which both the text and reader inhabit, a space that is neither one, nor the other, but somewhere in between: the Lacanian *vel* or space of non-meaning (lack, or as I have redescribed it, difference) that cuts through both the subject and the Other. This would mean that it is difference and the structure of repetition, not lack, that both joins and separates text and reader. Or in other terms, this would be the place where the reader both finds and creates the world of the text, where there is play between the text and the reader. Such a view of interpretation would not understand the reading process as the imposition of the reader on the text, or vice versa. Rather reading might be seen as a negotiation that does not have to diminish the difference between text and reader. The Third Space might be considered that 'space' which the reader both finds and creates, and which is *neither and both* text and reader. It is the space that both joins and separates text and reader, a space of difference produced when writing is doubled by reading, and vice versa.[28]

Interpellation into the Text

What might be said to initiate this negotiatory process? I would suggest that it is indeed the reader's interpellation by the text, the 'Hey you' of the text that calls the reader to identify with it in some way. Texts might be said to hail readers as subjects, through the use of second person forms. It might be obvious to point out that texts, and especially texts like prophetic texts, often deliberately address the reader using second person forms; the effect of such an address, however, is the possibility for the reader to respond as a speaking, acting, subject, *I*. In responding to the hailing of the text, the reader might be said to respond to the hailing of the text, followed by the demand of the text (*Che vuoi*, 'What do you want of me?'), as if the reader knows why she has been hailed in this way. And if the Lacanian logic is followed, in response, the reader may even internalize this demand ('What does the text want of me?'). In internalizing this demand, readers are urged to make identifications with images held out to them by the text. In this way the desires of the text become the desires of the reader. These identifications and desires are facilitated, in part, by the way the subject position is modified. To give an example, in the case of Micah the reader is hailed as *you*, 'O Daughter of Jerusalem', or *you*, 'my people', and so on. The reader is urged then to make the identification with the title (and corresponding image) that modifies *you*.

However this identification with the text is not immediate or complete; there are always the spatial and temporal aspects of language and text that mediate (and rupture) such an identification (see Bhabha 1994a: 36). In a model that takes into consideration the split between the subject of the statement and the subject of enunciation, such identifications can only ever be considered partial. The reader can never 'be' the subject of the statement (*you, my people, daughter of Jerusalem*, and so on); this subject position is always dissected by the reader's own subject position. Further, in a text such as Micah, the reader is interpellated into a series of quickly shifting positions, and the text demands the reader to

28. See Landy (1997: 162-65) for a discussion of Winnicott and biblical texts, specifically how biblical texts can both be part of, and intrude on, the child's play space.

identify with a number of differently repeated signs. This means that a sort of negotiation (which I will discuss in detail in Chapter 6) must occur in the interaction that takes place between the text and the reader.

Reading Pedagogical Objects and Discourses

However, I would argue (and will demonstrate in Chapter 5) that this negotiation is sometimes short-circuited if the text is considered as something to be 'known', dissected and understood (as is often the case with biblical or 'classic' texts), rather than read as an address and in this way allowed to 'enunciate'. It would seem that frequently, instead of answering the demand of the text, readers respond to a different demand, one perceived according to their own always-already ideological interpellation, and filled as such. I would suggest that sometimes readers find within texts—especially texts like Micah that seem to be 'lacking' in coherence—fantasy objects and ideal discourses which can be 'raised up' to the status of theme or interpretive key that can fill in the 'lack'. (In describing reading thus, I am following the connection I have traced above between Žižek's *objet petit a*—the fantasy object of desire that fills in for 'lack'—and Bhabha's pedagogical objects and discourses.) However, it would seem at times that these fantasy (pedagogical) objects and discourses are only raised up to the level of the master signifiers or *points de capiton* with which the reader has always-already identified and been interpellated. In this way, the 'lack in the text' is self-referentially filled by the *point de capiton* or master signifier, with which the reader has already been pinned.

Outside the Sentence

However Bhabha's attention to the undecidability of pedagogical objects and discourses causes me to consider that any accumulation of signs found in a text and raised to the status of master signifier (pedagogical discourse) or imposed on a text is just that, an accumulation of signs which, if attended to, or allowed to enunciate, will reveal their differences. Since the priority of any sign or image can only be established through repetition, it is replete with difference; these differences can be recognized, identified with and negotiated. If the signs of the text are 'allowed to enunciate', then the reader will be hailed to respond to the text's demand, hailed into difference—the difference within the text, and the difference between the subject position that the text offers and the reader's own subject position. Through this interpellation, the space for negotiation between text and reader opens up.

To use another of Bhabha's metaphors, this space is literally 'outside the sentence', or 'outside the text', a space through which the various

signs that accompany the discursive and textual positions of the reader
and the text circulate. All the differences between the repetitions of the
signs within a text circulate within this space, as do the (perhaps
conflicting) master signifiers by which readers have been always-already
interpellated. This space becomes, momentarily at least, a place of non-
meaning, a place in which the signifiers that make up the text and those
that have already pinned the reader overlap. In this overlap there is a
possibility for meaning to be negotiated. Many kinds of hybrid figures
can emerge in this space—between the signs of the text within the text,
between the fantasy pedagogical objects and discourses found in the text
and the text's repetition of these objects and discourses, and also
between the signs of the text and the *points de capiton* that have pinned
the reader (to which the textual fantasy objects may be raised).

Hybridity

What if in this moment, hybridity is produced as a result of the overlap,
repetition or re-presentation of signs with which readers are always-
already interpellated and those to which they may respond in the text?
The text may repeat the master signifier with which the reader has already
been pinned rather differently, forming hybridity. For instance, a text may
hold out a number of divergent points of identification to the reader. A
fantasy object that is held out for identification through direct address
('Hey you') in one part of the text might be configured differently in
another. If the reader were to try make these cohere with (or in Žižek's
terms, 'stand in for') the master signifier with which the reader has been
previously pinned, while at the same time identifying with each of these
positions in turn, there would always be some kind of excess formed,
some disturbing element that would not fit into a unifying image.

The appearance of the hybrid figure through the text's repetition of an
external master signifier could have several effects, all of which might, in
Bhabha's words, have the subversive effect of unsettling the 'mimetic or
narcissistic demands' of ideologically governed signification, by turning
the gaze of the text 'back upon the eye of power' (1994a: 112). First, by
creating a disturbance in the smooth repetition of a norm or ideal, the
hybrid figure might be said to bring into view the repetitive operation
that might otherwise go unnoticed, and by which a signifier is raised to
the level of 'master' signifier or *point de capiton* in the first place. The
very possibility that a norm might be repeated differently destabilizes the
authenticity of the norm itself. In this way the hybrid figure might
'unsettle the myth of origins', the myth of an authentic and pure master
signifier.

Second, the hybrid figure might have the effect of revealing the constraints and exclusions by which norms are established. Bhabha, following Žižek, suggests that the subject's accession (or pinning) to a master signifier always leaves an excess or a remainder behind (1994a: 184); this remainder is what is excluded from the signifying operation, or I might say that which cannot be contained by it. Bhabha argues that this remainder returns not as the repressed, but as the hybrid. In the case of difference within a text, the remainder might be those textual details that do not fit under the umbrella of the master signifier. The hybrid juxtaposes the 'norm' or master signifier with that which has been excluded from it (in order to arrive at a coherent interpretation according to the reader's ideological positioning). Thus, hybridity renders what has been excluded visible.

Third, and this is where hybridity relates to subjectivity, in displaying the master signifier differently, hybridity should, in theory, be able to displace the reader's own notions about self-identity. If the reader is formed as subject through a pinning to, and identification with, an external ideological master signifier, what happens to her identification with it, when it is transformed and hybridized through the operation of a text? Perhaps once its constructed and exclusionary nature is revealed, the reader is able to recognize her interpellation by it, and also oppressions inherent to this kind of ideological positioning.

Liminal Identification, Time-lag
This approach might be taken one step further to consider what might happen if, in this negotiation, the reader identifies with the differently repeated signs in the text and with the hybrid figure. Such an identification should, following Bhabha's description of the time-lag (retroactive signification), bring the subject—and meaning—down out of its trip through the text's symbolic order in a different place. In the time-lag between the sign's appearance in the text and its signification in reading—what Bhabha might call the moment between the 'event of the sign' and 'its discursive eventuality' (1994a: 182)—the reader can either identify self-referentially with the lack (of meaning) in the text, filling it in according to her own position within ideology; or she can identify liminally, with the differently iterated signs of the text, with the text's own discourse, thereby allowing the text to enunciate its difference. The point is that the reader's liminal identification with the text and subsequent repositioning as subject is intimately connected with the production of 'meaning', or in other terms, with the way the signs of the text signify. In the time-lag between the reader's interpellation into the text and the fastening down of meaning that takes place as she comes back out of her journey through the symbolic order of the text, a process of liminal identification with difference could occur that would affect the meaning of the text. This kind

of identification would avoid the ceaseless and narcissistic return of the reader as subject to the same place from which she started, thus simultaneously changing the way the text is understood.

Agency, Indeterminacy and Interpretation

Of course, thinking about interpretation as a negotiation of difference does not immediately resolve the problem set out in the discussion of textual determinacy (see Introduction); that is, is it the text, or the reader, or the reader's ideology that controls the production of meaning? Several questions remain. If the reader is so free to identify with the difference within the text and thus to affect her ideological positioning, would she not just do so if she wished, exhibiting a will that exceeds ideology in the first place and exemplifying readerly control over texts? Or if the reader is always-already formed in ideology and not necessarily aware of it, how would this kind of re-identification be possible? On the side of text, if, under this view, the structure of repetition in language always means that difference is produced, how can a text ever mean anything at all?

Bhabha's work on agency and contingency may be helpful in sorting out these problems. In the understanding of signification and subjectivity that Bhabha proposes, the sign and the subject (or agent) are both contiguous (dependent, related) and contingent (independent, indeterminate). Making the analogy to reading, I might say that the text *and* the reader are *both* determinate and indeterminate, and that meaning and subjectivity are determined in the negotiation between the two. The reader's agency as interpreter is contiguous with, and dependent on, the reader's ideological context, but it is also, in part, indeterminate, contingent on new questions, such as the question demanded by the text, '*Che vuoi?*' Likewise, the text's meaning is contiguous with the chain of signifiers in which it is written, but it is also contingent on the identifications made by the reader. This means that the *contours of the text are important to the kinds of identifications that can be made*. For example, there might be more *possibilities* for liminal identification in a text such as Micah which is notable for its shifts and for differences in the way it repeats images and addresses its readers.

The result of this four-way relation (text as determinate and indeterminate, reader as determinate and indeterminate) is a kind of negotiation that should allow both for re-identification with difference that shifts the reader's ideological positioning, and for the possibility of revaluation of symbols in the text. This is, as Bhabha says, an indeterminacy that does not mean free-floating signification. It is the negotiation that takes place in interpellation into the textual symbolic order, the response to the text's demand, that gives the reader a certain kind of agency (in Bhabha's terms, this might be the 'intersubjective relation with the Other' of the text). More than this, I might suggest, following Bhabha, that in this process, the oft-times subtly oppressive habitual readings of the text can be re-inscribed, reordered, resymbolized (catachresis).

To summarize this discussion about the reading process, I would say that according to this view, the negotiation that takes place between text and reader might be considered a negotiation of the difference—produced by the structure of repetition—within and between text and reader. This negotiation of difference can occur through a kind of liminal identification with the various iterations of the text, which can both replace and add to the reader's previous pinning by a master signifier. This process would, in theory, produce an excess, resulting in various kinds of hybrid figures, which in turn could put into question and displace the 'original' master signifiers at work in interpretation. Thus liminal identification and hybridity could disable the capacity of the master signifier always to pin the subject in the same way. This is how the subject might be enabled to come out of the signifying or reading process in a place other than where it started, and how different kinds of interpretations of a text might be proposed.

Reading Micah

It is my contention that the text of Micah is an excellent text with which to explore this kind of hypothesis regarding the possibility of the reader's repositioning as subject through a negotation of difference. Not only are the discursive contexts in which the text and its contemporary readers situated vastly different, but also, Micah is contoured by differences: differences in style, differences in the way particular words are used, differences in syntactic formations, differences in the type of content (for example, announcements of doom, or predictions of glory). Yet in spite of these many differences, it seems that Micah is often read by scholars as unitary and knowable; differences are read as incoherence (lack), which is solved (filled in) by emendments, hypotheses and translations. This has the effect of silencing certain voices and privileging other key concepts. It seems that the text is read as a kind of lack and therefore submitted to external master signifiers (as I illustrate in Chapter 5).

What I do in the next three chapters is to look carefully at the differences in Micah; at how various scholars have recently interpreted Micah in ways that disavow its difference and privilege certain themes; and at how readerly identification with the differently repeating signs of the text might affect subject positioning. In the next chapter I scrutinize the text of Micah and the many minute details of the shifting gender, nation and future found there, paying particular attention to the way readers are addressed. Following that, I look at the way several scholars have found within the text a cumulative fantasy image, a sort of pedagogical discourse of an oppressed, passive and suffering woman-nation who is rescued and led by the phallic active divine ruler. I show how this image seems to stand in for master signifiers of 'gender norms' and Israel's 'covenantal identity'—signifiers provided by contemporary discourses of gender and theology (which may of course have biblical roots, but that is not my argument).

In the final chapter of this book, I look at the way in which the text repeats this pedagogical discourse differently. I look at the kind of hybridity formed by repetitions in the text; at what kind of liminal identifications might be made with this hybridity; at whether such identifications can confront the ideological positioning of readers; and at what effect such a confrontation could have on the 'meaning' of the text. Because any real shift in the subjectivity of these particular readers (discussed in Chapter 5) would be difficult to ascertain, given that they have not read in the way I am proposing, I will only be able to suggest, for the sake of argument, that their work furnishes a sort of prototypical reader. I therefore suggest how identification with the differently repeated signs of the text *might* affect the ideological master signifiers that seem to be pinning such a reader. I also suggest how reading Micah in this way has affected my own ideological positioning.

Conclusion

In sum, Bhabha furthers Žižek's reading of interpellation to enable thinking about the possibility of repositioning the subject through identification with the *differently repeated signs* of the text rather than with the *lack* in the text. In this model, liminal identification is a negotiation that takes place between text and reader, a negotiation of the difference—produced by the structure of repetition—within and between text and reader. This negotiation through identification with the difference within the text produces an excess, a hybrid figure which in turn puts into question the reader's always-already interpellation into a particular ideology. Thinking this way allows for the possibility that the subject is not always rigidly predetermined and that even a highly difficult and disjunct text like Micah might have some determining role in the production of meaning. According to this view, texts and readers can be seen as both determined by, and freed for, new possibilities in the 'intersubjective', Third Space of the reading process. I turn now to look at various ways of reading Micah to see how this suggestion might bear out.

Part II
Readings

4

The Changing Subjects of Micah: Gender, Nation, Future

Having outlined how Bhabha's theory has caused me to consider the reading process as a negotiation of difference, through which the reader's subject position might be affected, I turn now to the text of Micah. To recall my overall argument for a moment, following Bhabha, I consider the possibility of the repositioning of the subject to hinge on the (re)identification of the subject with new objects of desire, made up of difference instead of filling in for lack. I wonder, therefore, how the text interpellates, or hails the reader into difference, and what images (objects of desire) this holds out for the reader to identify with. What effect might this have on the reader's always-already subject position?

One of my main concerns in this chapter is to give an exposition of the text in order to show, in detail, how I understand the Hebrew text of Micah to be a site of *difference* with which the reader has to negotiate. In order to illustrate this, I simply go through the text, looking at its difficulties and ambiguities, particularly with respect to gender, nation and future vision. I also show, throughout, how a number of scholars writing in the last thirty years have disavowed the difference in the text by 'solving' its problems.[1] This exposition of Micah will serve as a way of orienting my discussions of the text in subsequent chapters.

As will become evident, the Hebrew text of Micah is not always easy reading; its images shift from chapter to chapter, and even from verse to verse. In Bhabha's terms, it might be considered the 'Other' replete with difference. Indeed, as scholars have noted (e.g. de Waard, Shoemaker), one of the main problems of the book is in determining just who is being addressed or described, and what the relationships are between the various participants, speakers and addressees in the book—and here I use the word participant in the way that de Waard defines it: to denote any object or person that is related as agent, receptor, destination or instrument to an event in the text (1979: 509 n. 1). It is no simple task to identify the various participants—let alone interpret their metaphorical

---

1. Because many scholars make note of earlier scholarly suggestions, I have not repeated that material here (for an excellent compilation of earlier views, including medieval rabbinic thinking, see McKane [1998]).

significance—due to the frequent shifts in imagery in the book, as well as ambiguities and difficulties in determining the syntactic constructions. As stated in Chapter 1, it is not my intention to eliminate the problems in the text—nor to deal with all of them—but to let them stand. If at times my own text seems unresolved, it is because, at this stage especially, I try not to close down the text by providing answers or suggesting new readings (I do more of this in Chapter 6), but rather to represent and emphasize its openness.[2]

Because I will eventually be looking at how readers might identify with the various and differently repeated images in the text, I dwell particularly on the problems in determining the participants in the book. I look at how they speak, how they are addressed, how they are described, and how they seem to relate to the other participants in the book. I also notice the forms of address in the text (second person forms, including imperatives, vocatives and questions), because this is the most obvious way that texts can hail or interpellate readers (a theme to which I will return in Chapter 6). Further, because I am particularly interested in the kinds of readerly identifications that are and can be made with shifting contours of gender, nation and future vision in the book, and in the subsequent effect on readers' positioning as subjects, I pay special attention to the shifts in these configurations here.

Indeed—anticipating my eventual argument somewhat—I will point out shifts and ambiguities in the text as they pertain to two often ideologically overloaded sites of desire: *gender* (the linguistic and metaphoric distinction between masculine and feminine)[3] and *nation* (the various ways that Israel is understood). I am interested in the way that the text marks images of gender and nation as desirable or undesirable, through visions of the future (predictions of hope or doom). As a brief point of procedure, I should note that while I will notice the differences in the way the nation is described, where a general national term is needed, I use 'Israel'. Since I am not making any

2.   I will use the following set of abbreviations throughout the chapter: fs (feminine singular), 2fs (second feminine singular), 3fs (third feminine singular); 3fpl (third feminine plural); ms (masculine singular) 2ms (second masculine singular), 3ms (third masculine singular); mpl (masculine plural), 2mpl (second masculine plural), 3mpl (third masculine plural), 1cs (first common singular), 1cpl (first common plural); ptc (participle).

3.   Some might argue that linguistic gender in Hebrew is separate from issues of gender raised by feminists and others. However, to take a pertinent example, whether or not the noun עִיר, 'city', was originally understood as a personified feminine figure; the fact of the matter is that it has often been read as such along typical gender lines (see my Chapter 5). For this reason, the precise configuration of gender in the book bears some attention.

proposals about historical events, and since the text refers to both southern and northern kingdoms, for ease of reference, I simply refer to the entire nation as Israel.

I have chosen to use a less traditional (columned) format to try to show how technical and scholarly commentary relates to the text in a way that is slightly more organic than the usual use of notes. This format juxtaposes my own attention to the abrupt shifts and disjunctions in gender and number—shifts that affect understanding of participant identity in the book—with scholarly efforts to understand the text through solving its problems. Interspersed throughout is my own awkward translation of Micah, awkward because I wish to denaturalize English translations of the text for those who do not have access to the Hebrew, and also because I wish to show in another way the difficulty in smoothing out the text. Alternate possibilities for translation are inserted in parentheses, and I do not try to poeticize the English. It is my hope that this way of figuring textual ambiguities, alongside notes about scholarly solutions, will highlight the kinds of external unifying discourses (what Bhabha might call pedagogical objects and discourses) that are employed on texts.[4] The columns also show the way in which the text gets repeated differently (and infinitely multiplied) in translation and interpretation of the text. While my concern in this project is to focus specifically on the kinds of identifications that are made with the differently repeated signs *within* the text, the repetitive rendering of the text and commentary here may also point toward thinking about the kinds of liminal identifications that might be made with differently repeated signs produced in traditions of reading text.

---

4.   For an excellent discussion of the issues and problems that surround biblical translation, as well as the relation of translation to ideology see Aichele (2001: 61-83). My translation approaches a kind of hyper-literal translation, pushing the limit on the kind of translation that Aichele argues 'identifies…a shimmering opalescence of pure language that is always able to mean more (or less) than anyone could ever think. None of these Bibles is the same as any other Bible… This multiplicity of Bibles is not able to…speak authoritatively with a single voice. It cannot be universal, the same message in every language and in every age' (2001: 80).

Micah 1

The Hebrew in Micah 1 is quite complex, presenting a number of ambiguities as to who is being addressed, by whom. The chapter describes and laments destruction for the land, cities, and people of Israel. The precise cause and source of this destruction is not entirely clear, but seems to be related to the behaviour of Israel's cities. The participants in the chapter seem, for the most part, to be described in feminine (singular) terms, though sometimes a masculine (plural) group is addressed too; at points masculine and feminine syntactical forms and behavioural traits get mixed. The address seems to be extended to a large and varied audience, both masculine and feminine, while the first person voice seems to shift between Yahweh and the prophet, without any clear marker of the change. Because of the ambiguities, the audience or reader is positioned, in a sense, as both addressee and observer, as both masculine and feminine.

Micah 1.1-2

¹The word of Yahweh which was to Micah the Moreshite, in the days of Jotham, Ahaz, Hezekiah, the kings of Judah—which he envisioned concerning (against) Samaria and Jerusalem. ²Listen, O peoples, all of them (mpl). Pay attention, O earth, and all her fullness. Let Adoni (my Lord) Yahweh be amongst (against) you (mpl) as witness, Adoni (my Lord) from his holy temple.

The book begins with the requisite superscription stating that this is the word of Yahweh, by way of Micah, concerning, or against, Samaria and Jerusalem. Following this superscription imperatives and vocatives call *you*—O peoples (mpl), O land (fs)—to listen (1.2). Though it is not stated, Israel is undoubtedly included as one of the 'peoples' hailed, as is implied by the reference to its cities in the superscription. However, the address of the book is rather more all-encompassing than simply Israel (including the land and its peoples).

Scholars have debated whether the term 'peoples' (עמים) in 1.2 refers to the nations, or to Israel. For a discussion of the various suggestions about the audience intended by this term see Shoemaker (1992: 112-18), who concludes that the term refers to the inhabitants of the land. Petrotta (1991: 118-23) gives the interesting reading that the ambiguity is deliberately intended, so that 'the indeterminate terminology introduces a counter-movement right at the beginning of his message that creates an extended context that is neither restrictive (Israel only), nor exclusive (the nations *sans* Israel)' (1991: 123).

Micah 1.3-5

³For behold, the Lord is going forth from his place, and going down and treading upon the high places of the earth. ⁴The mountains will melt under him and the valleys will break, like wax before a fire, and like water flowing down a slope. ⁵All this is in exchange for the transgression of Jacob, and in exchange for the sin of the house of Israel. Who is the sin of Jacob? Is it not Samaria? And who is the high place of Judah? Is it not Jerusalem?

The text then moves into a third person prediction of divine wrath. Yahweh descends upon the earth wreaking havoc upon it. The reason for this fearful theophany is given in 1.5: Yahweh's wrath is caused by the transgression of Jacob (said to be Samaria), and the sins of the house of Israel (the high place of which is said to be Jerusalem). Israel is thus identified with its (feminine and transgressing) cities, which are the object of Yahweh's wrath, described to *you* (O peoples, O land).

For a discussion of the theophany tradition in Micah as it compares to Isaiah, see Stansell (1988: 9-33). For reference to Rabbinic discussion of the theophany in 1.4, see McKane (1995a: 424).

Micah 1.6-7

⁶I will make Samaria for a ruins, the field, for the places of planting a vineyard. I will pour her stones into a valley. I will uncover her foundations. ⁷And all her idols will be cut off, and her earnings will be burned in the fire, and all her idols I will make devastation. For from the earnings of a prostitute she gathers and to the earnings of a prostitute they will return.

The rest of ch. 1 seems to work out the disturbing theme of Yahweh's anger against feminine cities for their wickedness. To begin, the first person *I*, presumably Yahweh though the speaker is not identified, threatens Samaria (in the third person). *I* promise to strip Samaria and make her desolate—a ruined field, her foundations uncovered—for collec-

For a résumé of the various suggestions about the phrase 'for a ruin, the field' (לְעִי הַשָּׂדֶה) in 1.6 see Wagenaar (1996); McKane (1998: 32).

The *BHS* notes that the Syriac, Targum and Vulgate read the 3fs קִבְצָה ('she gathered') in 1.7 as the 3mpl Pual קֻבְּצוּ ('they are gathered'), to cohere with the masculine plural verbs at end of the line, reading 'from the wages of prostitutes they are gathered'.

The reference to prostitution in 1.7 has drawn considerable scholarly attention. Some scholars, like Hillers (1984: 20), Shoemaker (1992: 122 n. 75) and Ben Zvi (2000: 32), relate the reference to prostitution to the 'unfaithful woman' of Hosea. Many discuss the precise meaning of the term אֶתְנַן (the wage of a prostitute). P.D. Miller suggests that the

ting the wages of prostitutes. Samaria is not actually accused of prostitution, just of gathering their wages (1.7), and for this she is violently punished.

You—O peoples, O land addressed at the outset—implicitly watch the baring of Samaria as if an outside observer. Because the *you* whom the *I* addresses is not specifically situated in any more detailed way than at the opening of the book (land and peoples), the reaction to the scene is left open: it might be horror, guilt, approval, indignation or fear, depending on how *you* identify (both always-already as reader, and within the wide range that is land and peoples).

term is used to denote both the character of the sin and its punishment (1982: 27-29). W.G.E. Watson (1984b) finds the plural form in 1.7a to be an allusion to the Ugaritic snake tablet, a wordplay on the Ugaritic *tnn*, meaning serpent, thus accounting for the use of the word in the middle of a line which is otherwise focused on idols. McKane gives a range of views on the relation of the term to cultic practice (1995a: 429-32; 1998: 33-34). Petrotta argues that there is a pun on the senses—literal ('hire') and metaphoric ('idols')—of the word אתנן as it is positioned in the verse (1991: 85-89).

Micah 1.8

Concerning this I will lament and I will wail, and I will go barefoot and naked. I will make wailing like the jackal and mourning like daughters of an ostrich.

The speaker abruptly goes into a moment of angst—wailing and going barefoot. There is no clear indication whether the first person voice has changed or whether it is the same *I* that threatened Samaria in 1.6-7. Certainly if it is Yahweh that speaks here, his role has changed drastically, from one terrorizing the earth and Samaria, to one lamenting.

Because the language in 1.8 is anthropomorphic, most scholars assume that speech shifts to the prophet. Wolff notes that the Greek and the Targum use 3fs verbs here, to portray these acts of grief as Samaria's (1990: 43), but he himself considers the first person figure to be the prophet, so also Hillers (1984: 23); Allen (1976: 274). Ben Zvi suggests that this is deliberate fluidity in the text, designed to associate the prophet with Yahweh (1998: 113-14; 2000: 33, 39). Shoemaker argues that 1.8-9 play three roles: that of rhetorical bridge to 1.10-16; that of establishing the prophet as empathetic with the people; and that of stimulating anxiety in the audience (1992: 124-25). For a thorough discussion and rereading see Beal (1994), who is almost unique in arguing that this is the voice of Yahweh.

Micah 1.9

For she is an incurable one (a disastrous one)—her sickness (her wounds). For she comes to Judah. It/he strikes the gate of my people.

The speaker then recounts Jerusalem's encounter with catastrophe: some sort of incurable one (3fs), a sickness or

The words אנושה ('incurable' or 'disastrous') and מכות ('plagues' or 'wounds') in 1.9 seem to carry a double entendre, both sickness and warfare are implied; נגע ('strike') could be used in either context. The verse is difficult however, since the adjective and noun in 1.9a differ in number (אנושה מכותיה), and the disaster comes to Judah. It/he (3ms) strikes the gate of *my people* (1.9). Here the metonym 'gate' seems to affiliate the people with Jerusalem.

It is not clear what the introduction of 'my people' does to the position of the addressee. Is the addressee included in *my people*? It seems like the addressee is set up to take a certain observer's distance from the destruction (viewing it as happening to Samaria and to my 'people'.

It is also not clear who is responsible for bringing about this disaster; it is not the first person, *I*, who threatens to make this happen, it is not she, the incurable one either: '*it/he* (3ms) strikes', as if another participant in the text.

verbs shift from 3fs in 1.9a, 'she comes' (באה), to 3ms in 1.9b, 'he strikes' (נגע). Scholars have tried to solve these incongruities in a number of ways. Some emend the plural noun מכותיה ('her wounds') to the singular מכתה ('her wound') so that the phrase reads 'her wound is incurable'; so Hillers (1984: 22); R.L. Smith (1984: 20); Allen (1976: 267); Craigie (1985: 9); Shoemaker (1992: 124); McKane (1998: 57). Others assume that it is the adjective that should be plural, 'her wounds are incurable'; so Kaiser (1992: 30); Shaw (1993: 33). Some have emended to מכת יהוה ('the blow of Yahweh') to accord with the singular adjective and to provide Yahweh as a masculine subject for נגע ('he strikes'); so Mays (1976: 48); Wolff (1990: 43); Stansell (1988: 44). McKane emends the verb to the 3fs נגעה ('she strikes') to accord with the feminine subject (the incurable one) (1998: 39).

Allen also notes the shift to the suffix form in 1.9, suggesting this is the prophetic perfect (1976: 267), 'she will come, he will strike'.

Verses 10-16 seem to take up the theme of anger against cities and towns, but in a slightly different vein. The Hebrew in this segment of text is very complex, punning on place names as it does. The over all sense seems to be that the feminine towns Zaanan (1.11), Maroth (1.12), Lachish (1.13), Moresheth-gath (1.14), and Mareshah (1.15) are subjected to various, and often difficult to decipher, critiques, commentaries and punishments. However, it is not clear whether the poetry is directed to a feminine singular or masculine plural addressee, since the forms of address and their gender shift throughout. At first glance the passage *seems* to be addressed to the towns in Judah using feminine singular imperatives, which may correspond to the repeated femi-

The political significance of the town names in Mic. 1.10-16, in conjunction with the literary quality of the passage —albeit written in Hebrew difficult for the contemporary reader—has been the subject of much scholarly writing. Hillers gives thorough discussions of the puns on place names, as well as some of the other textual complications (1984: 24-28). Alfaro gives a very straightforward summary of the many discussions: 'It is difficult for us to understand in some cases the paronomasia, wordplay and alliterations used... In some instances the relationship between the name of the city and the punishment announced is partially clear even to us: Gath—*tagiddu* ("announce"), Beth-leaphrah—*aphar* ("dust, ashes"), Shaphir—*shophar* ("horn"), Zanaan—*yazeah* ("go out"),

nine singular participle in construct with a town name (e.g. יושבת שפיר, 'inhabitant of Shaphir'). But the passage is also punctuated by 2mpl forms, which trouble a facile identification of addressee.

To make matters of gender and address more convoluted, the place names can for the most part, either be read as vocatives (thus addressed to the 2fs), or as the subjects or predicates of the phrases (thus described in the third person). This is complicated by the fact that the relation of the verbs to the proper names is not always entirely clear. (Verse 15 seems to be an exception to this equivocal use of the construction, 'inhabitant of...'. There יושבת מרשה follows the 2fs לך, and so it seems necessarily to be read as a vocative, 'to you, O Mareshah'.) If the proper names in the passage are read as vocatives (O inhabitant of Shaphir etc.), the overall address is made directly to *you*. If, on the other hand, the town names are read in the third person (the inhabitant of Shaphir etc.), *you* are still present through the imperatives used, but positioned as an observer of the described towns. Thus it is not clear if the speaker is addressing these towns directly, or whether the towns are being described (in the third person) to another second person feminine figure, *you*. Could the 2fs figure, invoked through feminine singular imperatives, used periodically throughout and then in a more concentrated fashion at the end, be the Daughter of Zion of 1.13), so Shoemaker (1992: 132) and Hillers (1984: 27)? The text is ambiguous.

Lachish—*rekesh* ("chariot"), Moresheth —*meorashah* ("betrothed"), Achzib— *akzab* ("deception") and Mareshah— *yoresh* ("conqueror, possessor")' (1989: 19). For a detailed discussion of the complex kinds of wordplay at work, see Petrotta (1991: 65-85). Stansell notes that this kind of wordplay is characteristic of death laments (1988: 42). For a good overview of the earlier suggestions for emendation on this passage see Schwantes (1964). For discussion of the archaeological evidence related to the various towns see P.J. King (1988: 58-60); Shaw (1993: 44-47); and Schmitt (1990).

Micah 1.10-11

[10]*In Gath do not tell (mpl), certainly do not weep (mpl), in the house for (of) dust (Beth-leaphrah), roll (fs) (I roll) in the dust.* [11]*Pass (by) (cross over) (fs), to/wards (for) you (mpl). The (O)*

Reading Mic. 1.10-16 is tricky business, because of technical difficulties in the Hebrew. For instance, the feminine singular imperative in 1.10, התפלשי ('roll!') is read almost without exception, following the *qere* in the margin. Yet,

inhabitant of Shaphir (fs) (is) naked-
ness, shame (is) the (O) inhabitant of
Zaanan (fs) will not go out (fs). (The
inhabitant of Zaanan is) the wailing of
the house of Ezel (Beth-ezel) (ms) (he)
will take from you (mpl) his/its stand-
ing place.

In 1.10-11, the text moves through
variously gendered imperatives and
second person forms, beginning with
more masculine forms and settling
chiefly on feminine forms toward the
end.

The passage begins with masculine
plural imperatives addressing Gath: 'Do
not tell, do not weep'. Then abruptly a
feminine singular imperative tells Beth-
leaphrah, 'Roll in the dust', presumably
to express mourning. Someone is told to
'pass by', in 1.11, continuing the address
in the feminine singular. Perhaps it is
Shaphir who is told to pass by, but the
gender and number shifts momentarily
back to the masculine plural (לכם, 'you',
'to you', or possibly, 'all of you').

The text then moves into using
third person singular forms, oscillating
between feminine and masculine. The
feminine singular figures Zaanan and
Nakedness-shame are associated somehow with the 3fs verb 'she will not go
out' (לא יצאה), while masculine forms
seem to describe Beth-ezel, who will
take (3ms) *his* standing place from *you*
(2mpl) (יקח מכם עמדתו). Or perhaps it is
someone else, unnamed, who will take
his enigmatic 'standing place'.

Further, the poetic lines can be
divided syntactically in a number of
different ways, each associating verbs
and nouns differently, and resulting in
slightly different meaning. For example
1.11 might be divided as follows:

עברי לכם יושבת שפיר
עריה־בשת לא יצאה
יושבת צאנן מספד בית האצל
יקח מכם עמדתו

the *kethib* reads the first person
singular התפלשתי ('I roll') which might
indicate a continuation of the first
person speech of 1.8. The *kethib/qere*
marks the choices of ancient readers,
and because the text continues with
feminine singular imperatives, many
scholars since have made the same
choice. There are some exceptions
though: Shaw reads the *kethib* (1993:
34); McKane reads as a 2mpl (1998: 57),
as does Lescow (1997: 67), who also
emends the feminine singular imperative 'pass by' (עברי) to the masculine
plural imperative עברו (1997: 67). I read
the *qere*, following the MT, though the
possibility of a first person voice here is
interesting and might support the kind
of reading Beal gives (see n. 8 above).

Decisions about how to read this
verse are not made easier by the two-fold
occurrence of the 2mpl (לכם and מכם, 'to
you' and 'from you') amidst the feminine
forms, nor by the ever present possibility
of unmarked relative clauses. Further the
relationship between the two nouns, עריה
בשת ('nakedness' and 'shame') is not
obvious. Does the maqqep between the
two nouns in the MT indicate that the
Masoretes read עריה־בשת as a place name?
As such does it function as the subject of
the verb לא יצאה ('she will not go out')?
Or are the two nouns separate predicates
where יושבת שפיר stands as the subject for
two nominal sentences, though only
given once ('the inhabitant of Shaphir is
nakedness, the inhabitant of Shaphir is
shame').

There is also the difficulty of the
hapax logomena, עמדתו, which may
mean 'location' (KB) or 'standing place'
(BDB)—Hillers calls it 'nonsense' and
translates it as 'treasures' (1984: 24, 26).
Shoemaker translates it as 'support'
citing the cognate עמוד 'pillar, column'
(1992: 129 n. 103). And finally the
introduction of a 3ms subject with יקח
(he will take) could either refer back to

to be translated:

Cross over (fs) to you (mpl), O inhabitant of Shaphir (fs). Nakedness, shame will not go out. The inhabitant of Zaanan is the mourning of the house of Ezel. He will take from you his standing place.

Or the verse could be broken into lines as follows,

עברי לכם
יושבת שפיר עריה־בשת
לא יצאה יושבת צאנן
מספד בית האצל יקח מכם עמדתו

to be translated:

Pass by, you! The inhabitant of Shaphir is nakedness, shame. The inhabitant of Zaanan will not go out. The mourning rites of the house of Ezel will take from you its standing place.

Or possibly:

עברי
לכם יושבת שפיר
עריה־בשת לא יצאה
יושבת צאנן מספד בית האצל
יקח מכם עמדתו

to be translated:

Pass by! The inhabitant of Shaphir is for you [belongs to you]. Nakedness-Shame will not go out. The inhabitant of Zaanan is the wailing of the house of Ezel [which] will take from you its standing place.

Micah 1.12
For he grows tired (falls ill) for (the) good (of the) (O) inhabitant of Maroth. (The inhabitant of Maroth dances/ writhes in pain for good). For evil goes down from Yahweh to the gate of Jerusalem.

Beth-ezel, or indicate another, different participant.

Most scholars emend the verb חלה to the piel of the root יחל in 1.12 ('hope or wait for something'). Wolff and Hillers both note the various Greek versions are in favour of reading this way (Wolff 1990: 44; Hillers 1984: 26). Hillers reads

Suddenly *he or she* is in some way sick for good (with the strange construction כי חלה לטוב). The verb could be read as either the 3ms of חלה, 'grow tired or ill', or the 3fs of חיל/חול, 'dance around', or 'writhe in pain'. If read as a 3ms verb, perhaps, since there is no indication that a new participant is being introduced, this continues the action of the one (perhaps Beth-ezel) that takes something (a standing place) from *you* (mpl) just previously in 1.11. In this case, it is uncertain whether Maroth (יושבת מרות) is the recipient of this strange comment (i.e. a vocative), or the (indirect) cause of his tiredness/illness; that is, יושבת מרות could be bound to לטוב ('for the good of the inhabitant of Maroth'). If on the other hand Maroth is the subject, it is not clear whether she is in pain, or merely dancing, nor how this fits with the rest of the passage. Further, the terse Hebrew phrase seems contradictory, juxtaposing 'writhe' or 'be sick' (חלה) with what seems its opposite, goodness (טוב). Finally, at the end of 1.12, all of this is somehow related to the evil that descends (ms) from Yahweh to the gate of Jerusalem (recalling the gate of *my people* of 1.9).

'surely they waited for sweetness, the dwellers in Maroth' (1984: 24) citing the MT as 'unintelligible' (1984: 26). Wolff translates as 'how good can be "hoped" for the inhabitants of Maroth', following the LXX for the initial interrogative, reading מי instead of כי, and arguing that מי can be read as 'an interjection, "how!"' He also suggests the alternate reading, 'who can hope for good, O inhabitant of Maroth' (1990: 44). Likewise Mays translates, 'Who can hope for good, community of Maroth?' (1976: 49). Shoemaker emends to כי יחלה, arguing that the 'prefixal י was lost due to haplography', translating 'for the inhabitant of Maroth hoped for good' (1992: 129 n. 104). Shaw translates, 'they hoped for' (1987: 224) and 'they waited anxiously' (1993: 35), for the latter see also Craigie (1985: 13); Waltke (1988: 155). McKane takes this one step further, and interprets the phrase with the REB as, 'they are in the depths of despair' (1998: 45).

Micah 1.13

Harness (harnessing) (to harness) a chariot to the steed (of) the (O) inhabitant of Lachish. This (she) is the beginning of sin for the Daughter of Zion. For in (with) you (fs) are found the transgressions of Israel.

Something—'this' or 'she' (היא), possibly the harnessing of the chariot in Lachish, or perhaps Lachish herself—is said to be the beginning of sin for the Daughter of Zion. The sins of Israel are said to be found in *you* (fs) (כי בך נמצאו פשעי ישראל). Although this *you* (fs) may be the Daughter of Zion just previously mentioned, there may be an allusion to Samaria in the address too. The northern

For a brief moment, v. 13 seems to indicate a return to the masculine singular address with a command to 'harness the chariot to the steed' (רתם המרכבה לרכש)—though רתם ('harness') could also be read as an infinitive construct. This seems a strange shift from the more prevalent use of feminine singular imperatives in 1.13-16. Hillers comments that the 'imperative masculine singular is out of place before a feminine subject and most have preferred infinitive absolute רתם used as an imperative' (1984: 26-27); so also Wolff (1990: 44); Allen (1976: 277). An exception to this seems to be Mays who reads 'you harness' on

city is not mentioned explicitly, but the phrase 'transgressions of Israel' (ישראל פשעי) echoes the 'transgression of Jacob' (פשע יעקב) of 1.5, which was said to be Samaria.

Micah 1.14
Therefore, you (fs) will give a dowry on account of (to) (concerning) Moresheth-gath: houses of Achzib, as (for) (to) a deception (deceptive one), to (for) the Kings of Israel.

Then *you* (still fs) give a dowry or a parting gift to, or concerning, Moresheth-gath (תתני שלוחים על מורשת גת). This seems an unusually masculine behaviour. However, the identity of the dowry-giver is not given, the closest antecedent being *you* (fs) in whom the sins of Israel are found (1.13). Though the nature of this dowry is not very clear, and may only relate to Moresheth-gath, it could also possibly relate to the second line of the verse which speaks of the houses of Achzib, deception and the Kings of Israel (בתי אכזיב לאכזב למלכי ישראל). There is the possibility that the second ל ('for/to') in this line might link it to the previous line, since the usual idiom is נתן ל ('give to'). Thus it would be possible to read the dowry as a sort of deceptive gift (the houses of Achzib) given to the kings of Israel.

'the assumption that the beginning of each line is damaged' (1976: 49); the assumption of textual damage affects all of Mays's discussion on 1.10-16.

Scholars have wondered what to do with the 2fs subject of this phrase in 1.14. Allen notes that the feminine singular 'is not expected in view of the metaphor' (1976: 277), implying that the giving of dowries is not a common feminine comportment in the Hebrew Bible. Wolff notes the problem of addressee and solves it by translating as a third person form, following the Vulgate: 'let one give' (1990: 45). Hillers finds the feminine to be acceptable, if the addressee were taken to be the Daughter of Zion, giving a dowry to the departing Moresheth-gath (1984: 27). Mays suggests that the phrase implies that the inhabitants of the city are leaving (1976: 59). Shaw suggests an address to Lachish, announcing her exile, and drawing on divorce imagery as found in Deut. 24.1-4 (1987: 225; 1993: 42-43). The word שלוחים occurs only here and in 1 Kgs 9.16 where it is used as a term for the gift of the Canaanite city Gezer that Pharaoh made to his daughter when she married Solomon; BDB suggests that here the term is used in the sense of saying farewell to, or losing, Moresheth-gath.

The preposition על ('on account of', 'concerning', 'to') has troubled scholars in a minor way since נתן על does not occur elsewhere. Most scholars have translated 'you give...to Moresheth-gath'; Mays seems to be the exception, emending on the basis of his assumption of a damaged text, 'To you they give parting gifts, Moresheth-gath' (1976: 49). The relation of the dowry imagery to the second half of the verse does not seem to be considered.

The introduction of the 'Kings of Israel' in 1.14b, with no antecedent, nor follow-up, has also provoked discussion. Of the more recent commentaries, only Mays emends to the singular (1976: 49), though Hillers suggests this is a favoured option, without listing examples (1984: 27-28). Most scholars translate בתי אכזיב לאכזב למלכי ישראל as a nominal sentence, along the lines of 'the houses of Achzib are deception to the kings of Israel' (Shaw 1987: 224; Wolff 1990: 41; Hillers 1984: 24; Allen 1976: 277; McKane 1998: 58; Mays 1976: 49; Vuilleumier 1971: 19). See Demsky for a reading of Achzib as the 'site of a royal industrial plant' (1966: 215).

Micah 1.15

Again, my father is the one taking possession of (dispossessing) you (fs), O inhabitant of Mareshah. He will bring the glory of Israel to Adullam. (Again, I will bring to you an heir, O inhabitant of Mareshah. The glory of Israel will come to Adullam.)

Nearing the end of the passage, there seem to be several new developments. First, there is a momentary shift to a more hopeful tone which speaks of an heir (1.15a) and the glory of Israel (ms) to come to Adullam (עד עדלם יבוא כבוד ישראל) (1.15b).

Secondly, 1.15a contains the rather sudden introduction of a first person voice, not heard since the lamenting of 1.8 (or possibly—if the *kethib* 'I roll' is read—in 1.10). The MT reads עד הירש אבי לך יושבת מרשה, a phrase that does not contain a verb, and includes the cryptic אבי ('my father'). As the *BHS* notes, a number of manuscripts give the hiphil verb אביא ('I will bring') for אבי, reading something like 'Again I will bring to you (fs) an heir'. Thus there is some question as to the role that this first person plays, whether it is itself a kind of rescuing hero figure, or whether it defers to another hero (my father).

Scholars are not agreed upon whether to read 1.15 as hopeful or not. For instance, Shaw considers that this might be an announcement that these cities may too be conquered 'and brought back into the kingdom' (1987: 226); similarly see Mays (1976: 59-60). Many point out that Adullam was the site of the cave in which David hid, but they are at odds as to whether this is a hopeful image (Allen 1976: 282), or an image of doom (Wolff 1990: 63; Vuilleumier 1971: 23), or simply a lament (Schwantes 1964: 460). See McKane (1998: 50-52), for the equally varied readings of the versions and earlier commentators.

Many scholars follow the suggestions of the manuscripts to read אבי ('my father') as אביא ('I will bring'); so Hillers (1984: 28); Shaw (1987: 224; 1993: 36); Craigie (1985: 13). Wolff argues that the context excludes a first person voice, and suggests instead that the letters of יבא ('he will come') were reversed in a scribal error to produce אבי (1990: 45); so also Allen (1976: 277). In a similar fashion, McKane follows Rudolph in reading יבוא ('he will come') (1998: 52).

Micah 1.16

*Make yourself bald and shear (fs)
because of the sons of your daintiness.
Make large your baldness like the eagle,
for they (mpl) leave (go into exile) from
you.*

The hopefulness of 1.15 is only brief though, since in 1.16, somewhat contra-dictorily, an unidentified 2fs subject is urged (with fs imperatives) to crop *your* hair ('make yourself bald') in mourning for *your* departed children. Again there is a question as to addressee. It is not clear which of the feminine participants in the passage is the antecedent for the feminine forms here.

Wolff notes that the same fs imperative קרח is used in Jer. 7.29 as a lament for the disobedience of Israel. Wolff also lists examples where the baldness 'accompanies the lamentation over the destruction of a city or country (Isa. 3.24; 15.2; Jer. 47.5; 48.37; Ezek. 7.18; 27.31)' (1990: 64). Luker reads this as funeral rites (1987: 285).

In sum, this chapter seems to be an indictment of Israel's feminine cities and towns. However, there is a good deal of fluidity in the gendering of these participants, with cross-overs between masculine and feminine forms. The image of the *nation* offered is therefore not perfectly clear, nor unambiguously gendered. Further, it is not always evident whether what is being demanded of the towns is sarcastic or serious because of the vacillations in the type of statements made: e.g. 'do not weep', followed by 'roll in the dust' (1.10); or 'you give...houses of Achzib, for deception to the kings of Israel', followed by 'the glory of Israel comes to Adullam' (1.14, 15). Finally, because the place names can for the most part either be read as vocatives or as third person subject or predicates, the question of addressee is ambiguous. This gives the curious effect of positioning the party addressed as both addressee and observer. All of these difficulties combined make it difficult for the reader to find, let alone identify with, one image that depicts an ideal, or even a repudiated, 'Israel'.

Micah 2

Chapter 2 continues in the vein of difficult Hebrew with shifts in types of address throughout. However, rather than focusing on the feminine cities, the text seems always to return to an indictment of masculine plural leaders, with a sudden shift to a more hopeful tone in the last two verses of the chapter. Throughout the chapter, there is a constant shift between 2mpl and 3mpl forms—address that persistently flows into description and back again. There is also a first person voice that punctuates throughout, and at least one, if not two, unidentified masculine singular figures: *he/you* (3ms and 2ms). The dominant image evoked for a collective entity is *my people*, which is ambiguously related to the other participants in the chapter, particularly the masculine plural evildoers and prophets. It may be that the masculine plural evildoers and prophets are differentiated in some way from *my people*, as those that oppress them; however, this is a distinction that does not always hold since *my people's* role as oppressed or oppressor also seems to shift.

Micah 2.1-2

¹Woe, O (to the) ones (mpl) scheming evil and ones doing evil upon their beds. In the light of the morning they will do it, for their hand is for a god. ²They will desire fields and they will seize...houses and they will take. They will oppress a man and his house, a man (each one) and his inheritance.

The chapter begins with a woe oracle, using the exclamation '*hôy*' (הוי) and vocatives to address the ones (mpl) scheming evil (חשבי און). But the text move away from direct address when these schemers are described first using participles with 3mpl pronominal suffixes (e.g. ופעלי רע על משכבותם, 'the ones doing evil upon *their* beds') and then using third person verb forms that carry on into 2.2 ('*they* will do it...they will desire fields and they will take'). This shift from woe oracle to third person description gives the impression that the address is being made indirectly, that the prophet is speaking to the doers of evil, but by means of telling someone else about them. As in Mic. 1, the addressee is both addressed, and put into the position of observer at the same time.

Hillers suggests that *hôy*-oracles are related to address (1983b). He argues that the second person element of woe oracles may be obscured for contemporary readers by the traditional use of third person pronouns with vocatives. In *hôy*-oracles, he argues, 'a vocative element comes right after the *hôy* and pronouns referring back to this are for a time in third person in keeping with ancient usage; explicitly second person forms reassert themselves later' (1983b: 186). Mic. 2.1-3 is listed as an example of this pattern (1983b: 187), particularly because the second person form reasserts itself in 2.3, in the oracle of Yahweh.

For a discussion of 'desiring and seizing' as a possible allusion to the tenth commandment ('thou shalt not covet...'), see Andersen and Freedman (2000: 270-71); Ben Zvi (2000: 44).

Micah 2.3

Therefore, thus says Yahweh: see, I am the one scheming evil against this clan—from there you (mpl) will not remove your necks, and you will not walk with head high, for it is a time of evil.

Wolff argues that the 'therefore thus says Yahweh' formula beginning 2.3 changes the voice and scene completely (1990: 78-79). Ben Zvi, on the other hand, argues that because 'therefore' requires an antecedent, and because the language is so similar to that of the previous voice

An oracle of Yahweh speaks to *you* (mpl) the evildoers directly, parodying the evil behaviour described earlier, 'See I am one *scheming evil*' (הנני חשב...רעה). Where the evil doers scheme upon their beds (על משכבותם), Yahweh schemes, with assonance, upon this clan (על המשפחה הזאת).

Micah 2.4a
In that day he will raise a parable against you (mpl), and he will wail a wail (a wail). It has happened, he says, we are utterly destroyed.

Verse 4 continues, perhaps in the 'prophet's voice' (that is, the person who says, 'thus says Yahweh'), or perhaps continuing Yahweh's speech, though the first person forms disappear. It is predicted that a saying or a taunt (משל) will be raised against *you* (still mpl). The saying is then given, and seems to contain an emphasized lament (with 'wail' used two or possibly three times). The lament/taunt is of destruction, made by *he* about *we*. The use of the 1cpl draws the reader into this scenario of destruction.

Micah 2.4b
He exchanges a portion of my people (My people exchanges a portion). Surely he (my people) will remove to return to me our fields [that] he will divide. (Surely he will remove to return to me. He will divide our fields.)

The *we* figure seems to continue in the rest of 2.4, with the description of division and exchange of *our* fields or allotment. In this way, the addressee, already addressed as the threatened *you* (mpl), is also positioned to lament *our* destruction.

The lament/taunt also speaks of *my people*. It is not evident whether this 1cs voice is Yahweh's (of 2.3) or if it belongs to a member of *us*. Because the

of 2.1-2, divine and human voice blend together here (2000: 45).

The word נהיה ('it has happened') in 2.4a might also be read as a noun meaning, wail; but this would find two nouns meaning 'wail' in a row, following a verb meaning 'wail' (ונהה נהי נהיה). For an extended discussion of the wordplay of this taunt, see Petrotta (1991: 98-102), who argues that the taunt is a tight unit of 'sound and sense...point and counter-point' that contrasts the evildoers with Yahweh (1991: 102). Conversely, Wolff reads it as a textual error reclaimed by a redactor: 'an incorrect dittography... which was then understood by the redactor as a confirmation of the loss of the land that had taken place in the meantime' (1990: 69-70).

The translations scholars give for 2.4 are rarely the same.

Scholars deliberate over the switch from the 1cpl into the 1cs and back again. Ben Zvi notes that the text lacks determinacy here, perhaps blurring between human and divine speech (2000: 46-47). Wolff calls the phrases using the 1cs an interpolation which comments on the original bicola in the first person plural (1990: 70).

It is difficult to give a translation of חלק עמי ימיר איך ימיש לי לשובב שדינו יחלק that is not awkward, since the syntactical relations within the line are not straight-forward. Wolff reads חלק עמי ימיר as a kind of oppression, following the LXX: 'the land of my people will be

taunt is embedded in the speech of the earlier first person voice, with no clear break, in some ways, there seems to be a convergence of first person forms (*we* with *I*).

As well, another uncertain masculine singular subject appears here, perhaps performing an exchange, all in terms that are not very clear and that render ambiguous the role of *my people*. It is not evident whether *my people* is the subject of the verbs 'exchange' (hiphil מור), and 'remove' (hiphil מוש) and is therefore the one dividing fields, or whether *my people* is the object of the verbs, in construct with חלק, 'portion of my people' (and therefore acted upon). If the latter, some other masculine singular subject (*he*) would have to be acting as subject to divide *our fields*. Moreover, whether this kind of division and return is oppressive or restorative is also unclear, though it may still be part of the taunting parable (and therefore presumably oppressive). The ambiguous structure of the verse seems to have the effect of conflating *my people* with the possibly oppressive *he*. I might render this as follows, 'He [my people?] exchanges a portion [of my people?]. Surely he [my people?] will remove to return to me, he will divide our fields'.

Because it is difficult to tell who is doing what to whom in this verse, is also hard to know who the oppressed party is. Further, it is not obvious exactly where this saying ends, whether at the end of 2.4, or whether with the commentary in 2.5.

measured' (1990: 68, 70), reading 'my people' in the position of object; this seems in accordance with his overall way of thinking about 'my people' as oppressed and passive in the book. The phrase 'surely he will remove to return to me' (איך ימיש לי לשובב) is difficult in part because the hiphil of מוש, 'remove', normally takes an object (see Mic. 2.3; Zech. 3.9) which it seems to lack here (remove what?).

In addition, the *idea* of return (לשובב) is also odd and suggests perhaps some kind of change in fortunes. A number of scholars emend in order to make sense of it, reading, 'there is none to return it to me' (Mays 1976: 60; see McKane 1998: 71 for others who have suggested this). It might be possible here to apply Tucker's argument for a prophetic notion of punishment as the 'return' of wrong upon the wrongdoers in his article 'Sin and 'Judgment' in the Prophets' (1997).

Micah 2.5

Therefore, there will not be for you (ms) one casting a measuring line (portion) by lot in the assembly of Yahweh.

Verse 5 is addressed to *you* (suddenly ms), stating that as punishment (indicated by the introductory 'therefore',

In order to deal with the strange shift to the 2ms in 2.5, Hillers (1984: 32), Allen (1976: 285), McKane (1998: 72), Mays (1976: 61), and even Shaw (1993: 5) read 'to you (ms)' (לך) in 2.5 as the 2mpl, לכם, suggesting that the ם was lost by haplography. Wolff (1990: 70) does

לכן), there will be nobody to perform certain duties for *you* within the assembly of Yahweh. Exactly what these duties are is left somewhat up to the imagination, due to lexical ambiguities; however here again there seems to be some concern over allotted property. In short, the punishment seems to be that there will be no one to perform the service of dividing fields and land allotments. This sudden negative assessment makes one wonder if the previous line represents wistful thinking (he will return to me, he will divide) though it is uncertain how this would fit into the taunt.

It is hard to conjure up any image of 'nation' or 'people' on the basis of these verses, given the difficulties in discerning speakers and addressees (where speeches start and end etc.) and referents.

The relation between addressor and addressee becomes even more complex in 2.6-11. Because of the shifts in addressor and addressee, many scholars have concluded that Mic. 2.6-11 is a dispute between Micah and his opponents, whether these be false prophets or landowners. Certainly prophets other than Micah seem to be given voice here, though just where their speech starts and stops is somewhat vague.

not emend but reads 2.5 as a later addition.

The meaning of the phrase משליך חבל בגורל (literally: 'one throwing a portion by lot') is not immediately obvious. Usually when there is a preposition preceding 'lot', as there is here (בגורל), some other verb is used, like נחל ('inherit by lot') (e.g. Num. 33.54; 34.13; Josh. 19.51); or נתן ('give by lot') (e.g. Num. 36.2); even the verb חלק ('divide by lot') (e.g. Num. 26.55). For this reason most scholars have taken the sense of חבל as 'measuring line' rather than 'portion'; see Allen (1976: 285); Wolff (1990: 68); Mays (1976: 61); Shaw (1993: 69); Hillers (1984: 31); McKane (1998: 74). Some have read 'land allotment' instead of 'by lot': 'throw the measuring line over the land allotment'; so Wolff (1990: 68); Hillers (1984: 31); McKane (1998: 74).

For variations on the dispute theory, see Allen (1976: 294); Craigie (1985: 21-23); Mays (1976: 68-69); Neiderhiser (1981); Shaw (1993: 72); R.L. Smith (1984: 26); van der Woude (1969: 247-48); Waltke (1988: 159); Wolff (1990: 73). Scholars have also concluded that the text is corrupt (Allen 1976: 292-93; Hillers 1984: 34; Mays 1976: 68; Wolff 1990: 71). For instance, Mays says, 'the MT of these verses is in poor condition. It cannot be understood without emendations and reconstructions. Part of the difficulty in the transmission of these verses seems to stem from a confusion about the speaker' (Mays 1976: 68). Here, paradoxically, the difficulties which are *found in the text* (confusion between speaker/addressee) are also taken to be the *cause* of the problem (difficulty in transmission). Conversely, Ben Zvi finds the difficulties in the text to be indicative of its highly literate nature, i.e., originally written, designed to be read and re-read (2000: 58).

Micah 2.6

Do not prophesy (2mpl) (what) they (mpl) will prophesy, they will not prophesy to these. He will not be turned away, reproaches.

Micah 2.6-11 begins with what might be considered the words of a reported speech: *you* (mpl) are addressed by *them* (mpl), who are, apparently, some other prophets. ' "Do not prophesy (2mpl)", they will prophesy' (אל תטפו יטיפון). Alternatively, this could be read as a direct address and admonition: 'Do not prophesy [what] they will prophesy' (with an assumed relative pronoun). Two strange phrases follow introducing two new participants: 'they will not prophesy to *these*', and then the cryptic לא יסג כלמות, literally, '*he* will not be turned away, reproaches'. Are *these* the people, to whom the (antagonist) prophets speak? Is *he* the (protagonist) prophet? Any way it is read, the participants in this verse are many: a speaker (or narrator, depending on whether this is considered direct or reported speech) *you* (mpl), *they* (mpl), *he*, and possibly *these*.

As has been pointed out (e.g., Wolff 1990: 81), there is a derogatory *double entendre* at work in 2.6, since the primary sense of the verb נטף ('prophecy') is 'drip' or 'drivel'.

Wolff suggests that this is a demand for Micah's silence (in spite of the fact that the imperative is plural), and that the second half of the line, 'they will not prophesy to these' (לא יטפו לאלה), should be included as part of this prohibition, though he has to translate the 3mpl verb as 3ms to arrive at this reading: 'one should not preach about these things' (1990: 68; so also van der Woude 1969: 247).

The MT points the verb סוג ('turn away') as the passive niphal, 'be turned away', which seems to exclude כלמות ('reproaches') from the syntax of the phrase. Hillers (1984: 34) and Wolff (1990: 70) read the verb as hiphil of נשג, with the sense that the reproaches do not hit their target; McKane points out that this reading was also suggested by Rashi (1998: 75). Shoemaker makes the simpler suggestion of repointing to the hiphil, reading, 'He will not turn away reproaches' (1992: 141). This is one of the few places in the book where the syntax seems to me to be impassable, as opposed to ambiguous or difficult.

Micah 2.7

It is said, O house of Jacob, Is the spirit of Yahweh impatient? Are these his practices? Will not my words do good? (O) one walking with the upright one. (He is walking with the upright one.)

In 2.7, comes another saying regarding the house of Jacob; however, it is uncertain whether it is said to, about, or in, the house of Jacob, due to the lack of the preposition in the construction האמור בית יעקב. The most obvious reading is of a vocative, 'Is it said, O house of Jacob?'). What follows—presumably what is said—is a series of questions, 'Is

Because Mic. 2.7 is the only time in the MT that the past participle is used of אמר ('it is said'), many scholars have found that this phrase is 'not intelligible' (Wolff 1990: 70), and so have emended to ארור ('cursed'), or to the hiphil האמיר, a *binyan* that is rare for אמר. For the various possibilities suggested, see Hillers (1984: 61). By way of contrast, Ehrman suggests that אמר can mean 'curse' without requiring emendation, citing Job 3.3 (1970: 87). Neiderhiser also suggests that it can be understood without emendation as marking the beginning of a proverbial saying (1981: 105).

the spirit of Yahweh impatient? Are these his works?' Then suddenly, in a first person voice (2.7c), 'Do not *my words* do good?' It is not clear to whom the *my* refers, whether to the prophet, to Yahweh or to one of Micah's opponents. Words with the power to do good are often attributed to Yahweh; however, Yahweh is referred to in the questions just previous. The first person forms here (continued in 2.8) either signify that a change in voice has taken place midstream in the saying, or that this last question is not part of the saying about the house of Jacob.

The verse ends suddenly with an odd phrase describing one walking with the upright, but it is not clear who this is, or how it relates to the preceding questions, to *me*, or to Yahweh.

Micah 2.8a
Recently my people will be raised up as an enemy (recently he will raise up my people as an enemy).

The first person voice continues in 2.8-11, where again the relation of *my people* to oppression and to other participants is unclear. It is not clear if the first person voice is the same as in 2.7c (of 'my words'). Given the ambiguity there as to whether the speaker is Yahweh, the prophet, or an opponent, it is not obvious whose voice is heard here in 2.8. Whatever the case may be, *my people* is described as rising up like an enemy, as if it were itself the problem. The passage proceeds with some interruptions, speaking descriptively about *my people* as both oppressed and oppressor.

A number of scholars deal with the sudden first person voice by emending 'my words' to 'his words' (דבריו) (Allen 1976: 292; Hillers 1984: 35; Mays 1976: 66). Wolff reads the first person voice as a transition from the quoted speech to the prophetic voice (1990: 70). Because he makes this move, he also has to make sure that the sense of the verse is fitting for divine speech, so he translates the definite article as a relative pronoun in עם הישר הולך: 'Is it not so that my words mean well for him who lives uprightly' (1990: 68). In fact, this phrase is difficult because the adjective and the participle do not agree in definiteness, and so would not normally be read as one walking uprightly. If it were not for the troubling עם ('with'), הישר ('the upright one') could be read as the subject for the participle הולך ('the righteous one is walking'). For this reason, many read as Wolff does, as if the definite article were a relative pronoun; see McKane (1998: 86); Shaw (1993: 69); Craigie (1985: 21). Hillers reads 'with him' (1984: 34).

If 2.8a is left as is, an interesting discrepancy in tense appears, with the combination of the past time marker, ואתמול, ('and yesterday') and the prefix (future) tense, יקומם ('will raise up', polel of קום which KB notes can be either transitive or intransitive: raise or be raised). Many scholars emend the first word 'yesterday' (ואתמול) to 'but you (mpl)' (ואתם); see Hillers (1984: 35) for the ways with which the final two consonants are dealt with. Having done away with the ambiguity of tenses—by inserting a clear marker of address here, instead of the past time marker, and by reading the verb as a qal participle—and having removed the first person voice from the previous verse (emending 'my words' to 'his words'), most scholars confidently proclaim this as Micah's response to his opponents: 'But you are rising against my people' (Mays 1976:

67, 71; Craigie 1985: 21, 23; Wolff 1990: 70, 82; Allen 1976: 292-93, 296; McKane 1998: 86). Conversely, Lescow reads as an impersonal 'one is raised': 'Gegen mein Volk als Feind tritt man auf' (1997: 57).

Williamson notes that reading the text as is would (problematically) posit 'my people' as the source of oppression. He appeals to the next verse (2.9), saying that there 'my people' are seen as the object of oppression (1997: 361); he does not make the distinction that there it is 'the women of my people' who are oppressed.

Micah 2.8b-9

You (mpl) will strip off glory from the front of a mantle, from (more than) ones passing securely, ones returning from battle. ⁹You (mpl) will drive the women of my people from the house of her delight. You (mpl) will take my adornment (splendour) away from her children forever.

The address shifts back to *you* (mpl), who were last addressed in the (reported?) prophesy of 2.6 ('do not prophesy', 2mpl). *You* are now accused of stripping off glory, and in 2.9, of driving the women of my people from the house of *her* delights, of taking *my* splendour away from *her* children. The change in number (from the plural 'women' to the singular 'her') seems to indicate that the 3fs suffix represents a different entity than the plural 'women of my people', and perhaps refers back to one of the feminine cities. Nonetheless, both *she* and *her* children seem to be oppressed by *you* (mpl).

R.L. Smith (1984: 27), Craigie (1985: 23), Dearman (1984: 389) and Hillers (1984: 36-37) consider 2.8-9 to address wealthy landowners who were accumulating land; Wolff considers it to be about Judean occupational forces (1990: 83).

Hillers reads the shift from the feminine plural to the feminine singular as a reference to both the individual women of Israel and the nation personified as a woman (1984: 35); likewise, Andersen and Freedman (2000: 295). Others read the feminine singular suffixes as plural ('their delights', 'their children'), without necessarily emending; see Allen (1976: 293); Craigie (1985: 21); Mays (1976: 67). Wolff notes that Qumran, Syriac and Vulgate translate as plural (1990: 71).

Micah 2.10

Arise and walk (mpl), for this is not a resting place, because she is unclean (because of uncleanness), she (you, ms) will ruin, and destruction will be terrible.

The Hebrew in 2.10 has given rise to a number of differing readings. Hillers reads this verse as the speech of those chasing the women of my people out of their homes, though he does admit that the masculine plural imperatives pose a

Suddenly in 2.10, *you* (still mpl) are told to get up and go, because this is not a resting place. The phrase that follows—בעבור טמאה ('because of uncleanness' or 'because she is unclean') —acts as something of a hinge between the first part of the verse and the second, standing in the middle with no syntactic connectors to either the first or the last phrase (though it does come after the atnah, which marks the division of the line in the Masoretic tradition at least). Syntactically though, 'because she is unclean' could either be the reason that 'this is not a resting place', and so the cause for your (mpl) departure; or it could be the justification for the threat of ruin and destruction that follows; or poetically, speaking, it could be both.

Interestingly, the verb form in the last phrase, תחבל, could be read as '*you* (ms) will ruin' or 'she will ruin'. The former would introduce a new masculine singular participant here; the latter would be a strange reversal from the previous verse in which *you* (mpl) seem to be ruining *her* (driving her away from her home).

problem (1984: 36). Conversely, Allen reads it as an *address to* those very same ones chasing out the women (1976: 293). Wolff suggests that this is an address to the women and children themselves (1990: 84).

The word טמאה in 2.10 (either a noun, 'uncleaness', or a verb, 'she is unclean') has caused a some debate; see Hillers (1984: 36). In the MT, it only appears as a noun here, and may have been considered as such because it lacks the metheg that normally marks the *qames* in the first syllable of the feminine singular verb form; however in two other of the five times the feminine form of the verb is used in the MT, it appears without a metheg (Lev. 12.5; 22.6). Evan-Shoshan lists its appearance here as a verb. Wolff suggests it is a misreading for 'trifle', in the sense of placing financial burdens on people for a trifle (1990: 84).

The rest of the verse does not help clarify who or what is being described, since the piel verb תחבל 'ruin' seems to be missing an object, and could be read as either a 2ms, or a 3fs; the *BHS* suggests reading a masculine plural pual 'you will be ruined'. Several take the meaning of the qal for a different root of the same consonants: 'impound' or 'seize a pledge'; so Mays (1976: 72); Wolff (1990: 68). Hillers reads 'you do damage', but doesn't say why (1984: 36).

Micah 2.11
Would that (if) each one is walking (in) spirit (windily and deceptively) (he lies). And deceptively he lies (he lies deception), I will prophesy to you (ms) for wine and intoxicating drink. And this people will be one prophesying.

Returning in 2.11 to the theme of prophesy of 2.6, an equivocal statement is made that could either express a wish ('would that each is walking in spirit'),

Again the Hebrew is difficult in 2.11. Some read 'spirit' (רוח) as adverbial— 'walking windily' (Wolff 1990: 72)— though this means minimizing לו to 'if'. The adverbial construction seems also to be read as 'walking in spirit' (Andersen and Freedman 2000: 295; Shaw 1993: 77). What is unclear here is whether ושקר ('and deception') is part of the phrase רוח ושקר ('spirit/wind and deception'), therefore perhaps 'walking

or a doubt ('if each is walking windily and deceptively'). This is followed by a short, flat statement about a new masculine singular participant (or perhaps the masculine singular participant of the end of 2.6): 'he lies'. Then in 2.11b, suddenly a first person voice speaks, perhaps the words of the lie, saying that *I* will prophesy to *you* (ms) for wine. This declaration is perhaps clarified at the end of the verse as *this people's* prophecy ('this people will be one prophesying'), though it is not clear, if this statement continues the first person speech (I will prophesy to you for wine) or if it situates it. If the latter, it might indicate the speech as the voice of *this people.* Here again the roles of the participants are ambiguous. Are *you* (ms) the same 'ruining' *you* (or *she*) in 2.10b? Are there one or two speakers in this verse, and if two, is the main speaker (who quotes the other) different than the one speaking throughout the rest of the passage about my people, my splendour, and my words?

To sum up 2.8-11, not only is *my people's* activity in relation to oppression unclear but also there is some confusion between *I*, *my people*, *you* (mpl and ms), *her* and the inauthentic prophets. Because of the unmarked changes in subject and pronouns, crossovers seem to appear between the various participants.

windily and deceptively' (Hillers 1984: 36; Allen 1976: 293), or part of the phrase ושקר כזב ('and he lies deception').

Translations almost uniformly read והיה מטיף העם הזה as, 'He would be a prophet *for* this people', which assumes the preposition ל ('for') instead of the definite article on העם ('the people'). As far as I can see, no one but the *BHS* editors comment on this insertion, though it does change the position of העם הזה ('this people') from subject to object. Stansell distinguishes between 'this people' as the oppressors, and 'my people' as the oppressed (1988: 119). In fact, Stansell argues that the term 'my people' is used in Micah to refer to the oppressed 'true people of Yahweh, those who dwell in the towns and land of Judah', where the leaders 'are closely identified with Jerusalem and its destruction' (1988: 118).

Micah 2.12-13

[12]*I will certainly gather Jacob, all of you (fs). I will certainly gather the remnant of Israel. Together I will put him like a flock (feminine noun, צֹאן) of Bozrah. Like a flock (masculine noun, עֵדֶר) in the midst of his pasture, they (fpl) will make a chaotic noise more than a man.* [13]*The one (ms) breaking goes up before them, and they break. And they passed the gate and went out*

There are two general stances toward categorizing 2.12-13: one that they describe punishment, and the other that they are an affirmation of hope. McKane notes that these two divergent understandings of this passage are longstanding, citing medieval Jewish commentaries (Kimchi seems to understand it as a description of siege, while Rashi seems to see it as a hope for a return from exile) (1995b: 84).

with him, their king passed before them, and Yahweh at their head.

The final two verses of the chapter present what seems to be an abrupt change of pace. There are also a number of strange shifts in gender and tense in these two verses.

Beyond presenting a different vision for the future than seen previously in the book, these verses represent a turn to slightly more customary terms for the 'national' entity ('Jacob', 'the remnant of Israel'). However, there is some blurring of gender. In 2.12, a first person voice—perhaps Yahweh's, or perhaps still this people's prophecy of 2.11—speaks as a shepherd, '*I* will gather Jacob, all of *you* (fs)' (אסף אאסף יעקב כלך). The shift to the feminine singular pronominal suffix is rather surprising here, since Jacob is normally gendered as masculine. The gender ambiguity continues as it is announced that this first person figure will gather the remnant of Israel, making *him* like a flock. Here the text repeats 'flock' twice, using both the feminine noun צאן and the masculine noun עדר, and describing its noise with a 3fpl verb (תהימנה).

Then shifting again in 2.13, both into a third person description, and into the past tense, Yahweh the king went up and broke out before *them* (suddenly 3mpl).

On the more pessimistic side in recent commentary, Mays argues that this is not a disjuncture in the text, but rather an announcement of punishment: first Yahweh gathers his people into Jerusalem in the siege, and then leads them out in exile 'the siege and fall of the city is the work of YHWH ...the exile is a manifestation of his sovereignty and not his defeat' (1976: 76); Hagstrom agrees with Mays (1988: 53-57). Brin too argues for these verses as 'a description of judgment and punishment of Israel' (1989: 121). Van der Woude argues that these are the words of the pseudo-prophets (1969: 256). Mosala considers this a reflection of dominant imperialist ideology (1989: 127-34), the words of a formerly powerful class who have been hurt by the exile (1989: 134).

On the more positive side, Allen (1976: 301), Waltke (1988: 161) and Craigie (1985: 24) consider it to be a message of hope during the siege of Sennacherib. Wolff considers it an addition from the early Persian period, a message of hope to the diaspora (1990: 76). Shaw considers these words to the oppressed (1993: 90). Hillers considers the passage visionary, and also possibly reflective of the thoughts of the original prophet (1984: 40). Ben Zvi considers it to be an announcement of salvation which the text's readers would always imagine to be unfulfilled (2000: 68). Shoemaker considers it an 'oracle with both positive and negative aspects', that Yahweh will lead the people, but in a haphazard and tension-filled fashion (1992: 146-47).

Shoemaker argues that the gender ambiguity of 2.12-13 is because the passage moves from the collective you, to the third person, in what he calls the 'exclusive you' linguistic set; this discursive device, he argues, allows a 'multi-generational character' to be addressed: the current audience, the future collective audience, and within this, the city and town units that would be uprooted by Assyria and settled elsewhere (1992: 273-74).

Hillers follows the LXX in amending the 2fs suffix of כלך to a 3ms suffix כלו (1984: 38). Wolff (1990: 68, 72) and McKane (1998: 89) both comment on the versions but translate it as 'you', without commenting on gender. Mays notices that the second person is 'curious' (1976: 73) but does not comment on gender; likewise, a number of other commentators simply translate as 'you' without comment on gender (Waltke 1988; Allen 1976; R.L. Smith 1984; Stuhmueller 1986; Shaw 1993; Craigie 1985; McKane 1998; Wagenaar 2000). All apparently read it as a masculine singular pausal form, though it is not 'standard' for a rᵉbiaʿ to mark pause. However, there is some difficulty in checking this form, since the 2ms suffix on כל, כלך, is not attested. In Isa. 14.29-31 כלך is attested twice (both with regular accentuation and in pause) alongside predominantly 2fs forms in reference to the Philistines (a feminine noun); although interestingly a 3ms verb is also used in Isa. 14.31, נמוג פלשת כלך (usually read as an imperative, 'O Philistines despair, all of you'). Perhaps a shift in gender between name and address is not that unusual; see also Mic. 4.8.

The verb 'make noise' (הום) only occurs in the hiphil here and in Ps. 55.13; it most often occurs as niphal, with the sense of making a loud noise, or being riled up (KB translates 'go wild'), see 1 Sam. 4.5; 1 Kgs 1.45; Ruth 1.19. It is not a tranquil image.

Oddly, the verb forms shift from prefix (future) in 2.12, to suffix (perfective), to waw consecutive (past) in 2.13. Some read 2.13 as the prophetic perfect, so continuing the future tense

(Allen 1976: 300; McKane 1998: 94). Shaw reads it as 'the announcement of a successful military campaign' (1993: 85). Wagenaar reads it as a later addition (2000: 537-39). Wolff reads it as simply a different hand (1990: 85).

To sum up Micah 2, it seems clear that the masculine plural addressees are the object of some derision and some condemnation throughout. However, a number of questions remain. It is not clear how *they* (mpl), the evildoers and prophets, relate to *my people*. It seems that from time to time *my people* is vaguely related to *Jacob* (e.g. the saying to or about Jacob in 2.7-8), and to Yahweh (e.g. the assembly of Yahweh in 2.5); but it is not clear whether the shifts between 2ms and 2mpl addressees play any role in connecting the evildoers, the prophets and the people. Up to this point in the text, the references to *my people* have been sufficiently vague that it is not easy to tell. (To briefly recall the instances of *my people* (עמי) to this point: in 1.9, something unfavourable touches the gate of *my people*, presumably as a form of judgment for the sins of Jerusalem and Samaria described in 1.5-7, thereby equating the people with the sinful cities; in 2.4 it is not clear if *my people* is the subject or object of oppression; in 2.8 *my people* rise up like an enemy; in 2.9 the *women of my people* are driven out by *you* [mpl], acted upon, perhaps by leaders, or perhaps by some other colonizing force; and in 2.11 *this people* is prophesying in ways that may not be favourable.) Commentators seem to take the line that the people are oppressed, and the leaders or wealthy landowners are the oppressors, but this may be more a matter of readerly identification with *my people* than of textual clarity.

There is also some question about the significance of the shifts in gender of the participants in ch. 2. Both *my people* (2.9-10) and *Jacob* (2.12) are sometimes gendered as, or strongly associated with, the feminine. There is also some slippage between the uncertain masculine figures in 2.10 and *her uncleanness* which is said to create the demand for *you* (mpl) to depart, or possibly to be the reason for *your* (ms) ruin. In brief, though each has its own jurisdiction in the chapter, there also seems to be some blurring of boundaries between the evildoers, the prophets, the people, and what seems to be a feminine metaphor of the collective.

Micah 3

The Hebrew of Micah 3 becomes somewhat more straightforward, continuing the critique of *you* (mpl), here more clearly defined as leaders abusing *my people*. The leaders are accused of 'eating' the people (3.2-3), of dishonesty and false words (3.5, 11), and of twisting justice (3.9). Yet even here there is some blurring between the leaders and *my people* at points. In the middle of the chapter, as an interlude between two parallel attacks on the leaders (starting in 3.1 and 3.9), there seems to be a bid for prophetic authority: while prophets and diviners are threatened with failure and shame (3.6-7), *I* am filled with Yahweh's spirit (3.8). At the end of the chapter, the feminine Jerusalem takes the fall for the bad behaviour of her leaders (3.12).

Micah 3.1
And I said, Listen, O heads of Jacob and leaders of the house of Israel. Is it not for you (mpl) to know justice?

The chapter begins in the first person voice, 'And I said', addressing the (mpl) leaders of a nation. The *I* here is not identified; perhaps it is Yahweh's voice carried on from the previous chapter, where *I* gathers the flock (2.12), or perhaps it is the voice of the prophet.

For overviews of the various suggestions as to the import of the first person voice in 3.1 (whether as indicator of editorial connection or break with ch. 2, or as indicator of the continued debate between the false prophets), see Hillers (1984: 41) and Shaw (1993: 97). Andersen and Freedman consider it autobiographical (2000: 347).

Micah 3.2-3
[2](O) haters of good (mpl ptc) and lovers of evil, (O) ones tearing their (mpl) skin from upon them, and their flesh from upon their bones. [3]And who eat (3mpl) the flesh of my people, and they strip their flesh from upon them, and smash their bones. They spread out because in the pot, and like flesh in the midst of the cauldron.

The text then moves gradually from address into descriptive mode in v. 2, continuing the rhetorical technique—noted throughout, especially in 2.1-2—of positioning the addressee as both addressee and observer. Here, as in 2.1-2, the transition begins with masculine plural participles that retain a sense of address, even functioning as vocatives (O haters of good and lovers of evil). These participles give a caricature of men who act upon other men violently ('ones tearing *their* skin from upon *them*'). Verse 3 completes the shift from

The fact that there is no stated antecedent for the 3mpl pronominal suffixes in 3.2b—*their* flesh, *their* bones etc.—(עצמותם, ושארם) provokes many hypotheses. Some make this detail the basis for suggestions on the redactional process: Wolff suggests that the ואמר ('and I said') is a redactional connection that deliberately relates ch. 3 to ch. 2, so that the 3mpl suffixes are read as referring back to the oppressed people of 2.2, 8-9 (1990: 91); he points to Willi-Plein who suggests that 3.2b is a later addition to the text, since v. 2a and v. 3a seem to follow (1971: 81). Mays suggests that 3.2b should come after 3.3a where עמי ('my people') would serve as the antecedent for all of the 3mpl suffixes (1976: 79-80).

In order to maintain the same 3mpl subject throughout 3.3, scholars insert a 3mpl object for the verb 'spread' (פרש) without comment; they also change the sense of the verb to 'chop', reading

address into description, using 3mpl verbs that depict similar behaviours, 'they eat the skin of *my people*, they strip *their* flesh from *them*' (אכלו שאר עמי ועורם מעליהם הפשיטו). The 3mpl subject of the cannibalism being indicted seems to be the leaders, whereas, oddly the 3mpl object (of the pronominal suffixes) seems to be the normally singular *my people*.

At the end of v. 3, there seems to be a reversal or conflation in fortunes between the 3mpl subject and the 3mpl object of this violent culinary activity. *They* (the subject of the verbs), hitherto actively violent, are now 'spread out…in the pot'. This raises a question as to whether the subject has changed (that is, the hitherto 3mpl object becomes the subject of the verb 'spread'), or whether the violent leaders are suddenly themselves cooked too. While it is not syntactically problematic for the 3mpl object to become the subject of a verb, it is an unanticipated, unmarked shift which seems to have the poetic effect of conflating the oppressed with the oppressor.

Micah 3.4
Then they (3mpl) will cry to Yahweh and he will not answer them. Let him hide his face from them in that time, because their deeds do evil.

The ambiguity of the final line of 3.3 continues on in 3.4. Here it is unclear if *they* are the masculine plural *my people* of 3.3, or the leaders of Israel. Following from the last verse, it seems that both the leaders and the people might be in a state to cry out to Yahweh. The text qualifies the first statement with a second: *their* (3mpl pronominal suffix) works cause evil (הרעו מעלליהם), but—due to the use of the 3mpl pronoun to describe the people in 3.3— this does not necessarily clarify who is being described (the people or the

'they chop them' (though this sense for פרש is not attested elsewhere—some read פרס); and they read 'because' (כאשר) as a scribal misreading of 'like flesh' (כשאר) (as is also read in the LXX, as Hillers notes [1984: 42]); see Wolff (1990: 90-91); McKane (1998: 103); Hillers (1984: 41); Allen (1976: 304); Andersen and Freedman (2000: 374).

leaders). This ambiguity focuses the question raised in ch. 2 of whether *my people* in the text is vilified in any way, or whether it is just the leaders of Jacob and Israel that are indicted.

Micah 3.5

Thus says Yahweh concerning (against) the prophets, the (O) ones leading my people astray, the (O) ones biting with their teeth, but calling 'Peace', which he will not put upon their mouths. And they will proclaim a holy war against him.

In 3.5, there seems to be a clearer identification of the masculine plural *they* with the prophets/leaders, and there may also be some identification formed between Yahweh and the people. The verse states that Yahweh is to speak against leaders who act upon *my people*. At first glance this seems to assign the possessive 'my' to Yahweh; however, it is difficult to say whether Yahweh actually speaks until the next verse, because the text continues on for the rest of the verse with the description of these deceitful and hypocritical leaders against whom Yahweh speaks. But the text moves—as at the beginning of the chapter—from participle forms into third person verb forms: 'the/O ones biting with their teeth (mpl ptc). *They* are calling (3mpl verb), "Peace!"' This gives the sense of an address, as in 3.1-2, though here it seems more clearly to be a description. Once again the reader is equivocally situated as addressee and as observer.

The ambiguity as to where Yahweh's speech actually starts is also bound up with the question of to whom *he/him* refers: Peace is something which '*he* will not put upon their mouths and they will proclaim holy war against *him*' (וקראו). If (שׁלום ואשׁר לא יתן על פיהם וקדשׁו עליו מלחמה). Yahweh has not yet spoken, perhaps Yahweh is the 3ms referent; if this is all

Hillers solves the problem of determining where Yahweh's speech starts in 3.5 by emending יהוה על ('Yahweh concerning…') in 3.5, to הוי על ('Woe to you prophets'), 'supposing a haplography' (1984: 44); Wolff reads it as Yahweh's reported speech (1990: 90).

Commentators tend to avoid the problem of the referent for the masculine singular subject and object here ('*he* will not put…they proclaim a holy war against *him*'), by reading it as an impersonal 'someone' who deprives the prophets of their (culinary) desires, and so they make war on him (see Wolff 1990: 90, 102; Hillers 1984: 44; Craigie 1985: 25; Mays 1976: 80; Allen 1976: 310; Shaw 1993: 98; Shoemaker 1992: 156). Judging from the fact that many read in this way, which is not the most obvious reading, it may be that commentators are taking their lead from the Targum, which reads, 'Whoever gives them a banquet of meat they prophecy peace for him; but whoever does not offer them something to eat, they prepare war against him' (cited in Shaw 1993: 98). Along these lines, Wolff argues for reading 'mouth' (פה) as 'command' or 'wish' (1990: 102). To my mind, it seems less a statement about greed, and more like an accusation of hypocrisy and false prophecy. 'Peace' in 3.5 is prophesied by those who 'bite with their teeth'; peace is not put into their mouths by Yahweh, in fact they are so hypocritical that they make holy war on him (Yahweh, or perhaps his people). Along these lines, it may be possible that there is idiomatic play between, 'he will not put upon their mouths' (לא יתן על פיהם) and the opposite part of Yahweh's speech, perhaps *my people* is the referent. Or perhaps, the ambiguity here forms an identification between Yahweh and 'my people'.

Micah 3.6-7

⁶*Therefore night is for you (mpl) without vision, and darkness for you without divination. And the sun comes upon the prophets and the day is dark upon them.* ⁷*And the seers will be ashamed and the diviners will be ashamed, all of them will cover over the lip (mourn), for no one is one answered by God.*

Verse 6 starts with what is more clearly Yahweh's speech, using the typical announcement of judgment, 'therefore' (לכן) addressed to *you* (mpl): 'therefore night will be for *you* without vision, and darkness without divination'. Verses 6b-7, however, return to 3mpl forms, describing the lack of visions and inspiration, as well as subsequent shame to be brought upon these prophets.

This section of text (3.5-7) ends in a fashion similar to the last section (3.1-4), with the assertion of God's unwillingness to answer (using Elohim this time instead of Yahweh). Thus these two statements (3.4a and 3.7c) seem to form a kind of inclusio around the condemnation of the prophets.

Verse 4a also seems to be part of the earlier indictment of the leaders, perhaps acting as bridge between the two segments of text, and more importantly, between the participants (the leaders and the prophets) within these segments.

Micah 3.8

But indeed I am full of strength, with the spirit of Yahweh and justice and

affirmation in prophetic call pericopes, 'he touched my mouth' (ויגע על פי) (e.g. Isa. 6.7; Jer. 1.9). Reading this way would understand the 3ms subject ('...*he* will not put it in their mouths') as Yahweh, and the masculine singular object ('they will make holy war on *him*') as either Yahweh, or *my people*.

The idiom עטה על שׂפה ('cover the lip') of 3.7 seems to be a sign of humiliation (due to contamination, Lev. 13.45) or mourning (Ezek. 24.17, 22). Petrotta argues that 3.7 combines the images from the preceding two verses, mixing metaphors of mouth and speech (3.5) with darkness and sight (3.6) (1991: 94).

Ben Zvi reads 3.8 as a separate but pivotal unit between 3.1-7 and 3.9-12 (2000: 76-77).

strength, to tell to Jacob his transgression and to Israel his sin.

The speech returns to the prophet in 3.8, where *I* proclaim that *I* am filled with the strength, the spirit of Yahweh, to tell Jacob his transgression (ליעקב פשעו). The mention of Jacob's transgression once again recalls the feminine Samaria of 1.5, interestingly, again just prior to a text about Jerusalem (3.9-12).

Micah 3.9-12
⁹Listen (mpl) to this, O heads of the house of Jacob and rulers of the house of Israel, (O) ones regarding justice as an abomination and who will twist (3mpl) all uprightness. ¹⁰(O) one building (ms ptc) Zion with (in exchange for) blood and Jerusalem with (in exchange for) unrighteousness. ¹¹Her leaders will judge in exchange for bribes and her priests will teach in exchange for price and her prophets divine in exchange for silver. And they will lean upon (against) Yahweh saying, 'Is not Yahweh in our midst? Evil will not come upon us'. ¹²Therefore, because of you (mpl), Zion will be ploughed, a field, and Jerusalem will be ruins, and the mountain of the house for a high place of the forest.

The content of the prophetic proclamation announced in 3.8 seems to come in 3.9-12. Here, using language almost identical to that used at the start of the chapter (3.1-3) the speech begins with a masculine plural imperative, and moves into 3mpl forms in 3.9b-10. Although the text addresses and describes masculine plural leaders, it is Jerusalem/Zion who is accused and punished. Now in the third person, Zion is said to be built in bloodshed and Jerusalem in injustice. *Her* leaders sell their judgment, *her* priests sell their teaching, and *her* prophets prophesy for silver. The text marks these intellectual

The image of a woman being ploughed like a field in 3.12 might be read has having an aggressive sexual connotation. That it may be sexual is attested by parallels in ancient near eastern literature; for instance, in an example from Mesopotamian mythology, given by Frymer-Kensky in her study of ancient near eastern goddess imagery, the goddess Inanna sings, 'my vulva is a well-watered field—who will plough it?' (1992: 53). But here the image does not seem to be erotic, but rather violating.

Interestingly, almost perversely, scholars are intrigued by this description of violence against Zion. Gowan asserts that if the words of Micah are reduced to the threats in chs. 1–3, this may be his most memorable proclamation (1998: 52). McFadden seems to affirm the image, when he states that this passage is seen by many 'as a *climax* of an authentic Micah oracle of judgment' (1983: 142, emphasis mine). Using language that is similarly disturbing, Stansell finds this passage to be Micah's 'polemic against a Zion tradition and those who hold to a false security in the city's divine protection and *inviolability*' (1988: 51, 59, emphasis mine); Stansell also describes the rhetoric of 1.8-16 in the same way (1988: 47). Worded thus, it is as if *violation* (often a sexual term) will be what proves that her sense of security is false.

profiteers, with feminine possessive
pronouns, as hers. The punishment for
her ownership of them comes in 3.12,
where it is stated that because of *you*
(mpl)—suddenly jolted from observer
to addressee—Zion will be ploughed
like a field and turned into a heap of
ruins.

In this chapter then, there is an interesting shift back and forth between second and third masculine plural forms (vv. 1-2, 5-7, 9-10), which seems to have the effect of both drawing in addressees, and presenting them at the same time as distinct and alienated from some other group of listeners. There is also a fairly clear identification of guilt between the feminine city and her masculine plural leaders. Less clear is the relationship between the accused, *my people*, the prophet, Yahweh and the punished Zion. It seems clear that the leaders act maliciously, oppressing the people; but there is some ambiguity as to whether *my people* refers to Yahweh's identification with the people, or the prophet's identification with the people. Somewhat paradoxically, it seems that the feminine city is identified with and punished for the leaders' actions against *my people*, with whom she has previously also been identified (1.9, 2.9). Though the leaders' eating and smashing of the people is condemned, somehow violent punishment of Zion, who is in some way a representative of *my people*, is deemed as appropriate.

Micah 4

Chapter 4 begins with an abrupt shift from the imagery of Zion's humiliation to imagery of the exaltation of the mount of Yahweh, in a passage (4.1-8) that has been much celebrated for its utopic content. Here Yahweh's and Zion's relation to other nations is dealt with for the first time in the book (barring the call to the peoples in 1.2). It seems that Israel, represented by Zion as the mount of Yahweh, stands in a rather ambiguous relation to the nations, perhaps as superior, perhaps at their command, perhaps mutually accepting. At the start of the chapter, where the Hebrew is quite straightforward, it is clear that the masculine Yahweh is central. But this changes drastically in the latter part of the chapter, as the Hebrew becomes more complex again. Here an ambiguously gendered Zion takes the stage and is sharply distinguished from, and opposed to, the nations.

Micah 4.1-5

¹And in the days after, the house of Yahweh will be a mountain, one established at the top of the mountains. It will be lifted up more than (from) hills. ²Peoples will stream upon (against) it. And many nations will walk and they will say, 'Go' and we will go up to the mountain of Yahweh and to the house of the God of Jacob. And let him instruct us from his paths, and let us walk in his ways. (And many nations will walk and they will say, 'Come, let us go up to the mountain of Yahweh and to the house of the God of Jacob. And let him instruct us from his paths, and let us walk in his ways'.) For the law (Torah) will go out from Zion, and the word of Yahweh from Jerusalem. ³And he will judge between many peoples, and he will rebuke great nations until far away. They will beat (mpl) their swords into plowshares and their spears into pruning knives. And nation to nation, they will not lift a sword, and they will no longer learn battle. ⁴And they will dwell, each under his vine, and under his fig tree, and no one will cause fear. For the mouth of Yahweh of hosts has spoken. ⁵For all peoples will walk, each in the name of its God. And we will walk in the name of Yahweh our God, forever and ever.

The mountain of the house of Yahweh is described in the third person, in what is normally read as a bustle of utopic activity. This mountain seems to be some kind of metaphor for the nation. In v. 2 it is associated with Jacob; it also seems to be the feminine city, Zion/Jerusalem from which the word of Yahweh goes forth. This mountain of Yahweh seems to stand in contrast to the nations; it is raised up above other mountains and hills, indicating superiority; it is a high place to which other nations stream.

Yet depending on who the 1cpl 'we'

Most commentators translate the 1cpl verb of 4.2 as a cohortative, 'Come, let us go up' (Hillers 1984: 49; Wolff 1990: 112; Shaw 1993: 100; McKane 1998: 126; Andersen and Freedman 2000: 403).

The sudden shift into a more positive stance for the future is often explained as a later addition to the text. For instance, Wolff dates it to the Persian era, 'probably not until after the exilic period and the restoration of the temple' (1990: 117), noting Lescow's dating (1972b) of 4.1-4 to the dedication of the second temple. Mays also considers that it may have been written after the construction of the second temple (1976: 96). The details of dating differs from scholar to scholar, but in general those who opt for a later dating include Wolff (1990: 117); Mays (1976: 96); Renaud (1977: 161-62, 170-74); Lescow (1972a: 76). Those who consider these to be the words of Micah include Waltke (1988: 174-75); and Shaw (1993: 113-15). (See Waltke [1988: 172-73] for a discussion on universalism vs. nationalism that engages Renaud's view that 4.1-8 was late [Renaud 1977: 172-74].) Allen straddles the two views, considering 4.5 authentic, 4.1-4 to be older material (1976: 251, 323), and 4.6-8 to be added later (1976: 329). Alfaro treats this passage as well as the rest of chs. 4–5 as a debate between Micah and the false prophets (1989: 42-46), following van der Woude (1969).

The tolerance for other gods in 4.5 gives rise to a number of scholarly hypotheses. Wolff considers 4.5 a confessional statement which is joined in later liturgical use (1990: 118). Mays too considers it a response to the preceding prophecy of ch. 3 (1976: 99). Shaw agrees that it may have been a liturgical response, however he considers it to be written by Micah (1993: 106). McKane argues that this is a later hand, one

in the verb ונעלה is read (either as a regular prefix form, 'we will go up', or as a cohortative, 'let us go up'), the relation between 'us' and the nations changes. As can be seen in the translation, if ונעלה is read in v. 2 as a regular prefix verb, the nations' speech is much shorter, a command, 'Go' (לכו) to which *we* respond ('and we will go'). If read as a cohortative, the nations' speech is extended ('Come, let us go...'), and there is not the sense that *we* respond to the nations' will.

Reading a cohortative, as most scholars do, makes sense, especially in light of the jussive and cohortative that follow, yet the use of the 1cpl at the end of the section (4.5) might put this into question. The section 4.1-4 seems to conclude in 4.4 with a formulaic, 'for the mouth of Yahweh has spoken it'; but then carries on in 4.5a with the nations walking (mpl) again. Now each nation walks with its (ms) own God. Then in 4.5b, suddenly the 1cpl reappears: *we* are speaking again, '*we* will walk in the name of Yahweh our God'. This sounds similar to the words of *we*, the nations, with their cohortative, 'let us go up' in 4.2. Yet if *we* are *the nations* walking with Yahweh, then the statement in 4.5a that each nation will walk with its *own* God would seem to be contravened.

In short the relationship between 'us', the nations, and Yahweh is ambiguous. Perhaps, however, the use of the 1cpl in 4.5 does not support reading the 1cpl ונעלה in 4.2 as the nations' cohortative. But then the question is raised as to why *we* would be responding to the command of the nations in 4.2.

Micah 4.6-7
⁶*In that day, oracle of Yahweh, I will gather the lame and I will gather the scattered (outcast), whom I have done evil (done harm). ⁷I will put the lame one (fs ptc) for a remnant and the*

skeptical of the utopic vision put forth in 4.1-4 (1998: 124-26). Shoemaker asks if the significance of the arrival of the nations is ambiguous—he questions if this hints at attack (1992: 164).

A number of scholars break 4.1-8 up into various smaller units; all of which debates I will not list here. For a range of views concerning the relation of 4.1-4 to Isa. 2.1-4, see Hillers (1984: 51-53); Andersen and Freedman (2000: 413-27); Gosse (1993).

scattered (fs ptc) (far removed) for a mighty nation. And Yahweh will rule over them in the mount of Zion, from now until forever.

The oracle of Yahweh in 4.6-7 continues the image of the mount of Zion. From here I, Yahweh, rule over a gathered *remnant*, a collection of the lame, gathered to become a mighty nation. Here the verbs אסף and קבץ appear, also used in 2.12-13 where Yahweh is said to gather the remnant like a flock. This apparently positive image is marred only by the admission that the flock is the one 'whom I have harmed' (ואשר הרעתי) (4.6). Halfway through 4.7—as in 2.13—the address shifts from the first person ('I will gather', etc.) to the third person ('Yahweh will rule').

Micah 4.8

You (ms), O flock tower, O fortified hill of the Daughter of Zion (You, O flock tower, O fortified hill, O Daughter of Zion) (You are a flock tower; the Daughter of Zion is a fortified hill) (You, O flock tower, are the fortified hill of the Daughter of Zion). Unto you (ms), the former kingdom will come (fs); the kingdom will come (fs) to the daughter of Jerusalem. (Unto you she will come, the former kingdom will come, the kingdom to the Daughter of Jerusalem.)

Then suddenly in 4.8-14, Zion changes her attitude toward the other nations; s/he is no longer lame or contained. Now s/he appears as a very warlike but ambiguously gendered character. The passage begins with an address to a masculine singular *you*, which is followed by several noun constructions: first by the masculine singular 'flock tower' (מגדל עדר); then by the feminine 'Daughter of Zion' who stands in some relation to a (ms) fortified hill (עפל), parallel to the 'flock tower'. This is followed by two

The phrase (אתה מגדל עדר עפל בת ציון) in 4.8 could be read as two or three vocatives, modifying the initial pronoun; or as two nominal phrases; or as a vocative in apposition to the pronoun as the subject of a nominal phrase.

The masculine singular pronouns in the verse are twice lexically and syntactically parallel to the feminine 'Daughter of Zion'. In the first part of the verse, the masculine singular *you* (אתה) seems to be lexically parallel, in a chiastic arrangement, to the feminine 'Daughter of Zion' (בת ציון). The address then continues with a prepositional phrase in 4.8b, '*to you*' (ms) (עדיך), which is again chiastically parallel, this time syntactically, with another prepositional phrase, 'to the Daughter of Jerusalem' (לבת ירושלם).

The form of ממלכת in 4.8c is difficult. It looks like the construct of ממלכה ('kingdom'), but there is no noun to complete the bound form. The *BHS* notes that the LXX adds the noun 'Babylon'. However, the phrase ממלכת לבת ירושלם can be read as a construct before a prepositional phrase which is attested

synonymous 3fs verbs, 'she will come, she will come', followed by two more enigmatic feminine singular noun constructions meaning vaguely the same thing, 'the former kingdom' and 'the kingdom to the daughter of Jerusalem'. The structure of the verse with two almost synonymous verbs in a row is unusual, but the line seems to have a certain symmetrical structure: two verbs with two parallel noun constructions on either side.

(for this construction see Waltke and O'Connor [1990: 155, 9.6]); so also Hillers (1984: 56) and Shaw (1993: 100), who translate, 'Rule by Jerusalem'. Wolff translates '*kingship* of the *daughter* of Jerusalem'—itself an interesting gender hybrid (1990: 112, emphasis mine). Other scholars also tend to diminish the feminine aspects of this verse. Hillers leaves out 'Daughter' in both cases, since in his view the term serves 'primarily rhythmical purposes' (1984: 56). Shaw drops the second 'daughter' in his translation, without comment (1993: 100). Mays deletes the second feminine singular verb as a variant reading (1976: 102).

The masculine names at the beginning of the verse get more attention. Hillers notes that מגדול עדר is a place name in Gen. 35.21, but that this is more likely an image of fortification here, since it is parallel with עפל. It is not exactly clear what is meant by עפל here, but the references to עפל in 2 Chronicles and Nehemiah imply some kind of fortified hill in Jerusalem. Also, מגדול tends to suggest fortification: it seems to signify watchtower in 2 Kgs 17.9; 18.8; 2 Chron. 26.9; strong tower in Judg. 9.51; Ps. 61.4; Prov. 18.10; towers along the wall in 2 Chron. 14.6; 32.5. Shoemaker, following Yigal Shiloh, calls it the 'acropolis...the central area of the city which functions as the hub of political and social activity' (1992: 168, 334).

Micah 4.9-10
⁹Now for what will you (fs) raise a loud battle cry? (why do you cry aloud)? Is the King not with (in) you? (Is the King nothing to you?). Has the one counseling you perished? For trembling (anguish) seizes you like one giving birth. ¹⁰Tremble (writhe) and burst forth, O Daughter of Zion, like one giving birth. For now you will go out

Hillers accounts for the anomaly of the feminine form of רוע in 4.9, by stating that 'the text is doubtful at this point. The verb תריע is not well-attested in the sense "cry in distress"' (1984: 58); though he does end up by saying that the use is defensible here, reading it as a cry of distress.

Shoemaker suggests that in the image of birthing in the field, Zion is depicted

*from the town, and you will lie in the
field. And you will go until (as far as)
Babylon and there you will be
redeemed. There Yahweh will redeem
you from the hand of your enemies.*

The address becomes more definitively directed to a feminine singular
figure in 4.9, when the verb forms
become exclusively feminine. The gender ambiguity persists a little here
though, with two typically masculine
behaviours: the raising of the battle cry
and the going out from the town. The
verb רוע ('raise a battle cry') only occurs
here in the feminine; the verb יצא ('go
out') is infrequent in the feminine.

More feminine behaviours are suggested in 4.9-10 though: a birthing and
a rescue. The Daughter of Zion is
described as one in labour and told to
go out into the field, writhe, to give
birth and then to go to Babylon, in
order to be rescued.

as an animal, not necessarily as a
woman, in keeping with 4.6-7, 13; this,
he argues, is a taunt (1992: 171). For
more on this passage and its commentators see my Chapters 5 and 6.

Micah 4.11
*Now many nations are gathered
against you (fs). They are saying, let
her be (you will be, ms) desecrated, let
our eyes gaze on Zion.*

Then the nations are gathered against
you (fs), speaking in tones drastically
different than at the beginning of the
chapter. Here they seem to taunt, but
their speech is not directly to *you*, but
about Zion; or if it is read as direct
speech, then the addressee, designated
by the form תחנף ('you will be desecrated') is masculine.

It makes sense to read תחנף in 4.11 as
jussive, along with the following verb in
the phrase ותחז בציון עינינו ('and let our
eyes gaze on Zion'); however, because
the subjects of the two verbs are
different, I note the possibility that
formally, it could be 2ms—'*you* (ms) are
desecrated'—continuing the ambiguity
of gender in the passage.

Micah 4.12-13
*[12]But they (mpl) do not know the
schemes of Yahweh and they do not
understand his plans. For he will
gather them like swaths to the threshing
floor. [13]Arise and tread (fs), O Daughter
of Zion, for I will make your (fs) horn*

The language used to describe the
Daughter of Zion in 4.13 is similar to
that used of Asa and Josiah crushing
Asherah poles (2 Chron. 15.16; 2 Kgs
23.6, 15), of the King of Aram treading
down the army of Jehoahaz (2 Kgs 13.7),
of Yahweh treading down the nations

iron, and I will make your hoofs copper, and you will pulverise many peoples. And I will make herem (devote) their unlawful gains to Yahweh, and their wealth to the Lord of all the earth.

The fate of Zion seems to change again, because *they* (mpl), presumably the mocking nations, do not know the swathing schemes of Yahweh (v. 12); the use of 'schemes', מחשבות, here recalls the 'scheming', חשב, of evildoers and of Yahweh in 2.1-3. Then in 4.13, a first person voice steps in, demanding masculine behaviours, with feminine singular imperatives: 'arise, tread'. *I* promise to make Zion's body hard. Her horn will be iron and her hoofs copper to tread down and pulverize (דוש and דקק) many peoples. The language is the language of Kings.

It would, at first glance, seem that Yahweh is the speaker who promises to give the daughter of Zion an iron horn and bronze hooves; this seems to be the kind of thing that Yahweh would have the power to do. Yet this is rendered uncertain when in the second half of the verse, *I* promise to devote the gains made in war *to Yahweh* (והחרמתי ליהוה). Either there is a shift in voice here, or this could be the voice of someone else preparing Zion for battle.

(Hab. 3.12). For both verbs see Isa. 41.15; for דקק see also 2 Chron. 34.4, 7; Dan. 2.34, 45; 7.7, 19; for דוש, see also Amos 1.3; Judg. 8.7; Jer. 3.11; Isa. 25.10; 28.27. It is also the language used of the goddesses Anat (Bordreuil 1971: 21-28), Astarte (Hadley 1996: 123-24), and Ishtar (Frymer-Kensky 1992: 67) in ancient near eastern parallels.

Scholars have considered how to read the first person form והחרמתי ('I will make herem') in v. 13b. Hillers suggested that this is either an uncommon but attested form of the 2fs ('you will make *herem*') (so Shaw 1993: 129; Allen 1976: 335) or it should be corrected (1984: 60); so also Wolff (1990: 130). Mays suggests that this first person form has slipped in because of the preceding first person forms, but should be read as second person (1976: 107). Conversely, van der Woude considers this to be the voice of the pseudo-prophets building on a blind Zion tradition (1969: 254), here appropriating Yahweh's voice.

Micah 4.14

Now you (fs) will cut yourself, O Daughter of Mourning (O Daughter of the Troops). He lays (is one laying) a siege against us. With a staff they will smite the judge of Israel upon the cheek.

It does not seem that this victory is ever completed though, because out of the blue, it is predicted in 4.14 that *you* (fs) will cut yourself (תתגדדי), implying an act of mourning, or a sign of defeat. Your self-mutilation is followed by a siege which *he* lays upon *us*, and by a

For גדד as a sign of defeat or mourning, see 1 Kgs 18.28; Jer. 16.6; 41.5; 47.5, 48.37; it is forbidden as a sign of mourning in Deut. 14.1. Interestingly even here the vocative בת גדוד which plays on the verb גדד can also mean Daughter of the Troops, a rather masculine epithet.

The suddenness of the shift in Zion's fates is dealt with, in part, by a scholarly tendency to read this verse as the introduction to the 'promise of deliverance' in 5.1 (Willis 1968; Wolff 1990: 134; so also, Mays 1976: 111; Allen

chastisement of the judge of Israel, by an unknown *they* (mpl), perhaps the nations. It is not clear whether the 1cpl *us* includes the first person voice(s) of 4.13, or whether is this a new voice.

1976: 339; Craigie 1985: 38). Many read it as the first verse of ch. 5 (Mays 1976: 111; Wolff 1990: 129; Allen 1976: 339; Coppens 1971: 57-58). This has long been part of reading traditions, as reflected in English translations, as early as the KJV, which start ch. 5 with 4.14. McKane reads v. 14 as 'a fragment which bears no relationship either to the preceding verses, 11-13, or to what follows in 5.1ff' (1998: 143); similarly Hillers (1984: 62).

In the first part of the chapter then, it seems that the nation of Israel is one among others, though privileged to have the mountain—also the city of Zion—the seat of Yahweh's voice and judgment. Yahweh is central and active (judging, speaking, gathering), though it is not always clear how beneficent this rule is: there is a hint that Yahweh has also been the cause of some damage to those gathered (4.6). In the second part of the chapter, it is Zion who takes on the personality of the nation and is active. Here Zion exhibits a different, more aggressive kind of femininity than seen thus far in the book. Though she does seem to exhibit some traits typically assigned as feminine (birthing, being rescued, desecration), some of the metaphoric descriptions of her are more surprisingly reminiscent of masculine figures in the Hebrew Bible (she is a strong tower, she has an iron horn, she tramples the nations); as discussed, the syntax also bears out this gender bending. There is also ambiguity in her stance before other nations. She is alternately pitted against the nations, victorious over them, or taunted and punished by them; she is no longer one who lives in harmony with them.

Micah 5

Chapter 5, like ch. 4, seems to shift from the hopeful to the desperate, but the transitions in this chapter are even more bewildering, shifting suddenly between glory and desolation, using difficult Hebrew constructions. Here the focus seems to be on masculine figures (mainly singular), whether it be one ruling in the name of Yahweh, or Assyria invading the land, or those resisting Assyria, or Jacob ravaging other nations, or *you* (ms) being destroyed by Yahweh. The nation seems to be depicted either by its rulers or as a remnant; *my people* is not mentioned here at all.

Micah 5.1

*And you, O Bethlehem of Ephrathah,
are small (insignificant) to be among
the thousands of Judah. He will go forth
from you (ms) to me, to be one ruling
in Israel. And his coming forth (place of
departure) is from earlier times, from
the days of old.*

In what has often been considered a
'messianic prophecy', the first verse(s)
of ch. 5 contain an address to '*you* (ms),
O Bethlehem of Ephrathah', by '*me*' an
unidentified speaker. Here again, it is
difficult to say precisely where this
address ends. As has become a familiar
technique in the book of Micah, the
description changes from the second
person to the third person (5.1c). After
the clear signs of address (1cs, *I*, 2ms,
you) drop out, they do not reappear
until 5.8-9 (though the 1 cpl appears in
5.4-5). It is therefore uncertain whether
5.2-7 is part of the address; its third
person descriptions and predictions,
even with the 1cpl forms, do not carry
the same direct force of an address that
the *I* and *you* give in 5.1 and 5.9-14.

Because of the perceived messianic
reference in 5.1-3, Christian scholars
have paid much attention to these
verses. For examples of messianic
interpretation see Renaud (1977: 173-
75); Wolff (1990: 143-45); Waltke (1988:
181-82); Seebass (1992: 72-77); McKane
(1998: 148-64). Others focus on the
hope for a return to Davidic rule: Willis
(1968); Hillers (1984: 66); Shaw (1993:
144-47).

The first person voice in 5.1 ('he will
go forth from you to *me*') is odd here;
the brevity of its appearance makes the
speaker difficult to identify. Hillers
assumes it to be divine, comparing this
to the call of David in 1 Sam. 16.1 where
a similar construction is used (1984:
65)(כי ראיתי בבניו לי מלך) ('for I have seen
amongst his sons a king for me').
Conversely, Mays suggests that perhaps
לי ('to me') is short for ליהוה ('to
Yahweh') since 'the style of divine
speech is not present anywhere else in
the saying' (1976: 111). Wolff suggests
that the shift from the 1cpl in 4.14 to
the 1cs in 5.1 contributes to the 'liveli-
ness' of the passage, as does the shift
from feminine to masculine addressee
(1990: 134-35). Russell Fuller notes that
the Qumran text 4QMicah reads לא יצ]א
לי (1993: 194), which might mean 'from
you shall not come forth for me one
who is to rule in Israel' (1993: 201). He
suggests that this might say something
about the Qumran community's eschata-
logical expectation (1993: 202); but
instead of adopting this reading, he
considers that לי might be an alternate
spelling of לו (attested five times in the
Hebrew Bible), reading 'would that one
would come forth for me' (1993: 201).

Micah 5.2

*Therefore he will put them (3mpl)
(hand them over) (set them aside) until
a time that one giving birth gives birth.
And the remainder of his brothers will
return to (against) the sons of Israel.*

A number of scholars take 5.2a to mean
'he will give them up or over to enemies'
(Wolff 1990: 134; Craigie 1985: 38;
Hillers 1984: 64; Shaw 1993: 130); this
assumes that *he* is Yahweh and not the
king just previously described at the end

The scene seems to change again. There is no indication that a different participant from that of 5.1 (the ruler from of old) has been introduced as a referent for the 3ms *he*; but *his* behaviour does not entirely seem like that of a salvific ruler. Here *he* acts upon *them* (3mpl)—for whom we do not have a clear referent—until the one in labour gives birth. The construction of the phrase, 'he will put them until a time' (יתנם עד עת), is odd and does not seem to indicate where *they* (3mpl) will be put. Perhaps this is an act of 'handing them over', or perhaps 'setting them aside'. It does not give the impression of very heroic behaviour. In 5.2b *they* appear to be described as *the remainder of his brothers* (ויתר אחיו) who are returning in some fashion (to or against) to the sons of Israel (ישובון על בני ישראל). The way the preposition על ('to' or 'against') is read drastically affects the way in which one understands the relationship of *his brothers* to *the sons of Israel* (hostile or not). This in turn might affect how the 3ms figure is understood (as friendly to the sons of Israel or not).

of 5.1, so Hillers (1984: 65); Wolff (1990: 135). Mays solves both the issue of the identity of the 3ms figure and the problem of syntax by reading as an impersonal passive: 'they shall be handed over' (1976: 111). Wolff translates more literally, but says it should be understood in the passive (1990: 145). Coppens considers the verse to be a gloss about Yahweh's active role in the exile (1971: 69).

Although most scholars interpret the 3ms subject of 5.2a as Yahweh, they skip back to read the future ruler as the antecedent for 3ms pronominal suffix on אחיו ('his brothers') in 5.2b. There are various speculations as to who these returning brothers are; most consider it a reference in some way to the exile. Mays suggests this relates to the return of the remnant to the land (1976: 117). Hillers notes that the word 'remainder' (יתר) suggests the people left in the land, not the exiles; he mentions the possibility of, but does not take up, a reading by Ernst Sellin that considers יתר to mean 'surpassing', as in Gen. 49.3, thus, 'he who surpasses his brothers' (1984: 66-67). Allen sees this both as a reference to the exile and as a Davidic allusion (1976: 345). Wolff suggests that it refers to the exiled royalty, but also to the rest of the exiles (1990: 145). As far as I can see, no one reads על בני ישראל as 'against the sons of Israel', perhaps because this would not make sense within a messianic, or hopeful, understanding of the passage.

Many scholars make the connection of the woman in labour here (יולדה) to the woman bearing Immanuel in Isa. 7.14, and raise questions about the birth of the Messiah. Hillers suggests that the text leaves this possibility open (1984: 66). Mays argues that it is more likely a return of the image of travail that occurs in 4.9 (1976: 116), so also Shoemaker (1992: 176). Wolff suggests that the text makes the connection both to the metaphor in 4.9 and to Isa. 7.14 (1990: 145). Coppens argues that it is part of a later gloss about the exile (1971: 69-70); the woman in labour is not related to the woman of Isa. 7.14, but is Jerusalem who must suffer the exile (pains of labour) before her divine king will come.

Micah 5.3

And he will stand and shepherd in the strength of Yahweh. In the majesty (arrogance) of the name of Yahweh his God. And they will dwell (sit). For now he will be great until the ends of the earth.

In 5.3, *he* stands and shepherds in the strength of the name of Yahweh, and grows great, while—as denoted in a single word clause—*they* sit, or dwell (וישבו). Again the identity of the 3ms figure seems to shift, now aligned with Yahweh, and presumably more clearly friendly than in 5.2. However, his growing contrasts with their more static dwelling or sitting, which could be read negatively.

A number of scholars modify this one word clause, וישבו ('they will dwell') in 5.3, perhaps finding it too abrupt. Wolff (1990: 129) and Allen (1976: 339) insert 'undisturbed'. Mays inserts 'safely' (1976: 111) and Craigie 'securely' (1985: 38). Hillers (1984: 64) and Shaw (1993: 130) translate, 'they will remain'.

Micah 5.4-5

⁴And this will be peace, Assyria (And Assyria will be this peace). For he (Assyria) will come in our land and walk in our citadels. And we will raise up against him seven rulers and eight chiefs of humankind. ⁵They will rule (shepherd) (break) the land of Assyria with the sword and the land of Nimrod in her gates. And he will rescue from Assyria, for he will come in our land, and walk in our border.

Verses 4-5 mark another change in pace. Verse 4 begins with the phrase, 'and this will be peace' (והיה זה שלום). The phrase is sandwiched between the description of the divine ruler in 5.3 and of Assyria walking in *our* lands (5.4). It is particularly odd, placed as it

Wolff considers that the זה in the phrase והיה זה שלום (5.4) refers back to the ruler of 5.1, 3; he reads 'and he [this one] will achieve peace' (1990: 147). Similarly, Hillers links this passage to the previous verses by considering שלום זה a royal title, 'One of Peace' (1984: 67-68); so also Shaw (1993: 130). Some emend אשור of the next line to מאשור, assuming a haplography, reading 'peace from Assyria'; see Cathcart (1978: 39); Mays (1976: 117); Saracino (1983: 265). Conversely, R.L. Smith considers 'this' to refer to the time after Assyria has been defeated and rescue accomplished (1984: 45).

The resistance to Assyria is violent. The verb ורעו could either be from the stem רעע ('break') or from רעה ('rule/

is before a description of Assyria. Further, technically, the proper noun 'Assyria' (אשׁור) which immediately follows, could either stand as a rare one noun clause, followed by 'for he comes into our lands' (בארצנו); or it could be somehow attached to והיה זה שׁלום, perhaps in apposition ('and this will be peace, Assyria'); or it could function as the subject of the verb 'to be' (היה) ('and Assyria will be this peace'). The relationship between 'this peace', the one standing strong in 5.3, and Assyria is murky at best.

And then suddenly in 5.4b, a 3ms figure, *he*, previously the divinely appointed ruler in 5.1-3, seems to be Assyria, who comes into *our* lands and walks on *our* fortresses. One wonders if the entire passage could be about Assyria. This would clarify why *he* would give them up, and why his brothers would come against the sons of Israel.

However, an unidentified 1cpl voice, follows immediately, describing how *we* will resist his invasions. *We* say, in 5.4b-5a, that we will raise seven rulers and eight chiefs against him, and *they* will violently rule Assyria with the sword and Nimrod in her gates. It is uncertain whether this is a new collective voice, or whether it includes the *me* of 5.1.

Then abruptly, in 5.5b, *he* (no longer many rulers) will rescue *from* Assyria. Here the language is almost identical to that used to describe Assyria in 5.4b—'he will rescue, he will walk in our land, and tread on our border'. *He*, who may now again be the divinely appointed masculine singular figure of 5.2, seems to mimic Assyria.

In short these few verses are extremely complex and obscure. There is no clarity as to the relationships between the various participants, as to whether or not their actions display beneficent rule, or also as to where the speakers' favour lies.

shepherd'). The ruling of Nimrod 'in her gate' has possible violent sexual connotations. For commentary on the image of gate as vagina, see Magdalene (1995: 346); if read as such in 5.5, in conjunction with being ruled by the sword, this would seem to be an image of rape. Often 'her gates' (בפתחיה) is read as 'with a dagger' (בפתיחה) which both does away with the feminine singular pronominal suffix, and the rape imagery; so Wolff (1990: 132); Hillers (1984: 68); Craigie (1985: 38); Allen (1976: 339); Cathcart (1978: 39); Shoemaker (1992: 179); Shaw (1993: 130); Williamson (1997: 364). Saracino, translates 'with *his* very dagger' (1983: 266, emphasis mine).

There has been much speculation on the origin and incorporation of the material in Mic. 5.4-5; for an overview of scholarly discussion, see McKane (1998: 156-63). Wolff considers 5.4a and 5.5b to refer to the ruler in 5.1, 3 who will bring peace by saving Israel from its enemies; he considers 5.4b–5.5a to be a later gloss about the oppressed 1cpl of 5.4a and speaks of their resistance (1990: 147-48). Similarly McKane writes, 'Verses 4b, 5a are a larger addition and they create a tension between divine and human action so insupportable that their author cannot be the same person as the one responsible for vv. 1, 3, 4a' (1998: 160). He argues that 5.4-5 are very late additions that oppose reliance on the Messiah, and advocate self-help; the rulers raised up against Assyria are Maccabean heroes (1998: 13). Mays considers the oracle to be a redactional transition between Messianic and eschatological oracles (1976: 119). Van der Woude considers 5.4b-5 to be words of the pseudo-prophets who advocate coalition building (1969: 255). Cathcart takes this up to hypothesize the false prophets use of magical incantations to ward off evil; he compares the seven/

eight formula to Phonecian, Akkadian, Aramaic and Ugaritic incantations (1968, 1978). Building from this, Saracino (1983) compares Mic. 5.4-5 with a Ugaritic prayer to Baal which he relates to magical rituals. Hillers reads 'he will rescue' in 5.5b as the plural, 'they will rescue us', making the link with the rulers raised in 5.4b-5a (1983a: 137; 1984: 68-69).

Micah 5.6-7

6And the remnant of Jacob will be in the midst of many peoples, like dew from Yahweh and like many showers upon the grass, which does not wait (3ms) for anyone, and does not wait for the sons of Adam (humanity). 7And the remnant of Jacob will be among the nations, in the midst of many peoples, like a lion amongst the beasts of the forest, like the young lion among flocks of sheep, which if it passes and tramples and tears, no one can rescue.

Verses 6-8 shift again, now to a 3ms description of the *remnant of Jacob* who is said to be in the midst of many nations. The remnant is first described as gentle, like rain, but unrelenting, waiting for no one. Verse 7 repeats that the remnant of Jacob will be among many nations, but this time it is described rather differently, as a force among the nations, as a lion, tearing and destroying whatever it passes.

For various suggestions about the seemingly disparate nature of the dew and lion figures (e.g. pacifism followed by militarism), see Wolff (1990: 157), who ends by suggesting that they are parallel: one indicates the divine nature, the other the Messiah's rescue; similarly Hagstrom (1988: 67). Craigie suggests that 'they bring out clearly the dual character that had always been integral to the purpose of Israel: "I will bless those who bless you, and him who curses you I will curse", (Genesis 12.3)' (1985: 42-43); similarily Allen (1976: 354); Shoemaker (1992: 181). McKane argues the opposite, suggesting that they represent incompatible ideas: weakness vs. imperialism (1998: 168). Hillers suggests that the images may not be different, noting an earlier suggestion that dew might be a hostile simile; he cites a similar image in 2 Sam. 17.12: 'we shall light upon him like the dew falls upon the ground' (1984: 71). Anbar (1994) suggests that 5.7 was a later addition—signaled by its repetition of the first phrase of 5.6—by a scribe who didn't agree with the nations-friendly attitude of the original text.

Micah 5.8

Let your (ms) hand be raised against your oppressors and all your enemies will be cut off.

In 5.8 the 3ms descriptions shift abruptly back to an address in the 2ms, 'let *your* hand be raised against your

Though תרם in 5.8 is jussive, Mays (1976: 121) and Wolff (1990: 151) note that many mss and versions read the imperfect: 'you will lift'; so Hillers (1984: 70). Wolff suggests that the jussive might indicate this as an address to Yahweh (1990: 157), Mays argues

enemies'. *You* seem to take the place of the third person devouring lion-remnant of Jacob, though this connection is not explicitly stated. Or conversely, *you* could be Bethlehem of 5.1, or even the ambiguous ruler(s) of 5.1-5.

Micah 5.9-14

⁹In that day, oracle of Yahweh, I will cut your (ms) horses from your midst, I will destroy all your chariotry. ¹⁰I will cut off the cities of your land, and I will tear down all your fortresses. ¹¹I will cut off your sorcery from your hand. And there will not be soothsayers for you. ¹²I will cut off your idols and your memorial stones from your midst. And you will no longer bow to the work of your hands. ¹³I will remove your Asherah poles from your midst, and I will annihilate your cities. ¹⁴And I will make vengeance in anger and in wrath on the nations that do not listen (obey).

But the seeming victory of 5.6-8 is followed directly in 5.9-14, with no transition, by a first person oracle of Yahweh in which *I* threaten *you* (ms) with violence. I threaten to cut off your means of war and your cultural artifacts: I promise to cut off your horses and chariots, and your idols. I promise to annihilate your Asherah poles and destroy your cities (making an interesting connection between cities and the feminine goddess Asherah).

You are no longer the conquering, lion-like remnant, nor the majestic ruler, but now the target of destruction (perhaps Assyria?) There is, however, no indication that this is addressed to a different masculine singular *you* than the one who was just previously told would cut off his foes.

The chapter ends with the first person voice suddenly threatening vengeance upon the nations (3mpl) who do not listen (5.14).

that context suggests otherwise (1976: 121). McKane points it as an imperfect, but reads it as some kind of passive, 'your hand will be lifted up' (1998: 169).

Wolff asks 'why the "Asherim" and the "cities"...stand parallel' in 5.13 (1990: 159), and emends אֲשֵׁירֶיךָ ('your Asherim') to אֹיְבֶיךָ ('your enemies'), on the basis of the fact that the verb נתשׁ ('remove') normally implies deportation of peoples; he also emends 'cities' (עָרֶיךָ) to 'oppressors' (צָרֶיךָ) (1990: 152). This, he argues, would make a better connection between vv. 12 and 14. Knud Jeppesen considers 5.13 to be a critique of a popular Yahwism in which Yahweh had an Asherah consort (1984a: 463); he also considers that there was some 'parallelism between 'Asherim' and 'cities' (1984a: 464) and that perhaps Samaria was a center of Asherah ritual (1984a: 465). McKane conflates the two, reading this as a 'polemic against cities in Israel which have a foreign culture' (1998: 175).

Because the passage begins with וְהָיָה בַיּוֹם הַהוּא ('there will be in that day')—a phrase which, as Wolff notes, is a 'familiar connecting formula (Hos. 2.18, 20, 23; Amos 8.9; 9.11; Isa. 7.18, 20, 21, 23)' (1990: 69)—many commentators assume that 5.9-14 must also be 'a kind of salvation saying' (Mays 1976: 125); see also Wolff (1990: 154); Allen (1976: 356-67); McKane (1998: 173). Wolff likens 5.9-14 to 4.1-4, as a universal promise, a purifying act (1990: 154). Mays considers it a punitive yet salvific purging action (1976: 124). Hillers comments, 'the phrase "in that day" links this with the preceding predictions, and thereby helps determine its meaning. Whereas in itself the oracle is largely negative in tone, the context of the future glorious time makes it appear as the reverse side of the fabric: being deprived of cities, horses, and the rest prepares a time when God will rule unchallenged' (1984: 72). Other options are not often considered, for instance, that perhaps *you* might be other than Israel, or that the connecting formula might work in the other direction—by indicating punishment for the remnant's lion-like ravaging behaviour. Although, Jacob's appearance as a ravaging lion in 5.6-8 seems difficult to understand in any other way than a future promise of victory (so Wolff 1990: 155; Craigie 1985: 42-43; Allen 1976: 353-54; Hillers 1984: 139; Mays 1976: 121-23), the extreme violence that follows in 5.9-14 might indicate it as unacceptable (pun-ishable) behaviour.

Willis notes that the sudden appear-ance of the nations in 5.14 has been considered by many to be 'a later addition by a rabid nationalist' (1969b: 355). He also offers excellent surveys of the way that the issue has been dealt with; he himself considers the entire passage to be addressed to Israel's enemies, so this address to the nations is not out of place. Allen considers the attack on the nations the second part of Yahweh's plan—first Yahweh deals with Israel and then with its foes (1976: 360); so also Mays (1976: 125).

Chapter 5 then does not mention *my people*, but seems instead to refer to the nation—or collectivity such as it may be—as a remnant, who is gendered as male. Once again there is the same ambiguity as to whether the 'national entity' is oppressed or oppressing. The strange thing about this chapter is that the address seems to be made to contradictory figures. The 2ms figure seems to be both appointed by and destroyed by a first person figure. The 3ms figure seems both to be Yahweh's chosen ruler, and also Assyria, the one who is normally considered the enemy of Yahweh's people. The 3mpl figures seem to be those ruled by the special ruler, those who rise up against Assyria, as well as the nations who are destroyed. For the most part these shifts, as has come to be expected, are made without clear signals as to change in identity.

Micah 6

Chapter 6 returns to the disjunction between the masculine plural, the masculine singular and the feminine singular. Again the Hebrew is difficult to decipher, particularly in 6.9-12. The trope of unjust leaders returns here, as does the figure of *my people*, against whom Yahweh seems to have some kind of plaint. The feminine city also puts in an appearance, and again the connection between her inhabitants, the leaders, and the people is unclear. As always, there seems to be fluidity between the various addressees, as well as between speakers. Here, as in ch. 5, it is the 2ms figure who is threatened with destruction, perhaps for forgetting the past (6.4), or perhaps for the misdoings of the masculine plural leaders.

Micah 6.1-2

¹Listen (mpl) to what Yahweh is saying. 'Arise (ms), contend (ms) with the mountains, and the hills will hear (let the hills hear) your (ms) voice'. ²Listen (mpl), O mountains, and permanent foundations of the earth, to the case of Yahweh. For Yahweh has a dispute with his people and he argues with the people of Israel.

The chapter begins with the 2mpl *you* (a form not seen in chs. 4–5), by virtue of an imperative, calling *you* to listen to Yahweh. Then in 6.1b, the masculine plural imperative form changes and *you*, seemingly addressed by Yahweh's speech, become masculine singular again, called to rise up and dispute *with* the mountains. In 6.2, *you* (again mpl) are now the mountains called to listen to Yahweh's dispute, now with his people, instead of with the mountains.

Wolff accounts for differences in address in 6.1-2, by considering 6.1a redactional transition (1990: 167); so also Mays (1976: 129). Waltke considers 6.1a to be introductory, 6.1b to be Yahweh's voice to the prophet and 6.2 the voice of the prophet (1988: 192-93); similarly Hagstrom considers that 'v. 1a is addressed to the defendant (Israel), v. 1b to the plaintiff (YHWH), and v. 2 to the legal witnesses (the mountains and hills)' (1988: 26 n. 47). This latter follows the commonly held view that this is a lawsuit of Yahweh against his people. For the basic outline of the *rib* on which scholars tend to rely, see Daniels (1987: 351). For those who have provided detailed discussions of this 'genre' in the Hebrew Bible, see Hillers (1984: 77); for dissent to this view see Daniels (1987: 354); Shaw (1993: 182); De Roche (1983: 564-66, 570). Kessler makes the interesting comparison to Mic. 1.2-7, suggesting that both passages share the same basic structure (1999: 261). Shaw considers that the shifts in address 'fulfill the rhetorical function of establishing the relationship between the speaker and the audience' (1993: 184). Alternatively, Wolff considers the mountains and hills a 'cipher for the nations', reading this as a dispute with the nations 'against which comes the wrath of Yahweh' (1990: 173, see also 169).

Micah 6.3-5

³My people, what have I done to you (ms), and how have I cause you to be weary? Answer me. ⁴For I caused you to go up from the land of Egypt, and from the house of slavery I redeemed you. And I sent before you Moses, Aaron and Miriam. ⁵O my people, remember what Balak the King of Moab counseled, and what Balaam son of Boer answered him. From Shittim as far as Gilgal, in order that the righteousness of Yahweh be known.

I begin speaking, it would seem as Yahweh, giving voice to my complaint against *you* (ms), who are now identified as *my people*. In these lines, *I* straightforwardly ask how *I* have wearied *you*, and *I* remind you that I brought you out of Egypt, out of the house of slavery. I also refer *you* (still ms) to the tradition, asking you to remember the words of Balaam in response to Balak. As scholars point out, the reference to Shittim and Gilgal, though somewhat cryptic, seems to allude to the conquest, Shittim being the point of departure, and Gilgal the place of arrival (Hillers 1984: 78).

On the basis of the reference to the tradition, Wolff considers 6.2-8 a later deuteronomic didactic sermon which uses the lawsuit form (1990: 168, 174-77); McKane notes his skepticism toward Wolff's argument (1998: 180). Hillers finds the language deuteronomic in nature, but suggests that it may be earlier, a forerunner to Deuteronomy (1984: 79). Shaw does not consider the language to be close enough to deuteronomic texts, and so considers the oracle to be eighth century (1993: 167-70).

Micah 6.6-8

⁶With what shall I go to meet Yahweh, …will I bow to the God of heights. Will I meet him with offerings, with calves a year old? ⁷Will Yahweh be pleased with thousands of rams and ten thousand streams of oil? Will I give my firstborn, my transgression, the fruit of my womb, the sin of my soul? ⁸He has declared to you, O human (O Adam), (Adam has declared to you) what is good, and what Yahweh is seeking from

Some consider 6.6-7 to be an actual audience member's response to the prophet (so Daniels 1987: 351). Most consider it to be the prophet representing someone seeking priestly instruction (so Wolff 1990: 177; Allen 1976: 369; Mays 1976: 139); likewise Waltke considers these to be the questions of a 'representative worshipper' (1988: 194); in this vein, Hillers suggests that the questions posed are 'deliberately fanciful', invoking the

you (ms). Only to do justice and to love faithfulness and to walk wisely with your God.

Then rather abruptly in 6.6-8, *I* no longer seem to speak in the voice of Yahweh, rather, *I* am found asking what kind of sacrifices would please Yahweh. If the speaker is the prophet, he seems to have a different tactic than in the rest of the text. Here the concern is not with the future and with rhetorical forms of inciting change—such as indicting leaders for bad behaviour, or expressing anguish over coming punishment, or promising a glorious future—but instead, with describing proper living. This section of text ends, by way of an answer to *you* (ms)—no longer my people, but modified by the vocative 'O human' (אדם), told to do justice, to love faithfulness and to walk wisely with your God.

practices of a 'benighted people', i.e. child sacrifice (1984: 78).

In 6.8 I translate as 'human' since 'man' (אדם) often is a generic term in the Hebrew Bible. Some, however, have focused on this word to help sort out the force of the passage and the change in genre. Mays suggests that this is 'teaching meant for any *man* in Israel' (1976: 141, emphasis original). Dawes suggests 'mankind' (*sic*) in general (1988: 336-37). Hillers suggests that perhaps 'human creatureliness' (as opposed to divinity) is indicated (1984: 79); so also Allen (1976: 371). Shaw takes issue with these kinds of inter- pretations, arguing that it could not be reasonable to expect every Israelite to be just, and therefore this was directed to the king (1993: 177); by reading the king here, he chooses to understand the term as gendered (masculine).

The verb צנע, usually translated as 'humbly', only occurs in the MT here and in Prov. 11.2, where it is connected with 'wisdom'. Wolff points out that it also occurs in *Sir.* 16.25; 32.3; 34.22; 42.8, with the meaning 'well considered', 'prudent' or 'circumspect' (1990: 182); so Waltke (1988: 195). I have used 'wisely' to connote all of the above meanings; so also Hillers (1984: 76); Shaw (1993: 162).

Micah 6.9

The voice of Yahweh will call to the city, and your (ms) name will see success (wisdom). Listen (mpl) O tribe (O staff) (one leading away) and who appoints her (it)?

Verses 9-16 seem to shift gears again several times. First, in 6.9, the voice of Yahweh calls to the city, though which city is not indicated. The voice does not address a feminine participant but rather a masculine singular participant, saying, '*your* (ms) name will see suc- cess'. The address then moves into the

Mic. 6.9-16 is a difficult text, and so some consider it corrupt (Jeppesen 1984: 574; Mays 1976: 144); Hillers calls it rough and illogical (1984: 81). Wolff considers it to have been 'reworked by the insertion of secondary material' (1990: 188). Some supply context. For instance, in spite of the many shifts in gender and number throughout this passage, Cathcart and Jeppesen write, 'Mic. 6.9-14 is a diatribe against the cheating city, probably Samaria or Jerusalem' (1987: 110). Tournay considers the entire passage injected

2mpl with the imperative 'listen' (שמעו), followed by the masculine singular noun 'tribe' or 'staff' (מטה), and the short phrase, 'who will appoint her' (ומי יעדה). So the city, in spite of her linguistically feminine designations, is addressed as both the masculine singular (שמך and מטה) and the masculine plural (שמעו). Further, the feminine singular suffix on יעדה ('appoint her') may refer back to the city, but it is not clear what the relationship of the city is to the tribe, nor to the 2mpl addressee. In the short space of this one verse the gender and number shifts several times.

with an anti-Samaritan polemic by Judean scribes in the resettlement after the exile (1964: 514-24).

The meaning of the feminine noun, תושיה, 'success' (6.9), seems difficult to discern in this context; but it may have some relation to the success that comes with wisdom. The word occurs 12 times in the MT, most often in wisdom literature (Proverbs and Job); it is found in connection with 'counsel' (עצה) (Isa. 28.29; Prov. 8.14; Job 26.3); in connection with 'wisdom' (חכמה) (Prov. 18.1; Job 11.3; 26.3) and in connection with success (Job 5.12; 6.13). Given its association with wisdom, its use here may be related to the injunction to walk wisely with God in 6.8. (As an aside, Dahood, commenting on Moses' name in Mic. 6.4, finds the Canaanite etymology of Moses' name to be related to ושי 'be successful', the semitic root of תושיה [1983: 59]—though oddly he does not make the connection to this verse.) In order to render the connotation of wisdom some scholars repoint יראה ('see') to read 'fear'; so Allen (1976: 375); Hagstrom (1988: 93); many of the versions, see McKane who lists them (1998: 193). This repointing renders something like 'it is prudent to fear your name' (Wolff 1990: 185); similarly Allen (1976: 375); R.L. Smith (1984: 52); Hillers (1984: 80). Shaw reads without emending (1993: 162); so also Ben Zvi (2000: 158). Shaw suggests that it may be a gloss. The shift in gender from the feminine city to the masculine 'your name' is not generally commented upon.

The noun מטה could mean 'rod', or 'staff', or 'tribe'; or it could also be a masculine singular hiphil participle of נטה, 'one leading away', or 'one deceiving'—but this would be odd syntactically as there would be no object, and the problem of the shifts from plural to singular (and between genders) is not resolved. Most translate 'tribe' (Allen 1976: 375; Mays 1976: 143; Craigie 1985: 48; R.L. Smith 1984: 52; Wolff 1990: 185). Hillers translates 'tribe', but entertains the translation of 'rod' as 'the familiar figure for chastisement' (1984: 80-81); Shaw takes up this idea and considers Assyria as the rod (1993: 162).

The meaning of ומי יעדה ('who will appoint her') has also troubled scholars. Some follow a suggestion made by Wellhausen to emend the phrase to העיר ומועד ('the assembly of the city'); so Allen (1976: 375); Hagstrom (1988: 93 n. 13b); R.L. Smith (1984: 53); Mays (1976: 143); Hillers (1984: 80); Wolff (1990: 180); this is a way of dealing with the problems raised by both the 2mpl imperative שמעו ('listen') and the 3fs pronominal suffix on יעדה ('appoint her'). Jeppesen translates, 'who has made a decision about her' (1984: 574). Shoemaker reads, 'The tribe has heard, yet who testifies against her?' (1992: 198). Shaw translates, 'Listen! A rod— and who has appointed it again?', reading the first word of 6.10, עוד ('still', 'again') as part of the phrase (1993: 162, 173). Andersen and Freedman also append the particle, 'who appointed her *still*' (2000: 539). Shaw follows an earlier suggestion by Rudolph in considering the feminine singular pronominal suffix on יעדה as 'a neuter pronoun which takes the masculine noun מטה as its antecedent' (1993: 173).

Micah 6.10-12

[10]Is there still a wicked house, storerooms of wickedness and a cursed ephod of emaciation? [11]Will I be pure in the balances of wickedness, and in the purse of stones of treachery (false weights)? [12]Which her rich are full of violence and her inhabitants speak deception. And their (mpl) tongue is deceitful in their mouth.

Verses 10-11 continue in this cryptic

Scholars have found the question of purity unfitting in 6.11 in the first person voice. Wolff finds it 'not likely to have been spoken by Yahweh' and reads the piel, 'can I pronounce' (1990: 185-86). Hillers reads, 'can I tolerate' (1984: 80). Anderson and Freedman translate, 'shall I regard as pure' (2000: 542).

Because 6.12 begins the description of *her* rich and *her* inhabitants with the relative pronoun 'which' (אשר), for vein asking about the weight of the wickedness, and questioning whether *I* will be pure in the balance. This speaker seems to have the same kind of introspective tone as did the speaker of 6.6-7, seeming to focus on personal or ritual acceptability. By way of contrast though, here the suggestion is that the standards by which *I* will be judged are not trustworthy (where in 6.6-7, the concern is Yahweh's approval). As there, it is uncertain how this voice relates to the first person participant(s) in the rest of the book.

After this brief worry about personal measure, verse 12 then returns to the violence and deception of *her* rich and *her* inhabitants, presumably the inhabitants of the city in 6.9.

which there is no obvious antecedent, a number of scholars transpose 6.12 to some place prior to 6.10, keeping the references to the 3fs together (Mays 1976: 143; Hillers 1984: 80). For a clear overview of the various solutions and their problems, see Hagstrom (1988: 93 n. 13e) and McKane (1998: 196). Wolff reads אשר as 'because' (1990: 187), and does not transpose the text.

Micah 6.13-15

[13]And even I will make sore your (ms) smiting, making desolation against your sin. [14]You (ms) will eat and not be satisfied, your filth will be in your midst. And you will remove but you will not bring to safety, and what you save, I will put to the sword. [15]You will sow and not reap, you will tread olives but you will not pour oil, and grape stuff, but you will not drink wine.

Then in 6.13, *I* who was just a moment ago questioning *my* purity, now threaten and curse *you* (ms) with some kind of destruction, because of your sins. There is no indication, except for the type of threat issued, that the *I* has shifted from the prophet to Yahweh. Further, who are *you*? 'My people' is the figure to which 2ms pronouns refer most in the chapter. However, the closest referent for this (2ms) unnamed object of cursing is the already unclear 2ms suffix in 'your name will see success' (ותושיה יראה שמך), and previous to that, *you*, the individual told to do justice in 6.8 (who could be read as 'my

Wolff explains the switch to the 2ms in 6.13 after an accusation in the third person as typical of prophetic judgment, and in particular of Micah (2.3; 3.6, 12). The shift to the singular he relates to the fertility curses that follow, which he suggests are usually singular (1990: 196).

For suggestions about the problems of 6.14, see McKane (1998: 196-99). For the translation of ישחך ('filth') which only occurs as a noun here, see Williamson (1997: 367-69); Cathcart and Jeppesen (1987). Hillers follows the Syriac's translation as 'dysentery' (1984: 81), so also Ehrman (1973: 105).

Many scholars note the relation to the covenant curses in Deuteronomy (Allen 1976: 380-81; Waltke 1988: 198; Hillers 1984: 82; Wolff 1990: 189). Wolff finds evidence of later interpolations (1990: 189).

people' of 6.3-4). *You* could signify any of these entities. Verses 14-16 continue this threat, in language of Deuteronomic cursing.

Micah 6.16
Omri kept his own statutes (And he kept) (let him keep the statutes of Omri) and all the work of the house of Ahab. And you (mpl) walked in their counsels. Therefore I will make you (ms) as a waste and her inhabitants as an object of hissing. And you (mpl) will bear the reproach of my people.

Finally, in 6.16, there may be some direction as to the relationship between the various subjects and objects of this passage, though even this is not certain. The verse begins by speaking of Omri and Ahab, and their independence in keeping their own statutes (and presumably not those of Yahweh). *You* (mpl) are then accused of having walked in their counsels. This is said to be the reason (by means of the connecting 'therefore') for the attack on a masculine singular figure who seems to be equated through parallelism with *her* inhabitants. The address then returns to the plural: '*You* (mpl) will bear the reproach of *my people*'.

So it seems that *you* (mpl) may be leaders of some type, while both the destroyed *you* (ms) and the inhabitants of the city may be *my people* who reproach *you* (mpl), the leaders, for misguiding the people and bringing on destruction. And yet this conjecture is clouded by the fact that both *you* (ms) and the inhabitants of the city are accused of wrongdoing (6.12-13).

The use of the (self-reflexive) hithpael for שׁמר is odd. The two other times it occurs in the MT it is in the sense of keeping oneself *from* something (2 Sam. 22.24; Ps. 18.24).

In spite of the pervasiveness of the masculine addressees in this verse (both singular and plural), scholars tend to veer toward thinking of this as an address to the feminine city of 6.9. Andersen and Freedman take the two feminine singular pronominal suffixes to refer back to the city in 6.9, though they cannot decide if this is Samaria or Jerusalem (2000: 555). Craigie suggests that this is a warning to Jerusalem not to follow the example of Samaria (1985: 50). Shaw finds that the presence of Omri and Ahab in the text favours an address to Samaria (1993: 180); so also McKane, who also suggests that Samaria figures prominently and scandalously in the Deuteronomic literature, with which this passage resonates (1998: 203). Hillers finds that there is 'a pervasive disharmony in person and number and voice in this passage, which must be resolved somehow'; he emends to *the 3fs throughout*: from the 2mpl ותלכו to the 3fs ותלך ('she walks'), and from the 2ms אתך to the 3fs אותה ('you') (1984: 81). Wolff emends to the second person, 'your inhabitants', but does not specify gender (1990: 187).

A number of scholars read 'the peoples' instead of 'my people' (Wolff 1990: 187; Mays 1976: 144; Allen 1976: 377; McKane 1998: 206).

In chapter 6 then, what appears straightforward is that the address to the masculine singular *you, my people*, is spoken by Yahweh, who calls *you* to remember the tradition. It is also clear that *you* are called to justice in

6.8 and that *you* are violently punished at the end of the chapter (6.13-15). What is not clear is how the *you* of *my people* in 6.3-5 relates to the *you* called to do justice (6.8), to the feminine figure of the city to whom Yahweh calls (6.9), to her inhabitants (6.12), to *you* (ms) whose name will see success (6.9), to *you* (ms) who is punished at the end of the book (6.13-15), or to *you* (mpl) accused of following the wrong counsels (6.16). Do the conflations of gender and number in 6.9—which seems to be something of transitional verse—have any impact on how the various forms are read in the rest of the passage? Many scholars read it as such, but the text is ambiguous.

Micah 7

Chapter 7 is the conclusion to the book. It seems to move from doom to hope and perhaps also to give a voice to the people. Verses 1-6 carry on the lament of evil deeds after the fashion of 6.11-12. Then 7.7-20 shifts to a more generally hopeful tone and style to end the book, but there are still constant shifts in gender, speaker, addressee and tone. There is an unidentified speaker in 7.1-2, 7-10 who seems both to lament and to express hope, and whom many have considered to be one or other of the nation's cities. Throughout, the fluidity between the various participants in the book continues. The book ends with a flourish of praise to God.

Micah 7.1

Woe is me, for I have become like the gatherings of summer harvest, like the gleanings of vintage. There are no clusters to eat, ([no] first fruit [which] my soul desires). My soul desires first fruit.

The chapter begins with a cry of woe in the first person. This follows directly from the first person threat to *you* (ms) in 6.16, but once again it is uncertain if it is the same person speaking. As at the beginning of the book, with its lamenting voice of 1.8, here in 6.16–7.1, a lamenting, almost anthropomorphic, voice follows directly upon what seems to be a divine threat of punishment. The metaphor here seems clearly to be one of failed harvest, and unsatisfied desire. *I* lament that there are no

Most scholars consider the first person in 7.1 to be a different voice than in 6.16. Wolff considers it the prophet, though not Micah (so also Mays [1976: 150]), because of the terms used for the accused authorities (official, judge and great man) (1990: 203-206). Waltke considers it the voice of the prophet Micah who 'identifies with Yahweh at the beginning of the chapter and with the remnant in the latter half of the chapter' (1988: 199); similarly Allen (1976: 385); Shaw (1993: 172). Hillers considers it the prophet, quite possibly even Micah himself (1984: 85). Reicke considers 7.1-6 part of the liturgy that most scholars find in 7.7-20, so that the whole chapter might be considered a unity; he suggests that the liturgy was perhaps connected to an end of harvest festival (1967: 351). Hagstrom

clusters of fruit to eat in the harvest. *My soul longs for first fruit.*

considers that it might be a collective voice (1988: 97). Allen distinguishes between the individual lament in 7.1-7 and the communal lament in 7.8-20 (1976: 384). Shoemaker reads 7.1 as attached to 6.16 as a closure to 6.9-15; he considers the first person voice to be an 'embedded virtual quotation' (1992: 205), i.e. an unmarked quotation (1992: 281-89).

For a discussion of the versions translations of the phrase בכורה אותה נפשי ('my soul desires first fruit'), see McKane (1998: 208). Many carry over the particle of negative and insert a relative pronoun, 'no first fruit which my soul desires' (McKane 1998: 216; Wolff 1990: 200; Reicke 1967: 353; Shaw 1993: 165; Allen 1976: 383). Though this is plausible, the verse still makes sense as it stands; indeed, in some way the simple assertion makes the image of longing more forceful.

Micah 7.2-3

²The faithful one perishes from the land and there is no upright one among humans. All of them will lie in wait for blood, each of them will hunt his brother (with) a net. ³The prince is asking concerning (against) the (doing of) evil, hands to do good. (Upon evil, hands, for doing good). (The prince is asking), and the one judging with the vengeance, and the mighty one is saying [that] that (he) is the desire of his soul. They twist (weave) her (it) (fs).

Verse 2 speaks of the righteous (ms) having disappeared from the land, and *they* (mpl) are described hunting each other, while 7.3 describes evil behaviour with infinitives and masculine singular participles. A prince is asking for something, but it is not clear what. The one judging with vengeance seems to be a subject without a predicate. Finally the mighty one seems to mimicking the speaker in 7.1. Where in v. 1 the speaker

Verse 3a is particularly difficult. The word הרע could either be the noun 'evil' or it could be the hiphil infinitive construct of רעע ('do evil' or 'doing evil'); its relationship to 'hands' (כפים) and 'for doing good' (להיטיב, another hiphil infinitive construct) are unclear. The shift at the end of 7.3 to the 3fs pronoun on ויעבתוה ('they twist it') is also odd; the closest feminine singular antecedent is 'his soul', or 'my soul' of 7.1. For various suggestions as to possible antecedents such as 'justice' (משפט), see Hillers (1984: 84). McKane argues that 'twisting justice' is the sense of the phrase (1998: 211). Shaw calls it 'an indefinite neuter object' (1993: 164). Mays deletes the pronominal suffix reading טובם ('their good') at the beginning of 7.4 as the object of the verb, 'they twist their good' (1976: 149).

speaks of the first fruit which 'my soul desires', here the mighty one's speech is given indirectly: something is the desire of his soul. All of this is summed up with the single word phrase at the end of 7.3, 'and they twist it/her' (ויעבתוה), with no obvious antecedent for the feminine singular pronominal suffix.

Micah 7.4-6

⁴Their good is like a brier and upright-ness (an upright one) more than a hedge. The day of your (ms) waiting, your judgment, comes. Now it will be their confusion. ⁵Do not have faith (2mpl) in a friend, do not trust in an intimate (ms). Guard (ms) the entrances of your (ms) mouth from the one (fs) lying on your bosom. ⁶For a son will treat his father with contempt and a daughter will rise up with (against) her mother, a daughter-in-law with (against) her husband's mother. A man's enemies are the men of his house.

Verse 4 continues in the 3mpl, describing *their* (mpl) good (טובם)— perhaps the kind of good done by the hands in 7.3—as briar bushes. But the texts slips into direct address, speaking of the day *you* (ms) have been waiting for (יום מצפיך), *your* (ms) judgment, comes (פקדתך באה). Who *you* might be is a mystery, but the singular address in conjunction with the momentousness of the day, would make it seem like an address to a collective entity (as in 6.14-16), as opposed to one of the authorities mentioned just prior. And then abruptly, it will be *their* (mpl) confusion (תהיה מבוכתם). Verse 5 returns again to the direct address, giving warnings about traitors, first in the 2mpl and then in 2ms. Verse 6 continues on this general scene of distrust in the third person, warning of childrens' disrespectful attitudes, and of feminine uprisings.

Andersen and Freedman suggest that the shift from the plural to the singular in 7.5 is due to the emphasis on the individual and his wife (*sic*) (2000: 563); however, this does not clarify who the participants are here, or what relationship they have to the nation and its leaders.

For a discussion of the way 7.5-6 are taken up in the Gospels, early Jewish eschatology, and rabbinic texts, see Grelot (1986).

The daughters and daughters-in-law are without comment interpreted as rising up *against* the mothers and husbands' mothers. But the preposition ב ('with' or 'in'), is only rarely used in this sense (Deut. 19.15-16; Ps. 27.12; Hos. 10.4), and usually in some sort of legal context (witnesses accusing). If read in its more usual sense, the preposition could allow that the women, like the sons, are in contempt of fathers.

Micah 7.7-10

7And I will watch with Yahweh, I will wait for the God of my salvation. My God will hear me. 8Do not rejoice over me, O my enemy. Although (when) (if) I fall, I will rise; although (when) (if) I will dwell in darkness, Yahweh is a light to me. (Do not rejoice over me, my enemy, because I fell. I rose. When I will sit in darkness, Yahweh is a light to me.) 9I will bear the anger of Yahweh. For I sin (sinned) against him, until he will argue my case and he will make my justice. He will bring me out to the light, and I will look upon his righteousness. 10Let my enemy be afraid, and let shame cover her. The one (fs) saying to me, 'Where is Yahweh, your (fs) God'. My eyes look upon her. Now she (you, ms) will become a trampling place, like mud of the streets.

Verses 7-10 start out with what at first seems to be a statement of hope in the first person whose identity, once again, is not stated. This tone is a remarkable change from what has gone before, though this kind of shift to hope in Yahweh, following lament, is familiar in the complaint Psalms. This opening statement is followed by an address to *you* (fs), identified as *my enemy*, beginning in 7.8 with the imperative 'do not rejoice over me, my enemy'. However, the speaker's proclamation in 7.9 sounds almost like an ultimatum, a political *revendication*: *I* sin (and therefore will bear the wrath of Yahweh) *until* he brings me into the light and pleads my cause. One wonders if more than a clear and simple statement of hope and patient waiting, this might be a demanding response to all the accusations: 'I will continue sinning until I get justice'. In 7.10, *my* enemy is now described in the third person as one saying, 'where is *your* God' (with a fs suffix, אלהיך), as if he is

Wolff considers 7.7 to be part of the previous pericope, because the 'ו-*copulativum* in the first word of v. 7 connects it more closely to the preceding verses than v. 8' and because, starting in 7.8, the verbs become perfect (1990: 203); so also McKane (1998: 217), and Allen (1976: 389-90), who considers it the affirmation of confidence typical of the individual lament. Mays finds it transitional (1976: 153), so also Hagstrom (1988: 97); R.L. Smith (1984: 58); Ben Zvi (2000: 173). Most others follow Gunkel, who in his influential article 'The Close of Micah' (1928) finds 7.7-20 to be comparable to a lament psalm (1928: 125); within the passage, Gunkel finds 7.7-10 to be a lament, 7.11-13 to be a divine oracle, 7.14-17 to be a prayer for deliverance, 7.18-20 a hymn of assurance (1928: 142). Many scholars divide the passage up likewise, see Willis (1974: 66); Hillers (1984: 89); Wolff (1990: 215). Willis considers this text originally to have been from Northern Israel, preserved as ritual and reappropriated later for use in a Judean context (1974: 72-76); Hillers finds Willis's hypothesis unconvincing (1984: 89-90). Wolff considers that liturgical elements are present, but the final form is not 'a liturgy' (1990: 215). Shaw considers it liturgy with a rhetorical purpose of convincing the people to 'patient acceptance of punishment' (1993: 209-10).

Those who consider 7.7-20 to be liturgical also tend to follow Gunkel in considering the first person voice to be that of Zion (1928: 127) or Jerusalem; so Wolff (1990: 220); Hillers (1984: 90); Allen (1976: 394); Shoemaker (1992: 209); Andersen and Freedman (2000: 577). Shaw reads the city as Samaria (1993: 215-20). Hillers is more cautious, suggesting that the speaker 'is the devastated people, personified', *perhaps* the city (1984: 90).

not visibly meting out justice. The response to this taunt—that she, the enemy, will be put to shame, trampled like mud in the streets—repeats, more aggressively, the hope for Yahweh's appearance.

Interestingly, the feminine singular suffix in the enemy's address to the speaker indicates that perhaps it has been a feminine figure speaking all along. This is the only time in the book that the speaker is clearly feminine.

Micah 7.11-13

¹¹A day (is) for building your (fs) walls. That day borders are distant. ¹²That (is the) day, and he will come unto you (ms) from afar, Assyria and the cities of Egypt. From afar, Egypt, and until the river and the sea, from the sea and the mountain of the mountain. ¹³And the land will be for a desolation, on account of (against) its (her) inhabitants, because of the fruit of their (mpl) works.

Verses 11-13 seem to shift between hope and desolation. The possible triumph over the enemy in 7.10 is followed in 7.11 with a day for building *your* (fs) walls, a day when borders will be distant. This sounds like a time of expansion, or rebuilding. And in verse 12, in what seems to be a run-on sentence, a day breaks when Assyria and Egypt will come to *you* (suddenly ms) from afar. This is reminiscent of the utopic passage of 4.1-8, and could imply peaceful domination. But then, abruptly in 7.13, the land will be desolate, again because of *her* inhabitants and *their* (mpl) actions (recalling 3.12 and 6.12).

Micah 7.14-15

¹⁴Shepherd (rule) your (ms) people, with your staff, the flock of your inheritance, one dwelling in the isolation of

Scholars make much of the 2fs suffix on 'your God' (אלהיך). Here, because the language is read as distressed hope (and not, say, as political demand), scholars do not minimize the feminine, but consider a feminine city to be the speaker; cf. the commentary on 4.8 where the feminine forms are minimized in the description of Zion's fortification; or 2.12, where the 2fs suffix on כלך, ' all of you (fs)' (referring to Jacob and the remnant of Israel) is ignored.

Gunkel reads 7.11-13 as a hopeful divine oracle about Jerusalem: 'the city shall become a centre for the whole world ...the heathen shall seek the dwelling place of the most High, while the whole earth shall become a desert' (1928: 130); so also Wolff (1990: 225); Waltke (1988: 204); Allen (1976: 398). Hillers points out the problem with this hypothesis and resolves it: 'There would be a kind of illogicity in having foreigners come on pilgrimage to Zion, and at the same time have their own lands laid waste...but these are separate parts of the eschatological vision, not to be pressed' (1984: 91). Lescow considers these verses a later gloss (1997: 249). Willis considers the 'unnamed city' in 7.11 to be Samaria (1974: 69). Shaw is innovative in his suggestion that 7.12 refers to an attack by enemy nations and 7.13 describes the results (1993: 203-205).

Some emend the 2ms suffix on ועדיך ('unto you') in 7.12 to the 2fs (Wolff 1990: 213; Hillers 1984: 88; Allen 1976: 391). Williamson suggests emending to ועדרך ('your flock'), to provide a subject for the 3ms verb יבוא ('he will come'): 'your flock will come from afar' (1997: 371).

The identity of the second person addressee in 7.14 is almost uniformly taken to be Yahweh and 7.14-17 as a kind of prayer. However, if *you* are considered to

the forest, in the midst of a garden (Carmel). Bashan and Gilead will pasture as in the days of old. ¹⁵*As in the days of your (ms) going out from the land of Egypt, I will show him wonders.*

Verses 14-15 pick up the 2ms form of 7.12 beginning with the imperative, 'shepherd *your* (ms) people with *your* staff'. The verse recalls the predicted shepherding ruler of 5.3 and the return of this language here could possibly suggest an address to a ruler. This is complicated, though, by the first person voice that enters in 7.15, 'as in the days of *your* going out from Egypt, *I* will show *him* wonders'. The reference to *your* going out from Egypt would seem to indicate a switch from addressing a ruler to addressing the people as a whole, though this does not account for the odd 3ms *him*. The *I* would seem to be Yahweh, since Yahweh is usually associated with the exodus and with showing wonders.

be Yahweh (the shepherd) in 7.14, then the *I* in 7.15 raises questions about both the speaker and the addressee. Hillers accounts for the 2ms in 'your going out', by arguing that it refers to Yahweh's going out from Egypt (1984: 91).

The pronominal suffix on אראנו ('I will show') in 7.15 could be read as either 3ms ('him'), or as 1cpl ('us'); although it is not impossible to read 1cpl with the 1cs verb, the 3ms seems much easier ('I will show him'). However, because many scholars read this as part of a prayer, it tends to be emended to הראנו, reading it as a 2ms imperative and the pronominal suffix as a 1cpl ('show us'). This eliminates the sudden shift to the first person voice and the reference to the 3ms *him*; so Wolff (1990: 214); Barré (1982: 274); McKane (1998: 233); Mays (1976: 163); Lescow (1997: 245). Allen translates in the same way, but doesn't emend the consonants, rather, he reads it as a causative 'Aramaic-type Aphel' (1976: 392). Conversely, Waltke reads as an interruption of the prayer by Yahweh who promises to show Israel wonders (1988: 206); so also Hagstrom (1988: 101); Craigie (1985: 54).

Micah 7.16-20

¹⁶*The nations will see and be ashamed, from (because of) (without) all their greatness. They will put hand against mouth. Their ears will be deaf.* ¹⁷*They will lick the dust like the snake, like the things crawling on the ground. They will tremble (come trembling) from (without) their fortresses, to Yahweh our God. They will tremble and be afraid because of (more than) you (ms).* ¹⁸*Who, O God, is like you (ms), one who forgives sins, and one who passes over transgression, for the remnant of his inheritance. He does not make strong for ever his anger, for he delights in faithfulness.* ¹⁹*He returns, he has mercy on us, he tramples down*

Many scholars include 7.16-17 as part of the prayer in 7.14-17, reading the 3mpl forms of 7.16-17 as jussives (Gunkel 1928: 135; Wolff 1990: 212; McKane 1998: 233-34; Allen 1976: 392; Mays 1976: 163). In this general vein, Barré (1982) finds these two verses and Ps. 86.16-17 to be similar to an Amarna letter in which the idea of the humiliation of enemies is seen as a sign of the king's favour. Conversely Hillers translates as imperfect (1984: 89), so also Hagstrom (1988: 102); Craigie (1985: 55).

our sins. And you (ms) send all their (mpl) sins to the depths of the sea. [20]You will give faithfulness to Jacob, and faithfulness to Abraham, which you swore to our fathers from the days of old.

Verses 16-17 seem to be the start of a collective speech about Yahweh and the nations, using 1cpl forms (thus far used in the taunt/lament of 2.4, the more upbeat speech of the nations (or Israel) in 4.2, 5, the lament of chastisement in 4.16, and the resolution to resist Assyria in 5.4-5). Here the tone does not seem to be in keeping with the more inclusive and welcoming attitude toward the nations in 7.12. The promise is that the nations will see and be ashamed, they will lick the dust and come trembling from their fortresses to Yahweh *our* God, they will be afraid of *you* (ms). In 7.18 someone asks, 'Who is like *you* (ms), O God (אל)?' and elaborates on this using the by now familiar technique of participles moving from second person forms into the third person: 'one who passes over transgression (ptc)... he does not make strong his anger (ms verb)'. One might ask if this transition, as before, forms a kind of identification at a distance (addressee as observer). But this time the identification is with God, instead of with the accused.

Verse 19 proclaims his mercy (in the third person) to *us* and then moves back to address the deity, speaking of them (3mpl): '*you* (ms) (ותשליך) send all *their* (חטאותם) sins to the depths of the sea'. One wonders who is speaking here, why the shift from having mercy on *us*, to speaking about *their* sins. Is this some kind of distinction between people and leaders?

The book ends with a formulaic proclamation of *your* (ms) generosity. As appropriate to the close of a book, these last verses echo themes that have gone before ('transgression', פשע,

recalling 1.5, 13; 3.8; 'remnant', שארית,
recalling 1.12; 4.6; 5.6-7; 'faithfulness',
חסד, recalling 6.8; even 'return', שוב
recalling 2.4; 5.2). At the end of the day,
the indistinctions of the participants
even to the end of the book make no
difference, all are ultimately forgiven.

Thus chapter 7 picks up the themes from throughout the book: the
lamenting prophet, the feminine figure pitted against her enemies, the
nations streaming to Yahweh (though not necessarily on happy terms
here); the ruler shepherding. As in the rest of the book, it is not easy to
sort out who is speaking to whom and for what purposes. What is
different here is that the feminine figure also seems to speak in the first
person, and that the leaders are not mentioned at all (unless they are the
3mpl figure whose sins are spoken of in 7.19). There also seems to be a
kind of demand for justice from Yahweh, which may be a response to
the accusations and violence against the feminine cities throughout the
book. Perhaps the hopefulness of the last verses provides as close an
answer to this demand for justice as the book gets, while at the same
time proving true the speaker's assertions of Yahweh's help in making
this demand.

Summary

I would not like, at this point, to draw any conclusions about the text. I
have only tried to highlight some of the issues with which one is
confronted when reading the text of Micah. My task here was to
introduce the various participants in the text (my people, the feminine
cities, the corrupt leaders, the prophet(s), Yahweh, the masculine rulers,
the remnant, and the often unidentified masculine singular *you*), and to
show the frequent difficulty in distinguishing between these participants.
In addition, I have tried to point out the difficulty in knowing when
speeches start and end, and to whom they are addressed, as well as the
disjunction of the 'moods' or tones in the text (indicting or hopeful).
Throughout I have indicated how scholars have dealt with all the shifts
in the book, most often trying to mitigate the ambiguities thus produced.

With this exposition of these ambiguities of the text in place then, I
turn first to look at how, in spite of all these differences and ambiguities,
the text tends to be read in more homogenizing ways that seem to
employ particular notions of gender and of Israel's identity. When I
return to the text in Chapter 6, I will be interested in looking at these

various connections and disjunctions between the signs of the text, in order to see how they might both establish and disrupt constructs of gender and nation, as well as readers' investment in these constructs.

5

Damsels in Distress: Pedagogical Objects and Discourses

In this chapter I do a rather simple thing: I make the analogy between the way the nation of Israel is figured in scholarly work on Micah, and Bhabha's notion of pedagogical objects and discourses (cultural icons, stereotypes and historical narratives). More precisely, I show how scholars read the nation of Israel as an oppressed, contrite and passive woman in need of rescue or redemption by the active divine male ruler who leads the nation into a glorious future of dominion over other nations. I suggest that this image functions, in a very similar way to Bhabha's notion of pedagogical objects and discourses, to unify, and so to disavow, difference.

Like Bhabha's 'cultural icon', the image of the nation Israel as suffering, rescued, led and exalted tends to homogenize difference. Like Bhabha's 'stereotype', it is an image of the nation produced in scholarship that both fascinates and horrifies: the woman-nation is 'ideal' (most often Zion) when she is penitent and cognizant of her need for divine rule; but her salvation can only be realized in relation to 'that other image' of the bad woman (most often read as Samaria), justifiably punished. Like Bhabha's 'historical narrative', the image of the woman-nation is often linked to foundational historical events (the exodus and the Davidic kingdom), which it is intimated, will be repeated again in a glorious future. And like Bhabha's 'cultural icon'—recalling that it plays a role similar to Lacan's and Žižek's fantasy object standing in for an ideological pinning point or master signifier—this image seems to be a fantasy object that stands in for two more widespread discourses. These are: (a) the notion of gender (as binary), and (b) the 'theological' identity and destiny of Israel as intimately related to Yahweh's gift of the land in covenant, his retraction of it in punishment, and his restoration of it after requisite suffering and penitence. Like both Bhabha's pedagogical object and Žižek's elevated fantasy object, this image represents larger ideological discourses. As an ideological stand-in this image of the nation as a woman pins down difference in the text, stops the sliding of the signs of the texts in a particular place, and gives the reader a point of identification that accords ideologically.

I look at three instances in which scholars use this way of describing Israel in their readings of Micah: Lamontte Luker's article 'Beyond Form Criticism: The Relation of Doom and Hope Oracles in Micah 2–6' (1987); James L. Mays's commentary on Micah (1976); and Charles Shaw's monograph *The Speeches of Micah: A Rhetorical-Historical Analysis* (1993). I choose these scholars not only because this image of the nation of Israel appears in their work in particularly obvious ways, but also because it shows that this kind of reading occurs within a range of different methods (literary analysis, redaction criticism, historical-rhetorical analysis, respectively). These scholars are, however, by no means the only ones to read in this way, and I indicate points where others have read likewise.

I should note here that the images emphasized by these scholars *can* be found in the text. For instance, the image of Yahweh leading the remnant as a feminine flock is present in 2.12 and 4.6-7; the discourse of Yahweh's rescue from some kind of bondage is present in 2.13, 4.10, 6.4 and 7.15; longing for the divinely appointed ruler is present in 5.1-4; the image of a political entity passively waiting for Yahweh is present in 7.7-8; the image of the punished woman is present in 1.6-7, possibly 1.15-16, 3.12 and 4.14; the image of the woman in labour appears in 4.9, 10, and 5.2. But to conflate all of these images into the more overarching image of a woman's relation to Yahweh and his ruler is in a sense to allow the signs of the text to 'cumulate' (in Bhabhian terms) into a certain kind of discourse about the nation. What emerges is a discourse that highlights only a few of the diverse and differing signs of the text, thus smoothing them out into a seemingly natural biblical vision of the nation as an oppressed and suffering woman, one deserving of punishment, who will be transformed by Yahweh through the leading of the divine ruler.

Luker: Wounded Woman, Divine Warrior

I begin with the work of Luker, both because it is the shortest, and because it highlights the binary gender opposition at work in these kinds of readings. In his 1987 article 'Beyond Form Criticism', in which he presents in condensed form the findings of his 1985 dissertation, Luker is concerned with using literary analysis to account for the shifts between doom and hope oracles. He suggests that wordplay and the themes of 'lamentation, Divine Warrior and personification of the people as a woman' are the means by which the redactor ties the divergent oracles together to 'create a cohesive composition' (1987: 285). He finds these themes to be present in Mic. 1 and 7, which he suggests act together as the framework into which a redactor has fitted the oracles of chs. 2–6. Luker traces the themes of the people as a lamenting woman and the deity as a rescuing warrior as they repeat throughout the book. As he states in his dissertation and implies in his article, these images unify the text and blur the boundaries between the categories of 'hope' and 'doom' that have often been ascribed to the text (1985: 224-26).

The conclusions Luker draws as a result of tracing the repetition of these cohesive themes fall along particular gender stereotypes: a suffering woman as *passive* victim, rescued by an *active* male hero. Throughout his article, Luker seems to find a typical gender binary (active male, passive female) whereby, 'Daughter Zion wails alone, recalls the Exodus (7.15) and hopes for the return of the Warrior to fight on her behalf' (1987: 285). His own use of language also betrays this stance toward gender. He speaks of the text's rhetorical strategy of wordplay, 'hold-[ing] the listener's attention, as it was meant to *capture* Lady Zion's' (1987: 293, emphasis mine). 'Lady Zion' is portrayed, even in this explanatory metaphor, as helpless and imprisoned, and interestingly the listener is likened to her. Conversely, Luker describes Yahweh's relation to the feminine people in what might be considered highly phallic terms. He writes, 'note how the introduction of the remnant concept leads naturally to *need for the True Head*' (1987: 289, emphasis mine); or elsewhere, '[in 4.1-7] the *Mountain is raised. It points beyond* 3.12 where Zion is left desolate' (1987: 291, emphasis mine). Phallic or not, this language portrays the female figure as needing the ruler to prevent her total fragmentation and to be lifted beyond her desolation.[1] However, in this reading it is Yahweh's work that begins this fragmentation in the first place, violently culling and gathering the remnant (Luker builds on the two meanings of אסף: to gather, or to remove and destroy) (1987: 287, 89). Thus even the flock's identity as remnant is violently bestowed upon her, while she remains passive.

Along these same lines, Luker reads the various shifts in imagery that occur between 4.8 and 5.3 as the lament of a suffering mother and a celebration of the divine warrior through the Davidic ruler whom she will bear. The section, as Luker delineates it,[2] begins with 'the subject of

---

1.   For a similar binary—Israel as female victim, Yahweh as male rescuer—see Hillers on 5.9-14 (a passage in which if the addressee is Israel, it is clearly referred to in the 2ms: והכרתי סוסיך מקרבך האבדתי מרכבתיך). Hillers writes, 'Without these foreign, false sources of trust, Israel's protection will be carried out by *her* God. Israel's rights have already in the past been violated by other nations, but *she cannot and should not avenge herself*. Instead the supreme power will step in to vindicate *her* rights by punishing *her* adversaries' (1984: 73, emphasis mine).

2.   Cf. Shaw who, as noted below, reads 4.9–5.14 as a section.

Zion, personified as a woman who is nicknamed מגדל עדר [Tower of the Flock]', and ends in 5.3 with a 'picture of the ideal Davidic king shep-herding...[which] the prophet evidently understood...[as] a world-wide peace achieved by the Divine Warrior' (1987: 295). Because there is 'shepherding imagery' at the beginning and end of the passage (4.8 and 5.3), Luker argues that descriptions of Zion found in 4.8-14 'point to the messianic shepherd who will be born of Mother Zion' (1987: 292). In this view then, the descriptions about Zion are not really about Zion, but about her son; Zion's role is to bring the messianic ruler into the world. Zion 'will bear one fit to be [king] (4.9)...to rule for the Shepherd of the flock in the age of peace to come' (1987: 293). Zion's own actions in this passage are disavowed (see Chapter 6 for a thorough discussion).

Not only is Zion merely a mother in Luker's reading, but she also suffers in this role: '[the daughter of Jerusalem and the daughter of Zion] בת ירושלם (v. 8)/ בת ציון (v. 10) must shriek and cry out [like a woman in labour] כיולדה (vv. 9, 10; 5.2). It is a time of pain, but the *necessary pain* will *bear* the future in which the tables will be turned' (1987: 292-93, emphasis mine). And though she might suffer through military violence at the hands of the nations who 'discipline' her (1987: 195), and apparently even die in her time of travail, 'the Lady-of-the-Troops' *funeral ritual is part of the lancination which precedes the joy*' (1987: 293, emphasis mine). This 'lancinating' Lady of the Troops is also, for Luker, the 'lady in labour' who bears the king (1987: 293). In these ways, Luker interprets the woman as a sacrificing mother, enduring pain for the greater good, while the man is portrayed as a leader able to rescue and bring peace. Further, though Luker does not explicitly state it, as for instance Wolff does,[3] his language makes it clear that he under-stands Zion's suffering as requisite to her restoration. The stereotypic expectation for a sacrificially giving mother is all too present here.

In order to read this way, however, Luker makes a number of un-marked conflations. For instance, it seems that he considers the question in v. 9, 'why do you raise a battle cry?' (למה תריעי רע), to be a reference to the shrieking and crying of the woman in labour in v. 10 (יולדה), though he does not say why. And it seems he reads the 'Daughter of the Troops' (בת גדוד) of 4.13 as the same 'woman in labour' (יולדה) of 5.2, though there

---

3.   Wolff uses a similar image, but likens birthing to punishment and acceptance of that punishment: 'As certainly as the woman in labor will successfully give birth only after she has suffered birthpangs...just as certainly those expelled from Jerusalem will be saved from the violence of their enemies by Yahweh only after they make their way to Babylon. Israel arrives at the path to freedom only by experiencing the yes to the previously ordained punishment (cf. 1.16; 2.3f.; 3.12)' (1990: 148).

is a complete change of scene (5.1) that falls between. He also minimizes
certain features of the text, such as the fact that the male king and
counselor perish in 4.9, the gender ambiguity of the warrior Daughter of
Zion in 4.13, or the towering Daughter of Zion in 4.8 addressed by the
masculine pronoun. Luker maintains the unity of the feminine Zion
figure in 4.9–5.3, by arguing that the masculine address to Zion in 4.8 and
5.3 is simply a result of the influence of surrounding masculine imagery
and wordplay (1987: 292 n. 16). By omitting or downplaying textual
features, he glosses over a good many of the shifts and ambiguities within
these verses (see my Chapter 4).

Luker ends his article by pointing out that the Divine Warrior does not
in fact always rescue, but at times also judges and punishes the woman.
In Mic. 6, according to Luker's reading, 'the Divine Warrior is enthroned
as King and Judge' (1987: 298), and the prophet represents his complaint to the city (6.9). Although the reference to the city in 6.9 is
obscure, Luker uses it to conjure the image of the bad woman for the
whole of chs. 6–7, speculating, 'perhaps she [the city in 6.9] is Jerusalem,
perhaps Samaria, *perhaps another of Israel's prostitutes*' (1987: 299,
emphasis mine). In this, he makes the figure of the bad, punishable
woman (not even readily apparent in 6.9) that much more fascinating by
inserting the idea of prostitution where it is not otherwise present.[4] For
Luker, the violent reproach of 'pillage…at the hand of the Warrior' in ch.
6 is due to the fact that Israel, 'the covenantal people', does not listen.
However Luker suggests, condensing much of the material in chs. 6–7,
though the city/people/woman is punished 'her God can and will
[listen]' and 'will show his righteousness *as revealed in the Exodus* and
Conquest…[which are] the basis for a new [righteousness] (7.9)' (1987:
300, emphasis mine). Here, the female figure is both punished for being
inferior to the male figure (*not as good at* listening), and for a kind of
independence, a lack of contrition (*not listening*). Yahweh, on the other
hand is righteous, 'filled with [*hesed*] (7.18) [he] will share it with his
covenant people' (1987: 300). In response to this judgment, the 'lamenting lady of chapter 7 cries out…and she expresses her חרפה "reproach"
(6.16)…[she] laments due to the approach of the Divine Warrior' (1987:
300). In all of this, it seems that although Luker would have the woman
punished and penitent, he invokes the historical narrative of the exodus
and conquest as the future hope for this sorry figure.

---

4.   Interestingly, the very last line of Luker's dissertation reads, 'for though
corporate nation be engaged in prostitution, she is still [Yahweh's] dear daughter'
(1985: 228).

Mays: Power that Perfects Itself in Weakness

Where Luker takes some readerly license, making certain conflations and leaps to arrive at his reading, Mays tends to pay more attention to the details of the text in his *Micah: A Commentary* (1976). However, he arrives at essentially the same overall reading, using theological glosses and explanations to account for textual details as they relate to his analysis of the redaction of the book. In Mays's analysis, the arrangement of the book in its final redaction is specifically theological: 'within each section [1.2–5.15 and 6.1–7.20] the arrangement and shaping of material …bring[s] the individual units under the control of broader kerygmatic purposes' (1976: 3). Following these kerygmatic purposes, the first section is addressed to all people, but shows Yahweh's judgment of Samaria and Jerusalem, as well as his redemption of them for the purpose of showing the nations that they must either submit or be punished. The second section is addressed to Israel who must be judged, but who will be saved through God's forgiveness (1976: 3). Mays arrives at this reading by tracing what he finds to be the redactional layers of the book, and he finds that for both sections 'the *future of Jerusalem in the midst of the peoples* is a major concern' (1976: 33, emphasis mine). As he goes through the various layers of the text, it becomes clear that he sees Jerusalem's future strength as a result of Yahweh's rescue of Israel, from her (justified) suffering, by the divine ruler.

In a passage from his introduction that draws together these ideas, Mays writes:

> The election of Zion is to be the place where God's reign is manifest on earth will be fulfilled (*sic*). The judgment is not rejected or ignored. Its *suffering is incorporated*…as a fact which determines the present. The confident promises express the trust that YHWH will resume his former way with the daughter of Zion by redeeming, protecting, and *raising up a ruler* who will be the shepherd of Israel to keep them in the *strength that comes from* God (1976: 27, emphasis mine).

Here, as with Luker's reading, we have the notion of the suffering passive woman and the rescuing, enabling man.

Mays brings out this gendered theme of Yahweh's relation to Israel, when he comments on individual passages in the book. This can perhaps best be seen in his treatment of some of the details of chs. 4–5. As in Luker's reading, for Mays, the Daughter of Zion's birth pains in ch. 4 are necessary: 'they are the birth pains of a new phase of YHWH's dealing with Israel' (1976: 106). This new phase brings the 'supremacy of Zion over the nations as the site of YHWH's reign' (1976: 100). Yet Mays makes sure to show that Zion's 'supremacy' is fully supernatural, an act of salvation. For instance, Mays brings out the nation's ideal helplessness in his discussion of the gathered flock of 4.6-7 (described in the text using feminine singular participles). Here he gives a theological gloss on the lame flock, reading it as the weak and guilty feminine persona for the people of Judah (1976: 100),[5] 'cast out by YHWH because of their treason....YHWH's rescue of the flock, then, is a work of his power and grace overcoming their weakness and guilt' (1976: 100-101). Mays backs this position up through reference to other scriptures, saying, 'YHWH will make the wounded into the mighty, and show himself to be the God who *chooses what is small and weak to manifest his glory* (Deut. 7.7; 1 Cor. 1.28)' (1976: 101, emphasis mine).[6]

For Mays, it seems that the ideal nation is one that acknowledges her weakness, preferably after having been punished so that salvation can play its part. He suggests that such a nation appears in 7.1-6: she shows her weakness through 'lament at its human helplessness and turns to reliance on the salvation of Yahweh after she shall have undergone his punishment' (*sic*) (1976: 32). Her suffering 'leaves her cast on Yahweh alone' (1976: 32) and her lament 'acknowledges the rightful norms of justice and loyalty...and clears the ground for the resumption of the submissive walk with God' (1976: 151). Not surprisingly, Mays assumes that the speaker of 7.1-7 is a feminine figure, 'the city to whom the announcement is made (6.9), the feminine figure (Zion) who turns to YHWH in hope (7.7) and asserts her confidence in YHWH's salvation (7.8-10)' (1976: 151). The supposition of a feminine speaker here is something of a stretch, especially since the announcement to the city in 6.9-16 is addressed to the masculine *you* (both singular and plural). Although the text says that a voice calls to the city, the address is nowhere feminine, and the only reference to the feminine is through the noun 'city' and through a few third feminine singular pronominal suffixes. Mays acknowledges this, arguing that the second person masculine forms refer

---

5.   A few other scholars pay special attention to the feminine singular participles here too. Wolff asks if the feminine singular forms 'emphasize the tenderness of the promise' (1990: 123), and suggests that they likely correspond to the feminine singular noun 'flock' (צֹאן), as in Ezek. 34 (1990: 124); the word צֹאן does not, however, occur here, but the feminine singular noun 'remnant' (שְׁאֵרִית) does (though in 5.6-7 the remnant takes masculine verb forms). Ben Zvi suggests that 4.6-7 presents a 'self-image of Israel...as a lame female who has been driven away, as an afflicted woman' (2000: 112).

6.   Wolff makes a similar kind of gloss on 4.6-7 with reference to other scriptures: 'the small are made great, the weak are made strong (1 Sam. 16.1ff.; 1 Cor. 1.26ff.; Mt. 13.31-33)' (1990: 127).

to the 'tribe' or the (emended) 'assembly' of 6.9b, but that the call to the city in 6.9a was placed there by redactors to introduce this segment of text and to show that the punishment and humiliation proclaimed in 6.10-16 is of Jerusalem (1976: 10-11, 31-32) (though Jerusalem is not named in chs. 5, 6 or 7). Thus the feminine city (Jerusalem) is read as encompassing the sin of 6.10-12, the punishment of 6.13-16 and the lament of 7.1-7. Such a reading that finds a feminine figure central to a passage referring to the punishment of a *masculine addressee* might betray the assumption of a fundamental connection between woman and sin. Along similar lines, elsewhere Mays depicts the feminine Jerusalem as the embodiment of evil, arguing that 3.9-12 'makes it clear that Micah regarded Jerusalem as the urban incarnation of the crime he was commissioned to indict' (1976: 20).

Mays is also able to uphold the ideal image of the nation as weak, even in instances where the nation is not helpless or chastised, nor necessarily rescued by Yahweh, as for instance with the image of active, conquering, female warrior or goddess figure in 4.13. Here he argues that 4.13 was a later addition to the original prophecy, extending the redactional purpose of the book: 'a promise which looks *for the peoples to be brought under the reign of YHWH* by the divine power of Israel' (1976: 109, emphasis mine). Here Mays finds Yahweh's agency in victory, rather than Zion's, through the reference to *herem* in 4.13.[7] He argues that the reference to *herem* in this verse is 'acknowledgment that the victory was [Yahweh's]' (1976: 111); yet nowhere does the mention of the ritual of *herem*, even in de Vaux's discussion which Mays cites, give this kind of theological significance to the practice.[8]

---

7. So also Wolff: 'the "daughter of Zion" herself becomes the agent of Yahweh's punishment of his enemies, but she is empowered and authorized to do this only by the word and deed of Yahweh' (1990: 133); and McKane, 'the defeat of the mighty nations by the daughter of Zion is a miracle wrought by Yahweh (v. 13) and cannot be accounted for by weight of armour' (1998: 12).

8. Mays supports his position by citing Josh. 7, 1 Sam. 15 and Roland de Vaux's discussion of *herem*; but closer examination of these and other passages does not show a connection between *herem* and acknowledgment of Yahweh's agency in victory; see Lev. 27.28; Num. 18.14; Deut. 7.26; 13.18; Josh. 6.18; 7.1-15; 1 Sam. 15.21; Ezek. 44.29; 1 Chron. 2.7. Very often it has to do with utter destruction of property taken in war, as an act of conquest; see Num. 21.2; Deut. 2.34; 3.6; 7.2; 20.17; Josh. 20.28-39; Isa. 34.2; Jer. 25.9; Dan. 11.44; 1 Chron. 4.41; 2 Chron. 20.23; 32.14. It is true that conquest is often attributed to Yahweh, particularly in Deuteronomy and Joshua but the practice of *herem* does not seem to be an 'acknowledgment' of Yahweh's part in it, as much as some kind of designation of booty as sacred, and therefore not appropriate for human contact. Mays seems to conflate de Vaux's

Mays further reads this 'salvation'—Yahweh's victory through Zion—as a response to Zion's 'present distress' (1976: 108) of v. 11. The nations, as 'instruments of judgment' (1976: 109), are—and Mays embellishes somewhat suggestively on the nations' speech (תחנף ותחז בציון עינינו)—'bent on the desecration of Zion, the profanation of the sacred city... They *long for* the satisfaction of gloating over a defeated *prostrate* Jerusalem whose *humiliation* will fulfill their lust for power' (1976: 109, emphasis mine).[9] However, according to Mays, her humiliation 'is in fact the secret plan by which Yahweh gathers them as cut grain' (1976: 110); in this way Yahweh 'intervenes directly and mysteriously to vanquish them' (1976: 107). Mysteriously indeed, since it is Zion who threshes them. The point is that while it is true that the daughter of Zion does seem to be the passive recipient of her armoring, the image does not fully fit into Mays's power-in-weakness scenario; certain aspects of the text seem to be much exaggerated in his reading through theological gloss in order to enable a reading of punished-helpless-victim-woman whose punishment facilitates Yahweh's domination, and requires his salvation.

Where Zion is properly helpless and contrite in Mays's reading, the divine ruler, whether Yahweh or the 'messianic ruler' of 5.1-4, comes to the rescue (1976: 112): 'Yahweh will establish the capital of his reign in Zion, reclaim and transform the scattered remnant into an invulnerable manifestation of his power...by which the nations will find peace or punishment' (1976: 6). The messianic ruler meets 'the need' caused by Zion's humiliation or 'self-mutilation' (4.14) (1976: 112). In short, the divine ruler fills in where Zion is lacking: 'where the divinely chosen king is absent, the community lacks a concrete historical centre and social structure for actualizing their life within God's sovereignty' (1976: 112).

Shaw: A Helpless People Transformed by Yahweh

Yahweh's transformative power is a theme that Shaw picks up in his monograph, *The Speeches of Micah* (1993). Shaw's concern is to understand the rhetorical purpose for each of the sections in the book, in its historical context. Throughout his analysis, Shaw asserts the need for the feminine cities to be restored and transformed by Yahweh. He does this somewhat differently than other scholars, using a more pronounced good woman/bad woman dichotomy in which he finds Samaria to be

previous discussion of the necessity of faith in holy war with his discussion of *herem* (see de Vaux 1965: 258-61).

9.   McKane says, 'Mighty nations are now massed against Jerusalem and are titillated with the thought of its possession' (1998: 12).

ultimately guilty, while Jerusalem is struggling, needing only to be led by the divine ruler. In his conclusion (1993: 222-24), it becomes clear that Shaw considers the first and last sections (1.2-16; 6.1–7.7 and 7.8-20) to be concerned primarily with Samaria's guilt, and her need to acknowledge Yahweh. The middle sections of the book (2.1-13; 3.1–4.8; 4.9–5.14) show Yahweh's leading of Jerusalem through divine and human rule.

Shaw's depiction of the cities as properly passive feminine figures emerges in his discussions of the first and last sections of the book. Of the first section, Mic. 1.2-16, Shaw argues that the 'rhetorical situation' addresses 'national policies pursued by capital cities' (1993: 222). These national policies 'are viewed as the reason for the chaos described'. And while both Samaria and Jerusalem are seen as culpable, 'the greater guilt, however, lies with Samaria' (1993: 222). Although he does not say explicitly why this might be, it may be because he understands Samaria to have been politically dominant over Jerusalem, since later on in his discussion of this passage he writes, 'throughout much of her history Jerusalem appears to have been a subservient partner to Samaria' (1993: 61). He argues that the rhetoric of the passage shows that Samaria's *disease* spreads to Jerusalem. Because of this the sympathy in the passage lies with Jerusalem as a grieving mother (1993: 50), rather than with Samaria, the disease-spreading prostitute: 'the audience is allowed to imagine Samaria as a prostitute and Jerusalem as a mother mourning for her children' (1993: 51). Thus, even prior to a discussion of Yahweh's rescue, Shaw already inscribes the good woman, Jerusalem, as passive; she is guilty by association with her more active neighbours: she is 'a victim both of Samaria's illness and of the sins of Lachish [harnessing of the horses]' (1993: 50). For this reason, 'unlike the judgment on Samaria, the prophet suggests that beyond Jerusalem's misfortune lies restoration and renewal' (1993: 50). However, given the many difficulties in 1.2-16 (see my Chapter 4), these kinds of assumptions about the relationship between Samaria and Jerusalem, let alone between Jerusalem and Lachish, are very difficult to state so definitively.

Though Shaw describes the beginning of the book as fully anti-Samaritan, there does seem, in his mind, to be hope for Samaria in the final sections of the book (6.1–7.7 and 7.8-20). Shaw considers both sections to be addressed to Samaria and her rulers (1993: 223). He finds 6.1–7.7 to depict the punishment of Samaria through war, because of her rulers' actions, 'closing with a description of a chaotic society and the prophet's vow to trust in Yahweh' (1993: 223). The final section, 7.8-20, 'encourages the city to bear its judgment with lamentation and confession…[and] closes with a declaration of Yahweh's compassion and

faithfulness' (1993: 223). In spite of the fact that in chs. 6–7, the feminine
Samaria is only once tangentially present through the 'statutes of Omri
and the deeds of the house of Ahab' (6.10), in Shaw's descriptions of
both final sections, Yahweh's salvation is for Samaria.

Particularly in his description of the last section, Shaw reads the
speaker as Samaria—present only through the second feminine singular
suffix on אלהיך in 7.10—who is suffering and helpless, 'but expect[ing]
Yahweh to vindicate her' (1993: 211). Shaw emphasizes several times
that the city is both penitent and passive (1993: 197, 211, 214, 233). He
argues that this image is a rhetorical device, a way of encouraging the
audience to realize that 'Yahweh is the one who is to act while the
speaker waits and watches for restoration' (1993: 211). The text, he suggests, urges 'an acceptance of punishment as a means of averting even
greater disaster (vv. 8-10)' (1993: 219). For Shaw, the rhetoric works
through the audience's identification through liturgy with 'the passive
role assigned to it' (1993: 211): through the text's liturgy the people are
to realize that they 'are helpless to act and must wait for Yahweh who
has promised to show the enemy wonders like the exodus' (1993: 214).
He notes that each section of the liturgy, 'presupposes that the community is defeated and is powerless to act on its own behalf. Indeed,
Yahweh alone is able to intervene for Israel's vindication and restoration'
(1993: 197).

The middle sections of the book are, in Shaw's reading, more focused
on Yahweh's salvific action and rule. Within his discussions of these
passages, Shaw continues to emphasize that it is Yahweh alone who is to
be active, and that Jerusalem's proper role—since Samaria falls out of
the picture for a time—is to be passive and to endure her suffering. In
discussing 2.1-13, Shaw finds the oppressed people to be landowners
who are 'averse' to war, and who have been dispossessed of their lands
through military operations of the powerful (1993: 82-84). The women
and children driven away from 'her fair house' in 2.9 (1993: 83) are
metaphorically 'entire towns and their populations which are in some
way "driven away" from Jerusalem' (1993: 83). For Shaw, these metaphorically feminine towns and their children are 'victims', not because
they are poor but because they are 'adverse to war' (reading שובי מלחמה
in 2.8, as the 'ones turning away from war' [1993: 83-84]). By reading
this as an indication of voluntary surrender —'that they have chosen to
surrender their property rather than fight' (1993: 83)—Shaw seems to
idealize as self-sacrifice the victimization and oppression of (metaphoric)
women. But, according to Shaw, the prophet asserts that 'a radical
change in circumstances is imminent' (1993: 90) through the judgment
of Yahweh (2.4, 13) which will take the form 'of a military defeat of the

oppressors' (1993: 84). What will distinguish this military action from the violence of the oppressors is that it will be Yahweh's victory accomplished by Yahweh 'leading both king and army into battle' (1993: 86).

Following a similar pattern, in speaking of the transition from the destruction of Zion in 3.12 to the description of her glory in 4.1-4, Shaw contrasts the unacceptable activity within Zion to bring her own success with the acceptable activity of Yahweh. Zion's activity brings destruction, while Yahweh's brings glory. He writes, 'after human efforts fail to build up Zion, Yahweh himself will exalt the city by his own deeds' (1993: 102). While Shaw does acknowledge that these human efforts to build up Zion include bloodshed and violence (1993: 101, see also 121), his emphasis seems not to be upon the violence itself as questionable, but on the intent—the problematic 'efforts' and 'attempts to enhance the prestige and power of Zion' (1993: 121). He argues that the rhetorical movement in this passage is 'to make the possibility of judgment and disaster vividly real for the audience' (1993: 122), and to 'shake the false confidence of the leaders'. This has the effect of demonstrating 'that a glorious future in which Yahweh's protection of Israel is realized is only possible after the time of destruction' (1993: 123). In Shaw's reading then, as with the others, not only is Zion to be passive, but punishment is requisite to her exaltation. This exaltation will be (perhaps paradoxically) both a time in which Israel is a powerful nation ruling over all nations, and a time of universal peace (1993: 116-17).

All three themes—the divinely appointed leader, Zion as a suffering woman, and Yahweh's transformation of Israel—also appear in Shaw's discussion of 4.9–5.14. Here Shaw's discussion shows the pain of the woman as a rhetorical device that sets up recognition of Yahweh's transformation of Israel through his divine ruler. He argues that the 'leading questions of Mic. 4.9' (1993: 145) reproach the people for not recognizing Yahweh's rescue, and for 'allowing distress to overtake them so they act "like a woman in labor" '; instead the prophet 'exhorts the audience to turn their fruitless labor into productive labor' (1993: 151). (But the pain of labour is in fact necessary, and here Shaw cites Luker, saying 'the necessary pain will bear the future in which the tables will be turned' [1993: 151.]) Shaw argues that these questions invoking Zion's pain are *introductory* (1993: 150) and 'can be understood as a reproach to the people for failing to understand the significance of the king in their midst' (1993: 141). These questions 'are grounded in the belief that the Davidic king was a sign of Yahweh's presence' (1993: 145), and 'serve as reminders of the tradition that Yahweh will defeat Jerusalem's enemies on Zion' (1993: 151). Within all of this, Yahweh 'commands the city to take action [4.13]' (1993: 152); but the defeat of the nations to which Zion is called is dependent on 'the presence of the Davidic king' (1993: 145)—though this king is not mentioned in 4.9-14.

Shaw describes the rest of the section as showing the transformation of the punished Israel through the leadership of the divine ruler. In 5.1-8, Shaw finds the 'descriptions of a transformed Israel, united and secure among the nations and protected by Yahweh's power' (1993: 155), including the description of the 'remnant of Jacob as "a representative of the divine Victor"' (1993: 148). And finally, in 5.9-14, Shaw finds the violent imagery (the cutting off of cities and horses) to be 'the ideology of...the ideal ruler includ[ing] the destruction of weapons and the coming of peace' (1993: 155). Although Shaw emphasizes the peace (and presumably passivity) of this rule, neither peace nor rule (in the positive sense) is mentioned in 5.9-14. The violence of 5.9-14 is downplayed in Shaw's analysis, and is instead considered to 'point to the transformation of the nation into one that trusts solely in Yahweh' (1993: 155).

Pedagogical Objects and Discourses

I have undertaken the exercise of following the gendering of the nation in these three scholars' work for two related reasons, which I look at in turn. In brief, the first is that these readings exhibit the operation of unifying terms, stereotypes and historical narratives in a way that is akin to the manner in which Bhabha describes the operation of pedagogical objects and discourses. The second is that I am interested in how the imposition of pedagogical objects and discourses onto the text reveals something about readers' identifications and their ideological positioning.

In arguing the first point, evidently I am making the move of taking Bhabha's work away from its primary arena of analysis—that is, contemporary postcolonial cultures—and applying it to ancient text. These examples of the way Micah is read show that texts, like cultures, can be homogenized and stereotyped in ways that smooth over difference and authorize certain interpretations. The national image that scholars apply to the text of Micah might be said to illustrate precisely the kind of thing that Bhabha is trying to contest in his work, that is, images or discourses that are imposed on cultures (here text), disavowing difference and justifying discrimination (here interpretations that portray female figures inacurately and unfavourably and that valorize victory over other nations).

Each of these readings finds within the text what might be called pedagogical objects and discourses: cumulative images, stereotypes and narratives that elevate an image—of a damsel in (deserved) distress being rescued by her hero—which is then used to pin down and homogenize the differences and difficulties present throughout the text. This image is a *stereotype* of the fascinating yet horrifying figure of the nation as a woman; and it is a national identity—which invokes two *historical narratives or foundational events*, the exodus and the Davidic kingship—of an oppressed nation, being led by its deity into victory. As mentioned, these 'pedagogical discourses' both facilitate the process of reading by disavowing difference in the text and take up and even possibly justify oppressive stances outside of the text.

For example, the image of the horrifying yet desirable woman seems to operate in a way similar to Bhabha's stereotype as fetish.[10] Here, I might return to Luker's importation of the prostitute into Mic. 6; Mays's exaggeration of the sexual humiliation of Zion in 4.11; or Shaw's emphasis on Samaria's guilt and disease in Mic. 1, and her punishment and penitence in Mic. 6–7. Like Bhabha's stereotype as fetish, these are images of the nation that facilitate relations, in this case, between difficult text and reader, by supplying an object of horror and fascination. In each of these examples, the scholar finds textual details (feminine pronouns without obvious referents [1.9; 6.9; 7.10], or an odd jussive [4.11]), which are difficult to account for, and fills them in. The 'lack' in the text is filled in by titillating objects of desire—perhaps found elsewhere in the text, for example Samaria in relation to prostitution in 1.6-7, Zion 'ploughed like a field' in 3.12—that are both fascinating and repulsive at the same time. These horrifying yet titillating images may also help readers to account for the often disturbing unexplained vehemence of Yahweh's punishment on either Israel or the nations.

This kind of stereotyping shows how readers' desire plays into the reading process. Readers find or inflate fantasy objects, which can help them to read difficult passages and over which they can linger, yet ultimately repudiate, longing instead for what is acceptable: divine rule. This resonates with what Bhabha writes about national identity: 'This moment of the turn of the nation's subjects to a past then re-turns, rushes past—indeed, projects *the past*—into a paradoxical position of futurity. The national past is never simply an archaic assertion of ethnic or racial essentialism. The directionality of the past—its political destination as well as its designations of cultural identities—participates *in fetishistic forms of social relations*' (1994c: 103, emphasis mine). Here Israel's 'past' (as in sexual past) is projected forward, not only into a

---

10. Raymond Ortlund writes a whole book, *Whoredom: God's Unfaithful Wife in Biblical Theology* (1996), that fetishizes Israel's sin as sexual in this way. Of Samaria in Mic. 1.7 he writes, 'the harlotry referred to here is not only the literal sex act at the high places but also, and more searchingly, spiritual whoredom in violation of the covenant with Yahweh' (1996: 83).

justification for Yahweh's anger,[11] but also, on another level, into something that can facilitate what might be called the contemporary social relation and political destination of reading ancient and oft-times obscure text in faith contexts.

Longing for divine rule also gets taken up in slightly more complex ways in the construction of Israel's identity as a nation. Not only is it coded through gender (female nation needing to be rescued by male deity or ruler), but it also finds its authenticity and 'authority' through recourse to the historical traditions of Israel, in particular the formative event of the exodus and the idealized period of the Davidic ruler. These historical narratives then become the basis of a hope for Israel's future, and get taken up by scholars into descriptions of that hope. Perhaps not surprisingly, these two historical moments correspond respectively to the feminine and masculine elements of the pedagogical objects.

For instance, the exodus authorizes the reading of the nation as *passive and waiting* to be led. Though the text makes some reference to the exodus in 6.4 and 7.15, it is interesting that neither Shaw nor Luker make much of it in 6.4, where a masculine figure is admonished,[12] but both note its mention in 7.15 in the context of the (feminine) community's waiting for Yahweh (for Luker it is the woman's *wailing* waiting [1987: 285] and for Shaw it is the community's *helpless* waiting [1993: 214]). For Mays, commenting on 6.4, the exodus is 'the signature of the identity of Israel's God' and 'a metaphor of salvation pointing to the helpless bondage from which they were saved' (1976: 134).[13] The historical tradition of the exodus acts as proof, it would seem, that waiting is the (historically defined) appropriate position for the nation. The implication is that the exodus will eventually be repeated in Yahweh's rescue and the people will once more be restored.

The focus on the foundational Davidic tradition, on the other hand,

---

11. Though, as Stephen Moore points out in *God's Gym: Divine Male Bodies of the Bible* (1996), God's wrath and vengeance have perhaps only recently been viewed as problematic in Christian contexts (1996: 11-30).

12. Other scholars make more of the reference to the exodus in 6.4. Wolff reads it in relation to rescue as a call to repentance, through remembering that 'Yahweh has accomplished the redemption of Israel out of the house of bondage in Egypt by his own initiative alone' (1990: 175); for similar views see Craigie (1985: 45) and Waltke (1988: 204). Hillers argues that the exodus is listed along with the other 'saving acts of God which constituted the people as a community' (1984: 77) as a way of pronouncing that Yahweh is right and the people wrong in the ריב of 6.1-8.

13. Likewise, in discussing 6.4-5, Bruggemann, Parks and Groome describe the exodus as: 'the memory of *redemption…the moment of origin* [as] a particular match between *Israel's helplessness* and God's graciousness' (1986: 13, emphasis mine).

supplies the active male half of this gender binary. For Luker, Mays and Shaw, the Davidic ruler brings the appropriate response to the imagery of Zion's distress; as noted, he 'fills in' where Zion is lacking. In these readings, the Davidic ruler overshadows the imagery of Zion in his rescue, turning her role into one supporting to his own. Though the text makes almost no mention of the Davidic ruler (there is only the brief mention of the ruler coming from Bethlehem of Ephrathah[14] in 5.1, and of a former kingdom in 4.8), the Davidic or messianic ruler becomes a chief focus. The explicitly Davidic ruler seems to be parachuted in from the history and tradition of Israel as these scholars understand it. Further, this focus on the ideal ruler, mainly evident in commentary on 5.1-4, is obviously not only related to the narrative of Israel and hope for its future, but to the Christian narrative of the messianic ruler from Bethlehem, for which Mic. 5.1-4 is often understood as a prophecy. My point is simply that thinking about this readerly operation in terms of Bhabha's notion of 'pedagogical historical narrative' illuminates this focus on the specifically Davidic ruler as a simplifying inflation of one minuscule aspect of the text through recourse to a historical narrative.

These gendered images of both taboo and acceptable sides of Israel's identity (horrifying independent woman–cities and glorious past of male leading and rule) are projected into the future: to doom and hope. But as Luker suggests, though on a completely different register, the distinctions between these two kinds of future visions are not always as distinct in the text as reading through the eye of the pedagogical object might lead us to believe. In a more extended use of Bhabha in my next chapter, I explore how readerly identification with the differences in Israel's identity might disrupt these kinds of pedagogical discourses in ways that both affect understandings of the future visions in Micah and also reposition the reader as subject.

Ideological Discourses

The second reason that I have looked at these scholars' readings of Micah is that I am interested in how readers are positioned ideologically as they come to a text; how this shows up in the imposition of pedagogical

14.   Hillers points out that Bethlehem of Ephrathah is not identical to Bethlehem of Judah which was David's town of origin (1984: 64). Mays (1976: 115) and Wolff (1990: 143) point out that David's father Jesse was an Ephrathite from Bethlehem of Judah (1 Sam. 17.12). Ben Zvi notes that it is important to point out that 'the geographical term Ephrathah does not occur in the Deuteronomic History, nor is it associated with David elsewhere in the HB/OT, except in Ruth 4.11 and Ps. 132.6' (2000: 120); still he finds 5.1-4 to 'focus...clearly on a future David' (2000: 123).

objects and discourse onto the text (fantasy objects found in the text and raised to the level of an always-already ideological pinning point); and how identification with these images positions the reader. To my mind, these scholars' descriptions of Israel's 'identity' in Micah, seem to reflect two contemporary discourses, which might in some sense be considered ideological discourses: the first, a widespread biblical-theological discourse that understands Israel's identity as a nation to be theologically determined in its tumultuous relationship with Yahweh through covenant, vacillating between judgment and redemption; and the second, a widespread (contemporary, western) cultural discourse of binary gender roles. The image of the suffering penitent woman, rescued and led by male figures into a glorious future of domination matches both these discourses. I am also interested in how readers are positioned if they identify with this image of Israel, and the way in which this lines up with these two discourses. Without getting caught up in all of the complex debates that surround understandings of biblical theology or gender, I take a moment to explain how I understand them to be configured, describing them briefly, in very limited ways, using the work of two or three authors for each that seem to me to illustrate them well.

Judgment and Redemption

The pattern for understanding Israel's identity that I have tried to note in these three readings—of necessary judgment, followed by redemption into dominion over the nations—is one that seems to be a reflection of a more basic understanding that the prophetic texts are commentary on Israel's identity as a people in covenant with Yahweh. Covenant is a theme that has become popular in biblical theology,[15] though of course this is not the only type of biblical theology that is being done (for a good overview of the kinds of work currently being done in biblical theology see Bruggemann 1997: 71-114).[16] Though the thematic approach of biblical theology is repudiated by some (I will not rehearse the debate, with which many biblical scholars are familiar, around many of the assumptions

15. For more on biblical theology and the themes of covenant, judgment and redemption see: Bright (1955); Childs (1979, 1987); Clements (1965); Dumbrell (1988, 1997); House (1998); Lindblom (1962); Nicholson (1986); Von Rad (1965); Weems (1995); for an extended understanding of the theological significance of 'the land' in the Hebrew Bible, see Brueggemann (1977).

16. Interestingly, although Bruggemann characterizes his own efforts as 'post liberal' and 'non-foundational' (1997: 86), he also seems to read covenant, punishment, restoration, and rule over the nations as central (1997: 413-48, 453-54, 495-503, 552-55).

and methods of biblical theology[17]), it is still pervasive. The readings of these three scholars, and others, betrays a reliance on themes emphasized in the biblical theology tradition.

The 'covenantal' framework for reading the nation of Israel in Micah, appears clearly in a general article on prophecy by Wolff (whose work has no doubt greatly influenced scholarly work on Micah, since his commentary, which contains similar though less condensed views, is one of the most oft cited). Wolff's framework can be filled out with the more explicitly 'biblical theological' work of John Bright and Donald Gowan, both of whom have written about this judgment–redemption trajectory within the context of covenant.

Wolff, in his article 'Prophecy from the Eighth through the Fifth Century' (1987), argues that the prophetic pronouncements about the future follow a pattern in three stages: the end, the turning point, and the new (1987: 20-22). *The end*, he suggests, is the end of the 'salvation-and-election history', the end of the old covenant relationship (1987: 20), 'the loss of the land, the state, and the sanctuary' (1987: 21); those who have been graced by the exodus and conquest now have no further right to the land, and are deported. *The turning point* is, then, Yahweh's purifying punishment. These are Yahweh's corrective measures. As Wolff sees it, there is a sort of hope in the expressions of suffering—hope for 'a small community of believers who face a new future' (1987: 20).[18] Finally, *the new*, is a new covenant, with a new exodus that inaugurates a new time of salvation, which brings 'exaltation and peace' (1987: 21). The beginning of this new era, however, is conditioned on repentance, for which Yahweh patiently awaits (1987: 21). But, as Wolff emphasizes in conclusion to his discussion on the prophets' understandings of the future, each of these stages is Yahweh's doing. He writes, 'Diverse as the details of the future within classical prophecy may be, in one thing absolute unanimity prevails: it is Yahweh who brings in the end, the turning point and the *New*' (1987: 22). The pattern that Wolff describes is based on a particular understanding of Israel's history and literature,

---

17. These assumptions and methods are most forcefully contested by James Barr. For an accessible introduction to the issues that surround biblical theology movement in general, including the critique of it by Barr and others, see Penchansky (1995); see also Barr (1980). For a discussion of the related field of canon criticism, as it relates critically to historical criticism, theology and even literary criticism, see Davies (1998: 37-58).

18. This understanding of hope present in suffering can be see in Wolff's commentary on Micah, particularly in his description of the punishment of 5.9-14 as a purifying promise comparable in some ways to the hopeful passage of 4.1-4 (destruction of military weapons etc.) (1990: 154).

one that sees the events of the glorious past (the exodus, for example) as based on covenant; the covenant is undone by Israel's sin, and can only be reinstated through a time of punishment, suffering and forgiveness.[19]

A similar view can be seen in the work of John Bright in his *Covenant and Promise: The Prophetic Understanding of the Future in Pre-Exilic Israel* (1976). Bright discusses Israel's relationship to Yahweh through covenant with specific reference to various of the prophets, including Micah. He suggests that Micah's message is 'orientated upon the *traditions of Israel's formative period* and the stipulations of *covenant law*...which bound *the lesser party in the relationship, the people Israel*, to a full and willing obedience to the divine stipulations under threat of the direst penalties in the event of their failure to comply' (1976: 117, emphasis mine). Bright suggests that Micah decries crimes against justice that flout this law, and that disregard 'Yahweh's grace to *her* [Israel] in the formative events, *the events of exodus*, wilderness wandering *and land-giving*' (1976: 115, emphasis mine). Such crimes against covenantal law do not acknowledge and maintain the properly grateful relationship of vassal to lord, and so merit 'judgment of total proportion' (1976: 117). Yet, Bright suggests, prophetic announcements of doom look forward to a *renewal of Davidic rule*. He notes that while there may have been some tension in Israel between understandings of judgment under the Sinaitic covenant, and understandings of a promised eternal future under the Davidic covenant, 'the arrangement of [the] book in any event shows that its collectors saw no essential disharmony [between these two views]' (1976: 118).

One thing that might be emphasized about this understanding of Israel's identity is that it seems to be predicated on the idea that the making and breaking of covenant was intimately tied to the giving and taking of the land. This notion, central to many discussions of covenant, is brought out in Donald Gowan's recent discussion of prophetic theology in his book *Theology of the Prophetic Books: The Death and Resurrection of Israel* (1998). Gowan points out that 'the covenant with Abraham included the promise of the land to his descendants' (1998: 21), and that this was common knowledge in Israel. Thus, he suggests that Israelites also understood exile and restoration from exile—based on repentance—according to formulae laid out in Deut. 4.29-30 and Lev. 26.40-41, which state that Yahweh would always remember his covenant

19.   Carroll (who argues that the notion of covenant does not even belong in discussion of eighth-century prophecy) protests that the notion of repentance does not belong to covenant; broken covenant he argues, entails disaster, *point final* (1979: 16).

and the land (1998: 21). Such understandings of the promise of the land were taken up, Gowan argues, in the prophets' struggle to come to terms with the exile and 'the end' of the covenantal relationship between Israel and Yahweh (1998: 7). Certainly the notion of Israel's divinely ordained right to land, and dominion over other lands (and nations) is common and seems to reappear in scholars' discussions of Micah's portrayal of Israel's identity and future. [20]

These brief examples illustrate a view, which seems to be fairly commonplace in biblical scholarship. It is a view that understands Israel's identity as a nation to be theologically determined by covenant with Yahweh, and the unfolding of that identity to follow the trajectory of suffering for sin, penitence, redemption and restoration into a glorious future of domination over other nations within a specific territory. Certainly, this pattern is not hard to see reflected in the image of the suffering penitent woman, punished, passively waiting for rescue and led into glory over the nations by Yahweh.

The Gender Binary

It is interesting that this unequal covenantal relationship between Yahweh and Israel is often considered to be described in gendered terms, both within the biblical text (see Weems 1995, Galambush 1992) and by scholars describing the biblical text.[21] Yahweh is figured as the male lord, active and in control, while Israel is the female vassal, sinful, punished and rescued. This kind of gendered division of theological labour, as it were, does not seem unfamiliar. Indeed the way in which the relationship between Yahweh and Israel is gendered exemplifies what feminists have called binary gender norms. I turn now to feminist

---

20. For instance, in Micah studies, Hillers equates fulfillment with conquest: 'Thus the summary of sacred history leads from Exodus to conquest, from promise to fulfillment' (1984: 78). Likewise Waltke sees the conquest as the high point in Yahweh's work: 'The Lord...promises to show Israel in the future such salvation-wonders as when he smote the first-born of Egypt, provided a way through the Red Sea and Jordan river, preserved them in the wilderness and overthrew numerous nations mightier than they' (1988: 206). Wolff speaks of Israel's entrance into the land as God's saving gift (1990: 87, 176). When Gowan comes to reading Micah, he does not particularly emphasize the land, but focuses on the idea that chs. 4–7 were 'formulated originally in order to deal with the fact that although Judah was severely punished by the Assyrians, Jerusalem was saved, not destroyed, and *the Davidic dynasty continued*' (1998: 55, emphasis mine).

21. Conversely, Robert Carroll has argued that the image of husband and wife, which many scholars consider to be covenantal, is in fact a separate image, and has 'no necessary connection with covenant formulations' (1979: 15).

work and queer theory that analyses the way that this gender division is naturalized through societal prohibitions and norms.[22]

Here I give a thumbnail sketch of a particular understanding of gender made explicit by queer theorists and transgendered writers. I begin with poststructural queer theorist and feminist Judith Butler, who gives a good theoretical account of the way the gender binary is constructed, and its ideological nature. Butler's work can be further illustrated by the writing of Jan Morris and Kate Bornstein, two transsexual writers who have analysed their own transgressions of gender roles, and whose anecdotal descriptions of differently gendered positions bring Butler's explication of the gender binary clearly into view. This necessarily too-small piece of the recent discussions on gender (in queer and trans-gender theory—made smaller still because evidently I only present an extremely limited piece of even this debate) may be considered marginal by some;[23] however, I use it because I think it best gets at the idea of gender as an ideological discourse. To my mind, Butler, Morris and Bornstein, read together, are persuasive in showing how gender is ideo-logical (in the Althusserian and Žižekian sense of ideology as images and discourses with which people identify to make sense of their material relations) precisely because the processes of identification that form gender efface themselves, thoroughly naturalizing gender. As Althusser might say, 'gender' presents itself as the obviousness of obviousness. This way of thinking about gender will be helpful, not only for under-standing what is at work in scholars' readings of Micah, but also for thinking about how binary gender norms that readers bring to the text can be disrupted through a process of liminal identification.

In her book *Bodies that Matter: On the Discursive Limits of 'Sex'* (1993), Butler describes gender norms as binary and heterosexual ideali-zations (1993: 125), meaning that they are structured and constructed, on the paradigm of male–female relationships, as opposed to same sex relationships. The binary nature of gender (passive, bodily, irrational woman versus active, spiritual, rational man) is not a new observation

---

22. I am aware that some might consider the use of the term 'gender' a depoliticization of feminist issues, but that is certainly not my motivation here. I focus on gender because the use of the *gender binary* in readings of biblical texts is a political issue to be contested.

23. For more on gender, much of which is through the eyes of queer and transgendered theorists, see V.L. Bullough and B. Bullough (1993); Bolin (1988); Burke (1996); Butler (1991); Connell (1987); Ekins (1997); Ekins and King (1996); Feinberg (1992); Garber (1992); Gagné, Tewksbury and McGaughey (1997); Lewins (1995); Lorber (1995); H.L. Moore (1994); Newton (1972); Tyler (1991); Whittle (1996); Wittig (1992).

and has been discussed at length by many feminists. However, where some feminists have argued against the repression and oppression of an essential femininity, Butler falls into the range of feminisms that focus on the constructed nature of gender. Butler contends throughout her work that gender is 'performative': that is, it is constructed and reproduced through the lived repetition of socially encoded binary (male/female) norms under threat of punishment. Her contribution to the discussion has been to highlight the ideologically constructed, performative and heterosexual nature of this binary. For Butler, binary gender idealizations are naturalized as original and the norm (Butler 1990: 16-25; 1993: 125-26), through pathologizing and normalizing discourses that include rewards and prohibitions for appropriate and inappropriate behaviour. When these kinds of discourses are internalized, the constructed nature of this binary is hidden. In fact, Butler argues, gender ideals are so normalized that it is often unthinkable for individuals to live their sexuality another way or to alter their desire (1993: 94).

Butler's analysis of gender pushes toward an understanding of gender as an ideology, in that her analysis corresponds in many ways to an Althusserian analysis of ideology, and at points engages with it (see 1993: 7-8, 121-22). As I read her, Butler's concept of performativity theorizes the way in which gender, like any ideology, is realized in material practices (following a materialist view), and effaces itself as an ideology, appearing instead as natural or obvious. Butler suggests that gender attributes are not in fact natural, and dependent on sex, but enacted and encoded in a continually repeated performance. What she calls 'gender performativity' is a 'ritualized production' (1993: 95), that is, bodily norms and desires formed through habitual practice. A key element in performativity is its repetitive nature, its iterability. As she puts it, 'hegemonic heterosexuality is itself a constant and repeated effort to imitate its own idealizations' (1993: 125). Moreover, for Butler the repetitive performativity of gender is constitutive for subjects (1993: 95). The ritual repetition of gender norms is not a secondary process in the formation of the subject, it is what constitutes the subject (1993: 95, 99), constructing gender at the same time. This is a kind of interpellation. Subjectivity is constituted differently, depending on whether one is interpellated as a man or a woman, in other words on which gender role is (materially) practiced.

Butler's theory also coincides well with using Bhabha to think about repositioning subjects for two reasons. First, her understanding of the iterability of gender ideals is very similar to the Derridean understanding of the mark that Bhabha uses: the repetition of a mark of gender means that it can never be self-identical, it appears slightly differently each time it is repeated. Butler writes, 'iterability underscores the non-self-identical status of such terms; the constitutive outside means that identity always requires precisely that which it cannot abide' (1993: 188). This means that the imperfect repetitions of gender, like Bhabha's notion of hybridity, open up a space for new forms of identification, identifications that do not always bring the subject out of its trip through the symbolic order in exactly the same place.

Secondly, informed by a critical reading of Lacan, Butler understands gendered positions to be formed through identification and desire (see 1993: 99-105).[24] What Butler holds open in her reading of the relation between identification and desire—in ways that are complementary, though not identical to Bhabha's reading—is the idea that normative identifications can fail, precisely because of the relationship between desire and identification. Because identifications are the result of desire, she argues, they are never fully achieved: 'they are never fully and finally made; they are incessantly reconstituted and, as such, are subject to the volatile logic of iterability' (1993: 105). They are 'phantasmatic efforts of alignment...[that] unsettle the "I"'. Thus since identifications with ideological gender norms are never fully achieved, according to this way of theorizing gender, it might be possible for them to be made differently, and subjects repositioned with respect to the ideology of gender.

Two central aspects of Butler's understanding of the ideological nature of the gender binary (as heterosexual in orientation, and as constructed but naturalized) are illustrated in the writings of Bornstein and Morris. The heterosexual orientation that Butler argues is built into binary gender constructs can be seen in the statement made by Jan Morris in her autobiography *Conundrum* (1974):

> It is not merely the loss of androgens that has made me more retiring, more ready to be led, more passive: the removal of the organs themselves has contributed, for there was to the presence of the penis something positive, thrusting and muscular. My body then was made to push and initiate, it is made now to yield and accept (1974: 152-53).

There is no difficulty in recognizing the markers of gender here; there is no doubt of the direction of Morris's sex change, nor the ideals expected for either set of genitals: men are to be active initiators while women remain passive recipients of male activity.[25] Such ideals not only privilege

24. For Butler on Žižek's re-reading of Althusser, see her essay, 'Arguing with the Real', in Butler (1993).

25. Other accounts of men learning 'to pass' as women show up these binary ideals and their heterosexual orientation too. For instance, Bornstein cites Harold Garfinkel's account of Angie's change from male to female. Garfinkel describes how

men, but also correspond to 'typical' sexual activity between men and women (thrusting penises, receptive vaginas). This illustrates Butler's argument that binary gender ideals are profoundly heterosexual in orientation.

Along similar lines, Bornstein—who writes, speaks and performs on the need to abolish gender—describes in her book *Gender Outlaw* (1994) the way that gender constructs are effaced or hidden as 'natural'. Bornstein notices when she talks with her audiences that 'gender identity is assumed by many to be "natural"; that is someone can feel "like a man", or "like a woman". When I first started giving talks about gender, this was the one question that would keep coming up "Do you feel like a woman now?" "Did you ever feel like a man?" '(1994: 24). To illuminate assumptions that people accept about gender, she lists a series of 'rules' (in Butler's terms, normalizing and pathologizing discourses) by which people come to adopt their attitudes toward gender as 'natural', for example:

> 1. There are two and only two genders (female and male)...
> 2. One's gender is invariant. (If you are female/male, you always were female/male and you always will be female/male.)...
> 3. Genitals are the essential sign of gender. (A female is a person with a vagina; a male is a person with a penis.)...
> 4. Any exception to two genders are not to be taken seriously. (They must be jokes, pathology, etc.)...
> 7. The male/female dichotomy is a 'natural' one. (Males and females exist independently of scientists' [or anyone else's] criteria for being male or female) (1994: 45-51).

Bornstein's argument is that these assumptions 'naturalize' gender and efface the possibility that it might be constructed.

Bornstein also finds that *desire* operates to naturalize and normalize gender. She notices that desire, for many people, is related to an

---

Angie learned to 'act like a lady' sometimes through lectures from her boyfriend. On one occasion, 'she received a lecture on how a lady should conduct herself on a picnic. This he did by angrily analyzing the failings of a companion's date who had insisted...on wanting things her own way, of offering her opinions when she should have been retiring, of being sharp in her manner when she should have been sweet, of complaining instead of taking things as they were, of professing her sophistication instead of being innocent, of acting bawdy instead of abjuring any claims of equality with men, of demanding services instead of looking to give the man she was with pleasure and comfort'. His final admonitions were, 'Don't think the others are taking your part when you act like that. They're feeling sorry for the guy that has to be with her' (1967: 146-47). This kind of commentary not only shows up the enforced gender binary, but also gives a good example of 'pathologizing and normalizing discourses' operating in common parlance.

understanding to the naturalness of gender: 'when for example, I talk about the need to do away with gender, I always get looks of horror from the audience: "What about desire and attraction!" they want to know, "How can you have desire with no gender?"' (1994: 38). While these attitudes may be natural for many people, Bornstein makes it her work to question binary gender ideals as constructed as well as assumptions about the relation of sex and desire to gender.

Following from these reflections on the gender binary, I would say that each of the scholarly works I have looked at, both finds within, and imposes upon the text a gender binary that is heterosexual in its construction (thrusting man, receptive woman). In addition, the maintenance of gender ideals through pathologizing and normalizing discourses can be seen in the way that scholars speak about the bad woman, punished for her independent activity, and about the good woman passively enduring her suffering, waiting for her hero and ultimately being led into a glorious future. Desire also finds its way in here as human desire for future goodness and justice is depicted as feminine desire for masculine rescue.

Further, as I tried to highlight in my expositions of these scholars' work, the discourses of gender and of Israel's theological identity are fully intertwined in the image of the relation between Israel and Yahweh that I have described as a pedagogical object. The gender binary is fully implicated in—I might say overdetermined, both determined by and determining for—the theological idea that 'the nation's existence and role is wholly the work of [Yahweh's] purpose and power' (Mays 1976: 8). It almost seems as if the only way that the nation can be understood, especially its hopes and fears for the future, is through a gendered metaphor; somehow consideration of the future, perhaps because it is tied up with hope and desire, lends itself to gendered thinking (see Runions 1998). One might wonder whether the need to code theological ideas through gender resonates with Bornstein's audiences' question: 'How can we have desire with no gender?' It seems that, in these readings of Micah at least, gendered imagery facilitates, and may even be crucial to, the articulation of theological desire. One might wonder what interpretations of Micah might look like if theological desire was rendered without reference to gendered prohibition and desire.

Pedagogical Objects and Discourses as Ideological *points de capiton*

As I have pointed out, the binary image of the wounded woman rescued by her divine hero operates, in Bhabha's terms, as a kind of pedagogical object and discourse that helps to unify and minimize the alarming differences of the Other (the text).[26] The image of a wounded rescued woman filters out many of the differences in the text, resulting in a distilled—that is, more palatable—'message' of Micah. The images and signs in the text which are not necessarily easy to decipher (see my Chapter 4), are read together in a way that produces a clear and familiar image, one with which readers can identify in some way, and which functions to pin down the signs of the text in scholars' readings. To relate this to the question of ideology and reading, this kind of pinning point seems to be produced in and by the repetitions of extremely common cultural and theological discourses, with which readers have previously identified in some way. The signs of the text seem to be elevated to stand in for external master-signifiers. In this way, these readings of Micah could be said to rely on always-already interpellations into, and identifications with, particular discourses of gender and theology.

In the work of Luker, Shaw and Mays, such always-already identifications get taken up into idealized identifications with the text. Readers are assumed in these readings to identify with the passive woman, perhaps a reflection of these scholars' own identifications, or the identification that is presumed to be appropriate for the believing reader of the text. This kind of assumed identification is evident in Shaw's argument that the audience *identifies* (through liturgy) with the speaker in 7.10— penitent, suffering and passively waiting for rescue. Similarly, Mays seems to make a theological identification between the weak (feminine) nation Israel and the (masculine) Christian believer, when discussing the first person voice in 7.7, 'sometimes masculine, and sometimes feminine', who waits on Yahweh (1976: 157). Mays describes the first person voice in 7.7 using *masculine pronouns*: 'The *power that perfects itself in weakness* flows from the certainty with which *he* says "my God"... *He* [the speaker] holds to the election of Israel, actualizes its promise in *his* hope and commits *himself* to the help of God' (1976: 157, emphasis mine). Interestingly, he makes this shift in gender, even though he argues that 7.1-6 is in the voice of the feminine city (of 6.9), and that 7.8-9 is the voice of feminine Zion (1976: 158-60), and even though there is

---

26. Barr critiques the biblical theology movement in general along lines that resonate with Bhabha's discussion of the unifying and flattening role of pedagogical objects and discourses on cultures. Barr writes, 'biblical theology encouraged the use of sweeping and wholesale dominant terms rather than the careful and analytic dissection of what they might mean in this connection or in that. At the worst, terms became slogans...used wildly and generally, with little care for precision or for distinctions in sense' (1980: 4).

no particular indication of a change in person or gender for the speaker in 7.7. The use of masculine pronouns here perhaps betrays a view that this is how the generic believer (typically gendered as male) should behave (as feminine with respect to God—a view which would hardly be unique to these readers). Finally, though less obviously, Luker seems to identify the reader with the suffering Zion, when he describes the listener's attention 'captured' as was Zion's (1987: 293).

These kinds of identifications seem to be related to a certain kind of theological desire. While these readers seem to identify with the nation in some way, their desire is for the divine ruler. In this gendered theological framework, the desire of the reader, like the desire of the good woman, should be for the phallus or the active male ruler, 'raised up' for rescue. Punishment is also desired in a certain way, because it is understood as a necessary stage in the process of rescue, which will only be completed after suffering brings repentance and the bestowal of forgiveness. And ultimately dominance is desired, because this rescue is embodied in domination over other nations; but of course, the responsibility for this domination is not the responsibility of the passive woman–people, but of Yahweh.

While identification and desire seems to operate on the level of metaphor, between the reader and the participants in the text, I would argue it also seems to occur on the level of reading, between the reader and the text itself. Putting this into the more technical terms which I have outlined in Chapters 2 and 3, what these readings do, I would argue, is to raise several fantasy objects, or objects of desire, found within the text, to the status of a unifying master signifier, in order to fill in the 'lack' of coherence in the text. I might say that the fantasy objects found in the text operate like Bhabha's stereotype as fetish, or like Žižek's *objet petit a* raised to the level of *point de capiton*. Certain features of the text are raised to the level of pinning points through readers' identification with the lack in the text—an identification formed through desire for the fantasy object. These pinning points correspond to the ideologies with which the reader has already been interpellated, which might be called *the gender binary* (with attendant norms of active, phallic men and passive, suffering women) and *Israel's covenantal relationship with Yahweh* (with an understanding of Yahweh's beneficent bestowal of the land, and angry retraction of it). In this way, diverse features of the text act as (pedagogical) objects of desire to fill in the 'lack' in the text, by being raised (narcissistically) to the status of the master signifiers by which readers themselves have been pinned (gender and a theological understanding of Yahweh and Israel).

In other words, identification with, and desire for, these images does not bring readers/subjects out of their encounter with the textual symbolic order in another ideological place than where they started. Rather, they 'come down' out of the text (to allude to the Lacanian graphs) in the same place that they started. And this is not a particularly liberating or liberative place, since if the reader identifies with the nation of Israel as such, she may be positioned to accept gender oppression as ordained by God, and to affirm a larger colonial discourse that I might call 'ordained colonial rule'. She is invited to imagine a future where successful colonization is seen as a sign of God's favour and salvation from sin.[27] In this way, the reader is positioned (passively) to do nothing in the face of gender and colonial oppression and to feel no responsibility for it. And while one might protest that the reader is only positioned this way with respect to the text (and not in 'real life'), it does seem interesting that many of these kinds of readings are produced and digested by people in nations that have profited greatly by colonial and neo-colonial activity, and in theological contexts that encourage passive women. Thus, the subject positions produced for readers in reading the text this way are not all that different from the ideological contexts that produce the readings in the first place. In this kind of reading, the sign always returns to its 'proper place', since the reader's always-already interpellation as subject by particular master signifiers governs the reading process.

In the next chapter I would like to suggest what Bhabha's conceptual metaphors have to say to this kind of reading, and this kind of positioning of the reader. Namely, I would suggest that if readers read the difficulties in the text as difference, instead of as lack, and if they identify with that difference, then the unifying *point de capiton* or pedagogical object with which they are always-already interpellated might be put into question; consequently their positioning as subject might be shifted.

27. For a reading of the relationship between colonization and gendered stories, particularly '(Con)Quest' stories, see Maldonado (1995).

6

Outside the Sentence: The Performative Practice of the Text*

In the last chapter, I tried to show how several readers of Micah seem to have read the text's presentation of the nation of Israel and predictions of Israel's future according to an idealized image of a damsel in distress, punished and rescued by a male ruler. This image, I suggested, operates in a way similar to pedagogical objects and discourses as Bhabha describes them: it disavows difference, fills in for lack of coherence in the text, and poses as some kind of historically based ideal (akin to Bhabha's myth of origins). As such, I suggested that it might be operating as an ideological pinning point—in Žižek's terms a fantasy image raised to the level of the master signifier (*objet petit a* standing in for the *point de capiton*). I further argued that the (ideological) discourses for which this image stands in are common, and therefore perhaps ones by which many contemporary readers of this text are always-already interpellated. These are discourses of gender binaries and norms, and of Israel's identity formed through Yahweh's covenantal giving of the land, as well as his taking of it (in punishment) and restoration of it (in glorious future). I suggested that for readers 'always-already pinned' to these discourses when they come to the text, identification with the image of the nation thus conceived (the pedagogical object) would have no real impact on their subject positions.

In this chapter, I extend the Bhabhian metaphor to look at how the text of Micah might repeat or 'perform' these images of gender, nation and future differently, and how this might affect the way the reader is positioned to speak and act (that is, how it might affect her subject position). Drawing on the kinds of textual ambiguities and differences laid out in Chapter 4, I suggest that the text repeats the images proposed by biblical scholars differently and in a way that interpellates or hails the reader into a new kind of liminal identification with the text. I argue that ultimately not only can this kind of liminal identification with the differently repeated signs of the text shift the reader's positioning as subject,

---

* A number of the ideas in this chapter were initially worked out in Runions (1998, 1999, 2001).

but it can also present new possibilities for understanding the meaning of the text. It is important to note here, that I am not trying to say that I will be successful at leaving my own ideology behind, where others have not. To the contrary, my interests lie in considering the possibility of a process by which the ideological positioning of subjects, my own included, might come into view and be shifted.

This kind of reading of Micah follows the approach suggested to me by Bhabha's theory, outlined at the end of Chapter 3. I put this theory to work here in considering the negotiation that might take place between text and (contemporary) reader, if the text of Micah is considered to be site of difference and allowed to 'enunciate' as such. Not only is the text itself full of differences, but it is obviously culturally and historically completely different from any contemporary reader. Here I explore the idea of the reading process as a negotiation of difference that takes place 'outside the sentence', in a 'Third Space' of interpretation. That is to say, I consider the way in which the overlap between the difficult text and the set of images ('pedagogical objects') with which the reader has already identified creates an excess that can put these pedagogical objects into question. As proposed in Chapter 3, such a negotiation of difference might occur through the reader's careful attention to the various and different repetitions of the text which would both add to and replace the reader's previous pinning by an ideological *point de caption*. This process would, in theory, produce an excess, a hybrid figure which could put into question and displace the 'original' *point de capiton* and provide a new point of liminal identification. My goal is to see whether the reader (the subject) might be enabled to come out of the signifying or reading process in another ideological place than where she started, or at least more aware of her own positioning.

In order to pursue such a reading, I first look at the way the image (the pedagogical object) that scholars have used to pin down the signs of the text repeats differently in the book, producing 'hybrid figures'. I then consider whether or not the text seems to sanction and punish these hybrid figures, and instead, as scholars suggest, to reward passive acceptance of an identity of a nation led into domination over other nations. As I show, the hybridity of the figures in the text also moves toward an ambiguity concerning their future. In order to explore this more fully, I look more closely at two instances of hybridity—the oppressed–oppressing people and the female–male Yahweh–Zion—to ask what happens to notions of gender, nation and the future, if the reader identifies (liminally) with these hybrid figures, as the text seems to urge. Here I consider how readers are positioned—interpellated—by the text to identify with these images through the address of the text, and how the grammatical and

metaphoric shifts in gender and in address facilitate this kind of identification. As stated, I am interested in how identification with new images
might affect the reader's subject position, and also in how it might affect
the possibilities for interpretation of the text, particularly with respect to
the way in which the visions of the future are understood.

Before I turn to the text, several preliminary points should be made
clear. First, the 'pedagogical object' to which I refer throughout the
chapter is the one I have described in Chapter 4; it is the image of the
nation, Israel, as a punished and suffering damsel in distress, rescued by
her male hero/ruler/God and led into dominion over other nations. As I
noted in my discussion there, elements of this image *can* be found in the
text. What concerns me here though is how these elements that make up
the pedagogical object repeat differently in the text. Hybridity appears in
the text's imperfect repetition of the image with which readers have tried
to pin it down.

Second, for the purposes of this chapter, the 'reader' that I have in
mind is the reader that I described in the last chapter (made present
through the works of scholars). I imagine this reader to be formed as
subject, at least in part, through identification with discourses of gender
(binary gender norms) and of theology (the people of God formed as a
nation through covenant). As described more fully in the previous chapter, these discourses, and the fantasy objects they produce, naturalize
the ideal role of women (and God's people) as passive, suffering and
penitent, and the ideal role of men (and Yahweh) as active, initiating and
rescuing; this urges a certain passivity with respect to acceptance of the
role of colonizer. As I have shown, this is a position revealed in much of
biblical scholarship; it is also a position into which I have come to recognize myself (through the course of reading Micah) to have been interpellated (and I footnote several instances in which reading this way has
interrogated my own subject position).

Third, as I give these readings, I am not trying to argue that I have the
one right reading of Micah. Rather my concern is to show that this is one
approach to reading the text that may be useful for the study of Micah in
that it allows the difficulties in the text to play more fully, and it takes
into account the role of the reader. This is an approach that attempts to
take into account both the 'indeterminacy' of the text, and the determining factors that position readers as they come to the texts. Finally,
where I have discussed the textual issues in Chapter 4, I do not repeat
those discussions in the same detail; however, that work certainly under-
lies, and is assumed in my analysis here.

Hybridity

I begin then, with a discussion of the production of textual hybridity. I am guided by Bhabha, though the reading process does necessarily differ in some ways from Bhabha's conception of hybridity. To recall briefly, Bhabha suggests that hybridity is produced as a result of imperfect mimicry of a dominant culture by a colonized people; it is the dual effect of an imperfect imitation: it both justifies discrimination, and at the same time unsettles colonial 'authority' and the 'myth of origin' upon which that authority bases itself. In reading biblical text, obviously it is impossible to say that images written thousands of years ago are a deliberate effort to mimic a certain set of contemporary norms; however, it is possible to say that hybridity is formed through the text's imperfect repetition or re-presentation of the images that make up the reader's ideological pinning points. While the reader might bring external points of identification to the text, these norms are repeated differently there, to borrow a phrase from Derrida, 'varying each time according to context, to the network of other marks' (Derrida 1984: 16). And, as in Bhabha's theory, the hybridity that is produced by this readerly operation has the dual effect of being met with punishment and violent action on the one hand, and on the other, putting the authority and authenticity of imposed norms into question. As demonstrated (Chapter 4), there are many shifts in gender and in the way the 'nation' is described on both syntactic and metaphoric levels throughout the text of Micah. If the 'norms' of gender and of Israel's role prescribed by the pedagogical object are considered alongside these shifts in the text, they appear to be constantly mixed and transgressed, producing hybrid figures.

Hybrid Cities

For instance, though mention of the feminine cities seems often to be cryptic, what is depicted does not always adhere, either metaphorically or syntactically, to passive-feminine designations of lamentation (and perhaps this discordance from the norm contributes to the *perception* of the text's abstruseness). Certainly Israel's two main cities Jerusalem and Samaria can be read as ambiguously gendered (Jerusalem more clearly than Samaria), and not always, indeed rarely, as if in sackcloth. The figure of Zion seems to be consistently crossing lines between 'active male, triumphant ruler' and 'passive, suffering, female nation'. She is passively built (in blood) by her leaders, yet she seems to own them (3.10-12). Yet for this she suffers; she is ploughed under. In Mic. 4, Zion appears in a supportive role, the location from which the word of Yahweh goes forth,

the seat of his rule; but she is also 'lifted up' above the mountains and
the hills, a place where other nations come to learn and be judged (4.1-
8). 'She' is both addressed as *you* (ms), masculine and towering (מגדל עדר
אתה), and also as the Daughter of Zion (4.8). 'She' is said to raise a battle
cry, but also told to writhe in labour (4.9-10). 'She' is described 'going
out' from the town using the typically masculinely attributed verb יצא,[1]
but she is also rescued in Babylon. 'She' is told to trample nations in
battle like a king with an iron horn, but she is also said to gash herself,
presumably in mourning (4.13-14).

On a more metaphoric level, Samaria, Jerusalem's horrific counterpart
in the pedagogical object (the infinitely more punishable epitome of
feminine ills), is not actually herself a prostitute. Rather she actively
collects (קבצה) the wages of prostitutes (1.7). As the text stands, Samaria
enacts a kind of economic, even pimping, behaviour that tends to be
considered a 'male behaviour' within discourses on gender,[2] and a kind
of economic activity that is uncharacteristic for a female figure in the
Hebrew Bible. Interestingly though, this is a detail that most often gets
emended away to read, 'from the wages of prostitutes they [her idols] are
gathered'. While I might be tentative about saying exactly why this
emendation gets made, it seems that collecting prostitutes' wages, instead
of having idols collected, does not fit with what might be expected of a
biblical woman. Further, the result of this emendation is not simply to
undo, or disavow, Samaria's activity, but to render it as a different, titillating, more receptive, bad-biblical-woman kind of activity, a specifically
sexual activity, rather than as economic action. Her activity is further put
outside of the immediate picture where it can be imaginatively elaborated
and related to the punishment (e.g. Hillers 1984: 20; McKane 1995a: 429-
32; 1998: 33-34; Shoemaker 1992: 122 n. 75; Ben Zvi 2000). My point is
not one about the actual practice of prostitution, of which we know little,

---

1.   יצא denotes an active comportment reserved 90 percent of the time for male
subject.
2.   This is perhaps slowly changing on the margins of society, as at least some sex
trade workers begin to take charge of their work, and speak out about their
experiences. See, for instance, Shannon Bell's book *Whore Carnival* (1993).
While 'pimping' may be a highly anachronistic term, it seems that scholars, even
ancient readers of the text (e.g. the versions), cannot fathom the idea that Samaria
collects her own fees. McKane gives a number of scholarly views on who might
actually be collecting the fees, ranging from the Baal cult (Wellhausen) to the wealthy
temples of Samaria (Wolff); I would point out that all of these collectors are conceived of as male dominated (patriarchal) cultic institutes. Against this, Bird's study of
prostitution finds that the notion of a cultic prostitute cannot be found in the Hebrew
Bible, or other ancient Semitic languages (1989: 76, 85-89).

but that perhaps certain kinds of assumptions about gender, and biblical gender, underlie the usual emendation. If read as it is though, the text is ambiguous as to Samaria's role; she repeats the pedagogical object differently and hybridity emerges.

In like manner, the lesser known or unnamed cities in the book seem to resist the designations of the pedagogical object. For instance, the gender of the 'lamenting feminine' towns and cities of Judah (1.10-16) is not always clear, nor is the consistency of their lament. Masculine plural imperatives 'do not tell, do not weep' (אל תגידו, אל תבכו), are followed in the next breath by feminine singular imperatives, 'roll in the dust, pass by' (התפלשי, עברי), all of which seem to be addressed in some way to a masculine plural *you* (מכם, לכם) (vv. 10-11). The addressee also seems to take on active male behaviours, such as harnessing chariots to the steed (רתם המרכבה לרכש), and giving a dowry (תתני שלוחים), possibly to kings (vv. 13-14). Likewise, the unnamed city to whom a voice calls in 6.9 is initially addressed with masculine forms. In 6.9, it is said that *your* (ms) name will see success (ותושיה יראה שמך). *You* (mpl) are called to listen, hailed with the (ms) appellation מטה, 'O tribe', or as some have translated, 'O rod'—both of which have masculine connotations: of Israel's organization and governance for the first, and of aggression for the second. But at the end of 6.9 and in 6.12, the city also seems to be referred to in the feminine with feminine singular pronominal suffixes. Finally, a similar, though more obscure, ambiguity of a city's gender occurs in 7.11 where a day is proclaimed for building *your* (fs) walls, followed in 7.12 with the nations coming to *you*, suddenly masculine singular, with no indication that the addressee has changed.

Hybrid Remnant

The remnant of Israel is another figure that seems to repeat the pedagogical object differently. The role of the remnant is not static in these passages. At points the remnant is a favoured grouping, and at others it seems to be the sinful remains of former glory; at points it is a ravaging lion, and at others it is a flock wounded and ruled by Yahweh. In 2.12-13 and 4.6-7, the remnant is the dependent, gathered (feminine) flock, led by Yahweh. In 7.18, it is the remnant of El's inheritance, like an embarrassed leftover from better days, whose sins El passes over. But the remnant also appears—repeats again—as שארית יעקב, a roaring lion among the nations, who seems also to be the ruler that raises his 'hand' against his enemies (5.6-8).[3] Here the grammatical forms are masculine, and the only sign of the remnant's feminine attributes is his gentle appearance as dew

---

3. 'Hand' (יד) can refer to the penis, for example see Isa. 57.8.

from Yahweh; but even as divine dew he independently waits for no one. This is no passive remnant. The text acknowledges this in 5.8, slipping into 2ms forms: 'You (ms) will lift your hand amongst your oppressors, and all your enemies will be cut off'. The raised hand here evokes an image of (phallic) power, perhaps not unlike Zion's iron horn of power in 4.13. In fact, here the remnant seems to emulate the book's ideal male ruler more than the passive flock.

Hybrid Nation

Similarly, the figure of 'my people' is one that does not fit the scholarly pedagogical object, in which 'my people' is personified as a woman, passively led into a situation of divine rule over other nations. Over the course of the book, 'my people' appears sometimes to be punished, oppressed, rescued and led into conquest, and at others, to be accused of oppression. The gender (and number) of this image is not consistent; sometimes it is connected to the feminine cities, sometimes to the masculine rulers. At the beginning of the book (1.9), 'my people' seems to be the people of Jerusalem, afflicted by some kind of plague or attack, which could be related to the sin of Jerusalem and Samaria decried just previously (1.5). Yet the status of 'my people' as under attack becomes ambiguous as the book progresses. In 2.5 and 2.8, it is syntactically unclear whether 'my people' is the subject or object of oppression. At other points, 'my people' seems to be under physical and ideological attack from its leaders (3.3, 5). But then toward the end of the book, in ch. 6, 'my people' seems to be dealt with as if it were itself an oppressor and punished accordingly (though this is not entirely clear). For example, in 6.3-5, 'my people' is called to account for its attitude toward Yahweh, because it does not (as is properly flock-like) remember the exodus and conquest. Then at the end of ch. 6, a 2ms figure—perhaps 'my people'—is violently reproached through deuteronomic curses of unfruitfulness, devastation and the sword, as are 'her' deceitful and violent inhabitants (6.13-16). But then, it is not clear that 'my people' is punished as a (deceitful and violent) oppressor, since in 6.16 'my people' seems to be reproachful of someone, perhaps those responsible for bringing on the devastation.

Finally, Israel's identity as a nation ultimately ruling over other nations in peaceful dominion repeats differently. It is not always obvious that Israel either triumphs or rules graciously over the other nations, as the pedagogical object might have it. At points Israel seems to live as one with the nations (indeed in 1.2 it is not clear whether Israel is addressed separately from the other nations) and at other points the nations are portrayed in antagonistic relation to Israel. The nations live harmoniously in Zion alongside those walking with Yahweh (4.1-7); but they also gather against her (4.11); she trounces them (4.13), and is then taken under siege and her judge chastised (4.14). The divine ruler rules over the ends of the earth in a time of peace (5.3-4); but it is, at least momentarily, unclear whether it is the ruler, or the nation of Assyria's presence in the land, that brings peace (5.4). But then Assyria is resisted and ruled violently with the sword (5.4-5) and the remnant ravages the nations (5.6-7). At the end of ch. 5, it seems that both Israel (5.9-13) and the nations (5.14) are treated in the same way: destroyed by Yahweh's anger. Finally at the end of the book, it is predicted that the nations (Assyria and Egypt) will come to *your* (fs) enlarged borders from afar (7.11-12), potentially in peace; but suddenly, in an image which hardly seems to signify beneficent rule, the nations are ashamed and lick the dust, coming from their fortresses to Yahweh, trembling (7.16-17).

Disrupting Unified Images

All of these ambiguities of the identities in Micah, and the hybridity that they form with the pedagogical object, bring to mind Bhabha's critique of modernity's universal ideal of the nation as a homogeneous, sovereign, autonomous political entity. One might wonder if modernity's conception of the nation is also at work in scholars' reading of Israel in Micah. But, as discussed, Bhabha critiques this notion of the nation through a consideration of the 'ambivalence that haunts the idea of the nation' (1990a: 1). He looks at the articulation of cultural difference within nations, and the ambivalences that this creates, suggesting that narratives of nationhood are continually disrupted and destabilized by the different everyday cultural locations from which these narratives are spoken (what Bhabha calls the 'enunciatory present').

Following from this, I would suggest that a similar thing happens when the various articulations of the text are taken into account. In all of these examples, attention to the way that the text deviates from a perfect reproduction of an icon of the feminine Israel rescued by her divine ruler shows that certain meanings have to be excluded and details harmonized, fixed, or otherwise made to fit in order for the text to congeal into a unitary image of the nation and its God. When one looks carefully at the way the text repeats these images, one finds that the text resists the disavowal of difference, and hybridity is produced. In this way the hybridity that is produced between text and reader reveals the constraints that compel homogenous readings, and brings what has been excluded into view.

Hybridity and the Future

However, noticing this kind of hybridity does not simply disqualify more dominant readings; it becomes a little more complex than that when 'future vision' in the book is taken into account. It looks as if the text itself violently constrains hybridity in its visions of doom, and that this would appear to give weight to a cumulative reading that sees feminine activity punished and feminine passivity rewarded by colonial victory. And yet, as I will show presently, even the visions of the future become hybrid at points.

Punishment

It does seem on first reading that punishment for deviation from the norms outlined by 'the pedagogical object' is severe. For instance, the phallic and active woman–nation is not tolerated in any way. It seems that feminine passivity is violently enforced for the cities and the remnant. This trend starts right at the beginning of the book where Samaria is vilified, stripped and made desolate (1.6-7). She is stripped, as if to ascertain her real 'sex', and anything remotely phallic and thrusting, like idols, are cut off. Her earnings are burned. Thus she is stripped of any signs of male power, both physically and economically. Likewise, the ambiguously gendered addressee of 1.10-16 is penalized: she is told to become bald, as a sign of her exile and devastation. In 3.10-12, Jerusalem is punished as if responsible for her leaders (that is, as if she is really their owner, as the feminine singular pronominal suffixes imply). For their illicit activities she will be ploughed like a field, violently penetrated as if to prove her femininity, and turned into a heap of ruins. Similarly, the war-like Daughter of Zion is told she will cut herself, like one defeated. Her self-mutilation is followed by a chastisement of her judge, by an unknown (mpl) subject with a staff. The ravaging remnant of 5.6-7 is also undone. Everything is cut off: its ability to thrust (horses and chariots); its source of strength (cities), and anything remotely phallic (like idols or Asherah poles) (5.9-14). The ambiguously gendered addressee of 6.9-16, masculine and successful, yet somehow identified with the feminine city and her inhabitants, is thoroughly cursed, and threatened with devastation, with any escapee put to the sword. And finally in 7.13, the land is once more devastated after (city) walls are rebuilt and borders enlarged.

Indeed, it appears that the most violent acts of Yahweh's retribution come, not after instances of corruption and oppression, as one might suppose, but after instances of gender transgression. For example, the 'schemers of evil' who appropriate land and oppress others in 2.1-2 are threatened with some kind of evil which will result in their humiliation (2.3),[4] but the text only goes on to describe this humiliation as a kind of taunting (2.4)—a far cry from the stripping of Samaria in 1.7 or the (symbolic) castration of Jacob in 5.9-14. Likewise, the male rulers of 3.1-2, who are described metaphorically as flesh-eating, are only chided with the warning that Yahweh will not answer them when they call out (3.4). The prophets who lead the people astray in 3.5 are merely threatened with shame and darkness in place of visions (3.6-7). The leaders who deal corruptly in 3.10 are not themselves punished, but rather the gender transgressing Jerusalem is violated (3.12). The evil inhabitants of the city in 6.9-12 are not punished (nor the city this time), but threats are made instead to an unnamed 2ms figure, perhaps the not properly flock-like people of 6.3-5. All of this would seem to imply that gender transgression, more than injustice, is the problem.

Reward
In like fashion, the text of Micah does seem to reaffirm the normative images that make up the pedagogical object, many of which can be found in the text's visions of hope for a glorious future (2.12-13; 4.1-8; 5.1-8; and 7.8-20). In these visions, divine and divinely appointed male figures rule and shepherd. All of these rulers perform what could be read as aggressive and dominatory action-oriented activities, full of 'thrusting muscular' energy and phallic imagery (rising up, standing erect, shepherding with a staff). The corollary to this masculine thrusting is, of course, passive femininity. This is marked by the image in 2.12-13, 4.6-7 and 7.14 of the people as a flock: amorphous, passive and dependent, needing to be gathered, rescued, led, ruled. This helpless grouping is also the remnant, cared for by the shepherd (2.12; 4.7; 7.18). The dichotomy between passive and active bears out in the grammar too, as the feminine verb forms in these idyllic passages are few and far between.[5] It does seem on first reading that in these passages of

---

4. Ben Zvi notes the discrepancy between the crime and its punishment in 2.1-5. He suggests, on the basis of the change in verb tense between 2.1-2 and 2.3-5, that the evildoers were other than the ones suffering the punishment. He argues that this served the rhetorical function of defamiliarizing the genre of pronouncement against a group of individuals (2.1-2) (1999: 90), in order to explain the loss of land for monarchic Judah as caused by the policies of earlier kings (1999: 95). At the same time, he argues, it 'allows the intended (re)readers to identify the wrongdoers with multiple referents in their world of knowledge' (1999: 98).

5. One of two 3fpl verbs in the book (the other of the hills in 6.1) does occur to describe the flock's noise in 2.12; however, when the flock follows Yahweh out of the gate in 2.13, the verbs shift to masculine plural.

future hope, the ideal relation between Yahweh and Israel is of Yahweh
the active male to Israel the passive female.

Rescue?

However, if one looks at the way the shepherd/flock image (seemingly so
central to the idea of hope in the book) repeats differently, such clear
notions of reward and punishment begin to crumble. The male shepherd
king, *rescuing* his people from disaster, repeats differently to form a
hybrid figure, so that the idea of rescue is not always clear. In 2.12-13,
Yahweh is the shepherd who gathers his flock (with the verbs אסף and
קבץ) and then breaks out of their pen, and 'goes up' (עלה) before them.
Yet, as noted, there has been some discussion which suggests that this
image is not as pastoral and hopeful as it might seem. Indeed, the
militaristic image of breaking out, combined with the verbs אסף and קבץ,
could imply, as Willis suggests, 'the king gathering his army for battle'
(1966: 198).[6] The word used to describe the sheep's noise (הום) does not,
after all, generally connote well-being, but rather chaos or confusion. A
similar ambiguity occurs in 4.1-7 where again Yahweh is the king and
shepherd going up before his flock (once again using the verbs אסף, קבץ
and עלה). But here Yahweh says that he will gather up the lame, the ones
whom he has harmed (4.6). Given these ambiguities, the image of the
shepherd as a caring leader, as is so commonly asserted, is at best equivocal. This could equally be an image of controlling sheep so that they
could be made useful, or led to the slaughter.

Perhaps the same ambiguity about the goodness of the ruler can be
noted in the descriptions of the human rulers in chs. 5 and 7—though
here I might be a bit more tentative. In 5.1-3, the ruler comes from
Bethlehem, 'to stand and shepherd in the majesty (גאון) of the name of
Yahweh'. But might the 'majesty' (גאון) of Yahweh's name, by which the
human ruler stands and rules (5.3) connote arrogance as it does so often
elsewhere in the Hebrew Bible?[7] Since there is some ambiguity as to
whether this ruler hands over his people and allows his brothers to
return against the sons of Israel, perhaps this is a fraudulent (and

---

6.   See Willis (1966: 198 n. 1, 199 n. 2) for long lists of references for these verbs
in connection to preparation for battle.

7.   גאון seems most often to be a negative term, signifying arrogance or a pride
that needs to be brought down, see: Lev. 26.19; Job 35.12; Ps. 59.13; Prov. 8.13;
16.18; Isa. 13.11, 19; 14.11; 16.6; 23.9; Hos. 5.5; 7.10; Jer. 13.9; 48.29 (= Isa. 16.6);
50.44; Ezek. 7.20, 24; 16.49, 56; 30.6, 18; 32.12; 33.28; Amos 6.8; Zeph. 2.10; Zech.
9.6; 10.11. It much less frequently signifies majesty, splendour or pride in a positive
sense, see: Exod. 15.7; Job 37.4; 40.10; Ps. 47.5; Isa. 2.10, 19, 21; 4.2; 24.14; 60.15;
Nah. 2.3.

therefore arrogant) divine ruler. Or what of the shepherd-rulers (רעים)
raised up to lead resistance against Assyria in 5.4-5? This would seem an
appropriate thing for heroes to do, yet it culminates in a particularly
violent and perhaps sexual instance of domination whereby these
shepherd-rulers conquer Assyria with the sword and Nimrod in *her
gates*.[8] The prospect of even metaphoric sexual violation by the shepherds might not particularly assure the flock (even if Nimrod is read as
the enemy, embodying oppression [Wolff 1990: 147]).[9]

Finally, in 7.14 there is an appeal to a 2ms figure, either human or
divine,[10] to shepherd the people with a staff. But the use of the 'staff'
(שבט) in this shepherding activity is at best ambiguous, since שבט is used
most often as an instrument for smiting.[11] Even where used in the
context of shepherding, it has both positive and negative connotations.[12]
For instance, the idiom of separating sheep out for the tithe as they pass
under the staff (Lev. 27.32)—already not a very nice image from the
perspective of the tenth sheep—is used in Ezek. 20.37 in the context of
Yahweh's wrath, judgment and purging. Again one wonders about the
shepherd. It would seem that at points throughout the book, the
'rescuing, shepherding heroes' can be read as remarkably similar to the
evil rulers that are indicted for oppressing (and eating) the people.[13]

Thinking along these lines, the roles of the various participants in the
book become quite fluid, a fluidity which in turn questions why some are
rewarded while others are punished. At points, the feminine Jerusalem
and the passive remnant actively trample their enemies, strangely resem-
bling the ideal male rescuer (4.8-14; 5.6-8). Elsewhere, the seemingly
ideal rulers rule like Yahweh (5.1-5; 7.14), but as just discussed, may be
as equally oppressive for the people as their current oppressive leaders.

---

8.   As noted in Chapter 4, this image is not actually picked up by scholars, but
almost unanimously emended to 'they will rule...Nimrod with a dagger'.

9.   Mays argues that this is an exceptional instance in which the shepherd image is
used to depict 'harshness' with the nations (1976: 120).

10.   As noted in Chapter 4, most scholars read the 2ms figure in 7.14 as referring to
Yahweh, in spite of the clear intervention by Yahweh in the first person in the next
verse: 'as in the days of your going out from Egypt, I will show you wonders' (7.15).

11.   E.g. 2 Sam. 23.21 = 1 Chron. 11.23; Prov. 13.24; 23.13-14; 26.3 (in the context
of discipline); Job 9.34; Ps. 2.9; Isa. 10.24; 11.4; 28.27; 30.31; Lam. 3.1; Mic. 4.14.
Sometimes Israel's staff is used to crush or subdue other nations (Gen. 49.10; Num.
24.17). Sometimes the word is simply used to denote (military) power (Judg. 5.14;
Amos 1.5, 8; Zech. 10.11).

12.   Ps. 23.4 is a very rare, though well-known, example of a שבט used in calming
ways.

13.   Indeed, one might wonder if the critique of the people-hungry leaders in 3.2-3
might play on the expectation for rulers to act as shepherds.

The oppressive leaders are in turn identified with feminine cities (3.10-12; 6.9-12); and so the cycle begins again. This blurring between indicted and ordained therefore poses some questions about the doom and the hope foretold in the book. If the behaviours of all the various participants are similar, then why are some condemned, while others are celebrated? Why is the phallic remnant of 5.6-8 punished (5.9-14), while a very similar figure in 5.1-3 seems to be celebrated? Why are the feminine cities punished for their inhabitants' behaviour, when that behaviour (for example, building with blood in 3.10, or being filled with violence in 6.12) might resemble the heroes' behaviour? It seems that without the help of a clear pinning point to shut down or exclude certain meanings, the signifiers of the text do not easily stop their sliding and the 'meaning' of the visions of hope and doom remains obscure.

Liminal Identification

I will return to the question of the future further on, but first I would like to push this one step further by considering how the *text might position readers* to identify with these hybrid figures and what would happen—to the reader, and to understandings of the meaning of the text—if the reader were to identify with these figures. In my reading of Bhabha, I have termed such identifications with hybridity 'liminal identification'. Reading Bhabha alongside Žižek, I used Bhabha's notion of liminal identification to understand the subject's identification with the symbolic order in interpellation not as an identification with *the lack* of a privileged outside term (the phallus) by way of the fantasy object, but as an identification with *the difference integral to the production of that sign*. Put more simply, liminal identification is identification with difference rather than with an absent unifying sign.

Interpreting Bhabha, I argued that this difference is made visible by the hybrid figure, which offers itself up as a new fantasy object, a new point of identification. I further suggested, taking my lead from Bhabha's use of Derrida, that if such an identification were to be made in the process of (re)-interpellation (the subject being always-already interpellated), the new object of identification would substitute for, or supplement, the always-already object of identification (so destabilizing and displacing it). Thus the subject and the sign would come out of their circuit in a different place than where they started. Imagining that the text might interpellate or hail the reader, I also imagined that the reader could identify with the hybrid figure made up of the textual difference within the unitary signs with which the reader had always-already identified. This interaction resembles the overlap between meaning and being of the

Third Space; it is an overlap, a repetition and a doubling in which the unitary notion of a sign by which the subject has been always-already interpellated is disrupted.

Making the analogy to reading Micah, I would ask: what if the reader responds to the interpellation of the text differently? What if rather than making the more habitual move of filling in and identifying with the lack of the privileged terms in the text (in the example I am discussing, a clear gender binary and Israel's identity in relationship to Yahweh) the reader identifies with difference. What if the reader identifies with difference by identifying with the different textual signs (and the difference in the repetition of each of those signs) that cumulate into—and are disavowed by—privileged terms? Or put another way, what if the reader identifies with difference as it is revealed in the hybridity formed by the text's imperfect repetition of that pedagogical object? These are questions I pursue in the readings that follow, where I show, modifying Bhabha to my purposes, that in this process of liminal identification, the subject position of the reader is put into question and the habitual readings of the text (as evidenced in the pedagogical object) can be re-inscribed, reordered, re-symbolized, in short can effect what Bhabha calls catachresis.

Two issues mentioned in Chapters 2 and 3 become pertinent here: first, the reader's interpellation into the text, and second the split between the subject of the statement and the subject enunciating it. Both issues bear upon the way readers identify in reading. I would like to discuss the mechanics of how these two issues might play out in reading Hebrew text and then to give two more detailed examples of the negotiation of difference and the liminal identification that can take place in the Third Space of interpretation.

Textual Interpellation
In order to think at least about the formal aspects at work in texts' interpellation of readers, it might be helpful to keep in mind both Benveniste's reversible I–you subject position, and film theory's notion of 'suture'. As discussed in Chapter 2, Benveniste understands language to be intersubjective. He argues that *I* and *you* are reversible in nature, because the use of one automatically invokes the other. This is possible, he suggests, because 'language puts forth "empty" forms which each speaker, in the exercise of discourse, appropriates to himself' (1971: 227). As has been pointed out by biblical and cultural critics, this way of thinking about language is evocative of the way a reader, by responding to the *you* of the text as *I*, might take up a subject position offered to her by the text. Within the understanding of the reversibility of *I* and *you*, it

is possible to think of second person forms creating a space (Benveniste's 'eternally present moment' [1971: 227]) for a reader to respond as *I*, a speaking subject. It is possible to think of the text's *you*—in vocatives, imperatives and other second person forms—as Althusser's 'hey you' interpellating the reader, who responds as *I*. Likewise, the reader can take up the position of *I* in the text. Because the forms *I* and *you* are 'empty', any reader can take them up. However, they do not exist disembodied from a text, but rather are part of a textual context; this means that they are usually modified in some way. Thus newly formed subject positions, evoked by the *you* of the text, are also situated by the text.

This has something like relationship to film theory's notion of suture, as discussed in Chapter 2. The 'shot' shows the world as seen by an absent person, *I* (an empty form). In this way the viewer (*I*) is positioned to view the world as does the absent figure. But then the 'reverse shot' fills in the absence by giving an image of the absent *I*, so the viewer is told what her position is, and identification is urged between the viewer (*I*) and the reverse shot. Thus the viewer is positioned by the camera to identify and see the world in a certain way.

Applying this to Hebrew text, I might say that if the reader reading the text, finds herself addressed by an unmodified *you* (for example, אתה), she may respond as *I*—'who me?'—filling in that empty space with her own subjectivity. She therefore identifies with an empty form, a lack. However, this second person form may be modified (though it should be noted that in Hebrew even 'empty' second person forms are already modified by gender), either directly or eventually, as often happens in biblical text (for instance, the phrase אתה בית לחם אפרתה ['you, O Bethlehem of Ephrathah']). In this case, as in the reverse shot, the lack is filled in by another term, 'Bethlehem of Ephrathah' (and eventually again by 'insignificant to be among the thousands of Judah'). Following the principle of shot/reverse shot, if the reader has already identified with the designation 'you', an identification with the modifier (the term that comes to fill in the lack) is also imposed on her: in this example she would be positioned by the text to identify with Bethlehem of Ephrathah.[14]

14. Likewise, if a text uses a first person form, an identification is made with the empty form; but again this may be modified, for instance אני אל 'I am God' (e.g. in Isa. 43.22). The beauty of prophetic text, as religious/ideological text, is that sometimes *I* and *you* forms suture each other, as in the phrase, אני יהוה אלהיך מלמדך להועיל, '*I* am the Lord *your* God, one who taught *you* how to profit' (Isa. 48.17), giving the reader the curious sensation of identifying with both parties. Interestingly, this kind of textual suturing does not occur for first person forms in Micah, because first person forms are not modified by nouns or vocatives (so there is a fair bit of ambiguity as to their identity). In this chapter, however, I am only looking at the reader's positioning by

However, as has been discussed, formal analyses of textual interpellation can only go so far in talking about an effect on the reader's subject position, because they do not take into account the reader's always-already interpellation. Moreover, identifications with a text are always only partial, due to the split in language between the subject of the statement (in the text, here speaking of grammatical subject) and the subject of enunciation (either the reader, or the text allowed to enunciate). The reader can never 'be' the subject of the statement (*you, O Bethlehem/my people/ O human*). Inserted into the position of *you*, the reader is bound to some extent by the structures of the text, but the response to this *you* is always intersected by the reader's own always-already subject position. Even though the reader may momentarily be positioned as the subject of the statement by the text, she has an identity and subjectivity external to the text which stays consistent, presumably at least for the duration of a reading of the text. The *I* with which the reader responds to the *you* of the text is perhaps continuous, even where the text seems disjointed, and this compels, or at least allows, the reader to make connections between discrete instances of the *you* in the text. This urges affiliations between images that perhaps would not be made if they were described in the third person. Not only that, but these juxtapositions, held together by the *I* of enunciation may form hybridity with the signs and signifiers that have already pinned the reader in interpellation into the ideological order. In this way, by responding to the text's diverse hailings as *you*, the reader can also facilitate the production of hybrid images. A brief illustration of this, to which I will return, may help clarify. When the reader—whose always-already identification is with the passive, feminine nation—is interpellated at one moment as *you* (fs), the one in labour (4.10), and then at the next moment as *you* (fs), the aggressive Zion (4.13), the *I* of enunciation holds together these two positions along with the reader's own subject position, bringing to the fore the kind of hybridity that is formed with the repetition of signs.

With these issues in mind, I turn now to the hybridity that emerges between a reader—always-already pinned to discourses of gender and Israel's identity through an identification with the rescued damsel in distress (pedagogical object)—and the text. I consider the reader's possible identification with the new hybrid images that emerge, and the effect that this might have on her position as subject, as well as on the way in which the text is understood. To do this, I look at two components of the

the second person forms in the text, in other words, her response to the text's 'Hey you'.

pedagogical object and their repetition in the text. These are: the figure
of the oppressed people turned victor (chs. 5–6) and the figure of the
suffering, rescued mother, Zion (4.8-14). I choose these two passages
because between them, they contain most, if not all, of the elements that
get taken up and subsumed into one overall image in the pedagogical
object: the feminine city, the shepherd ruler and his flock, the people, the
remnant, and predictions of hope and doom; they also show these
elements repeating differently in the text. My two readings of these passages do not try to produce 'one' overall reading for Micah; there may be,
therefore, some discrepancies between them. Such is to be expected
when one reads through an identification with hybridity, since, as Bhabha
puts it, hybridity continually produces its own slippage (1994a: 87).

An Oppressed People, Turned Victor: Micah 5–6

The Pedagogical Object

As discussed in Chapter 5, a change in Israel's fortunes, from suffering to
dominion over other nations, becomes crucial for scholars' understanding of the nation in Micah. The shifts between doom and hope in the
book are understood as shifts between Israel's punishment and 'her'
rescue. Micah 5–6 contain one of the elements that is centrally integrated
into this understanding of the nation: the image of the oppressed people
turned victor. If the participants and their actions are combined to
construct an overall image for chs. 5–6, the nation may appear as an
oppressed remnant—connected in some way to Yahweh—that will triumph in the future. The figures accumulate: the ruler who comes from
the insignificantly small Bethlehem to rule in the name of Yahweh (5.1),
the rulers raised up to combat and overpower the invading Assyria (5.4-5)
(though no mention is made here of Yahweh); the remnant of Jacob, who
is like dew from Yahweh, yet eventually becomes a fierce lion (5.6-7), and
the call to the people to remember how Yahweh brought them from
exodus to conquest (6.3-4). Together these images can be seen to evoke
an enslaved and resistant people, on the verge of liberation. This accumulation of images fits with the theological pinning point 'Israel's covenantal identity' and so it is not interrogated much further.

Throughout the passage, the most consistent sign related to this image
of an oppressed remnant turned victorious, is the *masculine* singular *you*
(and here already hybridity with the notion of the nation as feminine
appears). This pronoun, more than any other sign, seems to represent the
oppressed people. In 5.1 there is the small insignificant *you*, Bethlehem,
from whom goes forth a ruler; this *you* seems also to be present in 5.2-3
through the continued description of a ruler, as if to that same addressee.

There is the *you* who cuts off your enemies in 5.8 and who, by virtue of similar behaviour, seems to be linked to the (third person) devouring, ravaging remnant of Jacob just prior (5.7). There is the *you*, my people, reminded of your exodus and conquest in 6.3-4. And there is the *you* whose name will see success in 6.9. In sum, *you* are the oppressed remnant turned victorious. *You,* I might say, is the short form for this image of the nation in the pedagogical object.

However, the repetition of the 2ms pronoun is not static, or identical, in this passage, and when one attends to these differences, a kind of performative rearticulation and disruption of the pedagogical object comes into view. This can be observed in several instances of the repetition and 'sliding' of the sign *you* in chs. 5–6. In particular, I examine three repetitions of this sign: the annihilated *you* in 5.9-14 and 6.13-16; the *you*, 'my people', in 6.4-5; and the call to *you*, O human, in 6.8. As I will show, these three slightly different repetitions of the sign *you* disrupt the image of the oppressed remnant turned victorious; further, if the reader responds to the text's shifting *you* and identifies with the hybridity that is so produced, the overall 'meaning' of the text is revisioned, particularly with respect to the future. All of this might resemble Bhabha's description of the time-lag, 'mov[ing] forward, erasing the compliant past…bringing the flow to a standstill in a reflux of astonishment' (1994a: 253).

Rearticulating the Nation

The repetitions of the sign *you* in 5.9-14 and 6.13-16 serve to illustrate the kind of slide that occurs in the reading process. These two passages within chs. 5–6 do not easily cohere with the pedagogical object because neither comes around to victory. In 5.9-14, *you*, just previously cutting off your enemies (v. 8)—with no warning (or marker of change in subject)—are suddenly told that you yourself will be cut off: your horses and chariots cut off (v. 9), your cities and fortresses devastated (v. 10), and your cultural practices plucked away; you will no longer bow down to the works of your hands (vv. 11-13). These things are predicted by a first person speaker, in an oracle of Yahweh. One moment *you* are an active and aggressive subject affiliated with Yahweh (assuming the *you* of v. 8 is the same figure as the dew from Yahweh and the roaring lion in vv. 6-7), the next moment *you* are a quite different subject, one whose activities are harshly curtailed by Yahweh. The resistant fighter in 5.7-8 is now set to be destroyed. A similar thing occurs in 6.13-16, where *you*, whose name has previously seen success, is cursed: all your efforts will be thwarted (eating, making wine, making oil, and so on). Within the

words of the curse there is no chance of success, nor victory; even if *you*
try to escape you will be put to the sword (v. 14).[15]

Although these shifts could be explained in a number of (text-
historical) ways, what is interesting for my purposes is that when they are
enunciated in the reading process, a connection can be made by the
reader between the disjointed *you*'s within 5.7-14, and similarly, within
6.9-16. The reader, interpellated into the text by the subject of the statement, *you*, responds as the subject of enunciation, *I*. But as a subject with
some continuity, the *I* of enunciation holds the two disjointed subjects of
the statements together: *I* once lifting my hand against my enemies am
now being destroyed by Yahweh; *I* once promised success, am now
promised destruction. Attention to the circulation of the various *you*'s in
these passages both allows the text to enunciate and also rearticulates the
pedagogical object. No longer is the oppressed remnant turned victorious. Here it becomes 'the remnant oppressed by Yahweh'.

Oppressed or Oppressor?
Leaving these jarring disjunctures aside for a moment, I turn to another
slightly different iteration of the sign *you* in chs. 5–6 which appears in
6.4-5 in the call to remember the exodus and the story of Balak and
Balaam. The call is to *you*, situated in 6.3 as *my people*. In 6.4 *you* are
reminded of the exodus; then in 6.5 an imperative calls *you* to 'remember Balak and Balaam'; it also calls *you* (the contemporary reader) to
engage with the intertext of Num. 22–24.[16] I would like to notice here
the way in which this intertext, while initially seeming to reinforce the
image of the oppressed nation turned victorious, actually hails the reader
in a manner that dissects the pedagogical object considerably.

In Num. 22–24, Balak, king of Moab, requests Balaam the seer to
'curse this people that came out of Egypt, because they are *too powerful
for me*, so that I can drive them out' (Num. 22.5-6). Balak's petition is a
plea of resistance by one certain to be overtaken by colonizing forces
(Israel). Balaam answers Balak counter to his wishes, by predicting
Israel's conquest, in full colonial rhetoric (Num. 23.24; 24.8-9, 17-18).

Numbers 22–24 appears then to be an intertext that would give
authority to the (pedagogical) image of a nation whose destiny is to

15. It is interesting to note that Luker (1987: 297-300) and Mays (1976: 127, 145)
consider these two passages to be depicting *your destruction* as purifying precursors
to repentance and a glorious future. Only Shaw considers the second of these (6.13-
16) otherwise: he considers it to be a shock tactic that announces an unabating
judgment (1993: 148-49).

16. I am not making any claims here about whether or not the author of the text
was referring specifically to Numbers as we have it written.

move from oppression to *conquest*. Read alongside Micah, it repeats the images of the exodus (Mic. 6.4) and of the lion (Mic. 5.7) which seem to bolster the notion that Micah is a text about the nation's hope for *rescue through conquest*. Twice, in Balaam's second and third oracles, the exodus theme appears just prior to the image of Israel as a lioness that will devour her foes and break their bones (Num. 23.24; 24.8-9). Thus the intertext serves to highlight the connection between the exodus and conquest in Micah, and so to justify the reading of Israel as a nation whose rescue will ultimately result in dominion over other nations.

However, the intertext articulates the text slightly differently, connoting Israel as an aggressive and colonizing power instead of as a force *resistant to* colonization and oppression (for example, 5.4-5). The focus is not on the exodus, but on the conquest. Thus, when this text is inserted into the Mican text, it has the effect of calling *my people* to remember an identity that seems to drop the 'oppressed' part of the oppressed remnant turned victorious. This process of repetition, it would seem, rather than allowing liberatory forms of cultural identification to emerge, as Bhabha suggests, reinforces an ethic of domination and colonization.

Yet in a strange reversal, this rearticulation of the nation, while constructing the remnant of Jacob as a colonizing power, at the same time places Balak and the Moabites in a position similar to that of Israel as a people resisting colonization (Mic. 5.4-5). This identification is strengthened in reading the intertext, where Moab is also addressed as *you* (ms); thus for the reader reading these texts together—responding to the 'hey you' of both texts—there is an odd connection made between Moab and *my people*. Moab, however, is not predicted to have a fate of future victory, but of destruction. Balaam, the reader recalls, prophecies devastation: 'Let me inform *you* what this people will do to *your* people in days to come... A scepter[17] comes forth from Israel, it smashes the brow of Moab' (Num. 24.14, 17, trans. Milgrom). Here then the intertext acts as displacing supplement: *you*, Barak/Moab, the nation resisting colonization (in the end defeated) repeats and substitutes for *you*, Israel, the nation resisting colonization (in the end victorious). The *you* in the address to Moab both replaces and adds to the *you* in the address to Israel in Mic. 6.4-5, and this substitution, held together in the reading process—connected in the *I* of enunciation—starts to blur the lines between the other nation and Israel. *You* (ms) are both the colonized

---

17. Interestingly the word for scepter here is שבט, the same word used to describe the chastisement of Israel's judge in Mic. 4.14 and to describe the shepherding of the flock in 7.14.

and the victor, the nation who already has land, and the nation who has been promised land.

Going one step further, it is interesting to notice that this supplementation of Mic. 6.4-5 (with Numbers 22–24) is framed by two passages in which *you* are suddenly destroyed (Mic. 5.9-14 and 6.13-16, discussed above). Thus, the reader, positioned to identify with the destroyed *you* in those texts, is here, in Mic. 6.4-5, positioned through intertext to make a (liminal) identification with *you* the enemy (Barak/Moab) under attack, about to be annihilated. At the same time, this identification also rearticulates these framing passages. In Mic. 5.9-13, *you*, like Moab, are threatened with violent destruction, and this identification is strengthened when in 5.14, with no transition markers, *the nations* (for example, Moab) are threatened in the same fashion that *you* have just been threatened in 5.9-13. Likewise, in 6.14, *your* escapees, like Moab's survivors (Num. 24.19), will be destroyed. *You*, who in the pedagogical object (and in the first reading of the intertext) were fully justified and authorized to conquer nations, are suddenly destroyed as they are. Once *you* are put into a position of identification with the aggressed nations, the position of conqueror, held up in the pedagogical object, is brought into a new light, and questioned as a positive behaviour.

Reading this kind of identification between Israel and the nations, facilitated by the repetition of the signs in the text and intertext, could have several potential, and perhaps contradictory, implications for the 'meaning' of the text, two of which I will mention here. First, if colonizing behaviour is critiqued through an identification between the remnant Israel and the destroyed nations, might the violence done to *you* in 5.9-14 and 6.13-16 be seen as retribution for the colonizing violence depicted in 5.6-8 and implied in 6.4-5? In other words, if these passages in which *you* are threatened are seen as punishment (which they normally are) might the crime punished be the now highlighted *colonization* depicted in the text, rather than the breaking of covenant, which is not mentioned directly in the text? If so, does this not at least question the pedagogical object in which *punishment is for unfaithfulness*, and *rescue is seen as conquest* led by divine rule?

Or alternatively, this recursive sliding of the signs of the text in the negotiation between text, reader and intertext could function to question the authenticity of the text's threats of punishment. By this I mean that the liminal identification made in this negotiation (*you*, Israel to be destroyed, like *you*, Moab to be destroyed) might be seen as a challenge to the veracity of Balaam's prophecy used by the Mican text, and so by extension as a challenge to the text of Micah. To spell this out, Balaam prophecies that Moab will be destroyed, but at the end of the oracles,

Barak goes on his way, not particularly nonplused it seems (Num. 24.25), and in reality Moab is never fully wiped out. In fact, in Num. 25, the Israelites are involved with Moabite women, and this is attributed in the tradition to the scheming of Balaam after he finishes giving his oracles (Num. 31.16).[18] The continuance of Moab, living intermingled with Israel—in spite of Balaam's oracles, and perhaps with his help—is a detail that not only further blurs the distinction between Israel and Moab, but also puts into doubt the authority of Balaam's clairvoyant powers, as well as his ability to comply with his own visions. With the curse of the intertext thus discredited, perhaps the text of Micah's own ability to curse *you* in 6.9-14 (as punishment for not remembering the events of intertext) is also put into dispute. The text's reliability is put into question by the circulation of its own signs.

Justice?: Repositioning the Subject

Finally, I arrive at the last repetition of the second masculine singular *you* in Mic. 5–6 that I will examine: *you*, O human called to do justice, love faithfulness and walk wisely with your God (6.8). Because this call follows questions in the first person—by a questioner who is concerned with what rituals will please Yahweh—it seems to be an answer addressed to an individual. In terms of the pedagogical object, this instruction, most often considered as related to covenant,[19] seems to bring onto a personal level the national covenantal identity established for Israel. The answer, 'he has told *you* [ms], O human', provides a point of identification for faithful readers: *you* are the individual called to do justice. The fact that this *you*, O human, acts as a point of identification for many readers is reflected in the literature. Much space has been devoted to trying to understand exactly how these desired behaviours should be lived out. 'Justice, kindness and humility' (the usual translation) have been interpreted variously: as 'kindness' (Shaw 1993: 175; Mays 1976: 142); as 'mutuality which recognizes the needy and responds in brotherly identification' (Mays 1976: 142); as 'the free taking on of that obligation to the other' (Sakenfeld 1985: 103); and as 'giving things back' (Brueggemann, Parks and Groome 1986: 5).

It is interesting to reflect on the way these desired behaviours for individuals compare with what is expected for Israel *as a nation* within the pedagogical object, as well as with the identifications I have just

---

18. For a thorough discussion of the Balaam tradition, see Milgrom (1990: 467-80).

19. So Shaw (1993: 175-76); Dawes (1988: 337); Sakenfeld (1985: 103-104); Achtemeier (1963: 277-79); Brueggemann, Parks and Groome (1986: 5); Alfaro (1989: 68-69); Hillers (1984: 79); Wolff (1990: 179-84).

described, made through the reader's enunciation of Mic. 5–6. The call to justice seems to be a call to an individual member of the nation, but because the 2ms pronoun has been used throughout chs. 5–6 to refer to the nation, the reader, now interpellated as an individual *you*, can make the identification between individual and nation. One begins to wonder what the implications of doing justice the way it has been prescribed for the individual might be, if applied to the nation. If the nation's identity is understood both as predicated on the exodus (the historical formative event), and as culminating in conquest (rescue into future dominion over the nations), the demand to 'give things back' might require a rethinking of that identity. Or if an identification can be made between Israel and the nations, between the conqueror and the crushed, a response compelled by 'brotherly identification' might mean more than charity: it might mean giving up on conquest. One might ask if 'unexpected' and 'kindhearted' acts (Shaw 1993: 175) include giving back the land.[20]

Reading this way, the reader is interpellated both as individual and as nation which brings into view a tension between individual will and national formation. What is interesting to me is the way in which this might also resonate with the reader's own ambivalence with respect to colonization and justice. The reader is at once interpellated into the position of an individual caring about justice, and into the position of a nation that exhibits a conflicted stance toward justice—engaged in resisting the threat of destruction and yet also struggling with an identity as a colonizer. This may be a position with which many readers are familiar: wanting to do justice, yet being part of a larger system that makes this difficult; trying to 'give things back', yet being caught up in a system in which they are ultimately benefiting from colonization or neo-colonialism. Read this way, the shifts and disjunctions in the text illuminate subject positions that are marked, like the text, with inconsistencies *vis-à-vis* colonization and justice.[21]

20. Hillers asks, 'but is "kindness" (חסד) expected outside Israel?' (1984: 79).

21. This is a point in reading this text where I have found my own position challenged. Reading the text this way has caused me to consider my own internal conflicts toward doing justice. Certainly the systemic oppression that I have faced as a woman has pushed me to be engaged in a wider range of resistances to colonizing forces, whether that be patriarchy, or transnational corporations. Yet, as white, educated, North American, and all-round privileged, I am also guilty of propagating many forms of oppression. Indeed by virtue of being North American, I am still the colonizer. When I am called to do justice, do I know what that is; would I even be capable of doing it? Thinking through the issues in these ways, I have had to re-evaluate my forms of resistance, particularly my role as a white activist working on issues that primarily affect people of colour.

But even more pointedly, the tension between interpellation as an individual wanting to do justice and interpellation as a colonized and colonizing nation also interrogates the always-already identification that the reader—at least the generalized reader that I am talking about in this chapter—has made with the Israel of the pedagogical object, that is, with Israel passively waiting for God's salvation through domination over other nations. As discussed at the end of Chapter 5, identification with this image may position the reader to accept colonization as a gift from God, and to feel no responsibility for it. However, the text's constantly shifting interpellations do not allow for this. The identifications instigated by the text's interpellation vacillate between Israel, the nations and the individual; this does not allow an individual believer responding to the call for justice to identify with Israel led to dominion over the nations without feeling some discomfort. Several things happen through the liminal identifications that the text urges: on the one hand the intertext emphasizes the active aggression of Israel; and on the other, identification with the colonized makes passive acceptance of the 'gift of colonization' more difficult; and finally the individual is called to be somehow active in responsibility for the 'other'. This means that the subject, identifying in these ways, is repositioned to resist, or at the very least, interrogate, passive acceptance of the role of colonizer.

So not only does the reader enunciate the text, opening it up into an ambivalent space, but the text, in a sense, also enunciates the reader. Just as the reader's subject position can open up the text, so also the text's subject positions can shed light on, and even disturb, the reader's always-already identifications. In other words, the new, liminal identifications the reader makes with the text, as a result of the text's interpellation, have the effect of bringing the reader's subject position into view, and even dislodging it from its always-already formations.

Time-lag
This kind of transformation brought about by liminal identification, I would argue, might also extend to thinking about the concept of future, and its 'meaning', in the book as a whole, in an operation similar to Bhabha's concept of the time-lag. Liminal identifications, Bhabha suggests, are the key to revisioning the future through the time-lag. For Bhabha, simplifying somewhat, the time-lag is the ability to use present identifications to change the past, in order to revision the future. The time-lag is the time and space between the 'event of the sign' and its (retroactive) 'signification'. Both meaning and the subject's positioning depend on the identifications the subject makes in its trip through the symbolic order.

Though I might be slightly more hesitant about offering the readings that contemplation of the time-lag might produce, nonetheless I would like to progress along these lines. It seems to me that the concept of time-lag is applicable to thinking about the visions of the future in Micah, especially in the light of the possible identifications with the repetitions of the sign *you* that I have been discussing. Since, as mentioned in Chapter 5, the past and the future are intimately linked in the peda-gogical image of Israel (the glorious past repeated in the glorious future), any disruption of the image of the past through liminal identification will also be a disruption of the future. So for instance, in the process of liminal identification, as I have outlined thus far, the reader is urged to make identifications with the trampled other, effectively, with the nations that are destroyed by the divine ruler. Because of this identification, suddenly the image of the exodus changes.[22] The pastoral leading of the flock into the promised land also becomes the invasion of *my* land by violent and colonizing forces (if identifying with the oppressed). Thus the image of rescue from oppression is inverted, and becomes an image of terror rather than of hope.

If such identifications and attendant transformations are entertained, even as *possibilities*, the entire scope of the future visions in the book changes. For instance, when—after all these liminal identifications have been made—at the end of the book in 7.14-17 a vision of a glorious future invokes the once-blissful-now-terrorizing exodus, this vision too mutates into something less pleasant. To spell this out, in 7.15 it is promised that *you* will be shown wonders, as in the days of *your* going out of Egypt (presumably including the conquest). By this *you* seem to be re-interpellated into identifying with the pedagogical object, that is, with one who has been (passively) lead into divinely ordained colonization (for which you do not have to take responsibility). Here you are interpel-lated into the position of looking forward to a glorious repetition of this event in the future. But though such prospects might once have appeared idyllic, now having made identifications with the oppressed nations, and having been called to justice, you might have some questions about your new exodus—particularly when in vv. 16-17 you see the nations lick the dust, be ashamed, and come trembling before Yahweh.

In a similar vein, but pushing it a bit further, the hybridity and liminal identifications formed thus far also begin to revision or reinscribe the future throughout the book, as the signs of the text continue their sliding. Just previous to interpellation back into identification with the pedagogical object in 7.15, *you* (ms) are the one ruling/shepherding your

22. The reading of the exodus as oppressive is of course not new (see Warrior 1989); my interest is in how identifications with the text might position the reader to realize this.

people with the staff (7.14). Nothing marks a shift from *you* the shepherd to *you* the one going out from Egypt. If the *I* of enunciation responds to both these interpellations, a connection is made between *you* going out in the now terrorizing exodus and *you* shepherding/ruling. This (composite) image of a shepherd as an initiator of the exodus resonates with the image of the shepherd in 2.12-13, gathering the sheep and leading them out of their pen. But if—through the various interpellations and liminal identifications discussed—the exodus is emphasized as conquest, suspicions noted earlier about the kindly nature of shepherd and the possible uses of his staff (here and throughout the book) begin to be confirmed. The shepherd leading his sheep into exodus metamorphizes into the king who forcibly gathers his troops for conquest. Suddenly it is not surprising that the flock's noise is chaotic and distressed (תהימנה) in 2.12. Nor is it surprising that in 4.6 the flock is wounded through an evil that Yahweh has done to it. Is the remnant-flock really an image of Yahweh's favoured people, or is it simply what is left of the troops after a colonial sally?

Following from this, one could begin to ask a number of other questions about the visions of future hope in the book, particularly about 4.1-8, often invoked in discussions of justice. For instance, why indeed does the image of the wounded flock in 4.6-7 come directly after the image in 4.1-5 of the nations gathered tranquilly on the mountain of Yahweh. Are the nations actually held there against their will, and have the flock-troops been used to bring them there? Is this why Zion is designated as some kind of fortified space in 4.8? Is the tower of the flock used for oppressive surveillance? Do the nations beat their swords and spears into gardening utensils because they want to, or because they must, to make the land yield produce? Is war no longer taught out of concern for people, or to ensure that the domination of Yahweh's mount will never be challenged? What exactly is the function of this apology for non-violence set next to the scene of the lame, enclosed and ruled remnant?[23] Why the need for a peaceful domain in the midst of a book that also valorizes aggression and conquest?[24]

23. I am not alone in wondering about the liberatory nature of this text. Mosala considers most of 4.1-8, with the exceptions of vv. 2-3, to be representative of an imperialist theology developed by the 'formerly powerful class, whose pride has been hurt by exile' (1989: 134). For Mosala, the imperialist *tendenz* in most of this passage makes it unusable as a liberatory text.

24. Brueggemann suggests that while this passage speaks out against the state's militarism and advocates for the right to adequate food and shelter, it gets taken up in 1 Kgs as state propaganda to normalize the force needed to maintain a royal

But, coming around again to the question of the subject's *repositioning* through the time-lag, one might ask how this kind of reading could possibly shift the reader's positioning in any kind of positive, liberatory way. I would propose that this type of consideration of 'divinely ordained future' might interrogate identification with the passive nation. For instance, if one were more suspicious of the sudden vision of non-violence in the midst of violence, and considered it, even possibly, as biblical manufacture of consent for a potentially oppressive regime, one's understanding of the mount of Yahweh and one's position on it might change. One might ask what violence is being done (to oneself and to others) in the name of non-violence. If non-aggression is not what it might seem, one might also reconsider the continual readerly demand for the nation to wait passively, non-violently, for Yahweh's violent rule; or— as this demand appears in commentary—to wait passively through the violence done to *you* (ms). The nation, it is claimed, is called to be peaceful.[25] One might ask if there is any connection between the desire for peace and the desire for passivity, and what the function of these ideals might be within violent contexts.

Perhaps thinking along these lines—and here I am taking this kind of reading to its limit—might also bring to light contemporary kinds of attitudes toward oppression. Could oppression be sustained, or at least ignored, by idealizing *peaceful and passive* comportment as divinely ordained (perhaps even through reference to this passage)? Given that many contemporary readers live in economies largely stimulated by, and successful through, the industry of war—an industry sustained by attack on, or exploitation of, other nations—what role might an identification with the passive, peaceful (yet ultimately powerful) nation play in allowing the violence of war-based economies to continue? One might be pushed to think about one's own nation's identity as 'peace-keeper', or 'peaceful' in the contemporary global economic context. Or one might think about those who are called to accept, passively, the violence done to them by the 'peaceful' state. Perhaps this image of gathering the nations, already maimed, to live peacefully under divinely ordained rule[26] is not as hopeful as it might be.[27]

lifestyle (1981). I might ask what is stopping it from being considered royal propaganda here too.

25. For instance, in commenting on 5.9-14, Hillers says, '*she* [Israel] cannot and must not avenge *herself*' (1984: 73, emphasis mine); though, as Luker comments, '[the Divine Warrior], ironically, must wage war to destroy militarism' (1987: 297).

26. And here I am thinking, in contemporary terms, of the United Nations.

27. This is another point at which I found my own position being illumined and confronted. Before I began reading this text I was an avowed pacifist. I believed in

Zion, Suffering Mother or Hybrid Figure?: Micah 4.8-14

Having looked at how liminal identification with the different repetitions of the masculine singular *you* in Micah 5–6 interrogates Israel's identity and future laid out in the pedagogical object, and with them the reader's subject position, I would now like to see how a similar—though not identical—operation might interrogate the discourse of gender that is used to describe the relationship between divinity and nation. In particular, my purpose is to look at the hybridity formed between the understanding of the nation personified in Zion as a suffering mother and the repetition of the imagery used to describe Zion in 4.8-14. I then consider what affect identifying with the hybrid image thus produced might have on the meaning of the text (in the time-lag) and on the reader's subject position.

Pedagogical Object: Suffering Mother

As pointed out in Chapter 5, it is not uncommon for scholars of Micah to understand the relationship between the (divine) Yahweh and the (human) nation of Israel in covenantal terms that are gendered. In this metaphor, the lesser party in the covenant treaty (the nation) is assigned a feminine identity, while the lord (Yahweh) is assigned a male identity. This kind of reading is supported with references to other prophetic texts, most often Hosea and Ezekiel. In this image, when the nation 'breaks covenant', the woman is punished until she repents and her fortunes are restored (see Weems [1995] for an extended discussion of this image). Thus when scholars come to read Micah, they tend to emphasize the woundedness and suffering of the feminine images in the text.

As with the image of the oppressed people turned victorious, the image of the suffering mother does seem to cumulate in the text (though

non-violent resistance, for me and for the rest of the world, and I had defended this position hotly in debate. Mic. 4.1-8 seemed like a perfect text to extol, with its abolition of weapons and regime of peaceful instruction. Yet, in the third space of interpretation, the text repeated my own prohibition on violence, but in repeating them, hybridity was formed between my ideal of non-violence, and the possibility of coercion suggested by the text. This has had the effect of supplementing my commitment to non-violence with my desire to try to stand in solidarity with the oppressed ('to do justice'). In this way, my knowledge of the 'best way to live' is displaced and the authority of my non-violent ideological stance challenged. Perhaps it is only through active resistance that oppressed peoples can break out of their situations of oppression. Perhaps it is active solidarity with this resistance (instead of against it) that will constitute a more glorious future.

with less pervasiveness). The image of the woman in labour appears in 4.9-10 and in a quite different context, in 5.2. The image of a mother's suffering seems also to be present in 1.16 where the 2fs figure is told to grow bald, and in 2.9 where the women of my people, whose children are deprived of splendour, are driven from some kind of pleasant abode. In addition an image of a woman's suffering appears in 4.14, where the 2fs figure is told she will gash herself. Of these, the only clear references to *Zion's* suffering as a woman *in labour* are in 4.9-10; following this it is predicted that she will be rescued and redeemed by Yahweh in Babylon.

Rearticulating the Mother: Hybridity

Yet this is not the only image of a woman that occurs in Micah. The text of 4.8-14 performs this image quite differently and creates a new liminal object of identification. It seems hard to suppress the hybridity that emerges in the text's 'enunciation' of the gender norms dictated by the pedagogical discourse. Thinking through the way the text repeats the image of a woman here disrupts a facile reading of the suffering mother, rescued by Yahweh. It is true that the suffering of the mother is what is most often drawn out in this passage; but Zion's male warrior-like behaviour (and iron appendage) in 4.13 is often rushed over. At best this behaviour is described by scholars in (unflattering) 'agrarian' terms that emphasize femininity. She is for example, 'an extremely large cow…the fem. pronominal references point to a "cow" rather than an "ox" ' (Ben Zvi 2000: 118); or 'a great heifer' (Hillers 1984: 61). Rarely is her masculine behaviour dwelt upon. Yet the figure produced in this verse is recognizably different: *you* (fs) *go forth* like a man; *she* could be *you* (ms) who is defiled; *your* (fs) *horn* is iron; and *you* (fs) *trample* nations. The signs of gender here have been repeated, but differently, producing an ambiguous mix of syntax and symbol.

This unusual hybrid behaviour has been noticed by some, who have been led to look at possible goddess-cognates. Such possibilities are rarely taken seriously by more mainstream scholarship,[28] but as Frymer-Kensky observes, 'Micah's picture of Zion as active and able to operate outside the city may owe its scope to several Near Eastern images' (1992: 174). Several examples might be tendered: the Akkadian 'Agushaya Hymn…[that] describes Ishtar as a fierce goddess who whirls around in her "manliness", whose feast is battle, who *goes out* in war' (Frymer-

---

28. Hillers, for instance, responds to Bordreuil (1971) by simply stating that the examples he gathers are unconvincing; but he does not say why (1984: 89). Interestingly, he accepts possible ancient near eastern parallels for the imagery in 5.4-5 (e.g. the seven/eight formula of 5.4; see Cathcart [1968, 1978]; and Saracino [1983]).

Kensky 1992: 67, emphasis mine; see also Sandars 1972: 25); the steles found in excavations of the Jezreel valley that depict a goddess wearing a headdress with horns (Hadley 1996: 123-24);[29] or Ugaritic portrayals of Anath, using the image of the horned ox trampling grain and enemies (Bordreuil 1971: 22-23; Rabinowitz 1998: 88-89). Or as Judith Hadley points out, the Ugaritic Astarte—who is often depicted similarly to the horned Anath and who was known as a goddess of war in Egypt—may also be a fertility goddess of the sheep (sometimes called 'Astarte of the field') who brings fertility to the land and the animals it sustains (1996: 116-17, 124-25, 129-31).[30] It would appear that parallels to this image in 4.13 abound in ancient near eastern portrayals of war and fertility goddesses.

What is interesting here is the way in which a new site of identification is brought into view by the *recognition* of hybridity (between what is expected of the text according to the pedagogical object and what is actually there). If the details that produce hybridity do not have to be disavowed to facilitate a certain kind of reading and are permitted at least to be contemplated, new possibilities also emerge, in this case consideration of a goddess image. By observing the gender hybridity in this text and looking at it a little more closely, scholars have arrived at an image that could provide new points of identification for contemporary readers. Thinking about a goddess image that holds together masculinity and femininity shows up an image that has been excluded, both from the larger biblical text, and more crucially, from readings of this text that favour an image of Zion as the passive, suffering mother. This kind of hybrid figure functions, as Bhabha suggests hybridity might, to bring into view what is normally excluded, to question authority, and to put the fantasy of origin and identity into question. As I will show, allowing the image to stand questions the 'authority' of the norms that are drawn out in many readings of the text; moreover, it puts into question the origin and identity of the covenantal relationship between deity and the nation in the text, and so also the legitimacy of the respective roles assigned in covenant.

The specifics of how this image came to be, or exactly which goddess figure is at work here are not the questions that concern me; indeed for

29. Hadley cites an excavation of the town of Beth-shan, documented by A. Mazar, 'located where the eastern extension of the Jezreel Valley meets the Jordan Valley' (1996: 122).

30. The image of the fertility goddess of the sheep is certainly interesting to consider in the light of the flock imagery in Mic. 4.6-8, just prior to this depiction of the horned Zion in 4.13.

my purposes it is enough to understand the ancient near eastern parallels as a bundle of fertility and war goddess images that illuminate the gender hybridity of the passage. Both fertility and warrior images are presented in 4.8-14, in both masculine and feminine terms, embodied by the figure of Zion. The general idea of a fertility–war goddess figure could tie together—for contemporary readers at least—the images that appear there of the woman giving *birth in the field*, and the woman *trampling her enemies* (4.10, 13). This might perform a montage comparable to the one that Jacob Rabinowitz has proposed for the image of (the male) Yahweh in the Hebrew Bible. Rabinowitz suggests that the figure of Yahweh can be seen to combine aspects of both Asherah (fertility goddess) and Anat (fertility goddess and war goddess) (1998: 83-95). As he puts it, 'Asherah and Anat were then apparently both assimilated to the Yahweh mythos, the one to account for his love, the other to explain his rage' (1998: 94). Here it seems that the figure of Zion combines images in a similar way.

Whether or not a similar thing *has happened* here cannot be said definitively (and is not really the point); what is interesting is what *does seem to happen* when the text overlaps with the images of the pedagogical object: a new and more astonishing hybrid figure appears. If, even hypothetically, the passage betrays submerged goddess imagery, then hybridity between goddess and god, Zion and Yahweh emerges when the birthing fertility goddess also takes on the role of conquering warrior—a role attributed to Yahweh alone in the pedagogical object. In other words, Zion appears in the text so much like the phallic-male-hero-Yahweh of the pedagogical object, that if the goddess imagery is permitted to stand, the two might be seen to merge into one divine figure. In fact, such hybridity might emerge as early as 4.1-7, where Zion is the exalted seat of Yahweh's judgment, the place from which the word of Yahweh goes forth.

You, a Yahweh–Zion Hybrid

With this kind of divine Yahweh–Zion hybrid in view, I would like to look a little more carefully at the details of the text, to see how it bears out and whether in fact it could operate as a new kind of pinning point, both for readerly identification, and for interpreting the shifting signs of the text. In other words, how would identification with a pinning point *made up of the text's difference* affect the reader and the reading of the text? What if instead of identifying with the wounded mother, a reader were to identify with an empowered (and powerful) female–male Yahweh–Zion hybrid, substituting this image in guiding her expectations and habitual ways of reading the text? In short, what might happen to a reading if the reader felt completely at ease—or at least tried to feel at ease—with this hybrid image and read the text accordingly? How would this affect the way she responded to the text's shifting modification of its empty form, *you*? Might the Yahweh–Zion hybrid provide a referent for what seem to be the text's unclear appellations (perhaps something like a reverse shot that suddenly explains erratic and seemingly indecipherable camera movements)? I explore these questions in the following pages by looking first at the details this new pinning point is able to accommodate, and even to 'make sense of', and then at the details that still resist containment.

The passage begins with ambiguous participants and mixed genders. In 4.8, *you* are hailed as masculine singular (אתה). It is not clear, however, who *you* is; the closest masculine singular referent would be Yahweh who rules 'over' his flock in v. 7. The masculine singular pronoun is immediately modified by both masculine (מגדל עדר) and feminine modifiers (עפל בת ציון): 'You are the tower of the flock, the fortress of the Daughter of Zion', combining the phallic, fortified, tower image, with the appellation 'Daughter'. Who are *you* then? Are *you* an unidentified masculine singular figure, are *you* Yahweh of 4.7? Or are *you* the Daughter of Zion? Yahweh would seem like a good candidate for the title '*you*, O flock tower', but then he is parallel to Zion. Having to choose between one or the other of these titles seems to exclude half the phrase. However, if one were to identify with the hybrid female–male Yahweh–Zion image, these shifts would not pose the same kind of problem; if identified with in this way, *you* could respond to all of these appellations.

The rest of 4.8 continues in the same vein, mixing masculine and feminine modifiers. Two syntactically parallel prepositional phrases are used to speak to *you* (ms) (עדיך) as if you were the Daughter of Jerusalem (fs) (לבת ירושלם): 'Unto you the former kingdom will come—the kingdom will come to the Daughter of Jerusalem'. Again the question of who *you* (ms) are arises, and here also the question of what the former rule refers to. Various suggestions have been offered, the most common of which is that this is a promise of the return of the Davidic kingdom to *you*, who is Jerusalem (Wolff 1990: 125; Mays 1976: 102; Hillers 1984: 56; McKane 1998: 131). (One might wonder if this is the case, why such an acclaimed tradition is not made more clear in the text.) Yet a different explanation of the meaning of the 'former rule' (v. 8b) might also be offered. What if this were read as the return of a former relationship between Yahweh and Zion (as Bhabha says of hybridity, a return of the excluded not as repressed but as excess)?

The text goes on to ask *you* (now fs), 'Why do you raise a battle cry, is the king not with you, has your counselor perished?' (v. 9). This has often been read as a cry of panic, related to the imagery of childbirth in

v. 10, followed by sarcastic or rhetorical questions.[31] Such readings tend both to inflate the punitive tone of the passage (along with the correlative pain of motherhood), and also to gloss the text with negative depictions of women (and their emotions). For instance, McKane reads these questions as '*histrionics*' and not to be taken seriously: ' "What are you making such a noise about"… "Why are you *bawling*?"… "as if you were a woman suffering birth pangs?" ' (1998: 135, emphasis mine). In contrast to this though, the verb רוע usually depicts militaristic or jubilatory cries and does not normally have a connotation of panic and pain. But, if *you* were considered to be the hybrid Yahweh–Zion figure (as opposed to the suffering woman), the sense of the text would not need to be changed in order to fit a demand for negative tone. The question could be read as an affirmation, in the sense that 'you do not need to sound the alarm,[32] your king is with you, your counselor has not perished'.[33] Reading in this way would set the tone for the whole passage in a very different fashion than is usual: no longer would it have to be read as a passage predicting doom for Zion.

Following on from this, if the reader continues to read through an identification with this hybrid figure, the birthing imagery of vv. 9-10 might be read as positive, in relation to fertility, rather than as negative; as scholars point out, the beginning of something new, but without the notion of requisite, punitive pain. Certainly, as noted above, *your* going out from the town to lie in the field (v. 10) fits with the notion of the Zion–goddess figure. Here again, for the most part, the sense of pain in birthing is inflated in translations of the passage. For instance the phrase כי החזיקך חיל כיולדה is often translated as something like, 'pain seizes you like a woman in labour' (NIV).[34] Yet the noun חיל ('pain') would more easily be translated as 'trembling',[35] which may imply fear, but not necessarily suffering. Likewise, the imperatives (חולי וגחי) are often translated

31. So Wolff (1990: 139); Mays (1976: 105); Hillers (1984: 59); Shaw (1993: 141); Allen (1976: 332).

32. Cf. Hos. 5.8; Joel 2.1; Num. 10.5, 9.

33. So Hillers, though he maintains the negative connotation by reading this as a reproach to the people of Jerusalem for 'forgetting that their heavenly king is in their midst' (1984: 59).

34. Interestingly, as some commentators note, 4QpMi reads a 2ms suffix, instead of a 2fs suffix on החזיקך (in the phrase 'anguish/trembling seizes you') (Wolff 1990: 130; Hillers 1984: 58; Collin 1971: 286).

35. KB lists four other instances of חיל, under the definition 'fear and pain'; yet with the exception of Jer. 22.23, when it occurs in parallel to חבלים ('labour pains'), in every example it is in parallel to words for 'trembling' (רעד) (Ps. 48.7), or 'anxiety' (צרה) (Jer. 6.24; 50.43).

something like, 'writhe in agony' (NIV),[36] though the verb חִיל ('to writhe') could be simply 'to be in labour', or even 'to tremble', while גיח is best translated 'to burst forth' (cf. Job 38.8; 40.23).[37] If the subject of these actions were imagined to be a divine Yahweh–Zion figure, the birthing image could be read along the lines of a colossal event, the trembling of the warrior held back, waiting to burst forth.

And indeed, the Yahweh–Zion figure does burst forth in v. 12. Yahweh gathers the nations to the threshing floor (v. 12), and Zion tramples them (v. 13). This is where the hybrid figure asserts itself most strongly. Not only do vv. 12-13 seem to present a combined action on the part of Zion and Yahweh, but also Zion is clearly figured as 'masculine' (if gender norms are followed). Her body is metallic; thrusting, not receptive. Her horn is made of iron, a terrorizing phallic symbol if ever there was one; her hoofs are copper. She is told to 'arise', and like the 'Divine Warrior', to trample the nations in kingly fashion.

The objection might be made that Zion is merely Yahweh's 'instrument', her body made hard for his purposes—thus separating the hybrid figure into its component parts. Indeed the text does render Zion's armouring as bestowed upon her by a first person figure: 'I will make your horn iron, I will make your hooves copper'. Traditional readings of the passage attribute these promises to Yahweh. Nevertheless, one textual detail persists, needing to be accounted for, or deleted, in order to understand the text this way: that is, it seems that the speaker is not Yahweh in v. 13, because *I* also promise to make *herem to Yahweh* (והחרמתי ליהוה), using a verb (חרם, 'to make *herem*') that is usually attributed to warriors themselves. If one lets this detail stand, several questions arise. What might be the implication for the hybrid figure? Who is the I? Might it be the collective voice of people who make up Zion, or the voice of the king that promises to make her strong? What is the significance of *someone else* (not Yahweh) arming this powerful hybrid figure, whether it be the people, the ruler, or another unknown voice? The answers to these questions are not provided, but at the very least this detail is imaginatively provocative, and suggests that Zion does not necessarily have to be

36. Some scholars are a little more faithful to the text, and translate, 'Writhe and bring forth' (cf. Wolff 1990: 129; McKane 1998: 143; Shaw 1993: 128). Some are more fanciful, e.g., Allen who translates, 'Writhe in agony and shriek' (1976: 332).

37. Hillers notes an interesting slippage of gender in the LXX—'not yet convincingly explained'—which reads 'act the man and draw nigh' (1984: 58). It seems the versions cannot contain the hybridity of the passage either; see n. 33 above.

read as subservient to Yahweh (as is the case when Yahweh is understood to be arming her).[38]

Reassertion of the Pedagogical Object?
While this kind of reading through an identification with a Zion–Yahweh hybrid does seem to provide a viable option for understanding much of the text, as with any pinning point, several textual details seem to resist containment, or at least to sit awkwardly on the edges of the reading. Some of these details are the same ones that get picked up as supporting evidence for scholarly depictions of the nation as a suffering woman rescued and restored to her land. But these details do not necessarily fit easily with the pedagogical object either, and may in some instances be read alongside the hybrid figure with no more contorted maneuvers than are habitually practiced on the text. They may be details that produce new excesses (and possibly new forms of hybridity with this hybrid figure). Nonetheless, because these are details that are integrated into the pedagogical object with which the (proposed) reader has identified, they require consideration. They perhaps serve to remind the reader momentarily of her own always-already identification, and to point out the tension between this position and any new identifications. Working through such details illuminates the negotiation between textual contours and readerly positioning; it also highlights the role of text and reader in the construction of meaning.

The first of these details that might support the pedagogical object occurs in 4.10 where it is predicted that *you* (fs) will go (בוא) unto Babylon, where Yahweh will rescue you. Here the hybrid figure (colossally in labour) seems to be disrupted by the pedagogical damsel in distress. It seems that the feminine figure is not only distinct from Yahweh, but rescued by him.

And yet there are textual quirks that do not fully support an identification of (or with) this figure as a suffering, punished woman either. It is interesting to note that the scene of the rescue and redemption is *in* Babylon; the rescue is not *from* Babylon. Twice the text says 'there' (שם): 'there' (שם) you will be redeemed, 'there' (שם) Yahweh will rescue you from the hand of your enemies. There is no restoration of land implied; there is no indication that the experience in Babylon is a purifying punishment. It is *there* that rescue happens. In addition, the circumstances by which Zion goes to Babylon are not clear. The use of עד ('until, as far as') which seems to indicate distance in some way (instead of the more

---

38. For instance, Hillers writes, 'God the harvester will use Zion as the beast' (1984: 61); Wolff calls Zion 'Yahweh's instrument against the nations' (1990: 142).

habitually used על, 'to'), may indicate that *you* have some control in the matter (i.e. initiative); for instance, you will go 'as far' as Babylon, and no further. Could this be an image of an advancing warrior?

Further, the trip to Babylon is a future prediction that stands in contrast to the suffix verbs and participles of the next verse (v. 11): 'But[39] *now* many nations are gathered against you, they are ones saying [horrible things]' (ועתה נאספו עליך גוים רבים האמרים). The shift in tense indicates that there is a more current and seemingly more painful moment occurring (now) in the nation's life. If one were to consider the hybrid Zion–Yahweh figure as the central character in this passage, the rescue *in* Babylon might be considered part of a self-preservative future plan to deal with these other nations (4.12-13).[40]

But then, Zion alone (without Yahweh) seems to be the subject of the nations' hostility, and this is another detail that might urge the pedagogical object to reassert itself. However, countering this, a tiny ambiguity emerges embedded in the nations' taunt in 4.11. The verb form תחנף could be translated as either a 2ms ('you will be desecrated'), to fit with the second person forms of the passage, or as a 3fs jussive ('let her be desecrated') to fit with the jussive that follows. Though the latter is usually chosen, the nations' speech in 4.11 *could* be read as 'you (ms) will be desecrated', followed by, 'and let our eyes gaze upon Zion' (moving from 2ms to 3fs as in v. 8). Reading this way would allow the masculine side of the hybrid figure to be implicated in what is normally read as particularly feminine violation (recall Mays's extended description of this moment).

Then at the end of ch. 4, another troubling element emerges. *You* are told you will gash yourself. He lays siege against *us*. Once again this threatens to undo the image of a powerful and divine Yahweh–Zion figure, and to reinscribe the suffering feminine image (or perhaps it merely points out a reader's demand for the divinity to be invincible). Having worked so hard to identify with this figure throughout the passage, struggling against a pre-formed readerly position, it seems painful to be chastised at the end of all these efforts. And yet this performs the same operation that consideration of the hybridity of the oppressed–oppressing people in chs. 5–6 performed in illuminating readerly positions. Suddenly, *I* (the *I* of enunciation), having just previously trampled

---

39. Translating the waw as disjunctive to reflect the contrast in tense.

40. Syntactically the phrase שם יגאלך יהוה *could* be read, 'there he will rescue you (fs), O Yahweh', exhibiting the same kind of gender slippage that happened in v. 8, between *you* (ms) and the names for Jerusalem (here the *you* is feminine and the name masculine).

nations, am positioned as defeated and oppressed. In this way, *I* am forced into a position of sympathy with those that I have just trampled. This turns the eye of power back upon itself.

Negotiation

As I suggested, if the 'empty form' *you* is filled in by the image of a hybrid Zion–Yahweh, the entire landscape of the passage changes. No longer need this be read as a passage about a suffering mother, rescued. No longer do the shifts in gender need to be explained away or corrected. No longer do awkward references to large cows need to be made, and seemingly obvious ancient near eastern parallels be dismissed. No longer does the violation of Zion at the hands of nations need to be inflated. Rather, many of the difficulties of the text suddenly come into their own. As noted, there are difficulties that remain; yet this is not surprising given the fact that hybridity is always constructed with what slips out of attempts at unification. It is precisely because of this kind of slippage that the meaning of the sign does not always come down in its 'proper place', nor can a new place necessarily be fixed.

Nonetheless, this is not free-floating signification. Reading this way is dependent on particular textual contours as well as on the reader's positioning. It is a negotiation that takes place 'outside the sentence' between the signs of the text and the signs that pin the reader. As in the understanding of signification and subjectivity that Bhabha proposes, meaning and the positioning of the reader by the text are both contiguous and contingent; they are dependent on the chain of signifiers that is the text, and on the reader's always-already formation as subject; and they are also subject to change depending on the interaction between the two. If the reader reads in response to the text's demand, 'What do you want of me?', and identifies with the differences found following that demand, she might come out in another place than where she started. In Bhabhian terms, I might say that in the reading of indeterminate text both the meaning produced and the possible repositioning of the subject are *effects of the intersubjective*.

Indeed, what is of significance for my purposes is the way in which working through the details of the text can bring into view and challenge the reader's always-already positioning and points of identification. For instance, reading this way—maintaining an identification with the hybrid figure instead of with the suffering mother—does not come easily, and has the effect of constantly interrogating the always-already positioning from which one reads the text. One is persistently confronted not only with the discourses of gender and biblical theology for which the image of a suffering mother stands in, but also with all of the prohibitions that give those discourses weight, starting with 'you shall have no other gods before me', moving through 'one cannot be both male and female',[41] to 'one cannot read biblical text without reference to the rest of the canon'.[42] In order to carry through reading as one identifying with this hybrid image, one is made constantly aware of these prohibitions, and therefore of what is excluded by them; as well as one's own formation by them. This brings into view and interrogates what is operating to form one as a reading subject.

Further the effect of this hybrid figure on the pedagogical object (which I have posited as an always-already point of identification for readers) is to put Israel's identity—in Bhabha's terms, the fantasy of identity and origin—into question. So not only does the hybrid figure disrupt the norms of gender operative in the pedagogical object, but with them, it disrupts the two essential components of the Israel/Yahweh relationship: humanity and divinity. As the distinction between the (feminine, human) nation personified here by the city, and the (divine, male) Yahweh begins to disintegrate, so too does the notion that in Micah, Israel's identity is based in the understanding of itself as the necessarily passive, because human, party in a covenant treaty. If Yahweh is seen as hybrid with the nation, his role of beneficent bestower of covenant grace and gifts (i.e. land) vanishes. With both the gender binary and the divinity–humanity binary turned upside-down, new images emerge: Yahweh as suffering mother, the people as phallic leaders. Such a reversal provides a less hierarchical and androcentric image of the deity (which may be theologically helpful for those who wish to keep the faith, but find the text too patriarchal); it also illuminates Israel's role as colonizer (which the pedagogical object effaces). And perhaps too—as in chs. 5–6—by illuminating Israel's role as colonizer, and by interpellating the reader into a position of identification with it, the text interrogates the reader's own role as conqueror (which the pedagogical object also effaces). Acknowledgment of this positionality would be in itself a slight shift in subjectivity.

Identification with this figure may have other kinds of effects on the reader's subjectivity as well. First, if the reader comes to the text identifying as gendered, that is, as male or female (which most readers are wont to do), she is likely positioned somewhere along the bipolar spectrum

41. See Bornstein's rules for gender (1994: 45-51)—discussed in my Chapter 5.
42. Cf. Childs's statement that 'the task of Old Testament exegesis is the interpretation of the canonical text as it has been shaped in the history of Israel's experience with God' (1987: 47, see also 48). See Aichele (2001) for a discussion of canon as a form of ideological control.

that the gender binary demands: as an active and powerful man, or as a less active, less powerful woman. However, if she responds to the constantly shifting and variously gendered *you*'s of the text, she responds to changes in placement within the gender binary. I might say that that the text's interpellation induces a kind of gender bending for the *I* of enunciation that holds together the various responses to the text's hailing. This means that if the reader lets herself be interpellated by the text, she sees herself positioned and repositioned with respect to behaviour, power and privilege. If the reader identifies with these shifts in power, this might make her more aware of her own functioning within the binary gender construct. This kind of gender bending, enacted through liminal identification with figures that undergo gender transformations, might put into question the natural fixity of gender roles in the first place. Indeed, this is one of the functions of gender bending in general; in the words of film theorist Annette Kuhn, it 'threatens to undercut the subject fixed in ideology...[and] highlights the centrality of gender constructs in processes of subjectivity' (1985: 54). The hybridity that interrogates gender might be able, again in the words of Kuhn, to 'open up a space of self-referentiality' which not only calls 'attention to the artifice of gender identity' but also 'effects a "wilful alienation" from the fixity of that identity' (1985: 54).[43]

Similarly, if the reader identifies, or tries to identify with the divine, phallic, active figure, instead of with the punishable and passive nation— the lesser party in the covenant treaty—her position with respect to power and with respect to desire (both of which, as Bornstein argues, are related to gender) changes drastically. No longer is she the passive recipient of divine rule. No longer is her desire for the deity's leading into a glorious future of colonial rule, for which 'gift' she does not have to take responsibility. Now she is in control of her destiny and fully

---

43. Reading this way certainly caused me to reconsider my position in gender. Before I began working on this text, I had not thought seriously about gender as an ideological discourse that affects the way I live. I hadn't ever spent time trying to see if I could perform gender ambiguously. I had rarely evaluated my wardrobe for its gender content. I hadn't ever walked down the street and tried looking at people in the eyes (male cue). I hadn't ever sat on the bus with my legs splayed to see what response I would get as a women in a male position. I hadn't ever shaved my head. Nor had I realized the kind of political privilege and voice gained by certain of my more masculinely-coded behaviours, and the problems that these posed for non-hierarchical organizing. Reading the text this way has propelled me to realize the ways in which I 'naturally' perform gender, as well as the way people 'naturally' respond to certain types of gendered behaviours. To my surprise, reading Micah pushed me to start breaking free of those gender confines.

responsible for her defeat of other nations. And yet the text, having urged this kind of identification, also immediately makes the reader aware of what such defeat feels like, in its command to 'cut yourself', and in its description of chastisement. Seeing and imagining the effects of power in this way might even have the result of putting into question the very desire for power, whether received as a divine *gift* (in the case of the feminine nation) or acted out as a divine *prerogative* (in the case of the hybrid figure). In short, through this kind of (liminal) identification, the reader's position is shifted from one prone to yieldingly accepting 'divinely ordained colonial rule' to one wary of the benefits of power thus configured.

Conclusion

What I have tried to show in this chapter is that the text repeats the signs of gender, nation and future much differently than attempts to unify it can allow. The text's repetition of the various components of the passive suffering woman–remnant–flock led into colonial glory by the active male deity disrupts this pedagogical object both as an image and as a viable pinning point for the text. The 'performative practice' of the text also brings into view identifications that readers might have made with the pedagogical object, and questions them. More than this though, the text's differently repeated signs disrupt the pedagogical object by producing hybrid images, such as the oppressed–oppressing nation, and the male–female, divine–human Yahweh–Zion which can provide new points of identification for readers. If readers identify with these images, or even try to identify with them, their own subject positions are brought into view, and possibly shifted. Finally, identification with these images changes the meaning of the text, and here I have looked primarily at the meaning of the future visions in the book. These kinds of readings are not meant to be final, it is the process of reading this way that concerns me; it is the process of reading as genuine *negotiation* that can have the effect of repositioning the subject in ways that engender resistance to oppression.

7

Conclusion

What I have endeavoured to do in this book is to come at the problems in reading the ambiguous Hebrew text of Micah by taking into account the question posed in discussions of textual determinacy: 'is it the text or the reader that controls meaning?' I have started from the position—common to much contemporary literary and cultural criticism—that the reader comes to the text already formed as a subject within ideology, and that this will necessarily affect the way she reads the text. But not satisfied with the idea that the reader, pre-determined by cultural and ideological discourses, is solely responsible for the meaning of the text, I have tried to see whether the contours of the text might also have something to do with meaning, and as well have an impact on the positioning of the reader as subject.

In order to come at this question I have taken up the work of post-colonial critic Homi K. Bhabha. I have argued first that Bhabha's theory has an important contribution to make in thinking about the possibility of repositioning the subject fixed in ideology and second that this can be applied to the reading of text. For the first, I argued that Bhabha's use of Derrida's critique of Lacan is pertinent for thinking about Žižek's use of Lacan in describing the subject's formation in interpellation. Žižek's reading of interpellation (following Althusser) seems to tend toward the fixity of the subject's positioning, as it is governed by identification with the absent master signifier (or *point de capiton*). Bhabha's theory takes up similar concepts but tries to envision the possibility that the subject need not always return to the same place, by imagining the potential for identification with difference within the master signifier (liminal identification). As for applying Bhabha to reading, I found his contrast between the pedagogical objects and discourses that pin down the identity of the nation and the performative practice of a nation, to be a useful analogy to the way the text of Micah has been, and can be, read. I suggested that in the reading process, the performative practice of a text—that is, the differently repeating signs of the text—is akin to Bhabha's negotiation of cultural difference, which takes place in 'the Third Space', produces hybridity, opens up spaces for liminal identification with difference, and revisions meaning in the 'time-lag'.

As I applied these concepts to reading Micah, I first tried to illustrate the text as a site of difference by looking carefully at the difficulties and ambiguities therein, particularly with respect to determining the various participants and their genders, given the shifting forms of address in the book. I then noticed that the text has often, if not predominantly, been read in ways that smooth out and unify these difficulties, through reference to what I labeled 'the pedagogical object', that is, the image of the damsel in distress, rescued by her male hero. This I argued, functions as a kind of fantasy object with which readers can identify, and corresponds to contemporary ideological and theological discourses of gender, and of Israel's identity formed in covenant. I tried to show that, as such, this pedagogical object serves to stop the sliding of the signs of the text and to impose 'coherence' on it, by determining the kinds of 'solutions' and readings that scholars posit.

But, I suggested, if one pays careful attention to the way the text repeats or performs this pedagogical object, not only does the pedagogical object with which the reader has been pinned come into view (through contrast to the difference in the text) but also, new hybrid figures emerge between the pedagogical object and the signs of the text. I further argued that the reader's identification with these hybrid figures affects the way that the text can be understood, and also enables the reader to see and to interrogate her own subject position. I tried to demonstrate how this negotiation with the text might disrupt the pedagogical object by looking at a number of hybrid images that appear in reading Micah. I particularly focused on the way in which the text repeats two of the elements of the pedagogical object: the oppressed remnant turned victorious, and the suffering mother rescued by Yahweh. I attempted to show that if the reader were to respond to the various interpellations of the text, hybrid images would emerge between colonizer and colonized, masculinity and femininity, hope and doom, humanity and divinity. Further I suggested that if readers were to identify with these hybrid images, the text would make sense differently, and so they might also find themselves positioned to do justice differently.

Possible Gains

Having worked through the text of Micah in this way, I have found this approach to be productive for thinking about the difficulties in the text and for thinking about the reading process. It is my hope that others will find even my first stage of simply laying out the ambiguities in the text (Chapter 4) helpful, and that the attention to all the shifts in the text may be suggestive for many other ways of reading than I have offered here. In addition, the exposition of normative theological readings of Micah (Chapter 5) may also help to open up the text, reminding readers of what might be at work in producing these readings. In my opinion, attention to the reading process in general can only lead to more careful readings of the biblical text (which in turn, as I have showed, can interrogate the reader's own subject position).

Moreover, I think that this way of looking at Micah can contribute to the discussions that are beginning to take place regarding Micah's 'indeterminacy' and its affect on readers (for example, Petrotta 1991; Ben Zvi 1998, 2000). I have placed the discussion within a theoretical framework that takes into account the problems that the concept of indeterminacy poses for positing texts' ability to actually have a rhetorical effect on readers. Along these lines, I hope that I have contributed in some small way to the larger theoretical discussion on textual indeterminacy that has been taking place in biblical studies by going past, as Gary Phillips suggests is necessary, the troubling either/or logic of 'text or reader' (1995: 197).

Further, I have focused on the question of justice in Micah slightly differently than is habitually done. I have argued that neither the text of Micah, nor readings of it, are as unproblematically aligned with discourses of justice as has often been supposed, but that at the same time, its call to justice does play a crucial role in the reading process. By mapping the work of Bhabha, who is concerned with liberation, onto a Marxist theoretical framework, which is concerned with understanding oppression, I have tried to consider a little more fully what it means to be called to justice, and what might have to happen for this interpellation to take effect.

In addition, in considering the problems of thinking about justice and liberation through biblical text, I have drawn on the work and insights of a range of biblical scholars thinking along these lines (liberation theologians, ideological critics, postcolonial critics, feminist critics, and so on). I have used a hermeneutic of suspicion, in order to be critical of the text, and to allow marginal voices (or readings) to be heard; but I have also been motivated by the impulse to liberation (from oppression, from determinism, from ideology) and (re)orientation (toward justice) with which much liberation theology is concerned. I would like to think that the kind of approach I have suggested here might be productive in drawing together the (anti-sexist, anti-colonial, anti-capitalist) issues raised by these various types of criticism, and in getting new conversations started between them.

Finally, I hope that I have taken one small step toward sorting out the difficulties in thinking about subjectivity, ideology and the possibilities for political struggle and change. Thinking about political change using Marxist frameworks *and* poststructural theory is not easy. Such theorizing is being done (for example in the works of Spivak, Butler, Laclau and Mouffe), but it has not been looked upon entirely favourably by some Marxist critics (for example, Žižek 1993; Eagleton 1996). Yet it is my contention that this must be thought through, especially for those who would like to see resistance to global market interests go beyond what sometimes seems to be the choice between public stand-offs with immutably brutish police forces on the one hand, and the writing of ineffectual political tracts to the converted, on the other. It seems to me that Bhabha's work is able to engage both the Marxist description of ideology which is concerned with oppressive structural determinants, and poststructural theory which is concerned with subverting dominant structures, but which does not necessarily want to work with absolutes. I hope that my reading of Bhabha's work has illuminated his ability to hold these two positions together.

Further Research

Following from this, several avenues for future research open up. First, because Micah is a text similar to a number of biblical texts, in that it is open and ambiguous, this kind of reading might be applied to other texts. At the end of the day, it is the approach to reading that concerns me, and though I do think it has provided some interesting results with Micah, I expect it needs to be tested further on other texts. It would be interesting to read other prophetic texts this way, for instance Jeremiah, Isaiah or Ezekiel, all of which have more space to develop a sustained view of Israel's identity and future prospects. I wonder, given my reflections on Micah, whether gender, nation and future are as predictable in the major prophets (aligned with notions of covenant, punishment and redemption) as might be expected, or if they too might repeat these signs differently, so that similar kinds of hybridity appear. Further, what I have argued here has some implication for a particular conception of prophetic theology that, to my mind, would benefit from an injection of gender criticism. (Renita Weems begins to move in this direction in *Battered Love: Marriage, Sex and Violence in the Hebrew Prophets* [1995], but in the end comes out in a place similar to other accounts of prophetic theology that find Yahweh's violence against the nation as a woman to be understandable and even productive [see 1995: 18-22, 113-19].) Trying to read these other prophetic books in the way I have proposed might be a place to begin such an line of investigation.

Second, where I have bracketed the *material nature* of ideology, in order to focus on the function of ideological *discourses*, materiality must be reinserted into the theoretical equation and a more thorough exploration of the relationships between materiality, ideology, politics, desire, text and interpretation be taken up. The kind of reading I have proposed seems to work when ideology is viewed in terms of ideological discourses; but what of material determinants for ideology? Can texts, read this way, disrupt ideology on the material level? If one's subject position is shifted on a discursive level, does it also shift with respect to material practice? Could this have an overall effect of changing ideology (as opposed to simply disrupting ideological discourses)? And perhaps most importantly, can this kind of technique actually be used in struggles for justice? Can *texts* have any impact on people's positioning within ideology, where ideology is understood to be structurally related to material practices of domination? If so, how precisely would they be used in struggles against oppression? More work is needed on the *textual capacity* to disrupt dominant or oppressive *practices* (which, at the end of the day, might have more implications for writing texts, than for reading them). My suspicion is that answers to these kinds of questions must take more fully into consideration the relation of desire to ideology and interpretation that I have outlined here. Further, while I have focused on the reader formed in ideology as a more or less unified subject (though split, lacking and decentered), it may be important to factor in the possibility—posited by those trying to theorize radical democracy—that individuals may hold multiple and even conflicting subject positions (for example, see Laclau and Mouffe 1985).

Third, while I have drawn on psychoanalytic theory in order to use Bhabha, I have treated identification and desire as something that can be, for the most part, negotiated consciously. In order truly to understand the processes by which change can come about, however, unconscious processes, desires and identifications must also be taken seriously. While what I have offered here lends itself to thinking about the unconscious processes in reading, I would suggest that this needs to be done in a more deliberate and thorough fashion. Indeed, in my view, theorizing the possibility of changing the subject through reading opens up new avenues for psychoanalytical criticism in biblical studies.

Finally, the consideration of ideology and biblical text opens out into a space for contemplating the role that the biblical text plays in contemporary culture. Occasionally in this book, I have hinted at how the biblical text may be read to *support*—as opposed to reproducing—particular cultural (ideological) views. It is my contention that because the biblical text is often used as both motivational metaphor and justification for many different types of political visions, desires and practices, its role as such must not only be examined, but perhaps confronted by the text itself, if ever it is to be used in struggles against oppression. For instance, I am curious about whether and how biblical images might give authority to nations' policies, as well as providing language by which to make these policies palatable. I wonder about the way that hope for an exodus (moving from oppression into conquest), and desire for glorious and peaceful *domination* have filtered into and support oppressive practices. It seems vital that careful work be done to show that these kinds of cultural appropriations of the Bible can crack and fissure along and through the fault lines of the text itself; to my mind this is the kind of work in which there might actually be ongoing hope for biblical studies to change subjects.

Glossary

CHE VUOI?: The (Italian) question the OTHER asks of the subject after it enters the SYMBOLIC ORDER: 'What do you want of me?' This question inaugurates desire.

DIFFÉRANCE: Derrida's term for the constantly differing and deferring structure of language.

DRIVES: Lacan's term for what Freud called the instincts (sexual needs and impulses, and also the death drive). When the subject enters into language it is split off from its drives, and from there on in they operate within the realm of the unconscious.

ENONCE: The French word for 'statement' that has been taken up in linguistics and theories of language and subjectivity to signify the subject of the statement, which could be either the subject matter (content) or the grammatical position (form), or both. Contrast ENONCIATION.

ENONCIATION: The French word for 'enunciation' that has been taken up in linguistics and theories of language and subjectivity to signify the subject of speech. Contrast ENONCE.

HYBRIDITY: Bhabha's term for what is produced in the imperfect repetition of colonizers by the colonized. This imperfect repetition is demanded by colonizers to justify discrimination, but the hybridity produced through the differently repeated colonial culture and norms also troubles the purity and authority of those very norms. This is to be distinguished from the notion of hybridity as simply a mixture.

IDEOLOGICAL INTERPELLATION: Althusser's conception of the way individuals come to be formed in ideology: they are hailed by social discourses and practices, in which they recognize themselves, and in this process are formed as subjects.

IDEOLOGICAL STATE APPARATUSES: Althusser's term for religious institutions, political parties, families, schools, media and so on, which ensure the smooth operation of the State, and offer the individual images and discourses with which to identify.

IDEOLOGY: According to Althusser (and Žižek), the imaginary relation that individuals have to their material conditions of existence (that is, the means and relations of production). Ideology is formed through identification with social discourses and images; it is lived out in everyday material practices; and it hides itself as the 'natural' or the 'obvious'.

IMAGINARY IDENTIFICATION: Lacan's term for the identification that the subject makes with an *image*, in the mirror stage; this image gives the subject a sense of coherence.

INTERTEXTUALITY: Julia Kristeva's term for the way that texts continually call to mind, and intersect with other texts, creating an infinite chain of reference and signification, and thus an endless play of meaning.

LIMINAL IDENTIFICATION: Bhabha's term for the kind of identification that can be made with HYBRIDITY, or with the difference that makes up the signs of culture (see: STRUCTURE OF REPETITION).

MASTER SIGNIFIER: Žižek's term for the signifier that hails and 'pins' the individual in IDEOLOGICAL INTERPELLATION; it determines the meaning of other signifiers in the chain of signification, and also the relations between signifiers. Coterminous with POINT DE CAPITON.

OBJET PETIT A: Lacan's term, also taken up by Žižek, for the fantasy object that comes to stand in for the subject's loss (of access to the DRIVES, what he calls being, or THE REAL) in entry into language. Paradoxically it is both the object and cause of desire.

OTHER: The English translation of Lacan's *Autre*; it is the realm of language into which the child enters, splitting it off from its drives to form the unconscious; also called the SYMBOLIC ORDER.

OVERDETERMINATION: Althusser's term (borrowed from Freud) for the process by which diverse and possibly contradictory cultural or social elements, determined by the economic base, are made to cohere in IDEOLOGY; this in turn results in adjustment and reworking of the economic structure. Ideology is thus overdetermined in that it is both *determined by* and *determining for* the material structure.

PEDAGOGICAL OBJECTS AND DISCOURSES: Bhabha's term for the images and discourses that are used to categorize cultures: stereotypes, cultural icons and historical narratives. He shows how these images and discourses are always unstable.

PERFORMATIVE PRACTICE: The everyday practices, repetitions and articulations of PEDAGOGICAL OBJECTS AND DISCOURSES that disrupt them.

POINT DE CAPITON: Lacan's term for the pure signifier, or pinning point, that represents the loss of being or the REAL. This pure signifier can only be known through fantasy. Žižek uses it to speak of the ideological pinning point, the MASTER SIGNIFIER.

THE REAL: The thing(s) (DRIVES, being, love object) that are traumatically lost in the subject's formation, which are never again accessible, but which still operate, giving rise to a series of substitutions (POINT DE CAPITON, OBJET PETIT A).

REPETITION COMPULSION: Freud's term for the repetitive behaviours and compulsions by which the individual tries to regain the lost love object.

RETROACTIVE SIGNIFICATION: An application of the Freudian notion of *Nachträglichkeit* (deferred action) to the process of signification. In psychoanalytic terms, this means that as a result of a later event an earlier memory can be restructured. For Lacan, it means that that subjectivity and meaning are only produced after the complexities of identification and desire have taken place.

STRUCTURE OF REPETITION: Derrida's understanding that any term is only known through its accumulated repetition; this puts into question the idea of origins, since 'an original' can only be known through its repetition.

SUBJECT: For the purposes of this book: the speaking, acting individual, positioned as such by language and IDEOLOGICAL INTERPELLATION.

SUPPLEMENT: Derrida's term for that which both substitutes for, and adds to meaning. Often that which has been excluded in order to establish meaning (e.g. for a signifier, text or culture) leaves a mark, a remainder, that then acts as a disturbing supplement.

SYMBOLIC IDENTIFICATION: The identifications that the subject makes with the OTHER; occurs after imaginary identification. It is Lacan's adaptation of the Freudian formation of the super-ego through the child's identification with the parent.

SYMBOLIC ORDER: see OTHER.

TEXTUAL INDETERMINACY: The constant play of text that renders meaning impossible to pin down. This endless play of text is inaugurated by the gaps or difficulties in a text which require the introduction of other texts to aid in interpretation, which in turn lead to yet other texts, all of which affect meaning. See INTERTEXTUALITY.

THE THIRD SPACE: One of Bhabha's concept metaphors, akin to the Lacanian VEL, where self and Other meet. The colonial self may try to pin the colonized Other, but in enunciating the position assigned to it, the colonial object becomes the subject, resisting the pinning of the Other.

TIME-LAG: One of Bhabha's concept metaphors which suggests that through new forms of identification, colonized peoples can resituate and reclaim histories of oppression in order to affect the present. Developed from the notion of RETROACTIVE SIGNIFICATION.

UNCANNY: Freud's term (in German, *unheimlich*) for the appearance of something that resembles what has been repressed; it seems somehow familiar yet haunting and disturbing.

UNDECIDABLES: Derrida's term for an idea or image that inhabits a (philosophical) binary, but which also does not quite fit, therefore troubling and disorganizing that binary.

VEL: A Lacanian term meaning 'or', taken from logic. Lacan uses it to describe the relationship (the overlap) between meaning (Other) and being (self) in the formation of subjectivity; see OTHER; Bhabha uses it as a model for THE THIRD SPACE.

Lacanian Graphs of Desire

(Lacan 1977: 303-15; Žižek 1989: 101-21)

Lower level of the graph: moving from imaginary to symbolic identification
(Retroactive signification)

Graph I

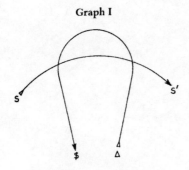

Graph II

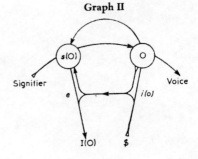

S–S¹ = chain of signifiers
Δ = pre-symbolic intention
$ = split, lacking subject

O = the Other
s(O) = final signification

Imaginary Identification (mirror stage)
e = imaginary ego (ideal ego)
i(o) = imaginary other
i(o)→e = imaginary identification

Symbolic identification
$ = (always-already) split subject
I(O) = ego-ideal
$→I(O) = symbolic identification

Upper level of the graph: takes place within the symbolic order

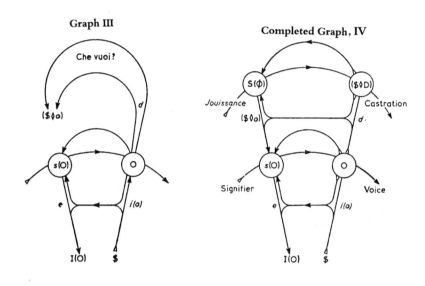

d   = desire
o   = *objet petit a* (fantasy object)
$<>o = desire of the $ for the *objet*
          petit a

$<>D = the drive
D   = symbolic demand
S(Ø)   = signifier of the lack of the
            Other (master signifier)

Bibliography

Achtemeier, Elizabeth R.
>   1963   'How to Stay Alive: Micah 6:6-8 and Mark 12:28-34', *Theology and Life* 6: 275-82.

Aharoni, Y.
>   1968   'Trial Excavation in the "Solar Shrine" at Lachish', *IEJ* 18: 157-69.

Ahmad, Aijaz
>   1992   *In Theory: Classes, Nations, Literatures* (London: Verso).

Aichele, George
>   2001   *The Control of Biblical Meaning: Canon as Semiotic Mechanism* (Harrisburg, PA: Trinity Press International).

Alfaro, Juan I.
>   1989   *Justice and Loyalty: A Commentary on the Book of Micah* (International Theological Commentary; Grand Rapids: Eerdmans).

Allegro, John
>   1968   *Discoveries in the Judean Desert*. V. *Qumran Cave 4 (4Q158-4Q186)* (Oxford: Clarendon Press).

Allen, Leslie C.
>   1976   *The Books of Joel, Obadiah, Jonah and Micah* (Grand Rapids: Eerdmans).

Althusser, Louis
>   1977   *For Marx* (trans. Ben Brewster; London: Verso [1965]).
>   1984   *Essays on Ideology* (London: Verso).

Althusser, Louis, and Étienne Balibar
>   1970   *Reading Capital* (trans. Ben Brewster; London: NLB [1965]).

Anbar, Moshé
>   1994   'Rosée et ondées ou lion et lionceau (Michée 5, 6-7)?', *BN* 73: 5-8.

Anderson, Benedict
>   1994   *Imagined Communities: Reflections on the Origins and Spread of Nationalism* (London: Verso).

Andersen, Francis I.
>   1994   'The Poetic Properties of Prophetic Discourse in the Book of Micah', in Robert D. Bergen (ed.), *Biblical Hebrew and Discourse Linguistics* (Winona Lake, IN: Eisenbrauns): 520-28.

Andersen, Francis I., and David Noel Freedman
>   2000   *Micah: A New Translation with Introduction and Commentary* (AB, 24E; New York: Doubleday).

Anderson, Janice Capel, and Stephen Moore (eds.)
>   1992   *Mark and Method* (Minneapolis: Fortress Press).

Anthias, Floya, and Nira Yuval-Davis
>   1992   *Racialized Boundaries: Race, Nation, Gender, Color and Class in the Anti-racist Struggle* (London: Routledge).

Barker, Kenneth L.
    1998   'A Literary Analysis of the Book of Micah', *BSac* 155: 437-38.
Barr, James
    1980   *Explorations in Theology* 7 (London: SCM Press).
Barré, Michael L.
    1982   'Critical Notes: A Cuneiform Parallel to Ps 86:16-17 and Mic 7:16-17',
            JBL 101: 272-75.
Barrick, W. Boyd
    1975   'The Funary Character of "High-Places" in Ancient Palestine: A
            Reassessment', *VT* 25: 565-95.
Barthélemy, D., and J.T. Milik
    1955   *Discoveries in the Judean Desert. I. Qumran Cave 1* (Oxford: Claren-
            don Press).
Barthes, Roland
    1974   *S/Z: An Essay* (trans. Richard Miller; New York: Noonday [1970]).
    1975   *The Pleasure of the Text* (trans. Richard Miller; New York: McGraw–
            Hill [1973]).
Beal, Timothy K.
    1992   'Ideology and Intertexuality: Surplus of Meaning and Controlling the
            Means of Production', in Fewell 1992: 27-39.
    1994   'The System and the Speaking Subject in the Hebrew Bible: Reading
            for Divine Abjection', *BibInt* 2: 171-89.
    1997a   'Opening: Cracking the Binding', in Beal and Gunn 1997: 1-12.
    1997b   *The Book of Hiding: Gender, Ethnicity, Annihilation and Esther* (Bib-
            lical Limits; London: Routledge).
Beal, Timothy K., and David M. Gunn (eds.)
    1997   *Reading Bibles, Writing Bodies: Identity and the Book* (Biblical
            Limits; London: Routledge).
Bell, Shannon
    1995   *Whore Carnival* (New York: Autonomedia).
Belsey, Catherine
    1997   'Constructing the Subject: Deconstructing the Text', in Robyn R.
            Warhol and Diane Price Herndl (eds.), *Feminisms: An Anthology of
            Literary Theory and Criticism* (New Brunswick, NJ: Rutgers Univer-
            sity Press): 45-64.
Benveniste, Emile
    1971   *Problems in General Linguistics* (trans. Mary Elizabeth Meek; Coral
            Gables: University of Miami Press [1966]).
Ben Zvi, Ehud
    1995   'Inclusion in and Exclusion from Israel as Conveyed by the Use of the
            Term "Israel" in Post-monarchic Biblical Texts', in Steven W. Holloway
            and Lowell K. Handy (eds.), *The Pitcher Is Broken: Memorial Essays
            for Gösta W. Ahlström* (JSOTSup, 190; Sheffield: Sheffield Academic
            Press): 95-149.
    1998   'Micah 1.2-16: Observations and Possible Implications', *JSOT* 77: 103-
            20.
    1999   'Wrongdoers, Wrongdoing, and Righting Wrongs in Micah 2', *BibInt*
            7: 87-100.

2000   *Micah* (FOTL, 21b; Grand Rapids: Eerdmans).

Bergbusch, Matt

2000   'Additional Dialogue, William Shakespeare: Queer Allegory and My
            Own Private Idaho', in Don Hendrick and Bryan Reynolds (eds.),
            Shakespeare without Class (New York: St Martin's Press): 209-25.

Bhabha, Homi K.

1984   'Representation and the Colonial Text: A Critical Exploration of Some
            Forms of Mimeticism', in Frank Gloversmith (ed.), *The Theory of
            Reading* (Sussex: Harvester Press): 93-122.

1986   'Remembering Fanon: Self, Psyche and the Colonial Condition',
            Foreword to *Black Skin, White Masks*, by Frantz Fanon (London:
            Pluto Press).

1989   'At the Limits: Homi K. Bhabha on the Power of the Text', *Artforum*
            May: 11-12.

1990a   'Introduction: Narrating the Nation', in Bhabha 1990b: 1-7.

1992a   'Freedom's Basis in the Indeterminate', *October* 61: 46-57.

1992b   'Double Visions', *Artforum* January: 85-89.

1992c   'Postcolonial Authority and Postmodern Guilt', in Lawrence Gross-
            berg, Cary Nelson and Paula A. Treichler (eds.), *Cultural Studies*
            (London: Routledge): 56-68.

1993a   'Beyond the Pale: Art in the Age of Multicultural Translation', in Ria
            Lavrijsen (ed.), *Cultural Diversity in the Arts: Art, Art Policies and
            the Facelift of Europe* (The Hague: Royal Tropical Institute): 21-30.

1993b   'Interview by Maria Koundoura and Amit Rai', *Stanford Humanities
            Review* 3(1): 1-6.

1994a   *The Location of Culture* (London: Routledge).

1994b   'Frontlines/borderposts', Afterword to *Displacements: Cultural
            Identities in Question* (ed. Angelika Bammer; Bloomington: Indiana
            University Press): 269-72.

1994c   'Anxious Nations, Nervous States', in Copjec 1994: 201-18.

1995a   'Dance this Diss Around: Homi K. Bhabha on Victim Art', *Artforum*
            April: 19-20.

1995b   'Black and White and Read All Over: Homi K. Bhabha on the New
            Black Intellectual', *Artforum* October: 16-17, 114, 116.

1995c   'Are You a Man or a Mouse?', in Brian Wallis, Maurice Berger and
            Simon Watson (eds.), *Constructing Masculinity* (New York: Rout-
            ledge): 57-65.

1996a   'Postmodernism/Postcolonialism', in R. Nelson and R. Shiff (eds.),
            Critical Terms for Art History (Chicago: University of Chicago Press).

1996b   'Laughing Stock: Homi K. Bhabha on Sokal Science', *Artforum*
            October: 15-16, 132.

1996c   'Unsatisfied: Notes on Vernacular Cosmopolitanism', in Laura Garcia-
            Moreno and Peter C. Pfeiffer (eds.), *Text and Nation: Cross-Discipli-
            nary Essays in Cultural and National Identities* (Columbia, SC:
            Camden House): 191-207.

1996d   'Rethinking Authority: Interview with Homi K. Bhabha by Gary Hall
            and Simon Wortham', *Angelaki* 2(2): 59-63.

1997a 'Editor's Introduction: Minority Maneuvers and Unsettled Negotiations', *Critical Inquiry* 23: 431-59.

1997b 'Queen's English: Homi K. Bhabha on Ebonics', *Artforum* March: 25-26, 107.

1997c 'Halfway House: Homi K. Bhabha on Hybridity', *Artforum* May: 11-12, 125.

1997d 'Designer Creations: Homi K. Bhabha on Diana's Subjects', *Artforum* December: 11-14, 130.

1998a 'On the Irremovable Strangeness of Being Different', *PMLA* 113(1-3): 34-39.

1998b 'The White Stuff: Homi K. Bhabha on Whiteness Studies', *Artforum* May: 21-24.

Bhabha, Homi K. (ed.)

1990b *Nation and Narration* (London: Routledge).

Bhabha, Homi K., Stuart Hall and Paul Gilroy

1991 'Threatening Pleasures: How the 1977 Jubilee, Music, Sexuality, Politics and Pleasure Come Together in "Young Soul Rebels" Wonder Paul Gilroy, Stuart Hall and Homi Bhabha?', *Sight and Sound* NS 1: 17-19.

Bible and Culture Collective

1995 *The Postmodern Bible* (New Haven: Yale University Press).

Bird, Phyllis

1989 ' "To Play the Harlot": An Inquiry into the Old Testament Metaphor', in Day 1989: 75-94.

Black, Fiona C., Roland Boer and Erin Runions (eds.)

1999 *The Labour of Reading: Desire, Alienation and Biblical Interpretation* (Semeia Studies, 36; Atlanta: Scholars Press).

Boer, Roland

1999 'David is a Thing', in Black, Boer and Runions 1999: 163-76.

2000 'Come Again: Repetition and the Insatiability of Desire in the Song of Songs', *BibInt* 8: 276-301.

Bolin, Anne

1988 *In Search of Eve: Transsexual Rites of Passage* (Massachusetts: Bergin & Garbey).

Bordreuil, Pierre

1971 'Michée 4:10-13 et ses parallèles ougaritiques', *Semitica* 21: 21-28.

Bornstein, Kate

1994 *Gender Outlaw: On Men, Women, and the Rest of Us* (New York: Routledge).

Bourdieu, Pierre

1998 'A Reasoned Utopia and Economic Fatalism', *New Left Review* 227: 125-30.

Brenner, Athalya (ed.)

1993–95 *The Feminist Companion to the Bible* (Sheffield: Sheffield Academic Press).

1995 *A Feminist Companion to the Latter Prophets* (The Feminist Companion to the Bible, 8; Sheffield: Sheffield Academic Press).

Brett, Mark G.
    1996   'The Ethics of Postcolonial Criticism', *Semeia* 75: 219-28.
Bright, John
    1955   *The Kingdom of God in Bible and Church* (Lutterworth Library, 46; London: Lutterworth Press).
    1976   *Covenant and Promise: The Prophetic Understanding of the Future in Pre-Exilic Israel* (Philadelphia: Westminster Press).
Brin, Gershon
    1989   'Micah 2,12-13: A Textual and Ideological Study', *ZAW* 101: 118-24.
Brown, J.P.
    1971   'Peace Symbolism in Ancient Military Vocabulary', *VT* 21: 1-23.
Brueggemann, Walter
    1977   *The Land* (Overtures to Biblical Theology; Philadelphia: Fortress Press).
    1981   ' "Vine and Fig Tree": A Case Study in Imagination and Criticism', *CBQ* 43: 188-204.
    1997   *Theology of the Old Testament: Testimony, Dispute, Advocacy* (Minneapolis: Fortress Press).
Brueggemann, Walter, Sharon Parks and Thomas H. Groome
    1986   *To Act Justly, Love Tenderly, Walk Humbly: An Agenda for Ministers* (New York: Paulist Press).
Bullough, Vern L., and Bonnie Bullough
    1993   *Cross Dressing, Sex, and Gender* (Philadelphia: University of Pennsylvania).
Burke, Phyllis
    1996   *Gender Shock: Exploding the Myths of Male and Female* (Anchor Books; New York: Doubleday).
Butler, Judith
    1990   *Gender Trouble: Feminism and the Subversion of Identity* (New York: Routledge.)
    1991   'Imitation and Gender Insubordination', in Fuss 1991: 13-31.
    1993   *Bodies That Matter: On the Discursive Limits of 'Sex'* (New York: Routledge).
    1995a   'Conscience Doth Make Subjects of Us All', in Lezra 1995: 6-26.
    1995b   'Subjection, Resistance, Resignification: Between Freud and Foucault', in Rajchman 1995: 229-50.
    1997a   *Excitable Speech: A Politics of the Performative* (New York: Routledge).
    1997b   'Sovereign Performatives in the Contemporary Scene of Utterance', *Critical Inquiry* 23: 350-77.
    1997c   *The Psychic Life of Power: Theories of Subjection* (Stanford: Stanford University Press).
Cadava, Eduardo, Peter Connor and Jean-Luc Nancy (eds.)
    1991   *Who Comes After the Subject* (London: Routledge).
Carroll, R.P.
    1979   *When Prophecy Failed: Cognitive Dissonance in the Prophetic Traditions of the Old Testament* (New York: Seabury).

1992   'Night without Vision: Micah and the Prophets', in F. Garcia Martinez, A. Hilhorst and C.J. Labuschangne (eds.), *The Scripture and the Scrolls: Studies in Honour of A.S. van der Woude on the Occasion of his 65th Birthday* (VTSup, 49; Leiden: E.J. Brill): 74-84.

Cathcart, Kevin J.
1968   'Notes on Micah 5, 4-5', *Bib* 49: 511-14.
1978   'Micah 5, 4-5 and Semitic Incantations', *Bib* 59: 38-48.

Cathcart, Kevin J., and Knud Jeppesen
1987   'More Suggestions on Mic 6,14', *SJOT* 1(1): 110-15.

Childs, B.S.
1978   'The Canonical Shape of Prophetic Literature', *Interpretation* 32: 46-55.
1979   'Micah', in *idem, Introduction to the Old Testament as Scripture* (Philadelphia: Fortress Press): 428-39.

Clements, R.E.
1965   *Prophecy and Covenant* (SBT; London: SCM Press).

Collin, M.
1971   'Recherches sur l'histoire textuelle du prophete Michée', *VT* 21: 281-97.

Connell, R.W.
1987   *Gender and Power: Society, The Person, and Sexual Politics* (Stanford: Stanford University Press).

Coote, Robert B.
1981   *Amos Among the Prophets: Composition and Theology* (Philadelphia: Fortress Press).

Copjec, Joan (ed.)
1994   *Supposing the Subject* (London: Verso).

Coppens, J.
1971   'Le cadre littéraire de Michée V: 1-5', in Hans Goedicke (ed.), *Near Eastern Studies in Honor of William Foxwell Albright* (Baltimore: The Johns Hopkins University Press): 57-62.

Coward, Rosalind, and John Ellis
1977   *Language and Materialism: Developments in Semiology and the Theory of the Subject* (London: Routledge & Kegan Paul).

Craigie, Peter C.
1985   *The Twelve Prophets. II. Micah, Nahum, Habakkuk, Zephaniah, Haggai, Zechariah and Malachi* (Daily Study Bible; Philadelphia: Westminster Press).

Crenshaw, James L.
1972   'Wedorek 'al-bamote 'ares', *CBQ* 34: 39-53.

Croatto, J. Severino
1981   *Exodus: A Hermeneutic of Freedom* (trans. Salvator Attanasio; Maryknoll, NY: Orbis Books [1978]).
1998   'The Function of the Non-fulfilled Promises: Reading the Pentateuch from the Perspective of the Latin-American Oppressed People', in Ingrid Rosa Kitzberger (ed.), *The Personal Voice in Biblical Interpretation* (London: Routledge): 38-52.

Cuffey, Kenneth H.
1987 'The Coherence of Micah: A Review of the Proposals and a New Interpretation' (PhD dissertation, Drew University, NJ, USA).

Culley, Robert C.
2000 'Orality and Writteness in the Prophetic Texts', in Ehud Ben Zvi and Michael Floyd (eds.), *Writings and Speech in Israelite and Ancient Near Eastern Prophecy* (SBLSymS, 10; Atlanta: SBL): 45-64.

Dahood, Mitchell
1970 *Psalms III: 101-150* (AB, 17a; Garden City, NY: Doubleday).
1983 'Minor Prophets and Ebla', in Meyers and O'Connor 1983: 47-67.

Daniels, Dwight R.
1987 'Is There a "Prophetic Lawsuit" Genre?', *ZAW* 99: 339-60.

Davies, Philip R.
1998 *Scribes and Schools: The Canonization of the Hebrew Scriptures* (Louisville, KY: Westminster/John Knox Press).

Dawes, S.
1988 'Walking Humbly: Micah 6.8 Revisited', *SJT* 41: 331-39.

Day, Peggy L. (ed.)
1989 *Gender and Difference in Ancient Israel* (Minneapolis: Fortress Press).

Dayan, Daniel
1976 'The Tudor-code of Classical Cinema', in Nichols 1976: 438-45.

Dearman, John Andrew
1984 'Prophecy, Property and Politics', *SBLSP* 1984: 385-97.
1988 *Property Rights in the Eighth-Century Prophets* (SBLDS, 106; Atlanta: Scholars Press).

Demsky, A.
1966 'The Houses of Achzib: A Critical Note on Micah 1:14b', *IEJ* 16: 211-15.

De Roche, Michael
1983 'Yahweh's *Rib* Against Israel: A Reassessment of the So-called "Prophetic Lawsuit" in the Preexilic Prophets', *JBL* 102: 563-74.

Derrida, Jacques
1974 *Of Grammatology* (trans. Gayatri Chakrovorty Spivak; Baltimore: The Johns Hopkins University Press [1967]).
1975 'The Purveyor of Truth' (trans. Willis Domingo, James Hulbert, Moshe Ron and M.-R. L.) *Yale French Studies* 52: 31-113.
1978 *Writing and Difference* (trans. Alan Bass; Chicago: University of Chicago Press [1967]).
1979a 'Living on: *Border Lines*', in Harold Bloom *et al.*, *Deconstruction and Criticism* (New York: Continuum): 75-176.
1979b 'The Parergon' (trans. Craig Owens) *October* 9 [1978]: 3-41.
1981a *Positions* (trans. and annotated by Alan Bass; Chicago: University of Chicago Press [1972]).
1981b *Dissemination* (trans. with an Introduction and Additional Notes by Barbara Johnson; Chicago: University of Chicago Press [1972]).
1982 *Margins of Philosophy* (trans. Alan Bass; Chicago: University of Chicago Press [1972]).

1984 'My Chances/*Mes Chances*: A Rendezvous with Some Epicurean Stereophonies', in Joseph H. Smith and William Kerrigan (eds.), *Taking Chances: Derrida, Psychoanalysis, Literature* (Baltimore: The Johns Hopkins University Press): 1-32.

1987 *The Post Card: From Socrates to Freud and Beyond* (trans. Alan Bass; Chicago: University of Chicago Press [1980]).

1995 ' "Eating Well", Or the Calculation of the Subject', in Elisabeth Weber (ed.), *Points...Interviews, 1974–1994* (trans. Peggy Kamuf and others; Meridian Crossing Aesthetics; Stanford: Stanford University Press): 255-87.

de Vaux, Roland

1965 *Ancient Israel*. I. *Social Institutions* (New York: McGraw–Hill).

de Waard, Jan

1979 'Vers une identification des participants dans le livre de Michée', *RHPR* 59: 509-16.

Dirlik, Arif

1994 'The Postcolonial Aura: Third World Criticism in the Ages of Global Capitalism', *Critical Inquiry* 20: 328-56.

Dumbrell, William J.

1988 *The Faith of Israel: Its Expression in the Books of the Old Testament* (Grand Rapids: Baker Book House).

1997 *Covenant and Creation: A Theology of Old Testament Covenants* (Carlisle: Paternoster).

During, Simon (ed.)

1993 *The Cultural Studies Reader* (London: Routledge).

Dussel, Enrique

1985 *Philosophy of Liberation* (trans. Aquilina Martinez and Christine Morkovsky; Maryknoll, NY: Orbis Books [1977]).

1996 *The Underside of Modernity: Apel, Ricoeur, Rorty, Taylor and the Philosophy of Liberation* (trans. and ed. Eduardo Mendieta; New Jersey: Humanities Press).

Eagleton, Terry

1976 *Marxism and Literary Criticism* (London: Methuen).

1978 *Criticism and Ideology: A Study in Marxist Literary Theory* (London: Verso).

1983 *Literary Theory: An Introduction* (Minneapolis: University of Minnesota Press).

1994 'Ideology and Its Vicissitudes', in Žižek 1994b: 179-228.

1996 *The Illusions of Postmodernism* (Oxford: Basil Blackwell).

Ehrman, A.

1970 'A Note on Micah 2:7', *VT* 20: 86-87.

1973 'A Note on Micah 6:14', *VT* 23: 103-105.

Ekins, Richard

1997 *Male Femaling: A Grounded Theory Approach to Cross-dressing and Sex-changing* (London: Routledge).

Ekins, Richard, and Dave King (eds.)

1996 *Blending Genders: Social Aspects of Cross-dressing and Sex-changing* (London: Routledge).

Eng, David L., and Shinhee Han
    2000   'A Dialogue on Racial Melancholia', *Psychoanalytic Dialogues* 10: 667-700.
Exum, J. Cheryl, and Stephen D. Moore
    1998   'Biblical Studies/Cultural Studies', in J. Cheryl Exum and Stephen D. Moore (eds.), *Biblical Studies/Cultural Studies: The Third Sheffield Colloquium* (Gender, Culture, Theory, 7; JSOTSup, 266; Sheffield: Sheffield Academic Press): 19-45.
Fanon, Frantz
    1986   *Black Skin White Masks* (trans. Charles Lam Markmann; London: Pluto Press [1952]).
Feinberg, Leslie
    1992   *Transgender Liberation: A Movement Whose Time Has Come* (New York: World View Forum).
Fewell, Danna Nolan (ed.)
    1992   *Reading Between Texts: Intertextuality and the Hebrew Bible* (Louisville, KY: Westminster/John Knox Press).
Fewell, Danna Nolan, and David M. Gunn
    1993   *Power and Promise: The Subject of the Bible's First Story* (Nashville: Abingdon Press).
Fewell, Danna Nolan, and Gary A. Phillips
    1997a   *Bible and Ethics of Reading* (Semeia, 77; Atlanta: Scholars Press).
    1997b   'Drawn to Excess, or Reading Beyond Betrothal', *Semeia* 77: 23-58.
Fish, Stanley
    1981   'Why No One's Afraid of Wolfgang Iser', *Diacritics* 11: 2-13.
Follis, Elaine R.
    1987   'The Holy City as Daughter', in Elaine R. Follis (ed.), *Directions in Biblical Hebrew Poetry* (JSOTSup, 40; Sheffield: JSOT Press): 173-84.
Forrester, John
    1990   *The Seductions of Psychoanalysis: Freud, Lacan and Derrida* (Cambridge: Cambridge University Press).
Foucault, Michel
    1972   *The Archaeology of Knowledge* (trans. A.M. Sheridan Smith; London: Routledge [1969]).
    1980   *Power/Knowledge: Selected Interviews and Other Writings 1972–1977* (ed. Colin Gordon; trans. Colin Gordon, Leo Marshall, John Mepham and Kate Soper; New York: Pantheon Books).
Fowler, Robert M.
    1985   'Who Is "the Reader" in Reader Response Criticism?', *Semeia* 31: 5-23.
    1992   'Reader Response Criticism', in Anderson and Moore 1992: 50-83.
Fox, Michael
    1995   'The Uses of Indeterminacy', *Semeia* 71: 173-92.
Freedman, David Noel
    1983   'Discourse on Prophetic Discourse', in Huffmon, Spina and Green 1983: 141-58.
Freud, Sigmund
    1953   'The Uncanny', in *The Standard Edition of the Complete Psychological Works of Sigmund Freud*, XVII (trans. James Strachey; London: Hogarth Press [1919]): 217-52.

1957a   'Instincts and their Vicissitudes', in *The Standard Edition of the Complete Psychological Works of Sigmund Freud*, XIV (trans. James Strachey; London: Hogarth Press [1915]): 109-40.

1957b   'The Unconcious', in *The Standard Edition of the Complete Psychological Works of Sigmund Freud*, XIV (trans. James Strachey; London: Hogarth Press [1915]): 159-215.

1989   *Beyond the Pleasure Principle: The Standard Edition with a Biographical Introduction by Peter Gay* (trans. James Strachey; New York: W.W. Norton [1920]).

Friedman, Jonathan

1992   'Myth, History, and Political Identity', *Cultural Anthropology* 7: 194-210.

Fritz, Von Volkmar

1974   'Das Wort gegen Samaria Mi 1, 2-7', *ZAW* 86: 316-31.

Frymer-Kensky, Tikva

1992   *In the Wake of the Goddesses: Women, Culture and the Biblical Transformation of Pagan Myth* (New York: Fawcett Columbine).

Fuller, Russell

1993   '4QMicah: A Small Fragment of a Manuscript of the Minor Prophets from Qumran, Cave IV', *RevQ* 16: 193-202.

Fuss, Diana (ed.)

1991   *Inside/Out: Lesbian Theories, Gay Theories* (New York: Routledge).

Gagné, Patricia, Richard Tewksbury and Deanna McGaughey

1997   'Coming Out and Crossing Over: Identity Formation and Proclamation in a Transgender Community', *Gender and Society* 11: 478-508.

Galambush, Julie

1992   *Jerusalem in the Book of Ezekiel: The City as Yahweh's Wife* (SBLDS, 130; Atlanta: Scholars Press).

Gallagher, Susan VanZanten

1996   'Mapping the Hybrid World: Three Postcolonial Motifs', *Semeia* 75: 229-40.

Gallissot, René

1987   'Sous l'identité, le procés d'identification', *L'Homme et la société* 83: 12-27.

Gallop, Jane

1985   *Reading Lacan* (Ithaca, NY: Cornell University Press).

1988   *Thinking Through the Body* (Gender and Culture; New York: Columbia University Press).

Garber, Marjorie

1992   *Vested Interests: Cross-dressing and Cultural Anxiety* (New York: Routledge).

Garfinkel, Harold

1967   *Studies in Ethnomethodology* (Englewood Cliffs, NJ: Prentice–Hall).

Gasché, Rodolphe

1986   *The Tain of the Mirror: Derrida and the Philosophy of Reflection* (Cambridge, MA: Harvard University Press).

Gordon, Pamela, and Harold C. Washington

1995   'Rape as a Military Metaphor in the Hebrew Bible', in Brenner 1995: 308-25.

Gordon, R.P.
    1978   'Micah VII 19 and Akkadian *Kabasu*', *VT* 28: 355.
Gosse, Bernard
    1993   'Michée 4, 1-5, Isaie 2, 1-5 et les rédacteurs finaux du livre d'Isaïe',
                ZAW 105: 98-102.
Gottwald, Norman K.
    1992   'Social Class and Ideology in Isaiah 40-55: An Eagletonian Reading',
                Semeia 59: 43-57.
Gowan, Donald E.
    1998   *Theology of the Prophetic Books: The Death and Resurrection of
                Israel* (Louisville, KY: Westminster/John Knox Press).
Grelot, Pierre
    1986   'Michée 7, 6 dans les évangiles et dans la littérature Rabbinique', *Bib*
                67: 363-77.
Grossberg, Lawrence
    1997   *Bringing It All Back Home: Essays on Cultural Studies* (Durham, NC:
                Duke University Press).
Gunkel, H.
    1928   'The Close of Micah: A Prophetic Liturgy', in *idem*, *What Remains of
                the Old Testament and Other Essays* (trans. A.K. Dallas; New York:
                Macmillan): 115-49.
Gunn, David M., and Danna Nolan Fewell
    1993   *Narrative in the Hebrew Bible* (Oxford Bible Series; Oxford: Oxford
                University Press).
Gupta, Akhil, and James Ferguson
    1992   'Beyond "Culture": Space, Identity and the Politics of Difference',
                Cultural Anthropology 7: 6-23.
Gutiérrez, Gustavo
    1973   *A Theology of Liberation* (trans. Sister Caridad Inda and John
                Eagleson; Maryknoll, NY: Orbis Books [1971]).
Hadley, Judith M.
    1996   'The Fertility of the Flock? The De-Personalization of Astarte in the
                Old Testament', in Bob Becking and Meindert Dijkstra (eds.), *On
                Reading Prophetic Texts: Gender-Specific and Related Studies in
                Memory of Fokkelien Van Dijk-Hemmes* (Leiden: E.J. Brill): 115-33.
Hagstrom, David Gerald
    1988   *The Coherence of the Book of Micah: A Literary Analysis* (SBLDS, 89;
                Atlanta: Scholars Press).
Hall, Stuart
    1997   'The Local and the Global: Globalization and Ethnicity', in Anne
                McClintock, Aamir Mufti and Ella Shohat (eds.), *Dangerous Liasons:
                Gender, Nation and Post-Colonial Perspectives* (Minneapolis: Univer-
                sity of Minneapolis Press): 173-87.
Hall, Stuart (ed.)
    1981   *Culture, Media, Language: Working Papers in Cultural Studies, 1972–
                79* (London: Melbourne).
Heard, Chris
    1997   'Hearing the Children's Cries: Commentary, Deconstruction, Ethics
                and the Book of Habakkuk', *Semeia* 77: 75-90.

Heath, Stephen
  1976   'On Screen, in Frame: Film and Ideology', *Quarterly Review of Film Studies* 1: 251-65.
  1978   'Notes on Suture', *Screen* 18(4): 48-76.
  1979   'The Turn of the Subject', *Ciné-Tract* 2(3-4): 32-48.
Hendricks, Osayande Obery
  1995   'Guerrilla Exegesis: "Struggle" as a Scholarly Vocation', *Semeia* 72: 73-90.
Hillers, Delbert R.
  1983a   'Imperial Dream: Text and Sense of Mic 5:4b-5', in Huffmon, Spina and Green 1983: 137-39.
  1983b   '*Hôy* and *Hôy*-Oracles: A Neglected Syntactic Aspect', in Meyers and O'Connor 1983: 185-88.
  1984   *Micah: A Commentary on the Book of the Prophet Micah* (Hermeneia; Philadelphia: Fortress Press).
House, Paul R.
  1998   *Old Testament Theology* (Downers Grove, IL: InterVarsity Press).
Holmlund, Christine Anne
  1991   'Displacing Limits of Difference: Gender, Race, and Colonialism in Edward Said and Homi Bhabha's Theoretical Models and Marguerite Duras's Experimental Films', *Quarterly Review of Film and Video* 13: 1-22.
Huffman, H.B., F.A. Spina and A.R.W. Green (eds.)
  1983   *The Quest for the Kingdom of God: Studies in Honor of George E. Mendenhall* (Winona Lake, IN: Eisenbrauns).
Irigaray
  1985   *This Sex Which Is Not One* (trans. Catherine Porter; Ithaca, NY: Cornell University Press [1977]).
Iser, Wolfgang
  1974   *The Implied Reader: Patterns of Communication in Prose Fiction from Bunyan to Beckett* (Baltimore: The Johns Hopkins University Press).
  1981   'Talk Like Whales: A Reply to Stanley Fish', *Diacritics* 11: 82-127.
Jameson, Fredric
  1981   *The Political Unconscious: Narrative as a Socially Symbolic Act* (Ithaca, NY: Cornell University Press).
  1982   'Progress Versus Utopia: Or, Can We Imagine the Future?' *Science Fiction Studies* 9: 147-58.
JanMohamed, Abdul R.
  1985   'The Economy of Manichean Allegory: The Function of Racial Difference in Colonialist Literature', *Critical Inquiry* 12: 59-87.
Jeppesen, Knud
  1978   'New Aspects of Micah Research', *JSOT* 8: 3-32.
  1979   'How the Book of Micah Lost its Integrity: Outline of the History of the Criticism of the Book of Micah with Emphasis on the 19th Century', *ST* 33: 101-31.
  1984a   'Micah V 13 in the Light of a Recent Archaeological Discovery', *VT* 34: 462-66.

1984b   'The Verb *Ya'ad in* Nahum 1, 10 and Micah 6, 9', *Bib* 65: 571-74.

Jeremias, Jörg
1965   *Theophanie: Die Geschichte einer alttestamentlichen Gattung* (Neu-kirchen–Vluyn: Neukirchener Verlag).

Jobling, David
1990   'Writing the Wrongs of the World', *Semeia* 51: 81-118.
1992   'Deconstruction and the Political Analysis of Biblical Texts: A Jamesonian Reading of Psalm 72', *Semeia* 59: 95-127.

Jobling, David, and Tina Pippin (eds.)
1992   *Ideological Criticism of Biblical Texts* (Semeia, 59/60; Atlanta: Scholars Press).

Jolly, Rosemary
1995   'Rehearsals of Liberation: Contemporary Postcolonial Discourse and the New South Africa', *PMLA* 110(1-6): 17-29.

Kaiser, Walter C. Jr.
1992   *The Communicator's Commentary: Micah–Malachi* (Dallas: Word Books).

Kapelrud, Arvid S.
1961   'Eschatology in the Book of Micah', *VT* 11: 392-405.

Kessler, Rainer
1999   *Micha* (Herders Theologischer Kommentar zum Alten Testament; Freiburg im Breisgau: Herder).

King, Dave
1996a   'Gender Blending: Medical Perspectives and Technology', in Ekins and King 1996: 79-98.
1996b   'Cross-dressing, Sex-changing and the Press', in Ekins and King 1996: 133-50.

King, Philip J.
1968   'Micah', in Raymond E. Brown, Joseph A. Fitzmyer and Roland E. Murphy (eds.), *The Jerome Biblical Commentary* (Englewood Cliffs, NJ: Prentice–Hall): 283-89.
1988   *Amos, Hosea, Micah: An Archaeological Commentary* (Philadelphia: Westminster Press).

Kofman, Sarah
1985   *The Enigma of Woman: Woman in Freud's Writing* (trans. Catherine Porter; Ithaca, NY: Cornell University Press [1980]).

Kristeva, Julia
1973   'The System and the Speaking Subject', *Times Literary Supplement* 12 October: 1249-50.
1980   *Desire in Language: A Semiotic Approach to Literature and Art* (ed. Leon S. Roudiez; trans. Thomas Gora, Alice Jardine and Leon S. Roudiez; New York: Columbia University Press).
1982   *Powers of Horror: An Essay on Abjection* (New York: Columbia University Press [1980]).
1984   *Revolution in Poetic Language* (trans. Margaret Waller; New York: Columbia University Press [1974]).
1995   *New Maladies of the Soul* (trans. Ross Guberman; New York: Columbia University Press [1993]).

Kuhn, Annette
 1985   *The Power of the Image* (London: Routledge & Kegan Paul).
Lacan, Jacques
 1966   'Le Séminaire sur "la lettre volée" ', in *Ecrits* (Paris: Editions du Seuil): 11-41.
 1968   *The Language of the Self: The Function of Language in Psycho-analysis* (trans. Anthony Wilden; Baltimore: The Johns Hopkins University Press [1956]).
 1972   'Seminar on "The Purloined Letter" ' (trans. Jefferey Mehlman), *Yale French Studies* 48: 38-72 [1966].
 1977   *Écrits: A Selection* (trans. Alan Sheridan; New York: W.W. Norton [1966]).
 1981   *The Four Fundamental Concepts of Psycho-analysis* (ed. Jacques-Alain Miller; trans. Alan Sheridan; New York: W.W. Norton [1973]).
 1982   *Feminine Sexuality: Jacques Lacan and the École Freudienne* (ed. Juliet Mitchell and Jacqueline Rose; trans. Jacqueline Rose; New York: W.W. Norton).
 1988a   'The Purloined Letter', in Jacques-Alain Miller (ed.), *The Seminar of Jacques Lacan. II. The Ego in Freud's Theory and in the Technique of Psychoanalysis 1954–1955* (trans. Sylvana Tomaselli; notes by John Forrester; Cambridge: Cambridge University Press [1954–55]): 191-205.
 1988b   *The Seminar of Jacques Lacan. VII. The Ethics of Psychoanalysis 1959–1960* (ed. Jacques-Alain Miller; trans. Dennis Porter; New York: W.W. Norton [1959–60]).
Laclau, Ernesto
 1977   *Politics and Ideology in Marxist Theory* (London: NLB).
 1988   'Metaphor and Social Antagonisms', in Nelson and Grossberg 1988: 249-58.
Laclau, Ernesto, and Chantal Mouffe
 1985   *Hegemony and Socialist Strategy* (London: Verso).
Landy, Francis
 1997   'Do We Want Our Children to Read This Book?', *Semeia* 77: 157-76.
Laplanche, J., and J.-B. Pontalis
 1973   *The Language of Psycho-analysis* (trans. Donald Nicholson-Smith; Intro. Daniel Lagache; New York: W.W. Norton [1967]).
Lavie, Smadar, and Ted Swedenburg
 1996   'Introduction', in Smadar Lavie and Ted Swedenburg (eds.), *Displacement, Diaspora, and Geographies of Identity* (Durham, NC: Duke University Press): 1-10.
Lefort, Claude
 1988   *Democracy and Political Theory* (trans. David Macey; Cambridge: Polity Press [1986]).
Lescow, Theodor
 1972a   'Redaktionsgeschichtliche Analyse von Micha 1-5', *ZAW* 84: 46-85.
 1972b   'Redaktionsgeschichtliche Analyse von Micha 6-7', *ZAW* 84: 182-212.
 1997   *Worte und Wirkungen des Propheten Micha: Ein kompositionsgeschichtlicher Kommentar* (Arbeiten zur Theologie, 84; Stuttgart: Calwer).

Levinas, Emmanuel
    1994   *Outside the Subject* (Meridian Crossing Aesthetics; Stanford: Stanford
              University Press).
Lewins, Frank
    1995   *Transsexualism in Society* (South Melbourne: Macmillan Education
              Australia).
Lezra, Jacques (ed.)
    1995   *Depositions: Althusser, Balibar, Macherey and the Labor of Reading*
              (Yale French Studies, 88; Yale: Yale University Press).
Limburg, James
    1988   *Hosea–Micah* (Interpretation; Atlanta: John Knox Press).
Linafelt, Todd
    1997   'Margins of Lamentations, Or the Unbearable Whiteness of Reading',
              in Beal and Gunn 1997: 219-31.
Lindblom, Johannes
    1962   *Prophecy in Ancient Israel* (Oxford: Basil Blackwell).
Lorber, Judith
    1994   *Paradoxes of Gender* (New Haven: Yale University Press).
Luker, Lamontte M.
    1985   'Doom and Hope in Micah: The Redaction of the Oracles Attributed to
              An Eighth Century Prophet' (PhD dissertation, Vanderbilt University,
              TN, USA).
    1987   'Beyond Form Criticism: The Relation of Doom and Hope Oracles in
              Micah 2–6', *HAR* 11: 285-301.
MacCabe, Colin
    1974   'Realism and the Cinema: Notes on Some Brechtian Theses', *Screen*
              15(2): 7-29.
    1976   'Theory and Film: Principles of Realism and Pleasure', *Screen* 17(3):
              7-29.
    1979   'The Discursive and the Ideological in Film: Notes on the Conditions
              of Political Intervention', *Screen* 19(4): 29-42.
Macherey, Pierre
    1995   'A Production of Subjectivity', in Lezra 1995: 42-52.
Magdalene, F. Rachel
    1995   'Ancient Near Eastern Treaty-curses and the Ultimate Texts of Terror:
              A Study of the Language of Divine Sexual Abuse in the Prophetic
              Corpus', in Brenner 1995: 326-52.
Maldonado, Robert D.
    1995   'Reading Malinche Reading Ruth: Toward a Hermeneutics of Betrayal',
              Semeia 72: 91-110.
Mannheim, Karl
    1970   *Ideology and Utopia: An Introduction to the Sociology of Knowledge*
              (trans. Louis Wirth and Edward Shils; New York: Harcourt, Brace &
              World [1936]).
Marin, Louis
    1973   *Utopiques: Jeux d'espaces* (Paris: Les Editions de Minuit).
Mason, Rex
    1991   *Micah, Nahum, Obadiah* (OTG; Sheffield: JSOT Press).

Mays, James Luther
    1976   *Micah: A Commentary* (OTL; Philadelphia: Westminster Press).
    1983   'Justice: Perspectives from the Prophetic Tradition', *Int* 37: 5-17.
Mays, James Luther, and Paul Achtemeier (eds.)
    1987   *Interpreting the Prophets* (Philadelphia: Fortress Press).
McComiskey, Thomas Edward
    1985   'Micah', in Frank E. Gaebelein and Richard P. Polcyn (eds.), *The Expositor's Bible Commentary*. VII. *Daniel—Minor Prophets* (Grand Rapids: Zondervan): 395-445.
McFadden, W. Robert
    1983   'Micah and the Problem of Continuities and Discontinuities in Prophecy', in William W. Hallo, James C. Moyer and Leo G. Perdue (eds.), *Scripture and Context. II. More Essays on the Comparative Method* (Winona Lake, IN: Eisenbrauns): 127-45.
McKane, William
    1995a   'Micah 1, 2-7', *ZAW* 107: 420-34.
    1995b   'Micah 2: 12-13', *JNSL* 21(2): 83-91.
    1998   *The Book of Micah: Introduction and Commentary* (Edinburgh: T. & T. Clark).
McKnight, Edgar V.
    1988   *Post-modern Use of the Bible: The Emergence of Reader-oriented Criticism* (Nashville: Abingdon Press).
Meyers, Carol L., and M. O'Connor (eds.)
    1983   *The Word of the Lord Shall Go Forth: Essays in Honor of David Noel Freedman in Celebration of his Sixtieth Birthday* (ASOR, 1; Winona Lake, IN: Eisenbrauns).
Milgrom, Jacob
    1990   *Numbers* (JPS Torah Commentary; Philadelphia: Jewish Publication Society).
Milik, J.T.
    1952   'Fragments d'un midrash de Michée dans les manuscrits de Qumran', *RB* 59: 412-18.
Miller, Jacques-Alain
    1978   'Suture (Elements of the Logic of the Signifier)', *Screen* 18(4): 24-34.
Miller, Patrick D.
    1982   *Sin and Judgment in the Prophets: A Stylistic and Theological Analysis* (SBLMS, 27; Atlanta: Scholars Press).
Mitchell, Juliet
    1982   'Introduction-I', in Mitchell and Rose 1982: 1-26.
Mitchell, Juliet, and Jacqueline Rose (eds.)
    1994   *Feminine Sexuality: Jacques Lacan and the École Freudienne* (trans. Jacqueline Rose; New York: W.W. Norton).
Moore, Henrietta L.
    1994   *A Passion for Difference: Essays in Anthropology and Gender* (Bloomington: Indiana University Press).
Moore, Stephen D.
    1989   *Literary Criticism and the Gospels* (New Haven: Yale University Press).

1995 'True Confessions and Weird Obsessions: Autobiographical Interventions in Literary and Biblical Studies', *Semeia* 72: 19-50.

1996 *God's Gym: Divine Male Bodies of the Bible* (London: Routledge).

2000 'Postcolonial Criticism and Poststructuralism' (Paper given at the Annual Meeting of the Society for Biblical Studies, November 18-21, Opreyland, Tennessee).

Moore-Gilbert, Bart

1997 *Postcolonial Theory: Contexts, Practices, Politics* (London: Routledge).

Morley, Dave

1980 'Texts, Readers, Subjects', in Hall 1980: 163-73.

Morris, Jan

1974 *Conundrum* (New York: Harcourt Brace Jovanovich).

Mosala, Itumeleng

1989 *Biblical Hermeneutics and Black Theology in South Africa* (Grand Rapids: Eerdmans).

Mouffe, Chantal

1988 'Hegemony and New Political Subjects: Toward a New Concept of Democracy', in Nelson and Grossberg 1988: 89-103.

1993 *The Return of the Political* (New York: Verso).

Moylan, Tom

1982 'The Locus of Hope: Utopia Versus Ideology', *Science Fiction Studies* 9: 159-66.

Na'aman, Nadav

1995 'The House-of-No-Shade Shall Take Away Its Tax from You', *VT* 45: 516-27.

Neiderhiser, Edward A.

1981 'Micah 2: 6-11: Considerations on the Nature of the Discourse', *BTS* 11: 104-107.

Nelson, Cary, and Lawrence Grossberg (eds.)

1988 *Marxism and the Interpretation of Culture* (Chicago: University of Illinois Press).

Newsom, Carol A.

1989 'Woman and the Discourse of Patriarchal Wisdom: A Study of Proverbs 1–9', in Day 1989: 142-60.

Newton, Esther

1972 *Mother Camp: Female Impersonators in America* (Anthropology of Modern Societies Series; Englewood Cliffs, NJ: Prentice–Hall).

Nichols, Bill (ed.)

1976 *Movies and Method: An Anthology*, I (Berkeley: University of California Press).

Nicholson, Ernest W.

1986 *God and his People: Covenant Theology in the Old Testament* (Oxford: Clarendon Press).

O'Brian, Julia

1995 'On Saying "No" to a Prophet', *Semeia* 72: 111-24.

Oosthuizen, M.J.

1988 'Scripture and Context: The Use of the Exodus Theme in the Hermeneutics of Liberation Theology', *Scriptura* 25: 7-22.

Ortlund, Raymond C.
1996   *Whoredom: God's Unfaithful Wife in Biblical Theology* (New Studies in Biblical Theology; Grand Rapids: Eerdmans).

Otto, Eckart
1991   'Techniken der Rechtssatzredaktion israelitischer Rechtsbücher in der Redaction des Prophetenbuches Micha', *SJOT* 5(2): 19-50.

Oudart, Jean-Pierre
1978   'Cinema and Suture', *Screen* 18(4): 35-47.

Papastergiadis, Nikos
1996   'Ambivalence in Cultural Theory: Reading Homi Bhabha's "Dissemi-Nation"', in John C. Hawley (ed.), *Writing the Nation: Self and Country in the Post-Colonial Imagination* (Critical Studies, 7; Amsterdam: Rodopi): 176-93.

Parry, Benita
1987   'Problems in Current Theories of Colonial Discourse', *Oxford Literary Review* 9: 27-58.

Pêcheux, Michel
1982   *Language, Semantics and Ideology: Stating the Obvious* (trans. Harbans Nagpal; London: Macmillan).

1995   *Automatic Discourse Analysis* (ed. Tony Hak, and Niels Helsloot; trans. David Macey; Utrecht Studies in Language and Communication, 5; Amsterdam: Rodopi [1969]).

Pellegrini, Ann
1997   *Performance Anxieties: Staging Psychoanalysis, Staging Race* (London: Routledge).

Penchansky, David
1992   'Up for Grabs: A Tentative Proposal for Doing Ideological Criticism', *Semeia* 59: 35-42.

1995   *The Politics of Biblical Theology: A Postmodern Reading* (Studies in American Biblical Hermeneutics, 10; Macon, GA: Mercer University Press).

Perkinson, Jim
1996   'A Canaantic Word in the Logos of Christ; Or the Difference the Syro-Phoenician Woman Makes to Jesus', *Semeia* 75: 61-86.

Petrotta, Anthony J.
1991   *Lexis Ludens: Wordplay and the Book of Micah* (American University Studies, VII; Theology and Religion, 105; New York: Peter Lang).

Phillips, Gary A.
1995   ' "You Are Either Here, Here, Here, or Here": Deconstruction's Troublesome Interplay', *Semeia* 71: 193-213.

Pixley, George V.
1991   'Micah—a Revolutionary', in David Jobling, Peggy L. Day and Gerald T. Sheppard (eds.), *The Bible and the Politics of Exegesis: Essays in Honor of Norman K. Gottwald on His Sixty-fifth Birthday* (Cleveland: Pilgrim): 53-60.

Poe, Edgar Allen
1960   *The Fall of the House of Usher, and Other Tales* (Signet Classic; New York: Penguin).

Pui-lan, Kwok
    1996   'Response to the Semeia Volume on Postcolonial Criticism', *Semeia* 75: 211-18.

Rabinowitz, Jacob
    1998   *The Faces of God: Canaanite Mythology as Hebrew Theology* (Woodstock, CT: Spring Publications).

Rajchman, John (ed.)
    1995   *The Identity in Question* (New York: Routledge).

Reicke, Bo
    1967   'Liturgical Traditions in Mic. 7', *HTR* 60: 349-67.

Renaud, B.
    1977   *La Formation du livre de Michée* (Paris: Gabalda).
    1987   *Michée, Sophonie, Nahum* (Sources Bibliques; Paris: Gabalda).

Richard, Pablo
    1998   'The Hermeneutics of Liberation: Theoretical Grounding for the Communitarian Reading of the Bible', in Segovia and Tolbert 1998: 272-82.

Ricoeur, Paul
    1975   'Biblical Hermeneutics', *Semeia* 4: 29-148.
    1978   'Can There Be a Scientific Concept of Ideology?' in Joseph Bien (ed.), *Phenomenology and the Social Sciences: A Dialogue* (The Hague: Martinus Nijhoff): 44-59.
    1980   *Essays on Biblical Interpretation* (ed. Lewis S. Mudge; Philadelphia: Fortress Press).
    1981   *Hermeneutics and the Human Sciences* (trans. John B. Thompson; Cambridge: Cambridge University Press [1981]).
    1986   *Lectures on Ideology and Utopia* (ed. George H. Taylor; New York: Columbia University Press).
    1992   *Oneself as Another* (trans. Kathleen Blamey; Chicago: University of Chicago Press [1990]).

Robinson, Robert B.
    1988   'Levels of Naturalization in Obadiah', *JSOT* 40: 83-97.

Roof, Judith, and Robyn Weigman (eds.)
    1995   *Who Can Speak: Authority and Critical Identity* (Urbana, IL: University of Illinois Press).

Rose, Jacqueline
    1982   'Introduction-II', in Mitchell and Rose 1982: 27-58.

Rothman, William
    1976   'Against "The System of Suture"', in Nichols 1976: 451-59.

Runions, Erin
    1998   'Zion is Burning', *Semeia* 82: 225-46.
    1999   'Playing it Again: Utopia, Contradiction, Hybrid Space and the Bright Future in Micah', in Black, Boer and Runions 1999: 285-300.
    2000   'Hysterical Phalli: Numbers 16, Two Contemporary Parallels and the Logic of Colonization', in George Aichele (ed.), *Culture, Entertainment and the Bible* (Sheffield: Sheffield Academic Press): 182-205.
    2001   'Called to do Justice?: A Bhabhian Reading of Micah 6:8', in A.K.M.

Adams (ed.), *Postmodern Interpretations of the Bible* (St Louis: Chalice): 153-64.

Rushdie, Salman
1988   *The Satanic Verses* (New York: Viking Penguin).

Sakenfeld, Katherine Doob
1978   *The Meaning of Hesed in the Hebrew Bible: A New Inquiry* (HSM, 17; Missoula: Scholars Press).
1985   *Faithfulness in Action: Loyalty in Biblical Perspective* (OBT; Philadelphia: Fortress Press).

Salomon, Willis
1995   'Deconstruction, Postcoloniality and Objective Interests', in C.W. Spinks and John Deely (eds.), *Semiotics 1995* (New York: Peter Lang): 41-48.

Sandars, N.K.
1972   *The Epic of Gilgamesh: An English Version with Introduction by N.K. Sandars* (Harmondsworth: Penguin).

Sanderson, Judith E.
1992   'Micah', in Carol A. Newsom and Sharon H. Ringe (eds.), *The Women's Bible Commentary: Expanded Edition* (Louisville, KY: Westminster/John Knox Press): 215-16.

Saracino, Francesco
1983   'A State of Siege: Mi 5:4-5 and an Ugaritic Prayer', *ZAW* 95: 263-69.

Saussure, Ferdinand de
1986   *Course in General Linguistics* (ed. Charles Bally and Albert Sechehaye, with Albert Riedlinger; trans. Roy Harris; La Salle, IL: Open Court [1916]).

Schmitt, Gött
1990   'Moreschet Gat und Libna mit einem Anhang: Zu Micah 1: 10-16', *JNSL* 16: 153-72.

Schor, Naomi, and Elizabeth Weed (eds.)
1994   *The Essential Difference* (Bloomington: Indiana University Press).

Schüssler Fiorenza, Elisabeth
1995   *Bread Not Stone: The Challenge of Feminist Biblical Interpretation* (Boston: Beacon Press).

Schwantes, Siegfried J.
1964   'Critical Notes on Micah I 10-16', *VT* 14: 454-61.

Scott, Joan
1992   'Multiculturalism and the Politics of Identity', *October* 61: 12-19.

Seebass, Horst
1992   'Der Herrscher aus Betlehem (Mi 5, 1-4a)', in *Herrscherverheissungen in Alten Testament* (Biblische Theologische Studien, 19; Neukirchen–Vluyn: Neukirchener Verlag): 41-82.

Segovia, Fernando F.
1998a   'Pedagogical Discourses and Practices in Biblical Studies: Toward a Contextual Biblical Pedagogy', in Segovia and Tolbert 1998: 137-67.
1998b   'Biblical Criticism and Postcolonial Studies: Toward a Postcolonial Optic', in Sugirtharajah 1998b.

Segovia, Fernando F., and Mary Ann Tolbert (eds.)
  1995a   *Reading from this Place*. I. *Social Location and Biblical Interpreta-*
            tion in the United States (Minneapolis: Fortress Press).
  1995b   *Reading from this Place*. II. *Social Location and Biblical Interpreta-*
            tion in Global Perspective (Minneapolis: Fortress Press).
  1998   *Teaching the Bible: The Discourses and Politics of Biblical Pedagogy*
            (Maryknoll, NY: Orbis Books).
Shaw, Charles S.
  1987   'Micah 1:10-16 Reconsidered', *JBL* 106: 223-29.
  1993   *The Speeches of Micah: A Rhetorical-Historical Analysis* (JSOTSup,
            145; Sheffield: Sheffield Academic Press).
Sherwood, Yvonne
  1996   *The Prostitute and the Prophet: Hosea's Marriage in Literary-*
            theoretical Perspective (JSOTSup, 212; Gender, Culture, Theory, 2;
            Sheffield: Sheffield Academic Press).
Shoemaker, Kenneth W.
  1992   'Speaker and Audience Participants in Micah: Aspects of Prophetic
            Discourse' (PhD dissertation, Graduate Theological Union, CA, USA).
Silverman, Kaja
  1983   *The Subject of Semiotics* (New York: Oxford University Press).
  1996   *The Threshold of the Visible World* (New York: Routledge).
  2000   *World Spectators* (Stanford: Stanford University Press).
Sinclair, L.A.
  1983   'Hebrew Text of the Qumran Micah Pesher and Textual Traditions of
            the Minor Prophets', *RevQ* 11: 253-63.
Smith, Abraham
  1997   ' "I Saw the Book Talk": A Cultural Studies Approach to the Ethics of
            An African American Biblical Hermeneutics', *Semeia* 77: 115-38.
Smith, Paul
  1988   *Discerning the Subject* (Theory and History of Literature, 55;
            Minneapolis: University of Minnesota Press).
Smith, Ralph L.
  1984   *Micah–Malachi* (WBC, 32; Waco, TX: Word Books).
Snaith, N.H.
  1967   *Leviticus and Numbers* (Century Bible; London: Thomas Nelson).
Snyman, Gerrie
  1997   ' "Tis a Vice to Know Him", Readers' Response-Ability and Responsi-
            bility in 2 Chronicles 14-16', *Semeia* 77: 91-114.
Spivak, Gayatri Chakravorty
  1990   'Poststructuralism, Marginality, Postcoloniality and Value', in Peter
            Collier and Helga Geyer-Ryan (eds.), *Literary Theory Today* (Ithaca,
            NY: Cornell University Press): 219-44.
  1993   *Outside in the Teaching Machine* (London: Routledge).
Stansell, Gary
  1988   *Micah and Isaiah: A Form and Tradition Historical Comparison*
            (SBLDS, 85; Atlanta: Scholars Press).
Sternberg, Meir
  1985   *The Poetics of Biblical Narrative: Ideological Literature and the*

Drama of Reading (Indiana Literary Biblical Series; Bloomington: Indiana University Press).

Stuhmueller, Carroll
    1986   *Amos, Hosea, Micah, Nahum, Zephaniah, Habakkak* (Collegeville, MN: Liturgical Press).

Sugirtharajah, R.S.
    1998a   'Biblical Studies in India: From Imperialist Scholarship to Postcolonial Interpretation', in Segovia and Tolbert 1998: 283-96.

Sugirtharajah, R.S. (ed.)
    1991   *Voices from the Margin: Interpreting the Bible in the Third World* (Maryknoll, NY: Orbis Books).
    1998b   *The Postcolonial Bible* (The Bible and Postcolonialism Series, 1; Sheffield: Sheffield Academic Press).

Tarlin, Jan William
    1997   'Utopia and Pornography in Ezekiel: Violence, Hope and the Shattered Male Subject', in Beal and Gunn 1997: 175-83.

Thompson, John B.
    1984   *Studies in the Theory of Ideology* (Cambridge: Polity Press).

Tournay, R.
    1964   'Quelques relectures biblique antisamaritaines', *RB* 71: 504-36.

Tucker, Gene M.
    1997   'Sin and "judgment" in the Prophets', in Henry T.C. Sun and Keith L. Eades, with James M. Robinson and Garth I. Moller (eds.), *Problems in Biblical Theology: Essays in Honor of Rolf Knierim* (Grand Rapids: Eerdmans): 373-88.

Tyler, Carole-Anne
    1991   'Boys Will Be Girls: The Politics of Gay Drag', in Fuss 1991: 32-70.

Utzschneider, Helmut
    1999   *Michas Reise in die Ziet: Studien zum Drama als Genre der prophetischen Literatur des Alten Testaments* (Stuttgarter Bibelstudien, 180; Stuttgart: Katholisches Bibelwerk).

van der Wal, Adri
    1990   *Micah: A Classified Bibliography* (Amsterdam: Free University Press).

van der Woude, A.S.
    1969   'Micah in Dispute with the Pseudo-prophets', *VT* 19: 244-60.
    1982   'Three Classical Prophets: Amos, Hosea and Micah', in Richard Coggins, Anthony Phillips and Michael Knibb (eds.), *Israel's Prophetic Tradition: Essays in Honour of Peter R. Ackroyd* (Cambridge: Cambridge University Press): 32-57.

Vanhoozer, Kevin J.
    1990   *Biblical Narrative in the Philosophy of Paul Ricoeur* (Cambridge: Cambridge University Press).

Von Rad, Gerhard
    1965   *Old Testament Theology* (2 vols.; New York: Harper & Row).

Vuilleumier, René, and Carl A. Keller
    1971   *Michée, Nahoum, Habacuc, Sophonie* (Commentaire de l'Ancien Testament, 11b; Neuchâtel: Delachaux & Niestlé).

Wagenaar, Jan A.
    1996   'The Hillside of Samaria: Interpretation and Meaning of Micah 1:6',
                BN 85: 26-31.
    2000   ' "From Eden He Went Up...": Some Remarks on the Text and
                Interpretations of Micah II 12-13', *VT* 50: 531-39.
Wallace, Mark I.
    1990   *The Second Naiveté: Barth, Ricoeur and the New Yale Theology*
                (Studies in American Biblical Hermeneutics, 6; Macon, GA: Mercer
                University Press).
Waltke, Bruce
    1988   'Micah', in D.J. Wiseman (ed.), *Obadiah, Jonah and Micah* (TOTC,
                23a; Downers Grove, IL: InterVarsity Press): 137-207.
Waltke, Bruce, and M. O'Connor
    1990   *An Introduction to Biblical Hebrew Syntax* (Winona Lake, IN:
                Eisenbrauns).
Warrior, Robert Allen
    1989   'Canaanites, Cowboys and Indians: Deliverance, Conquest and Libera-
                tion Theology Today', *Christianity and Crisis* 49: 261-65.
Watson, Wilfred G.E.
    1984a   'The Hebrew Word-pair 'sp//qbs', *ZAW* 96: 426-34.
    1984b   'Allusion, Irony and Wordplay in Micah 1, 7', *Bib* 65: 103-105.
    1989   'Internal or Half-line Parallelism in Classical Hebrew Again', *VT* 29:
                44-66.
Weaver, Jace
    1996   'From I-hermeneutics to We-hermeneutics: Native Americans and the
                Post-colonial', *Semeia* 75: 153-76.
Weedon, Chris
    1997   *Feminist Practice and Poststructuralist Theory* (Oxford: Basil Black-
                well, 2nd edn).
Weedon, Chris, Andre Tolson and Frank Mort
    1980   'Theories of Language and Subjectivity', in Hall 1980: 195-215.
Weems, Renita J.
    1995   *Battered Love: Marriage, Sex and Violence in the Hebrew Prophets*
                (Minneapolis: Fortress Press).
Weinfeld, Moshe
    1977   'Ancient Near Eastern Patterns in Prophetic Literature', *VT* 27: 178-95.
West, Gerald
    1991   *Biblical Hermeneutics of Liberation* (Pietermaritzburg: Cluster Publi-
                cations).
West, Gerald, and Musa W. Dube (eds.)
    1996   *Reading With African Overtures* (Semeia, 73; Atlanta: Scholars Press).
Whittle, Stephen
    1996   'Gender Fucking or Fucking Gender? Current Cultural Contributions
                to Theories of Gender Blending', in Ekins and King 1996: 192-214.
Williamson, H.G.M.
    1997   'Marginalia in Micah', *VT* 47: 360-72.
Willi-Plein, Ina
    1971   *Vorformen der Schriftexegese innerhalb des Alten Testaments:*

Untersuchungen zum literarischen werden der auf Amos, Hosea and Micha zurückgebenden Bücher im hebräischen Zwölfprophetenbuch (BZAW, 123; Berlin: W. de Gruyter).

Willis, John T.

1966 'The Structure, Settings and Interrelationships of the Pericopes in the Book of Micah' (PhD dissertation, Vanderbilt University, TN, USA).

1968 'Micah IV 14—V 5—A Unit', *VT* 18: 529-47.

1969a 'The Structure of Micah 3-5 and the Function of Micah 5, 9-14 in the Book', *ZAW* 81: 191-214.

1969b 'The Authenticity and Meaning of Micah 5, 9-14', *ZAW* 81: 353-68.

1974 'A Reapplied Prophetic Hope Oracle', in *Studies on Prophecy: A Collection of Twelve Papers* (VTSup, 26; Leiden: E.J. Brill): 64-76.

Winnicott, D.W.

1971 *Playing and Reality* (New York: Basic Books).

Wittig, Monique

1992 *The Straight Mind and Other Essays* (Boston: Beacon Press).

Wolff, Hans Walter

1981 *Micah the Prophet* (trans. Ralph D. Gehrke; Philadelphia: Fortress Press [1978]).

1987 'Prophecy from the Eighth through the Fifth Century', in Mays and Achtemeier 1987: 14-26.

1990 *Micah: A Commentary* (trans. Gary Stansell; Minneapolis: Augsburg [1982]).

Woods, Tim

1995 'A Review of the *Location of Culture*, by Homi K. Bhabha, Routledge, 1994', *British Journal of Aesthetics* 35: 292-93.

Xie, Shaobo

1996 'Writing Boundaries: Homi Bhabha's Recent Essays', *Ariel* 27(4): 155-66.

Young, Robert

1990 *White Mythologies: Writing History and the West* (London: Verso).

Yuval-Davis, Nira

1997 *Gender and Nation* (Politics and Culture; London: Sage Publications).

Žižek, Slavoj

1989 *The Sublime Object of Ideology* (Phronesis; London: Verso).

1990 'Eastern Europe's Republics of Gilead', *New Left Review* 183: 50-62.

1991a *For They Know Not What They Do: Enjoyment as a Political Factor* (Phronesis; London: Verso).

1991b *Looking Awry: An Introduction to Jacques Lacan through Popular Culture* (October Books; Cambridge, MA: MIT Press).

1993 *Tarrying with the Negative: Kant, Hegel and the Critique of Ideology* (Durham, NC: Duke University Press).

1994a 'Is There a Cause of the Subject?', in Copjec 1994: 84-106.

1997 *The Abyss of Freedom/Ages of the Word: An Essay by Slavoj Žižek with the Text of Schelling's* die Weltalter *(second Draft, 1813) in English Translation by Judith Norman* (Ann Arbor: University of Michigan Press).

Žižek, Slavoj (ed.)

1994b *Mapping Ideology* (London: Verso).

Index of References

Old Testament

New Testament

Matthew		*Mark*		*1 Corinthians*	
13.31-33	188	7.24-30	41	1.26	188
15.21-28	41			1.28	188

Apocrypha

Sirach (Ecclesiasticus)		32.3	168	42.8	168
16.25	168	34.22	168		

Index of Authors